The Battle of the Sambre, 4 November 1918, was a decisive British victory. The battle has, however, been largely neglected by historians: it was the last large-scale, set-piece battle fought by the British Expeditionary Force on the Western Front: the Armistice was only one week away. Seven Victoria Crosses were won and the poet Wilfred Owen was killed in action. In scale it was similar to the first day of the Battle of the Somme: thirteen divisions of the BEF led the assault on a frontage of approximately twenty miles, supported by over 1,000 guns, with initial plans presuming an involvement of up to 70 tanks and armoured cars. The German Army was determined to hold a defensive line incorporating the Mormal Forest and the Sambre-Oise Canal, hoping to buy time for a strategic withdrawal to as yet incomplete defensive positions between Antwerp and the Meuse river and thereby negotiate a compromise peace in the spring of 1919. This is the only book devoted solely to this battle and includes original, bespoke, colour maps covering every inch of the battlefield.

The work analyses the battle at the operational and tactical levels: the BEF was no longer striving for a breakthrough – sequential 'bite and hold' was now the accepted method of advance. Drawing on information largely from unpublished archives, including over 300 formation or unit war diaries, Dr Clayton casts a critical eye over the day's events, examining the difference between plan and reality; the tactical proficiency of units engaged; the competence of commanders, some of whom proved capable of pragmatic flexibility in the face of stubborn enemy resistance and were able to adapt or even abandon original plans in order to ensure ultimate success. The role of the Royal Engineers is also highlighted, their tasks including devising improvised bridging equipment to facilitate the crossing of the waterway. Other questions are raised and answered: to what extent was this an 'all-arms' battle? Where does this engagement fit in the context of the BEF's 'learning curve'? Was it necessary to fight the battle at all? Was it indeed decisive?

Dr Clayton's analysis places the battle into its wider strategic context and reaches important, new conclusions: that this victory, hard-won as it was by a British army hampered by logistical, geographical and meteorological constraints and worn down by the almost continuous hard fighting of the summer and autumn, irrevocably and finally crushed the will of the German defenders, leading to a pursuit of a demoralized, broken and beaten army, whose means of continued resistance had been destroyed, thus expediting the armistice.

Derek Clayton was born in Yorkshire and attended Batley Grammar School before beginning a long association with the University of Birmingham. He graduated in 1979 with a BA in French and German and went on to teach Modern Languages in three Birmingham schools before retiring in 2015. His fascination with military history began in childhood, but the discovery almost thirty years ago of photographs of his great-uncle in his KOYLI uniform and his grandfather in the RFC focused his interest squarely on the Great War. He returned to the university in 2004, following the publication of his battalion history: *From Pontefract to Picardy: the 9th King's Own Yorkshire Light Infantry in the First World War* (Tempus, 2004), and completed his MA in British First World War Studies, as one of the initial cohort of this course, in 2006, having produced a dissertation on the 49th (West Riding) Division. He then went on to write his doctoral thesis 'The Battle of the Sambre: 4 November 1918' – a subject suggested by Professor Peter Simkins - under the supervision of John Bourne, and was awarded his PhD in 2016. He is currently working on a history of the 21st Division in the Great War. Derek is a member of the Western Front Association. He lives in Worcestershire.

Decisive Victory

The Battle of the Sambre, 4 November 1918

Derek Clayton

Helion & Company Limited

Helion & Company Limited
Unit 8 Amherst Business Centre
Budbrooke Road
Warwick
CV34 5WE
England
Tel. 01926 499 619
Fax 0121 711 4075
Email: info@helion.co.uk
Website: www.helion.co.uk
Twitter: @helionbooks
Visit our blog http://blog.helion.co.uk/

Published by Helion & Company 2018
Designed and typeset by Mach 3 Solutions Ltd (www.mach3solutions.co.uk)
Cover designed by Paul Hewitt, Battlefield Design (www.battlefield-design.co.uk)
Printed by Gutenberg Press Limited, Tarxien, Malta

Text and maps (unless latter specifically credited) © Derek Clayton 2018
Illustrations, some maps © as individually credited
Front cover artwork by Peter Dennis © Helion & Company Limited 2018

ISBN 978-1-912174-90-4

British Library Cataloguing-in-Publication Data.
A catalogue record for this book is available from the British Library.

For details of other military history titles published by Helion & Company Limited contact the above address, or visit our website: http://www.helion.co.uk.

We always welcome receiving book proposals from prospective authors.

Contents

List of Illustrations

Diagrams

All IWM images are from a Royal Engineer's Report by Colonel Sankey (ref: IWM LBY 73281).

List of Maps

List of Abbreviations

BA: MA	Bundesarchiv: Militärarchiv
BEF	British Expeditionary Force
BGC	Brigadier-General Commanding
BGGS	Brigadier-General General Staff
BGHA	Brigadier-General Heavy Artillery
CHA	Commander Heavy Artillery
CRA	Commander Royal Artillery
CRE	Commander Royal Engineers
DAQMG	Deputy Assistant Quartermaster General
DRLS	Despatch Rider Letter Service
DSO	Distinguished Service Order
GHQ	General Headquarters
GOC	General Officer Commanding
GSO 1/2/3	General Staff Officer grade 1/2/3
IWM	Imperial War Museum
MC	Military Cross
MGC	Machine Gun Company
MGGS	Major-General General Staff
MGRA	Major-General Royal Artillery
MM	Military Medal
OR	Other Ranks
QMG	Quartermaster General
RAF	Royal Air Force
RE	Royal Engineers
RFA	Royal Field Artillery
RGA	Royal Garrison Artillery
TNA: PRO	The National Archives / Public Record Office

Acknowledgements

The research and writing of this book would have been impossible without the welcome assistance from the following people and institutions.

Special thanks to my PhD supervisor, Dr John Bourne, for his direction, support, encouragement and unfailingly wise counsel.

Thanks to Professor Peter Simkins who, having supervised my MA dissertation, suggested the Battle of the Sambre as a subject ripe for further study. He then kindly supplied data on divisional performance during the Hundred Days and granted permission to use it in this work.

Thanks also to the excellent staffs of the National Archives (Kew), Imperial War Museum, Bundesarchiv – Militärarchiv, Freiburg and the National Library of New Zealand.

Former University of Birmingham colleagues have been a constant source of friendship and encouragement: my grateful thanks to the late Geoff Clarke, who allowed access to some of his doctoral research on logistics, and to Trevor Harvey, Peter Hodgkinson, Alison Hine and Michael LoCicero.

Foreword

Some 25 years ago I found myself sitting at the back of the cinema in the Imperial War Museum listening to Peter Simkins, then the Museum's Senior Historian, deliver a lecture to an audience of sixth formers from the south-east of England on the last four months of the Great War on the Western Front. He began with a statement: 'During the last 100 days of the First World War the British Army in France and Belgium fought the biggest land battles in its history, recording an unbroken series of victories.' This was followed by a pause and a baleful stare. 'Who can name one of these battles?' he continued. Two hundred young people looked at their feet and prayed for someone to break the embarrassing silence.

I am not sure that an equivalent audience today would do better, though they would have less excuse. The battles of 1918 have never captured the British public's imagination like those of 1914, or of the Somme and 'Passchendaele'. They were, however, even more costly in British lives: 1918 was truly 'the year of killing' as well as 'the year of victory'. The battles of the 'Hundred Days' in the summer and autumn of 1918, in particular, do not readily evoke the iconic images of the Western Front – trenches, barbed wire, no man's land, 'attrition', 'deadlock'. Fighting was often semi-mobile, presenting new weekly, even daily, operational and tactical challenges, crossing rivers and canals, fighting in woods and through hedgerows, and in built up areas. Movement forward, if not rapid, was constant.

The members of Peter Simkins's audience 25 years ago had some excuse for their ignorance. It was not until Harris and Barr's pioneering study, *Amiens to the Armistice* (1998), that the 'Hundred Days' were subjected to a modern, scholarly analysis. In more recent times, as the centenary of the war approached, there has been a steady stream of excellent accounts: Peter Hart's *1918: A Very British Victory* (2008); Jonathan Boff's *Winning and Losing on the Western Front* (2012); Nick Lloyd's *Hundred Days: The End of the Great War* (2013); and Peter Hodgkinson's *The Battle of the Selle* (2017). To these must now be added Derek Clayton's fine study of the very last battle, on the Sambre. The First World War in the west did not drift to a conclusion. This was a mighty battle, involving 13 British divisions on a front of almost 20 miles, comparable with the first day of the Somme. Although Germany's allies were collapsing all around her, the German High Command [OHL] clung to the belief that the Western Front could still be held, a powerful defensive line established between Antwerp and the Meuse and the war extended into 1919, when better peace terms could be brokered. The Sambre disabused the OHL of this belief. Its strategic effects were therefore profound. At the operational and tactical levels the performance of the British Army showed how much it had learned in four years of hard fighting, but its limitations were also exposed. Divisional performance was patchy and in some cases unimpressive. But despite operating at the very limits of its logistical chain, short of tanks and with deteriorating weather making an 'all arms' battle impossible, the combination of a powerful artillery and a determined infantry that retained 'the will to combat', wonderfully supported by the heroic professionalism of the Royal Engineers, the BEF prevailed.

John Bourne
University of Wolverhampton
April 2018

Introduction

The almost forgotten Battle of the Sambre, 4 November 1918,[1] was a decisive British victory. On that cold, gloomy, damp and misty pre-dawn late-autumn morning, close on 80,000 troops of Third and Fourth Armies[2] were in their jumping off positions, ready to advance across the very same fields that, during those sweltering August days of 1914, had witnessed the Old Contemptibles'[3] retreat from Mons. Forcing the Germans out of their prepared defensive positions would prove to be neither easy nor straightforward.

The Sambre was the last large-scale, set-piece battle fought by the British Expeditionary Force [BEF] on the Western Front. If the battle is known at all in the public domain, it is for the death of the poet Wilfred Owen.[4] The battle was on a huge scale: 13 divisions of the BEF led the assault on a frontage of approximately 20 miles, supported by over 1,000 guns, with initial plans presuming an involvement of up to 70 tanks and armoured cars. This engagement was therefore not dissimilar in scale to the attack of 1 July 1916 on the Somme, yet other battles of the summer and autumn of 1918 overshadow this one in current historiography, notably the Battle of Amiens (8-11 August), and the Hindenburg Line, including the crossing of the Canal du Nord (27 September-1 October). This book hopes to go some way toward redressing this imbalance.

Analysis of the Battle of the Sambre raises a number of questions. Was the battle indeed decisive? What had the BEF learnt in the previous four years' fighting and therefore where does the battle fit in the context of the 'learning curve'? To what extent was this engagement an 'all-arms' battle? This raises the further question of plan versus reality: did the battle go entirely to plan? If objectives were not reached, did it matter? Was it necessary for officers on the spot to adopt a pragmatic approach rather than adhere strictly to instructions? The battle cannot be viewed in isolation: what other factors influenced the rapidity of the German Army's disintegration and was it necessary for the BEF to fight the battle at all?

---

1   The battle ran officially from 4 to 6 November 1918.
2   Commanded by General Hon. Sir Julian Byng (Third Army) and General Sir Henry Rawlinson Bt. (Fourth Army).
3   Sobriquet adopted by the original units of the British Expeditionary Force that helped stem the German advance of summer 1914.
4   Lieutenant Wilfred Edward Salter Owen, 5th Battalion (attached 2nd Battalion) Manchester Regiment, 32nd Division, was killed in action on the Sambre-Oise Canal, approximately 1,000 yards north of the village of Ors. He is buried in Ors Communal Cemetery, Grave A.3.

This work focuses on the level of tactical and operational effectiveness of the BEF at the very end of the 'learning curve' and shows how it managed to storm a challenging, prepared defensive position without involvement of the much-vaunted Australian and Canadian divisions.[5] This assault also gives a fascinating and starring role to the Field Companies of the Royal Engineers who rarely receive the attention and recognition they deserve and is also a battle with immediate strategic and political consequences. The work also argues that the British victory was decisive – at the strategic level it expedited the Armistice – and that it was necessary to fight the battle: until the German Army was pushed off its last prepared defensive line, German High Command [OHL[6]] was still hoping to be able to make a strategic withdrawal to an as yet incomplete line between Antwerp and the Meuse, to hold out through the winter and pursue a more favourable negoti-

General Hon. Sir Julian Byng, Commander Third Army. (Australian War Memorial)

ated peace settlement in the spring of 1919. What the BEF had learned in the previous four years' fighting is examined and the extent to which this final battle was its ultimate expression analysed.

By describing and analysing the fighting methods used, the question to what extent this engagement was an 'all-arms' battle can also be answered. At the operational level, the dilemma that dogged British High Command was that of which methodology would best lead to the strategic victory that would defeat the German Army on the field of battle and throw it out of France and Belgium. Breakthrough or attrition? The repeated failure of the former led eventually to an acceptance of the latter in the form of 'bite and hold' tactics, where attacks would be limited in both time and geographical scope so as to avoid overstretching attacking troops and ensure that ground captured could be held against counter-attacks. This work explains how this tactic developed and shows how the methods of late 1918 fit into this paradigm.

It also demonstrates that the levels of fighting efficiency and of training were not uniform, showing how some units fared better than others. In places the assault went largely to plan. In others, it took improvisation, the adaptation or discarding of original plans, for some units to achieve success in the face of serious initial setbacks. The execution of the battle plan is shown to be far from perfect, with some units underperforming at the tactical level.

The nature of the Hundred Days campaign is examined, along with the effect on the German leadership of the collapse of their Allies. The battle of 4 November did not initiate German

5   There were Dominion troops involved: the 3 New Zealand Rifle Brigade and 1 New Zealand Infantry Brigade assaulted the fortified town of Le Quesnoy, and a small contingent of the 1st Australian Tunnelling Company were involved in building a bridge over the Lock near the village of Rejet de Beaulieu at the southernmost point of the attack frontage.
6   OHL – *Oberste Heeresleitung*.

requests for an armistice. Negotiations had been ongoing since early October 1918, but the effect of the defeat on the Sambre will be shown as pivotal in the process. The concepts of 'bite and hold', 'all-arms battle', the 'learning curve' and an overview of the Hundred Days campaign, including Germany's peace negotiations, are dealt with in Chapter 1, "Contexts". The performance of the German Army is not examined except through the eyes of its opponent. Detailed analysis of this kind is beyond the scope of this work, but an overview can be found in Jonathan Boff's *Winning and Losing on the Western Front.*[7]

Malcolm Brown's *The Imperial War Museum Book of 1918, Year of Victory* covers the events of 4 November in a little under two pages,[8] focusing on the Victoria Cross winners and the unfortunate poet. He does, however, in one sentence, evoke the question of the need for the battle: in quoting an officer present at the time (John Glubb, later Lieutenant-General Sir John Glubb), who commented "The enemy has melted away before us like snow",[9] he raises the matter of whether the battle was necessary at all, with the BEF by now pushing on what was surely an open door with the Armistice an imminent certainty. Gary Sheffield, in *Forgotten Victory – The First World War, Myths and Realities*,[10] hints at a possible answer, reinforcing Niall Barr's opinion that it was defeat on the Sambre-Oise Canal and in the villages in

General Sir Henry Rawlinson, Commander Fourth Army. (Australian War Memorial)

front of the Forêt de Mormal that persuaded the OHL that the game was finally up.[11]

General Sir Henry Rawlinson's diary gives us a brief insight into his own opinion on this matter. On 20 October he wrote: "I think the Boche mean to go back gradually to the line of the Meuse. [...] Our railways are not getting on as fast as I should like".[12] Indeed, on 22 October, when contemplating the progress of peace talks, he was envisaging the possibility of the war continuing into 1919:

7   Jonathan Boff, *Winning and Losing on the Western Front. The British Third Army and the Defeat of Germany in 1918* (Cambridge: Cambridge University Press, 2012). See pp. 16-17, 45-53, 68-69, 105-122, 160-178, 226-242.
8   M. Brown, *The Imperial War Museum Book of 1918 – The Year of Victory* (London: Sidgwick & Jackson, 1998).
9   Ibid. p. 281.
10 G. Sheffield, *Forgotten Victory – The First World War, Myths and Realities* (London: Headline, 2001).
11 Ibid. p. 215.
12 Churchill Archives Centre, Churchill College, Cambridge: Rawlinson Papers, RWLN 1/11.

The negotiations are like selling a horse: we have to fix the reserve price – If it is too high the Boch won't buy and we shall go on fighting. – I am inclined to keep up the pace and to insist on unconditional surrender. It will probably prolong the war but it is better so than having an unsatisfactory peace. If the Bosch continues to destroy all railways we shall not be able to get to the German frontier before Feb'y [...] we will then enter Germany and dictate terms. After all it is worth another 3 or 4 months' delay.[13]

After a conference of the commanders of First, Third, Fourth and Fifth Armies on 31 October, Field Marshal Haig wrote in his diary that after each commander had expressed his views on the current situation, the consensus was that

The Enemy is fighting a very good rear guard action and we are all agreed that from a military standpoint, the Enemy has not yet been sufficiently beaten as to cause him to accept an ignominious peace.[14]

The attitude of the Germans varied from day to day during the last weeks of the war,[15] but the OHL stubbornly clung on to the possibility of a negotiated peace that would allow Germany to keep some of its conquered territories and the Army to remain largely intact. Hindenburg wrote: "By the end of October the collapse was complete at all points. It was only on the Western Front that we still thought we could avert it".[16] Delaying the Allied advance at the line of the Sambre-Oise Canal and the Forêt de Mormal could keep alive the possibility of a compromise peace. The success of this rearguard action thus assumed huge importance.

Historiography

The Military History of the BEF on the Western Front
The historiography of the BEF on the Western Front is vast. This review therefore concentrates on recent works and cannot claim to be exhaustive. Divisional or regimental histories produced in the decades following the conflict gave their readers largely non-critical accounts of events, basking to some extent in the reflected glories of recent victory. It is the next wave of literature that remains deeply rooted in the public perception of the conduct of the war. Graves, Liddell Hart, Lloyd George, Sassoon and Owen portray a war of shattered ideals, of futility, suffering, of a generation of innocents sacrificed by incompetent and uncaring generals. This view is perpetuated post-Second World War by Taylor, Clark, Laffin and Winter.[17]

---

13   Ibid. It is interesting to note that throughout his journal, Rawlinson never adopts a consistent spelling of the word 'Boche'.
14   Sheffield & Bourne (eds), *Douglas Haig, War Diaries and Letters 1914-1918*, p. 483.
15   See Erich Ludendorff, *My War Memories 1914-1918 Vol. 2* (London: Hutchinson), pp. 739-71.
16   Quoted in Barr, 'The Last Battle: the Crossing of the Sambre-Oise Canal, 4th November 1918', in *Changing War*, p. 74. Originally taken from Charles Messenger, ed., Field Marshal Hindenburg, *The Great War* (London: Greenhill, 2006), p. 222.
17   A.J.P. Taylor, *The First World War. An Illustrated History* (London: Hamish Hamilton, 1963); Alan Clark, *The Donkeys* (London: Random House UK, 1961); John Laffin, *British Butchers and Bunglers*

John Terraine offered a reappraisal of the BEF's Commander in Chief in 1963 and his vindication of Haig has stood the test of time, serving as a catalyst to new waves of historians prepared to take a more dispassionate view of events.[18] Bidwell and Graham[19] and Tim Travers[20] took up the argument, the former championing the BEF's achievement in developing an all-arms system of warfare, the latter echoing this, but with the claim that it was achieved within a system where high-level commanders failed to come to terms with the technological advances and the tactical changes required to integrate and implement them successfully. Paddy Griffith[21] accepts the importance of technology, but concludes that High Command, through the dissemination of ideas, can claim some responsibility for the levels of skill and tactical awareness of the BEF in 1918.

Much of the literature of the 1970s, 1980s and 1990s prefers the worm's eye view of battle and attempts to reclaim the war for the common man: this includes works by Martin Middlebrook, Lyn MacDonald and the series of 'Pals' histories. The emphasis is on the major attritional battles of the middle years of the war and little is said on the subject of tactical, operational or strategic development.

Robin Prior and Trevor Wilson's military biography of Sir Henry Rawlinson[22] looks at the development of the formations under his command and assesses his contribution to "the ultimate success of British arms".[23] They conclude that the victories of 1918 were as much due to the decentralisation of command as to the applied wisdom of the upper echelons of the command structure. John Bourne's *Britain and the Great War*[24] takes the evolution of the BEF from imperial police force to modern, mass army and places it within its military, political and social contexts and argues that objectivity of viewpoint is skewed by the prism of the Second World War.

The last 15 years have seen a continuation of serious scholarship on the development of the BEF: Simon Robbins examines the BEF's path toward a winning formula at the strategic level, affirming that divisional commanders were the key leaders;[25] Andy Simpson looks at British Corps command and shows how this level of the command structure became instrumental in the planning and execution of operations, recognising a flexibility that allowed the

of World War One (Stroud: Alan Sutton Publishing, 1988); Denis Winter, *Death's Men: Soldiers of the Great War* (London: Allen Lane, 1978).

18   John Terraine, *Douglas Haig: The Educated Soldier* (London: Hutchinson & Co Ltd, 1963) See also Gary Sheffield, *The Chief: Douglas Haig and the British Army* (London: Aurum Press Ltd., 2011); Walter Reid, *Douglas Haig: Architect of Victory* (Edinburgh: Birlinn Ltd., 2006); Gary Sheffield and John Bourne, eds, *Douglas Haig: War Diaries and Letters 1914-1918* (London: Weidenfeld & Nicolson, 2005).

19   S.Bidwell & D.Graham, *Firepower: British Army Weapons and Theories of War 1904-1945* (London: Allen & Unwin, 1982).

20   T.Travers, *The Killing Ground: The British Army, the Western Front and the Emergence of Modern Warfare 1900-1918* (London: Allen & Unwin, 1987).

21   Paddy Griffith, *Battle Tactics of the Western Front: The British Army's Art of Attack 1916-18* (London: Yale University Press, 1994).

22   Robin Prior and Trevor Wilson, *Command on the Western Front* (Oxford: Blackwell, 1992).

23   Ibid, p. 3.

24   J.M.Bourne, *Britain and the Great War 1914-1918* (London: Edward Arnold, 1989).

25   Simon Robbins, *British Generalship on the Western Front 1914-1918. Defeat into Victory* (London: Frank Cass, 2005).

Corps commander to centralise control where necessary, but delegate to subordinates when appropriate.[26]

Revisionist literature is now accepted within academic circles and emerging views have appeared in volumes of collected essays by respected historians. Strategic, operational and tactical developments are treated in detail in works edited by Gary Sheffield and Dan Todman,[27] and by Spencer Jones[28] and Gary Sheffield and Peter Simkins have compiled some of their writings into single volumes,[29] the former looking at the nature of the war from the viewpoints of politicians and the exercise of command at all levels, the latter reassessing the theory and practice of the BEF as it developed into a war-winning army in 1918.

Studies of the Great War in single volumes cannot delve into the operational and tactical levels of warfare, but any campaign must be viewed within its wider context, and David Stevenson[30] and Ian Beckett[31] have produced recent works that combine breadth of approach with clarity of thought to debunk comprehensively many of the myths that still linger in the public perception of the conflict. Stevenson has also produced a detailed work on 1918, in which he bemoans also that "whereas comprehensive investigations now exist into the outcomes of other modern conflicts, the First World War still lacks one".[32] Stevenson then goes on to provide one. His wide-ranging assessment of 1918 rarely dips below the military strategic level but includes analysis of technology, logistics, manpower levels and morale. The study widens in scope to include sea-power and the war economies and politics of the belligerent nations. He divides the war in the west into three distinct phases: 1914-17 was an era of deadlock, dominated by the superiority of the defence, where countless attacks by both sides of varying scale failed to break through the increasingly complex trench lines. 1918 saw both sides throw all they had into attempts at decisive victory. The first, the German Spring Offensives, prompted by victory in the east and the threat of growing American involvement in the west, failed through strategic miscalculation and logistic deficiencies. Thereafter, they "had no alternative but to attempt a desperate exercise in damage limitation, which largely failed them."[33] The second, the Allies' Hundred Days offensives, proved victorious. The German Army was pushed back from a series of defensive lines until it was forced into headlong retreat once the Battle of the Sambre had "settled the matter".[34]

26   Andy Simpson, *Directing Operations: British Corps Command on the Western Front 1914-1918* (Stroud: Spellmount, 2006).
27   Gary Sheffield & Dan Todman, eds., *Command and Control on the Western Front: The British Army's Experience 1914-18* (Staplehurst: Spellmount, 2004).
28   Spencer Jones, ed., *Stemming the Tide: Officers and Leadership in the British Expeditionary Force 1914* (Solihull: Helion & Company, 2013) and *Courage Without Glory. The British Army on the Western Front 1915* (Solihull: Helion & Company, 2015). This series will expand to one volume for each year of the war.
29   Gary Sheffield, *Command and Morale. The British Army on the Western Front 1914-1918* (Barnsley: Pen & Sword Books, 2014) and Peter Simkins, *From the Somme to Victory: The British Army's Experience on the Western Front 1916-1918* (Barnsley: Pen & Sword Books, 2014).
30   David Stevenson, *1914-1918. The History of the First World War* (London: Allen Lane, 2004).
31   Ian F.W.Beckett, *The Great War 1914-1918* (Harlow: Pearson Educational, 2001).
32   David Stevenson, *With Our Backs to the Wall: Victory and Defeat in 1918* (London: Allen Lane, 20111) p. xvii.
33   Ibid, p. xviii.
34   Ibid, p. 168.

The major attritional battles such as the Somme or Third Ypres have been studied in exhaustive detail at the operational and tactical levels. This treatment has yet to be applied to the battles of the Hundred Days.

The Hundred Days

The historiography of the Hundred Days and of the operational and tactical methodology of these sequential attacks is not yet definitive, but there has been a surge of interest amongst historians over recent years in the events of 1918. Published accounts are still few and far between, however. The histories of the two British armies, Third and Fourth, that played the major roles in the events of the Hundred Days were published 92 years apart. Archibald Montgomery's volume on Fourth Army appeared in 1920 and in style resembles many of the formation histories written at that time:[35] General Rawlinson's preface is a justification of BEF strategy, claiming that the events of the summer and autumn of 1918 "constitute the greatest military triumph the world has ever seen",[36] and goes on to praise the "genius and foresight"[37] of Foch[38] and Haig. The text traces Fourth Army's advance in a style that is less self-congratulatory, but that nevertheless constantly honours the memory and efforts of the officers and men of an "army [with] the will to conquer, and the confidence in victory, that foreshadow success".[39] Montgomery's closing chapter, rather than concluding as its title might suggest, reads like a tactical manual for use in future conflicts, giving advice on, amongst other things, the rate of advance of the creeping artillery barrage, the efficacy of the flank attack and the advantage of the surprise assault.[40]

Jonathan Boff's book on Third Army is a much more analytical work and sheds much light on this neglected period of the Great War, asking important questions on the relative performances of the BEF and the German Army, tracing their efforts to adapt methodologies to this ever-developing phase of the conflict.[41] After a brief narrative of events,[42] he adopts a thematic approach, analysing manpower and training, materiel, morale, the BEF's combined arms tactics and the German response, communications, command and control. Boff concludes that the picture is a complicated one: "The armies were locked in a deadly evolutionary struggle where measures and counter-measures continually interacted in highly dynamic fashion".[43]

He also argues that 'all-arms' tactics declined in October and November 1918 and that progress along multiple learning curves was hampered by the BEF's difficulty in shaking off some of the habits of trench fighting.[44] This book, in its detailed treatment of operations and tactics, substantially adds to the body of evidence that corroborates these theories.

---

35   Sir A. Montgomery, *The Story of the Fourth Army in the Battles of the Hundred Days, August 8th to November 11th 1918* (London: Hodder & Stoughton, 1920).
36   Ibid, p. vii.
37   Ibid, p. viii.
38   Maréchal Ferdinand Jean Marie Foch (1851-1929) Allied Commander-in-Chief from 26 March 1918.
39   Ibid, p. 146.
40   Ibid, pp. 263-272.
41   Boff, op cit.
42   Ibid, pp. 22-38.
43   Ibid, pp. 248-9.
44   Ibid, pp. 245-6.

J.P. Harris and Niall Barr's 1998 work constitutes the first single-volume account of the BEF's advance to victory.[45] It is, as Harris explains in the introduction, a "fairly short book on a very big campaign",[46] and as such can rarely delve below the operational level of war. The BEF's contribution (and that of the Dominion Forces) is assessed against that of its allies and the fighting methods used are carefully analysed, resulting in an assertion that the allies' weapon system was "fallible" and that "[t]o think in terms of the constant application of a set formula would be to underestimate the dynamism and complexity of the campaign".[47] This book, by examining the final battle at the tactical level, goes some way toward substantiating this premise.

Nick Lloyd tells the story of the Hundred Days in his 2013 work, skilfully weaving together the stories and testimonies of individual soldiers and of the military and political leaders of the time.[48] He explores two main questions: how effective were the BEF's fighting methods and was the German Army actually defeated in 1918? His conclusion on the former is that the allies had "finally mastered a tactical and operational system that could achieve victory on the battlefield."[49] On the latter, he argues that the allied victory was "partial",[50] that in facing an increasingly tired and logistically challenged enemy, "a complete collapse of German resistance in 1918 [was] unlikely",[51] but admits that, had the war continued, a collapse in the following spring would have been the probable outcome.

A sparse and therefore far from complete historiography of the Hundred Days means that some questions on the conduct and outcome of the Great War lack definitive answers. Battles are won and lost at the tactical level, and it is only through detailed study of these final encounters that such gaps may begin to be filled.

Existing accounts of the Battle of the Sambre
These are rare. In *Amiens to the Armistice*,[52] Harris and Barr devote more than most to this final engagement: six pages.[53] They give a comprehensive, yet brief outline of the day's events and sum it up as a "grand slam".[54] Peter Hart, in *1918, A Very British Victory*,[55] devotes three and a half pages,[56] but concentrates almost exclusively on the attack of the 2nd Battalion Royal Sussex at Lock No.1 and the two Victoria Crosses won there. Wilfred Owen merits half a page and the travails of the eight divisions of Third Army are encapsulated in less than three lines. Niall Barr's contribution to *Changing War* runs to 17 pages, largely devoted once more to Fourth Army, but rightly emphasises the role of the Royal Engineers, which was vital to the success of the attacks. He concludes with the thought that this battle merits closer and more detailed study.

45   J.P. Harris with Niall Barr, *Amiens to the Armistice* (London: Brassey's, 1998).
46   Ibid, p. xiii.
47   Ibid, p. 298.
48   NickLloyd, *Hundred Days: The End of the Great War* (London: Viking, 2013).
49   Ibid, p. 278.
50   Ibid, p. 278.
51   Ibid, p. 277.
52   Harris & Barr, op cit.
53   Ibid. pp. 227-83. The account includes a map – a rarity for this battle.
54   Ibid, p. 283.
55   Peter Hart, *1918: A Very British Victory* (London: Weidenfeld & Nicolson, 2008).
56   Ibid, pp. 487-90.

Books that set out to tell the story of 1918 as a whole tend to focus their narratives elsewhere: John Terraine, *To Win A War – 1918, the Year of Victory*,[57] sums up the events of 4 November in one page, concentrating largely on the New Zealanders' audacious "storming" of the fortified town of Le Quesnoy; J.H. Johnson, *1918 – The Unexpected Victory*,[58] gives two pages of narrative; Simon Robbins, in his brilliant *British Generalship on the Western Front 1914-1918 – Defeat into Victory*,[59] does not attempt a narrative, but highlights IX Corps' tactics of reinforcing success and outflanking troublesome pockets of enemy resistance.[60]

It is no surprise that Prior and Wilson's study of Sir Henry Rawlinson, *Command on the Western Front*,[61] concentrates on the deeds of the Fourth Army, putting its success down to the use of tanks in the villages along the western edge of the Forêt de Mormal, demoralisation of defenders at Landrecies, skilled infantry tactics and overwhelming use of artillery. The parts played by the British Third Army and French First Armies are dismissed in one sentence as supporting roles.[62] Nick Lloyd's *Hundred Days*[63] gives us four pages of narrative concentrating on Wilfred Owen and the Manchester Regiment, but includes first-hand German testimony.

The two publications that contain the most extensive accounts of the action on 4 November 1918 are *The Story of the Fourth Army in the Battles of the Hundred Days, August 8th to November 11th 1918* by Major-General Sir Archibald Montgomery[64] and the Official History, *Military Operations France and Belgium 1918, Volume V*, by Brigadier-General Sir James Edmonds and Lieutenant-Colonel R. Maxwell-Hyslop.[65] The former gives an 18 page, detailed account with numerous photographs; the latter presents 29 pages of familiar, if rather dry, narrative, along with its usual short sections on the French, American and German perspectives. It is interesting to note its late publication date of 1947 (only two Western Front volumes appeared after this one – Passchendaele, 1917 Vol. II and Cambrai, 1917 Vol. III): in the Preface, written in December 1945, Edmonds bemoans the passing of many combatants and the fading memories of others, with the result that he has not been able to call upon as much help from them as in previous volumes. Indeed, he comments that Montgomery's *Story of the Fourth Army* "has been of consider-able value".[66] The sections on Third and Fourth Armies, running to 23 pages, are narrated in a matter-of-fact tone: successes are under-played and setbacks or failures are either glossed over with unwarranted brevity or are camouflaged by false positivity. Analysis is notable by its almost total absence: the success of tactical and operational methodology is taken for granted. The method of advance on Third Army front is described in broad terms whereby three objective lines are proposed and units leap-frog onto each subsequent line, thus not overstretching the troops. Pauses are built in, during which artillery can be moved forward to support the final stages of the assault

57   John Terraine, *To Win A War – 1918, the Year of Victory* (London: Papermac, 1978).
58   J.H. Johnson, *1918 – The Unexpected Victory* (London: Arms & Armour Press, 1997).
59   Robbins, *British Generalship on the Western Front*.
60   Ibid, p. 104.
61   Prior & Wilson, *Command on the Western Front*.
62   Ibid. p. 388.
63   Lloyd, *Hundred Days*.
64   Montgomery, *The Story of the Fourth Army in the Battles of the Hundred Days*.
65   J.E. Edmonds & R. Maxwell-Hyslop, *Military Operations France and Belgium 1918, Vol. V* (London: HMSO, 1947).
66   Ibid. Preface, p. viii.

that were originally out of range.[67] The initial stages of the assault dominate the narrative, the later stages being reduced almost to irrelevance by the repetition of phrases such as "[machine guns were] easily overcome"; "resistance then collapsed"; "very little opposition"; "success was gained".[68] Indeed, the final summing up of Third Army's advance suggests a certain effortlessness: "The Third Army's objective had, therefore, been reached on its whole front, in places overpassed, and little more than the advanced guards of eight of its 15 divisions had been engaged."[69] It was not that simple, as the detailed analysis in this book shows.

Two examples serve to illustrate the lack of interpretive detail. The difficulties encountered by 96 Brigade (32nd Division) and their subsequent failure to cross the canal south of Landrecies as planned are dealt with in six lines of narrative, devoid of explanation or analysis.[70] The tactical naivety of 17th Division, and in particular 50 Brigade, is not mentioned: its failure to gain its objectives, in stark comparison to 38th Division on its immediate right, is explained away by the simple assertion that "resistance was obstinate".[71]

It is the lack of detail that mars the official narrative. Edmonds makes his excuses for this in the volume's preface, stating that "[i]n dealing with such large forces it was impossible within a reasonable space either to enter into much detail or to mention every unit engaged; the scale of the narrative had to be different from that of earlier volumes".[72] The final advance did not merit detailed treatment, it would seem, yet the Battle of Cambrai (20 November – 7 December 1917) was thought worthy of its own 400-page volume.

It is in the 'Preface' and 'Reflections' chapters that some analysis – of a general nature – can be found. Edmonds bemoans "too much blue, red and green line", limiting units to fixed objectives even when commanders were exhorting them to "go all out", but argues that "the system of limited advance was inevitable", otherwise troops would have "fallen out of control". At the same time, however, he describes the small-unit tactics used to deal with enemy machine guns as "magnificent: the use of ground, the value of the indirect approach and envelopment [being] well understood".[73] This book expands on these premises, describing the action in sufficient detail to show that the BEF's tactical and operational methodology was, in November 1918, much more complicated that Edmonds' superficial treatment suggests.

Other works, formation or unit histories, written for the most part soon after the end of the war, are numerous. Some of these are referred to in later chapters, though they largely help to add narrative 'colour': they were never meant to be treatises on operational method, and any analysis included can be an attempt to put a positive spin on an unsuccessful episode or to defend the reputation of a unit by stating the difficult circumstances under which they had been required to operate. They were aimed, after all, at the former officers and men of the unit: offending them would do nothing to boost sales. They also rely heavily on battalion war diary entries, often transcribing them verbatim, and rarely add anything substantial or significant to the original first-hand accounts.

67   Ibid. p. 478.
68   Ibid. pp. 479, 482, 482 & 486.
69   Ibid. p. 488.
70   Ibid. p. 470.
71   Ibid. p. 480.
72   Ibid. Preface, p. iv.
73   Ibid. p. 576.

Sources

This work is based largely upon unpublished, archival sources: the documents contained in over 300 formation or unit War Diaries held at the National Archives, Kew.[74] War Diaries chronicled the day-to-day activities of the BEF and are described by Jonathan Boff in his study of the Third Army in the Hundred Days as "the most important single primary source".[75] They were kept by all formations, from GHQ down to Battalion and give unrivalled insight into the events on the front-line. Each battalion had its own adjutant, one of whose jobs was to complete the War Diary. This was done on a day to day basis, though in busy times, entries could be written some time after the events described. Above battalion level, the diary was the domain of the Staff Officer: orders sent down to lower formations, narratives of engagements, after-action reports and advisory documents were also compiled by these often largely anonymous men. Some of these documents were distributed widely: 117 copies of the 32nd Division's "Notes on Future Operations", for example, issued 1 November 1918, were sent out to lower formations/units, including 17 to each of the division's three brigades, thus ensuring that every company commander would receive a copy. As Majors, Captains and occasionally Lieutenants, the Staff Officers were able to sign the documents in the absence of their commanding officer at Brigade and Divisional level, and it would seem rare that the Brigadier-General or Major-General added his signature prior to despatch. It would seem unlikely that he himself would have compiled the document anyway, but one might hope that he had read it. At Corps and Army level, it fell largely to the MGGS or BGGS to sign off the documents: illustrative examples of this would be Brigadier-General I. Stewart, BGGS XIII Corps, and Major-General A.A. Montgomery, MGGS Fourth Army, whose signatures adorn almost every document issued by these formations in the period leading up to and during the Battle of the Sambre. It must be added, as a cautionary note, however, that a signature is not necessarily an indicator of authorship.

Some War Diaries are sparse,[76] but the majority are, thanks to the meticulous approach of many of the adjutants charged with their compilation, a rich seam of original, first-hand accounts, including maps, orders received and sent, narratives of battles, casualty figures and coherent after action reports that contain valuable operational and tactical analysis. Some are incomplete, with appendices lost or misplaced over the years, but careful analysis of division, brigade and battalion documents can give a coherent picture of occurrences at the operational level: the planning; the events; the outcomes. They were written at the time, by the man on the spot, free from a century's-worth of hindsight, undistorted by the prism of decades of changing attitudes and mores. They cannot be totally free from bias, from omission or error: they were written by human beings with opinions of their own, survivors of dramatic and even traumatic events, with limited fields of view, but they are honest and leap fresh from the page almost a century later. Multiplicity of authorship and viewpoint helps to smooth out the wrinkles of inconsistency. An accurate analysis of events cannot be achieved without heavy reliance on these invaluable documents.

74   See Bibliography.
75   Boff, *Winning and Losing*, p. 17.
76   The account of the day's actions in the diary of 1st Battalion King's Own Yorkshire Light Infantry, 151 Brigade, 50th Division, for example, runs to just four hand-written lines.

Secondary sources – listed in the bibliography – serve a dual purpose: they can sometimes be used to plug any gaps in the accounts contained within the War Diaries, but more importantly are essential in placing the Battle of the Sambre within its wider contexts.

The inclusion of analysis of the battle from the German viewpoint would not materially help to answer the questions posed in this book. Primary German sources are in any case incomplete, particularly for the final months of the war, and relatively difficult to obtain. The German Official History is of limited value: as the armistice approaches, the work is lacking in operational and tactical detail and concentrates exclusively on the strategy of retreat and the political machinations relating to the pressing issue of capitulation. Leutnant Alenfeld's account of his tribulations on 4 November 1918 has been included in Chapter 7 as being representative of many similar experiences endured by German combatants on that day.

Structure

The book is divided into seven chapters and a conclusion. Chapter One places this final battle into its wider context by examining briefly the events of the 'Hundred Days', the attempts by Germany to broker a peace settlement with the United States, the collapse of Germany's allies and the different character of the fighting after 4 November. The terms 'learning curve', 'all-arms battle' and 'bite and hold' are also explained and placed within the wider context of the Great War and its historiography. The chapter also considers the planning stages of the battle, detailing the orders that were sent down the chain of command, the infantry units chosen to execute the assault and their relative performances during the Hundred Days, the viability of the objectives set for the day's fighting and the resources available across all branches of the services. The expected cooperation between infantry, engineers, artillery, tanks and RAF is examined to assess just how much this was to be an 'all-arms battle'.

Subsequent chapters involve detailed accounts of the events of 4 November 1918. The narrative moves, chapter by chapter, from the north to the south of the battle frontage. Chapter Two deals with the attack of XVII Corps. Two divisions, the 19th and 24th, already in possession of some of their 4 November objectives, were to cross the Petit Aunelle River, capture the large twin villages of Wargnies le Grand and Wargnies le Petit and then advance up the gentle slopes to the east toward the ridge line where the fortified villages of Eth and Bry blocked their path. The terrain here was "open country",[77] with scattered villages, small streams and rivers, orchards and fields. Some fields were cultivated, but "the area as a whole was pasture land intersected by hedges and wire".[78]

Chapter Three describes the actions of VI Corps, which was faced by similar ground to that of their northern neighbours: the ground rose gently to the east and was crossed by the Rhonelle and Petit Aunelle rivers which cut the ground into spurs running north-west to south-east. The main obstacles of the Guards and 62nd Divisions were the villages of Frasnoy and Preux-au-Sart.

---

77   Harris & Barr, *Amiens to the Armistice*, p. 273.
78   Edmonds & Maxwell-Hyslop, *Military Operations France and Belgium 1918, Vol. V*, p. 464.

The assaults of IV Corps are assessed in Chapter Four. This Corps contained the only non-British unit involved in the battle, the New Zealand Division, and it was given the task of capturing Le Quesnoy. This town was fortified in the 17th Century by Vauban and retains its classic star-shaped ramparts, with ditches, moats and fortified gates.[79] To the south, the 37th Division, bolstered by the presence of tanks, were to cross the defended railway line east of Ghissignies, capture Louvignies and continue their advance into the north-western corner of the Forêt de Mormal.

In Chapter Five we reach the southern limits of the Third Army frontage: V Corps. The 17th Division on the left, again with the help of tanks, was confronted by an area of orchards, hedges and villages just west of the Forêt de Mormal and then by an advance through the forest to and then beyond the isolated village of Locquignol in its centre. To the south, 38th Division, on a narrow, single-brigade front was quickly into the forest and thus deprived of armoured assistance. They advanced mainly along its rides and tracks, attempting to outflank the isolated German machine-gun posts.

Chapter Six deals with the left flank of Fourth Army: XIII Corps had three divisions in the front line: 18th; 50th; and 25th. Between them, they had 24 tanks at their disposal. On the left of the Corps frontage 18th Division faced the fortified towns of Hecq and Preux-au-Bois. With 50th Division to the south, the advance was to continue deep into the forest, where vehicles of the 17th Armoured Car Battalion were to cause havoc along the forest tracks. The ultimate objective was a spur beyond the eastern limits of the forest overlooking the Sambre north-east of Landrecies. This town on the Sambre-Oise Canal was the objective of 25th Division: it was hoped that a crossing could be forced and the town occupied by the end of the day.

Chapter Seven analyses the actions of IX Corps. Its two divisions, 32nd and 1st, directly faced the obstacle of the Sambre-Oise Canal. The Germans still held ground on the western banks and attempts to force a passage across the canal met with mixed fortunes: 32nd Division was mauled badly as it came up against determined opposition and was forced to improvise in order to ensure the success of the attack; one of the most daring efforts was made by 1st Division on the right flank of the Corps frontage at Lock No.1, where the width of the canal was reduced to 17 feet at the lock gates. The lock buildings on the eastern bank were heavily defended, but success here would allow a general advance into the open country beyond.

Each chapter includes analysis of the number of objectives gained in relation to those projected; the levels of casualties suffered; the efficacy of 'all-arms cooperation' – what were the relative values of the contributions of the infantry, the artillery, engineers, tanks and aircraft? The question of the difference between 'plan' and 'reality' is examined: to what extent did the plan work, and how far were the successes, failures and recoveries down to the 'man on the spot', the formation or unit commander, who, faced with a faltering or stalled attack, was able to adapt or even abandon the original orders and yet still achieve his overall objectives?

The conclusion assesses the extent to which the assault can be deemed a success. It shows that the BEF was able to adapt its operational and tactical methodology to suit the conditions it faced and that it was a dynamic force that could learn from experience and assimilate new technologies. It also demonstrates clearly, however, that the Battle of the Sambre was not a

---

79   Sébastien le Prestre de Vauban (1633-1707), military engineer and builder of a chain of forts for
      Louis XIV.

true 'all-arms' battle, for reasons logistical, meteorological and topographical, but one where victory could nevertheless be won by an army confident enough in its own abilities to attack with the resources available. Neither was this battle a true example of 'bite and hold': Professor William Philpott describes the 'Hundred Days' battles as a "sophisticated attritional offensive" that would go on "until one side or the other broke".[80] By 4 November the German Army was on the point of breaking and the 'bite' could be repeated a number of times as units leapfrogged each other into the attack, the 'hold' becoming largely irrelevant as the paucity of German reserves rendered meaningful counter-attacks impracticable.

The conclusion also shows that it was necessary for the BEF to fight the Battle of the Sambre. Foch's great offensive "never broke the German front", advancing at "less than a mile a day [...] over the period from 8 August to 11 November", and the German defence remained tenacious, "exacting a steady toll on their pursuers".[81] It was the decisive victory on the Sambre that finally broke the will of the German Army and prompted OHL to accept peace at any price.

80   William Philpott, *Attrition: Fighting the First World War* (London: Little, Brown & Co., 2014), pp. 327-328.
81   Ibid, pp. 333-334.

1

Contexts

The historiographical context was dealt with in the 'Literature Review' in the Introduction. This chapter places the Battle of the Sambre into its political, strategic, operational and tactical contexts before looking at the formations involved and outlining the planning process.

The Political Context

This section examines Germany's increasingly fraught attempts to broker a peace settlement, which run concurrent to their desperate defensive battles of the autumn. It then shows how the loss of its allies, as they exited the military stage one by one, each comprehensively defeated, left Germany alone in its attempts to hold out. Not only was she alone, but she was facing an ever-growing number of enemy troops. The entry of the USA into the war – as an 'associate' power, rather than an 'ally' – had helped to precipitate the German Spring Offensives in March 1918. In the autumn it was the rate at which the number of American troops was growing that alarmed OHL: the Americans were still tactically naive and logistically inefficient, but sheer weight of numbers was becoming a decisive long-term factor.

It was on 28 September, two days after the start of the Meuse-Argonne offensive, at OHL's headquarters in Spa, Belgium, that Ludendorff, faced with news of a German collapse in Flanders, and possibly suffering a nervous breakdown,[1] confided to Hindenburg that an armistice offer must be made as soon as possible. He was "responding not only to events in the West, but also to the news that Bulgaria was suing for peace".[2] An offensive begun on 25 September had broken the Bulgarian lines and German reinforcements were sent too late to avert the crisis. A ceasefire agreement was signed on the 29th.

Austro-Hungarian forces were also on the verge of collapse: "defeat and rout"[3] at the Battle of Vittorio Veneto, which began on 24 October, prompting the surrender of half a million men to the Italians, led to a rapid disintegration of the Habsburg Empire with Austria signing an

---

1   See David Stevenson, *1914-1918: The History of the First World War* (London: Allen Lane, 2004), p. 431 and Lloyd, *Hundred Days*, p. 178.
2   Stevenson, *1914-1918*, p. 431.
3   Ibid, p. 485.

armistice on 3 November. Meanwhile, the Turkish army had been defeated at Megiddo, with Damascus and Beirut falling to Allenby's[4] troops on 1 and 2 October respectively, but it was the Bulgarian surrender that expedited the Ottoman Empire's final collapse. Turkey's best divisions were still centred in the Caucasus, leaving only four divisions guarding Constantinople and the Straits. Rather than helping to prop up Germany, the boot was on the other foot: in order to defend their territory, Turkey needed money and armaments from Germany, but the allied offensives against Bulgaria had cut the rail link. General Milne,[5] commanding officer of British forces in Salonika, would also soon be in a position to move on Constantinople, prompting the Turks to request peace terms on 16 October. The armistice document was signed two weeks later.

By the time of the Battle of the Sambre, Germany had therefore lost all its main allies, but "although [their] surrenders coincided, they were all defeated separately, and tellingly, each negotiated for an armistice independently. [Defeats] on other fronts did not determine the outcome of the battle in the west, or have much impact on the cohesion of an alliance which existed in name only by this point".[6] The mood at OHL remained belligerent: they were aware of the deteriorating condition of the German army: they were being driven back step by step on the Western Front, unit strengths were falling, owing to battle casualties and to sickness,[7] and there were almost no reserves left. Nevertheless, Germany was not yet prepared to accept unconditional surrender: if nothing else, the army must remain intact to serve as a buffer against revolution at home. Paul von Hintze, Secretary of State,[8] saw a chance to "play off America against Britain and France"[9] by appealing directly to President Wilson, proposing acceptance of peace terms based on his Fourteen Points, but also realised that a change of political system might win Germany better terms: he tried to instigate a "stage-managed democratisation", a revolution from above to avert one from below.[10]

The German government resigned on 3 October and the new Imperial Chancellor, Max von Baden, head of a government with a majority comprising the SPD,[11] the Catholic Centre and the Liberals was empowered to salvage what he could from an increasingly perilous situation. Max was not at first inclined to take precipitate action, but on Ludendorff's insistence the cabinet was persuaded to send a note to the American President. Despatched on 4 October, it was "short and simple, requesting Wilson to take in hand arrangements for an immediate armistice and for peace negotiations in which Germany would accept as a basis the Fourteen Points".[12]

In the exchange that followed, with Wilson sending three notes on 8, 14 and 23 October and the Germans replying on 12, 20 and 27 October, the American President's stance gradually

4   Edmund Henry Hynman Allenby (1861-1936). GOC Cavalry Division in the original BEF; GOC V Corps, and then from October 1915, GOC Third Army. Promoted to command Egyptian Expeditionary Force in June 1917.
5   George Francis Milne (1866-1948) GOC 27th Division, then GOC XVI Corps, and finally GOC British Forces in Salonika.
6   Philpott, *Attrition*, p. 337.
7   Ibid, p. 325.
8   Paul von Hintze (1864-1941) Diplomat. Chosen as Foreign Minister in July 1918.
9   Stevenson, *1914-1918* p. 470.
10   Ibid, p. 470.
11   *Sozialdemokratische Partei Deutschlands* – German Social Democratic Party, founded 1863.
12   Ibid, p. 471.

hardened. By 20 October, Wilson was insisting that a ceasefire "must render Germany unable to resist any eventual peace treaty [...] and that he must demand an end to Wilhelm's control of policy. His minimum requirements were for a fully constitutional monarchy and parliamentary control over the high command".[13] The Germans must also agree to Allied commanders dictating the terms of any armistice.

As early as 9 October, however, Ludendorff had emerged from his breakdown and insisted to the new Chancellor that "the Army could defend the frontiers for a long time yet".[14] The cabinet met on 17 October and discussed the current situation. Ludendorff advised that an allied breakthrough was possible rather than probable and that Germany could achieve better peace terms by continuing the war into 1919. David Stevenson states: "In fact there were genuine grounds for saying that with the campaigning season ending and the army retreating in good order, Ludendorff had [earlier] overestimated the danger and his new opinion was more realistic."[15]

The German government was unconvinced and decided that negotiations must continue. Wilson's third note brought the situation to a head: essentially it stated that the USA would enter into negotiations, but not while the Kaiser and OHL continued to dictate policy: "if it had to deal with the military masters and the monarchical autocrats then America would demand not peace negotiation but surrender."[16]

This was the end for Ludendorff: he and Hindenburg issued a proclamation to the army denouncing, as they saw it, Wilson's threat of unconditional surrender, and imploring the soldiers to continue their resistance. This document blatantly undermined the authority of the Chancellor and his government and on 26 October the Kaiser dismissed Ludendorff, replacing him with Wilhelm Groener,[17] who was recalled from his post as Chief of Staff of Army Group Kiev. On arrival in Spa, he soon formed the opinion that the retreat to the Antwerp-Meuse line could not be postponed for long. His troops would have to hold out on the Hermann Line in order to allow all the vehicles and ordnance currently stranded between the two positions to be moved east to safety, or risk losing a huge amount of materiel should the retreat come too soon. It was the allied success on the Sambre on 4 November that was to precipitate his decision, orders for the retreat being issued that day.

So, by the end of the day on 4 November, the German High Command knew that their efforts to hold out against Allied attacks until the winter had failed.

Am 4. November wurden die Bedingungen für Deutschland endgültig festgesetzt.[18]

Groener was desperate for an armistice: on 5 November he spoke to the cabinet, intimating that the army could "hold out long enough for negotiations", but adding, on the following day, that

---

13   Ibid, p. 474.
14   Ibid, p. 475.
15   Ibid, p. 475.
16   Lloyd, *Hundred Days*, quoting from President Wilson's reply to the German note of 21 October 1918 on 24 October in *United States Army in the World War 1917-19*, Vol. X, pp. 17-18.
17   Erster Generalquartiermeister Karl Eduard Wilhelm Groener, (1867-1939) Commander in Chief on the Western Front from 29 October 1918.
18   Bundesarchiv: *Der Weltkrieg 1914-18. Vol. XI. Die Kriegführung an der Westfront im Jahre 1918* (Berlin: Mittler & Sohn, 1944) p. 746. Loosely translated, this means: "On the 4 November, Germany's fate was irrevocably settled."

"even Monday will be too late: it must be Saturday[19] at the latest".[20] Later that day, the German armistice delegates set off for the front. Ideas of a negotiated peace in the spring of 1919 with Germany still holding on to occupied territories were dashed.

The situation in Germany was grave: the Navy had mutinied at Wilhelmshaven on 27 October and this had spread to several other northern ports; within days "most of the provincial capitals were in revolutionary hands".[21] It was announced by Max von Baden that Kaiser Wilhelm had abdicated and a Republic was declared from the Reichstag building by SPD leader Scheidemann on 9 November. The declaration of the abdication was premature: Wilhelm only agreed to step down once his generals had been consulted. Thirty-nine of them were gathered at Spa and asked whether they would march back to Germany and "recapture the homeland"[22] in the name of the Kaiser. Only one answered in the affirmative, with 15 unsure and the rest against. Without the backing of the army, Wilhelm could hang on no longer: he left for exile in Holland the following day.

All the political machinations had, by this stage, been rendered irrelevant by the fact that the German representatives had already crossed French lines and had been presented with the Allied conditions for surrender by Maréchal Foch. These terms had been decided not by President Wilson, but by two Allied conferences in Paris, running from 6 to 9 October and from 29 October to 4 November. The demands were as follows: cessation of hostilities within six hours of signing; evacuation of occupied France and Belgium, including Alsace and Lorraine, within two weeks; the surrender of 5,000 artillery pieces, 36,000 machine guns, 2,000 aircraft, along with rolling stock and military stores. The allies would occupy the left bank of the Rhine with substantial bridgeheads at Mainz, Cologne and Koblenz. There would be no cessation of hostilities until a signature was received. Matthias Erzberger, leader of the German delegation, countered these with a document claiming that the terms were too severe. Foch dismissed it, making only minor concessions. A courier was sent back to Berlin carrying Erzberger's advice that Germany accept the terms. By the time he arrived, Prince Max's government had fallen. The new Chancellor, Friedrich Ebert, instructed Erzberger to sign on any terms. The signature was duly appended at 5:10 a.m. on 11 November.

The Strategic Context

Being the last large-scale set-piece attack by the BEF in the Great War, the Battle of the Sambre fits neatly into the pattern of events that punctuate the Hundred Days, demonstrating the "new operational art",[23] which comprehensively defeated the German army on the Western Front. This battle has so far escaped detailed study: it has, as Niall Barr puts it, been "overlooked perhaps because of the rush to reach the Armistice which seems to afflict most studies of the Great

19   9 November 1918.
20   J.E. Edmonds & R. Maxwell-Hyslop, *Military Operations France and Belgium 1918, Vol. V* (London: HMSO, 1947), p. 516.
21   Stevenson, *1914-1918*, p. 496.
22   Lloyd, *Hundred Days*, p. 260.
23   Gary Sheffield, *The Chief: Douglas Haig and the British Army* (London: Aurum Press, 2011), p. 303.

War".[24] It was the last of a sequence of battles that began on 18 July 1918, not with the BEF, but with the French Tenth Army under General Mangin.[25] They had stopped in its tracks the last German offensive of the war, which had aimed to capture the city of Rheims, and turned the tables with a counter attack by 18th Division of XX Corps, including American troops from 1st and 2nd Divisions, spearheaded by almost 500 tanks. There was no preliminary bombardment, "nothing to warn the Germans of the impending assault".[26] A creeping barrage commenced at Zero Hour as the infantry and tanks began their advance. The resulting French victory, which cleared German forces from the Marne salient, shocked the OHL into suspending all plans for future offensives. "They had lost the initiative. The tide had turned irrevocably, and on 2 August 1918 Ludendorff ordered his subordinates to adopt a strategic defensive policy",[27] although he also resisted requests to fall back immediately to the Hindenburg Line and to begin preparations for a new defensive position running from Antwerp to the Meuse. It would therefore be incumbent upon the Allies to push the German army back step by step, with the last big effort coming on the banks of the Sambre-Oise Canal on 4 November 1918.

Haig required Rawlinson, now commanding Fourth Army, to plan an assault that would drive the Germans away from the strategically vital rail hub of Amiens. In what was almost a throwback to the days of 1916, Rawlinson's initial idea was for an advance of seven miles, but Haig was looking for something rather more ambitious: 27 miles. What emerged was a plan with many similarities to that implemented by the French on the Marne, and arguably a scaled-up version of the Battle of Hamel (4 July 1918), a "laboratory for ideas", where Australian and Canadian infantry (again with some American involvement) had captured the town in two hours, helped by gas shells, a creeping barrage, 60 tanks and a liberal scattering of Lewis Guns and grenade-throwing rifles.[28]

Some historians argue that the assault launched on 8 August 1918 east of Amiens was the apogee of this methodology, when artillery, infantry, armour and aircraft were used together in "one of the most remarkable days of the war":[29] counter-battery work had severely disrupted German artillery capabilities and over 400 tanks had rumbled forward in support of the infantry. Over 1,000 aircraft were employed in reconnaissance, ground attack, contact patrols, artillery spotting, bombing and the suppression of German aerial response. An advance of around six to eight miles was achieved with casualties of around 48,000 (33,000 of those being taken prisoner or missing) inflicted upon the defenders.

---

24   Niall Barr, 'The Last Battle: The Crossing of the Sambre-Oise Canal, 4 November 1918', in Gary Sheffield & Peter Gray, eds., *Changing War The British Army, the Hundred Days Campaign and the Birth of the Royal Air Force 1918*, (London: Bloomsbury Academic, 2013), p. 73.
25   Charles Marie Emmanuel Mangin (1866-1925). Nickname "The Butcher". Recaptured Forts Vaux and Douaumont as Commander of 5th Division. Sacked as Commander of Sixth Army after the failure of the Nivelle Offensive in 1917, but reinstated as Commander of Tenth Army by Foch in1918. Most famously said of war: 'Whatever you do, you lose a lot of men'.
26   Lloyd, *Hundred Days*, p. 3.
27   Ibid, p. 7.
28   Stevenson, *1914-1918*, p. 426.
29   Lloyd, *Hundred Days*, p. 54.

This kind of effort took its toll, however. Advances on subsequent days struggled against stiffening German resolve as reserves were rushed in from other sectors to stem the tide.[30] The levels of artillery support could not be maintained and on the second day, less than half the tanks were still operational. "Almost as significant as the attack itself, however, was its suspension."[31] On 11 August Rawlinson called a halt. Foch was all for a resumption of the attack at the earliest possible moment, but Haig resisted these demands. "The Allies would no longer batter away along the same sector beyond the point of diminishing returns. The secret of success lay not only in the new technology and good preparation, but also in a willingness to halt while the going was good before starting again elsewhere."[32]

Gary Sheffield calls the Battle of Amiens "an unrepeatable one-off".[33] Indeed, British commanders would never be able to call upon such numbers of armoured vehicles again: by 4 November the Tank Corps could only muster 40 tanks to support the planned attack. Diminishing hours of daylight and adverse weather conditions would also restrict RAF involvement as the summer turned into autumn. The BEF fell back inevitably on the two mainstays of contemporary operational practice: artillery and infantry.[34]

Ten days later the emphasis shifted to Third Army, who opened the Battle of Albert. This was not a repeat of Amiens, but showed that the "optimum conditions" of 8 August "were not essential for success", and that "[s]tandard British Divisions with weaker artillery and armoured support could win dramatic victories as well".[35]

Fourth Army took up the cudgel again astride the Somme two days later and on 2 September the Canadians "smashed one of the strongest German defences",[36] the Drocourt-Quéant Line. By the evening of the same day, Australian troops had captured Mont St Quentin and the town of Péronne was in their hands. OHL immediately ordered Below's Second Army to retreat to the Hindenburg Line, other Armies following suit in the next few days. At an OHL conference at Avesnes on 6 September, Lossberg[37] suggested an immediate withdrawal to the Meuse. Ludendorff would not countenance such advice, even if it was "sensible and realistic".[38] Instead he ordered the construction of the 'Hermann Stellung', part of which would form the defences assaulted on 4 November.

Allied attacks continued: the Franco-American offensive in the Meuse-Argonne sector began on 26 September; British First and Third Armies launched attacks towards Cambrai the following day and on the 28th, Belgian and British forces pushed eastwards from what remained of the Ypres Salient. By this time, the Allies were facing an enemy who no longer had sufficient reserves available to replace losses, and although allied losses were also mounting, "Foch would accept the reciprocal wearing down of his own forces' fighting strength, secure in

30   By the third day, 14 extra German divisions had been moved into the Amiens sector. See Lloyd, *Hundred Days*, p. 60.
31   Stevenson, *1914-1918*, p. 426.
32   Ibid, p. 427.
33   Sheffield, *The Chief*, p. 308.
34   See Boff. *Winning and Losing on the Western Front*, pp. 245-46.
35   Sheffield, *The Chief*, p. 308.
36   Stevenson, *1914-1918*, p. 428.
37   Friedrich Karl von Lossberg (1868-1934). Defensive tactician who pioneered the 'defence in depth organisation' tactic.
38   Lloyd, *Hundred Days*, p. 112.

the knowledge that a steady supply of new American divisions […] would be able to support them if the French and British armies could not complete his grand design that year."[39]

On 29 September, in what was another set-piece attack – the British had been nibbling away at the German defences in the days leading up to the attack in order to establish realistic jumping-off positions – the Fourth Army "punched through" the Hindenburg Line, the high-light being IX Corps' audacious crossing of the Canal du Nord: "46th Division's assault [here] unhinged the German position. A three-mile deep gash had been ripped in the Hindenburg Line."[40] Six days later the BEF was "through the last of the prepared defences and could look to contesting 'unfortified' ground".[41] Other 'fortified' positions, even if hastily prepared, would cause the BEF to pause and prepare further 'set-piece' assaults.

It was becoming clear to Haig, if not to the politicians in London, that a victory in 1918 was possible. Henry Wilson (CIGS) had warned Haig that incurring heavy losses against the Hindenburg Line would be unacceptable and a memorandum from Churchill had advised the conservation of resources in readiness for 1919 and 1920. Haig replied to the latter on 3 October, re-emphasising his desire to "beat the enemy as soon as possible", having scrawled "What rubbish" on the original document adjacent to the mention of 1920.[42]

It was also becoming clear that the onus for this victory lay squarely with the BEF: the offensives in Flanders and the Meuse-Argonne sector having stalled owing to serious logistical problems, decisive results could best be achieved against the sector facing the British Third and Fourth Armies and French First Army. Haig consulted Byng and Rawlinson on 1 October and recorded in his diary that "both consider that Enemy has suffered very much and it is merely a question of our continuing our pressure to ensure his breaking".[43] It was a question of how many more setbacks the German army suffered, and which one would prove ultimately decisive. It would be the fourth, the Battle of the Sambre, that would cause the crumbling house of cards finally to collapse.

Cambrai fell on 9 October and the forcing of the Selle river began eight days later, the BEF coming up against stronger than anticipated resistance.[44] The Germans had, however, begun construction of the *Hermann Stellung* on 30 September and assurances were given that "within eight days artillery positions could be posted, sites selected for anti-tank guns, and dug outs and machine gun nests built".[45] The reality fell somewhat short of these estimations: by the end of October "nowhere had there been the time to construct the concrete dug outs and pill boxes and string out the acres of barbed wire that might have held the Allies up for any extended period".[46] The Germans would instead rely on natural obstacles such as forest, water courses and forti-fied villages to prevent any breakthrough. Douglas Haig, his forces taking a logistics-enforced breather after inching their way during that month up to the Sambre-Oise Canal and the Forêt de Mormal, was of the opinion that the job was not yet done. On the other side of the canal

39   Philpott, *Attrition*, p. 329.
40   Sheffield, *The Chief*, p. 323.
41   Stevenson, *1914-1918*, p. 431.
42   See Lloyd, *Hundred Days*, p. 191 and Sheffield, *The Chief*, p. 324.
43   Gary Sheffield & John Bourne, eds, *Douglas Haig. War Diaries and Letters 1914-1918* (London: Weidenfeld & Nicolson, 2005), p. 468.
44   See Sheffield, *The Chief*, p. 329 and Sheffield & Bourne, *Douglas Haig*, p. 474.
45   Lloyd, *Hundred Days*, p. 193.
46   Ibid, p. 214.

OHL believed in the possibility of continued resistance: Hindenburg still thought that all was not yet lost. The Battle of the Sambre was acquiring crucial significance.

The Operational Context

An army does not suddenly acquire the skills and techniques to defeat its enemy. The learning process had been a long and tortuous one: Professor William Philpott defines the term 'learning curve' as "a process of improvement based on battlefield experience".[47] The phrase appears to have been coined by Professor Peter Simkins in 1991[48] and was meant as a shorthand term for rejecting the 'Lions led by Donkeys' approach adopted by some historians. It has been criticised as being too simplistic, but the basic principle is now commonly accepted in academic circles. It is equally understood that the process was neither smooth nor constant. Philpott asserts that it was a "dynamic process of adjustment to new technologies, more sophisticated and flexible tactics, novel operational doctrines, complex logistics and fundamental change in the systems of command, control, communications and intelligence".[49] Christopher Duffy challenges the idea that the learning curve was a smooth one, declaring that "it was more of a series of steps, some of which led downwards"[50] – these would include the failure to learn from the successful use of artillery in the opening phase of the Battle of Neuve Chapelle, 10 March 1915, when a short but intense bombardment of sufficient concentration allowed the attacking troops to break into the German forward positions – but it is correct to say that the curve was both steep and significant. Paddy Griffith argues that "the first two years of the […] war effort […] represent the time of greatest amateurism, blundering and fumbling"[51] and later asserts that pamphlet SS143 (February 1917) was "a stormtrooper's handbook".[52] It is argued by Gary Sheffield and Peter Gray that some of the developments achieved by the BEF represent a "Revolution in Military Affairs", particularly in the fields of artillery and airpower, adding that "operations in 1914 looked back to Napoleon. In 1918 they were very different".[53]

The concept of multiple learning curves is a compelling one: the advances ranged widely in the areas of infantry tactics, developments in weapon technology, the invention and integration of light machine guns, grenades, mortars, tanks and aircraft; the emergence of the platoon as an effective fighting formation, a miniature all-arms unit in its own right as it evolved to include rifle grenade and Lewis Gun sections. Field survey and the consequent production of large-scale

47   Dr W. Philpott, *Beyond the Learning Curve: The British Army's Military Transformation in the First World War* (https://rusi.org/commentary/beyond-learning-curve-british-armys-military-transformation-first-world-war) Accessed 8 January 2016.

48   Peter Simkins, *World War One: The Western Front* (Godalming: Colour Library Books, 1991), p. 171.

49   Philpott, op cit.

50   C.Duffy, *Through German Eyes: the British and the Somme* (London: Weidenfeld & Nicolson, 2006, quoted in P. Simkins, *From the Somme to Victory: The British Army's Experience on the Western Front 1916-1918* (Barnsley: Pen & Sword, 2014), p. 54.

51   Paddy Griffith, *Battle Tactics of the Western Front: The British Army's Art of Attack 1916-1918* (New Haven & London: Yale University Press, 1994), p. 11.

52   Ibid, p. 194.

53   Gary Sheffield & Peter Gray (eds), *Changing War: The British Army, the Hundred Days' Campaign and the Birth of the Royal Air Force 1918* (London: Bloomsbury Academic, 2013), pp. 6-7.

maps became vital to the planning of infantry attacks and artillery barrages. Battlefield communication remained problematic throughout the war: wireless technology never properly replaced the need for visual signalling or the simple 'runner'. In the field of artillery emerged the creeping barrage, improved fuses and effective counter-battery work.[54] Training pamphlets proliferated and lessons learnt were disseminated and integrated into infantry training schemes. At the operational level in 1918 the BEF was capable of maintaining a high tempo of attacks that the Germans could not withstand; sufficient materiel and a logistics system capable of delivering it; the decentralisation of command in order to allow the 'man on the spot' both input into planning and the freedom to improvise on the battlefield;[55] the gradual move from successive deep assaults aimed at breakthrough that characterised most allied attacks of 1915-17 to sequential, limited offensives on a widening front through the summer and autumn of 1918 – a programme of rolling 'bite and hold' operations. The acceptance that the German Army could not be defeated by one single blow[56] was slow to reach prominence: there was no sudden damascene conversion of the General Staff. Bite and hold had been suggested by Lieutenant-General Sir Henry Rawlinson (commanding IV Corps) and Major-General Sir Thompson Capper (commanding 7th Division) for the Battle of Neuve Chapelle in March 1915, but Sir Douglas Haig (then commanding First Army) insisted on deepening the range of objectives to include Aubers Ridge. The break in succeeded, the breakthrough did not.[57] The "chimera" of the breakthrough[58] persisted, and British soldiers were sacrificed on its altar at Aubers Ridge, Festubert, Loos, Somme and the early phases of Third Ypres. Attacks with limited objectives, such as Bazentin Ridge (14 July 1916), Flers-Courcelette (25 September 1916) and Messines Ridge (7 June 1917) are notable for their scarcity, but Simon Robbins asserts that the General Staff became more predisposed to the latter method by the second half of 1917,[59] with Plumer's successive, methodical and limited assaults through September and October 1917 on the approaches to the Passchendaele Ridge lighting the way forward.[60] Indeed, Haig had told a conference of Army Commanders at Doullens on 7 May 1917 that he "intended to use 'step by step' methods" and an official communication to Armies on 7 August 1917 "advocated striking a series of blows in each of which 'our furthest objective must not only be within the power of our artillery, but within the power of our infantry'".[61]

The Battle of Amiens, 8 – 11 August 1918, is often cited as the high point of British operational 'all-arms' art, but it also serves to illustrate the General Staff's disinclination to persist in the idea of the breakthrough when Haig brought it to a halt after four days, as diminishing returns and stiffening German opposition persuaded him to defy Foch's order to continue.

54   Simkins, *From the Somme to Victory*, p. 58.
55   Boff, *Winning and Losing*, pp. 12-13.
56   Simon Robbins, *British Generalship on the Western Front 1914-1918. Defeat into Victory* (London: Frank Cass, 2005), p. 139.
57   Patrick Watt, "Douglas Haig and the Planning of the Battle of Neuve Chapelle". Spencer Jones (ed) *Courage without Glory. The British Army on the Western Front 1915* (Solihull: Helion Publishing, 2015), pp. 183-200.
58   Robbins, *British Generalship*, p. 118.
59   Ibid. p. 125.
60   Menin Road, 20 September: Polygon Wood, 26 September: Broodseinde, 4 October.
61   Paul Harris & Sanders Marble, 'The Step-by-Step Approach: British Military Thought and Operational Method on the Western Front, 1915-1917', *War in History* 15 (1) (2008), pp. 38 & 39.

Thereafter it was a series of "shallow battles" that defeated the German Army in autumn 1918 rather than "futile attempts to fight deep battles of penetration".[62]

Jonathan Boff suggests, however, that the use of "combined arms declined" through October and November 1918,[63] leaving the infantry and artillery as the major components of an assault as they came to terms with dwindling numbers of available tanks, problems associated with a struggling logistics system, the curtailments of RAF involvement as daylight hours shortened, less favourable terrain (including forest and water courses) and suggests a renewed "de-skilling" of the BEF by persistent high casualty rates.[64]

This study will illustrate and expand the main points of this contention, while taking issue with the final point, showing that the British Army, by the end of the war, had progressed to a point where it was able to adapt to circumstances and defeat the German defenders with whatever means were at its disposal, unhampered by the absence or paucity of certain weapons or where their use was prohibited or limited by topography or weather. It will also show, however, that whereas some units had "reached [this] high level of sophistication, [...] some had not".[65]

This book will locate the Battle of the Sambre firmly on the learning curve, demonstrating that the BEF had developed tactics that were well-suited to the prevailing conditions and that developments in weapons technology, along with a renewed faith in the doctrine of fire and movement were well understood, on the whole, and that the integration of artillery, tanks and aircraft with the infantry, plus the ingenuity and bravery of the Royal Engineers combined to defeat the German Army and push it from its last prepared defences on the Western Front.

Any attempt to discern a smooth learning process for the British Army within this series of encounters would prove difficult: the tempo of the attacks differed, owing to logistical issues, geography, the rate of German withdrawal and the strength of their defensive positions. On occasion it was deemed advisable to be at the Germans' heels. At others, an operational pause prior to an assault on prepared defensive positions was preferred, if indeed it was not imposed by external factors. The battles of Canal du Nord, Selle and Sambre are examples of the latter, where substantial topographical obstacles, such as water courses or forests, faced the attacker. The need for artillery pieces and sufficient ordnance to be brought forward to ensure that well-coordinated and appropriately heavy artillery support along a broad front could be relied on was required at a time when the British transportation system was beginning to reach breaking point.[66]

The British had also known for a long time that artillery support was by far and away the most vital requirement for operational success, and were forced to respect the limitations of the logistical systems and thereby abandoned the idea of breakout: "the BEF settled on the less glamorous, but more logistically feasible, limited-objective, set-piece attack".[67] They were not going to repeat their mistakes of 1915 – 17, nor those of the German offensives of Spring 1918. Bite and hold, albeit on a large scale, was the way forward.

62   Sheffield, *Forgotten Victory*, p. 206.
63   Boff, *Winning and Losing*, p. 245.
64   Ibid, pp. 245-246.
65   Ibid, p. 247.
66   See Boff, *Winning and Losing*, pp. 74 – 91 and I.M. Brown, *British Logistics on the Western Front 1914-1919* (West Port, Connecticut, USA: Praeger, 1998), pp. 198 – 204.
67   Brown, *British Logistics on the Western Front 1914-1919*, pp. 201-202.

The concept of 'bite and hold' is summed up by Paddy Griffith as "occupy[ing] a limited portion of the defender's front line before the latter could react. The attacker could then rapidly revert to a defensive posture on his newly won position, to beat off the inevitable counterattacks".[68] Peter Simkins adds the longer term view to this tactic: "…the BEF would capture a section of the German trenches, hold it against counter attack and – when the enemy had exhausted themselves – carry out the process again".[69]

Defeating the German army by such means would be a long and costly business, and British High Command clung onto the hope of breakthrough and cavalry exploitation even as realism slowly began to set in. Assaults with limited objectives and with any advance not exceeding the range of the attacker's artillery had proven successful as early as March 1915 at Neuve Chapelle, even if bite and hold was not the original intention. Bazentin Ridge and Delville Wood in July 1916, Vimy Ridge in April 1917, Messines Ridge two months later and the three limited offensive battles of Menin Road, Polygon Wood and Broodseinde in September and October 1917, just before Third Ypres ground to its costly and exhausting conclusion, all serve as examples of the efficacy of this "not only entirely sensible but probably […] only successful form of warfare which lay open to Britain".[70]

By 1918, once the German offensives had again proven that breakthrough was beyond the capabilities of either side, the Allies, now fighting a war with almost unlimited materiel available, were able to "conduct a series of operations, both concurrent and sequential, which allowed [them] to place enormous pressure on the German defenders. It enabled the tactically-effective bite and hold techniques […] at long last to have operational significance".[71] It was by this method that the BEF finally defeated the German Army.

The Battle of the Sambre does not, however, fit neatly into the accepted definition of bite and hold: by November 1918, as this study will illustrate, the 'bite' was effective; the 'hold' was almost unnecessary, as the risk of counter attack had all but disappeared. As a result, the 'bite' stages could be extended and there was the acceptance that three forward bounds, as brigades leapfrogged each other onto increasingly distant objectives – the last of those with (or occasionally without) improvised artillery support – constituted a good day's work. German units, by the end of 4 November 1918, had received orders to withdraw, so not only had the threat of counter attack evaporated, but also any objectives not gained that day as troops declined to over-extend themselves were often taken unopposed the following morning. "Tactical possibilities were at last allowed to dictate the course of events."[72]

By November 1918, most of the nails had already been driven into the German coffin: the Third and Fourth Armies were about to hammer in the final, decisive one and the fighting after 4 November 1918 took on a very different character. General Rawlinson wrote in 1919 that the "rapidity with which the armistice was forced upon the enemy […] was the direct consequence

---

68   Paddy Griffith, *Battle Tactics*, p. 32.
69   Peter Simkins, *From the Somme to Victory*, p. 43.
70   Robin Prior & Trevor Wilson, *Command on the Western Front* (Oxford: Blackwell Publishers, 1992), p. 79.
71   Gary Sheffield, *Command and Morale: The British Army on the Western Front 1914-1918* (Barnsley: Pen & Sword, 2014), p. 108.
72   Shelford Bidwell & Dominick Graham, *Firepower: The British Army Weapons & Theories of War 1904-1945* (Barnsley: Pen & Sword, 2004), p. 133.

of overwhelming defeat on the field of battle".[73] Sir Archibald Montgomery states that the Battle of the Sambre was instrumental in breaking the enemy's resistance, adding that "after this defeat, the German forces had no alternative but to fall back along the whole front, and the Allied pursuit only required to be pressed home in order to compel the enemy to accept whatever terms the Allies were prepared to offer".[74] From 5 November a completely new 'end phase' of the Hundred Days emerged. The German army, whose battalion strength was now estimated at an average of 150 men,[75] was beaten and in full retreat. Its fleeing infantry, screened largely by machine gun teams and occasionally artillery batteries, made a series of temporary stands where battlefield topography allowed, along the line of watercourses, railway lines and embankments[76] or in farm buildings and villages. All the BEF had to do, it seemed, was to continue to pressure the German rearguards, giving them no opportunity or time to create another viable line of resistance.

There is a great deal of compelling evidence in both contemporary and secondary sources that this 'end phase' was one of 'pursuit' by the BEF. Indeed, the title of the chapter in the British Official History covering events from 5–7 November 1918 is entitled "The Pursuit after the Battle of the Sambre".[77] Fourth Army War Diary of 5 November states that "yesterday's success [was] exploited along the whole army front. [...] With the exception of isolated machine gun nests there was no opposition".[78] VI Corps War Diary also states that "the enemy not offering much resistance except for the machine Guns covering his rear Guards (sic)".[79] In divisional war diaries phrases such as "without opposition", "little opposition met", "resistance slight or negligible" and "progress unopposed" are numerous. The Germans had no reserves left: the additional losses of men and materiel on 4 November meant that no units of "fighting strength" were available to send forward.[80]

Jonathan Boff describes the BEF's advance as a pursuit, but adds that the rate of advance was never spectacular, "at least two miles per day, but never more than three".[81] There are reasons for this: firstly, German resistance in some places was stubborn, notably on Third Army front, particularly on the banks of the Sambre river north-east of Landrecies and on the Hogneau river opposite 24th Division. It was sometimes deemed necessary to assault these positions under artillery barrages, with all the inherent delays that this tactic involves. On occasion, however, the German units had retired before the prepared assault could go in.[82] Secondly, the BEF had to battle against the weather conditions: "The heavy drizzly rain [...] restricted observation and the rate of advance was slow".[83] The rain turned the roads and tracks into quagmires. These

73   Foreword to Sir A. Montgomery, *The Story of the Fourth Army in the Battles of the Hundred Days,
       August 8th to November 11th 1918* (London: Hodder & Stoughton, 1920), p. ix.
74   Ibid, p. 256.
75   Bundesarchiv, *Der Weltkrieg 1914-18*, p. 699.
76   The National Archive (TNA):PRO WO95/2192 War Diary 24th Division HQ.
77   Edmonds, *Military Operations Vol. V*, pp. 492-517.
78   TNA: PRO WO95/439 War Diary Fourth Army HQ.
79   TNA: PRO WO95/775 War Diary VI Corps HQ General Staff.
80   *Der Weltkrieg*, p. 700.
81   J.Boff, *Winning and Losing*, pp. 211-12.
82   Edmonds, *Military Operations, Vol. V.*, p. 496.
83   Montgomery, *Fourth Army*, p. 256.

"dreadful"[84] conditions slowed the advance. It was difficult to get the guns forward and food and ammunition supplies were subject to serious but unavoidable delays.

Thirdly, Jonathan Boff argues that British commanders, perhaps understandably, "took their foot off the pedal" after 8 November as it became clearer that an armistice might be imminent. By that time the German armistice delegates had arrived behind French lines, but it would not be surprising if this phenomenon predated that event. Lieutenant-General Fergusson, GOC XVII Corps, is not so kind. His diary entry of 5 November 1918 sums up the situation as he saw it: "Wet day. We made very fair progress in the morning, but somehow it fizzled out later and the general impression of the whole day was stickiness."[85] Fourthly, the retreating German army left a trail of destruction in its wake. Roads and railways were damaged, bridges were demolished and craters were blown at most road junctions. If this were not enough, those men of the BEF toiling to repair them had to face the danger of delayed-action mines.[86] Getting materiel forward was no easy task. The BEF was working, by this stage, under logistical, topographical and meteorological constraints, and with reduced manpower. Logistics had dictated a pause after the advances made on 24 – 25 October. Supplies of ammunition, weapons, food, engineering equipment and other materiel had to be brought forward from railheads that had not advanced significantly since the Selle crossings of 17 to 25 October. These railheads were around 12 miles from the front line as the crow flies,[87] but geography dictated that journeys of over 15 miles were necessary to re-supply forward units by road. The roads along which the supplies were being transported had until recently been behind German lines, and as the occupiers had paid little attention to their upkeep, unprecedented levels of traffic meant that road surfaces were continually breaking up, requiring constant maintenance, and thus lengthening journey times. There was no shortage of materiel – shipments into France were keeping up with demand – but delays were inevitable along the last links of the supply chain.[88]

The experience of the British troops varied depending upon the stubbornness of German resistance, which was uneven along both army fronts. Isolated machine gun nests "concealed in hedges or enclosures necessitate[ed] in most cases a turning movement for their capture".[89] Resistance could always be overcome by the advance of troops on either flank. Where resistance was met, small unit tactics were up to the challenge.

In places there were echoes of 1914: on IX Corps front, a thin cavalry screen preceded the advance, with the infantry of 46th and 32nd Divisions struggling along the roads behind them. "The cavalry successfully prevented the enemy's rearguards offering any serious resistance and captured a number of guns."[90]

The German retreat continued even as the British advance slowed. By 8 November V Corps had lost touch with the enemy and once the Avesnes-Maubeuge road was reached it was decided, largely, it seems, for logistical reasons, that the majority of units would halt and consolidate their

---

84   Edmonds, *Military Operations Vol. V*, p. 496.
85   TNA: PRO WO95/936 War Diary XVII Corps General Staff.
86   See Lloyd, *Hundred Days*, pp. 262-263.
87   Fourth Army railheads were at Busigny, Honnechy, Bohain, Fresnoy and Vaux-Andigny, whereas Third Army relied on a single depot at Caudry. By 10 November, railheads were anything between 17 and 50 miles from the front.
88   I am grateful to Geoffrey Clarke for allowing me to use material here from his doctoral research.
89   TNA: PRO WO95/897 War Diary XIII Corps HQ. Narrative of Operations.
90   Montgomery, *Fourth Army*, p. 256-257.

positions, allowing "the task of keeping touch with the enemy on the whole [Third] Army front [...] to be taken over by an advanced guard under the command of GOC VI Corps. 4 Cavalry Brigade would form a screen".[91] V, IV and XVII Corps troops would be responsible for the road, but were ordered to thin out their men and echelon as far back as possible "in order to facilitate the supply of the advanced guard".[92] On Fourth Army front similar orders were issued and 'Bethell's Force'[93] was formed and designated as advanced guard, 5 Cavalry Brigade forming the screen.

It can be shown, therefore, that the Battle of the Sambre, 4 November 1918, instigated the 'end phase' of the war on the Western Front. The German Army was defeated and forced into headlong retreat with no hope of turning back the tide. Rearguards could only delay the inevitable for a short time and the rate of the BEF's advance was in the end not dictated by the strength of German resistance, but by topographical, meteorological and logistical factors.

The Tactical Context

In order for 'bite and hold' to be effective, there had to be a parallel development of the weapons systems that would give attackers the necessary advantage over the defenders. New weapons had to be integrated, often by trial and error, into battle plans. The move toward an 'all-arms' system was inexorable, if uneven.

War accelerates technical and scientific advancements: the British infantryman of 1918 was very different from his 1914 counterpart. The overriding problem facing commanders once the deadlock of trench warfare had established itself was how to overcome enemy defences. Concealment by, and protection of, earthworks, quick firing rifles, machine guns and artillery allowed dominance over the attackers who, by necessity, were forced to advance across open ground armed only with the weapons they could carry, albeit with the support of their own artillery. The problem ranges wider than this purely tactical conundrum: "the [...] object was to break through a highly organised defensive system protected by fire-power of hitherto unimagined intensity and occupied by some of the best and bravest soldiers in history, coupled with the flow of new weapons, new methods, new inventions, and the base administrative apparatus that had to be built to support the new citizen armies, and the difficulties of training this mass of men who, unlike their opponents, had no military tradition – it is hardly surprising that costly mistakes were made, but truly amazing that the efforts of the staff and fighting soldiers were finally crowned with such an overwhelming success."[94] The fire-power balance had to be reversed to favour the attacker, but the development of an all-arms system that could deliver this would take time.

Inventions, both lethal and non-lethal, were, sometimes reluctantly, introduced and attempts made to integrate them into the operational and tactical art of the attack. In 1914 the infantry's 'weapons system', such as it was, consisted of the rifle, the bayonet and the entrenching tool. External support came from artillery that was largely limited to firing shrapnel at targets that

91   TNA: PRO WO95/228 War Diary Third Army HQ. Narrative of Operations p. 66.
92   Ibid.
93   Major-General Hugh Keppel Bethell, GOC 66th Division.
94   Bidwell & Graham, *Firepower*, p. 3.

could be directly observed. By 1918, this arsenal had widened considerably to include grenades, rifle-grenades, trench mortars and the Lewis Gun: the re-organisation of the structure of the platoon to include all these weapons produced an integrated combined-arms unit capable of fire and manoeuvre tactics supported by its own increased fire-power capabilities. They were supported by an artillery arm firing not only shrapnel, but also high explosive, gas and smoke shells; the 106 instant percussion fuse allowed easier destruction of barbed wire and other obstacles without cratering the ground; the creeping barrage had been developed into a highly sophisticated entity and effective counter-battery work was facilitated by aerial photographic reconnaissance, sound-ranging and flash-spotting; to these can be added machine gun barrages, tanks, armoured-cars and aeroplanes, the latter performing contact patrols, artillery spotting, ground-attack and bombing of the enemy's rear areas. All these innovations had to be tried and tested through the painful and often costly process of trial and error, acquired wisdom in their use being disseminated through 'after action reports' and pamphlets, their efficacy improved through training, until a functioning weapons system that crosses inter-service boundaries finally reversed the fire-power equation.

Mistakes were made, and two examples will serve to illustrate the point. Long artillery bombardments prior to assaults, such as before the first day of the Battle of the Somme, could be ineffective and would rob the attacker of the element of surprise: artillery barrages that began only as the infantry advanced from their jumping-off positions eventually allowed fire *and* manoeuvre to replace the fire *then* manoeuvre doctrine that had held sway through the middle years of the war. This latter system is described by John Bourne as a "crucial mistake".[95]

The tank was seen by some, after the war, as a potentially war-winning weapon: it took time to realise that it was not. Its vulnerability to enemy artillery fire (not to mention mechanical breakdown) was illustrated, for example, at Cambrai when tanks were pushed ahead well in advance of the infantry resulting in heavy losses for both, the latter from machine guns that the tanks had failed to neutralise. It was eventually conceded that the tank "had no effective independent role. [It was] essentially [an] infantry support weapon".[96] They would learn to advance together, thus allowing mutual protection.

The battles of Hamel (4 July 1918) and Amiens (8–12 August 1918) are often heralded as the shining examples of successful all-arms co-operation on the Great War battlefield. It is not within the scope of this work to justify or counter this claim, but it will show how, and to what extent, the Battle of the Sambre fits into this paradigm, particularly as it took place in a period when "the use of combined arms declined, leaving the infantry and artillery as the major components of the assault".[97]

To borrow the metaphor of the orchestral score,[98] this book will show that the BEF was capable of adapting to circumstances and of mounting a successful assault when some sections of the orchestra were either absent or much reduced in number. "Firepower-based combined arms

---

95   J.M. Bourne, *Britain and the Great War* (London: Edward Arnold, 1989), p. 39.
96   Ibid, p. 79.
97   Boff, *Winning and Losing*, p. 245.
98   Lieutenant-General John Monash, commander of the Australian Corps from June 1918, wrote: "A perfected modern battle plan is like nothing so much as a score for orchestral composition, where the various arms and units are the instruments, and the tasks they perform are their respective musical phrases." Quoted in Lloyd, *Hundred Days*, pp. 299-300.

tactics were central to success"[99] against a German army that was demoralised, out-manned and out-gunned, but the BEF's weapons system had reached a level of "maturity"[100] which meant that victory could be extemporised from what resources were at hand. Combined arms need not imply *all* arms.

Both sides fought the final encounters of the war with dwindling numbers of infantry, the Germans having lost a huge number of their best fighting men during their abortive spring offensives, being "reduced not just in size but, very markedly, in quality".[101] As mentioned above, however, this kind of "mobile attrition"[102] also cost the Allies dear. German estimates for the end of October 1918 were that French battalions were, on average, 600 strong, the British 700, the Americans 1,200 and their own 500.[103] These figures are backed up by Jonathan Boff, who states: "In 37th Division battalions on average went into action with fewer than 500 fighting men during the campaign. The Guards Division worked on the assumption that even an 'up to strength' battalion could now place only 400 rifles (including Lewis gunners) in the firing line".[104] Average German figures for *17th Army* went from 807 in February 1918 to 456 by 30 October, but with the caveat that although rifle strength had almost halved, "Machine gun fire-power declined by less than a quarter".[105] The Germans were to rely more and more on machine guns as the mainstay of their defence as the autumn encounters were played out.

The Institutional Context

The battle frontage was occupied by Third Army (General Sir J.H.G. Byng) in the north, and Fourth Army (General Sir H.S. Rawlinson) to the south. Third Army was made up of four corps: XVII Corps (Lieutenant-General Sir C. Fergusson); VI Corps (Lieutenant-General Sir J.A.L. Haldane); IV Corps (Lieutenant-General Sir G.M. Harper) and V Corps (Lieutenant-General C.D. Shute). Fourth Army had two corps in the line: XIII Corps (Lieutenant-General Sir T.L.N. Morland) and IX Corps (Lieutenant-General Sir W.P. Braithwaite). The following British divisions formed up in the firing line on 4 November 1918, north to south: 19th, 24th, Guards, 62nd, New Zealand, 37th, 17th, 38th, 18th, 50th, 25th, 32nd and 1st, the first eight listed being part of Third Army, the rest belonging to Fourth Army.[106]

All these divisions had been involved in attacks launched since 8 August – a total of 332 between them, the New Zealanders being the most frequently engaged on 42 occasions, the

---

99   Boff, *Winning and Losing*, p. 6.
100 Sheffield, *Forgotten Victory*, p. 198.
101 Harris & Barr, *Amiens to the Armistice*, p. 20.
102 Boff, *Winning and Losing*, p. 37.
103 Bundesarchiv: *Der Weltkrieg 1914-18*, p. 708.
104 Boff, *Winning and Losing*, p. 43. Figures come from TNA: PRO WO95/2515 37th Division General Staff War Diary and TNA: PRO WO95/1195 Guards Division General Staff War Diary.
105 Ibid, pp. 47-49. Figures quoted apply to *206th Reserve Infantry Regiment*.
106 Of them, two were Regular (1st & Guards), two were Territorial (62nd & 50th), one was Dominion (New Zealand) and eight were New Army (17th, 18th, 19th, 24th, 25th, 32nd, 37th & 38th) For details of which divisions belonged to which corps, and for details of their commanders, see Map 1 and Appendix I.

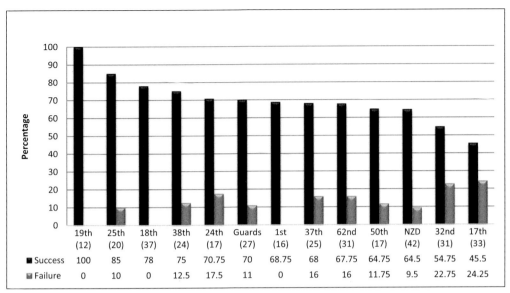

	19th (12)	25th (20)	18th (37)	38th (24)	24th (17)	Guards (27)	1st (16)	37th (25)	62nd (31)	50th (17)	NZD (42)	32nd (31)	17th (33)
■ Success	100	85	78	75	70.75	70	68.75	68	67.75	64.75	64.5	54.75	45.5
▨ Failure	0	10	0	12.5	17.5	11	0	16	16	11.75	9.5	22.75	24.25

Performance of Divisions in the Attack, August – November 1918

19th Division at the other end of the scale on 12. Their success rates can be seen in the bar-chart above.[107]

The selective use of statistics can prove almost anything, but it is interesting to note that eight out of the 13 divisions crowd into the 75–60 percent success rate bracket. Only three exceed this figure and two fall short. The disappointing performances of 17th and 32nd Divisions on 4 November do provide instant correlation, however.[108] Paddy Griffith identifies the elite 'assault spearhead', naming most of the Regular divisions, but only the 18th and 19th from our list. [109]

The efficacy of a unit is often linked to the reputation of its commanding officer. John Bourne asserts that the quality of the army's 'middle-management' was, by 1918, high, most of those then in command of battalions, brigades and divisions having survived, learnt and, tellingly, proven themselves where it mattered, on the battlefield. They were in position on merit. It is perhaps enlightening to take a snapshot of this middle-management layer of Third and Fourth Armies in November 1918.

The average length of service of the six corps commanders was 316 days, Fergusson of XVII Corps having served longest with 894 days, with Haldane of VI Corps a close second with 819, whereas the rest had only 690 days between them, with Braithwaite of IX Corps having only been in post since the middle of September 1918.[110]

107 I am indebted to Professor Peter Simkins for the data: he describes a 'success' as being "some forward progression in an opposed attack against meaningful opposition". Failure is described as "no progress, not even limited, made". Email communication with the author on 31 July 2013.
108 See Chapter 5 (V Corps) and Chapter 7 (IX Corps).
109 Griffith, *Battle Tactics of the Western Front.* pp. 79-83.
110 Braithwaite had therefore been in post for only 53 days. For a complete table of commanders' dates of appointment and days in post, from Brigadier upwards, see Appendix II.

Divisional commanders had been in position, on average, for 445 days, the three longest serving being Russell (New Zealand Division), 1086 days, Strickland (1st Division) 876 days, and Robertson (17th Division) 845 days. Pure length of service was no guarantee of quality, however. Indeed, 25th Division, which had been recently reconstituted, faced one of the more challenging tasks on 4 November – a 2,000 yard opposed advance, followed by the forcing of a canal crossing and the capture of a town, all of which were completed successfully – and was commanded by Major-General J.R.E. Charles, who had been appointed only three months before.

The position of Brigadier General was inevitably more fluid: average time spent in post being 203 days. Of the 38 brigade commanders, only 10 had been there for more than 10 months. Ten had tenures of less than two months.

A full analysis of all commanders' career paths is beyond the scope of this work, but two examples of divisional commanders will serve as pointers to the calibre of men who planned and led the attack on 4 November. The choice of 1st and 17th Divisions will contrast a regular and a 'New Army' formation, the former performing well throughout its involvement in the Hundred Days advance, the latter struggling to implement the latest tactical methodology and performing less well as a result. 1st Division had experienced no outright failures in the attack during the summer and autumn of 1918, whereas 17th Division had made no progress at all in almost a quarter of its engagements, succeeding in less than half.

1st Division had been involved in the war since the Battle of Mons and the subsequent retreat. It saw action in, amongst others, First Ypres, Aubers Ridge, Loos, Somme, Third Ypres and Lys. During the advance to victory it joined Fourth Army from First Army on 11 September and then spent the best part of a month in the front line, taking part in the Battle of Epéhy, the advance to and capture of the Hindenburg Line and the Battle of Beaurevoir. Thirteen days out of the line was followed by the crossing of the Selle, with 1st Division troops reaching the outskirts of Catillon on the west bank of the Sambre-Oise Canal.

The division had had six commanding officers during the war, Major-General A.E.A. Holland being the longest in post, from 11 September 1915 to 12 June 1916, before Major-General Strickland took over and then remained in command for the rest of the conflict.

Edward Peter Strickland ('Strick') was born on 3 August 1869 and was educated at Warwick School. He was commissioned into the Norfolk Regiment in 1888 and served in Upper Burma before fighting at Atbara and Omdurman in 1898. Service then took him to Nigeria where in 1909 he commanded the North Nigeria Regiment. At the outbreak of war in 1914 he was in India, commanding 1st Battalion Manchester Regiment, part of 8 Jullunder Brigade, 3rd (Lahore) Indian Division. They reached the Western Front in October 1914, just in time to meet the German onslaught at First Ypres. By the time of the Battle of Neuve Chapelle, Strickland was in command of the Jullunder Brigade. He also took them through Second Ypres in April 1915, before assuming command of 98 Infantry Brigade, 33rd Division on 16 November that year. On 12 June 1916 he was promoted to command 1st Division. Between August and November 1918, the division took part in 16 opposed attacks, succeeding almost 70 percent of the time, and failing completely in none.[111] It is surely not by accident that 1st Division was given one of the more demanding sectors of the attack frontage on 4 November – the forcing of

---

111 See bar chart on p. 41.

the canal at Lock No.1 and the capture of Catillon, one of the few places where German troops were still occupying the western bank of the canal.

17th Division came into being as part of Kitchener's Second New Army in September 1914. It was sent out to France in July 1915 and spent some time in the trenches in the Ypres Salient before taking part in the actions on the Somme the following summer, then at Arras and the latter stages of Third Ypres during 1917. They were involved in stemming the German 'Operation Michael' offensive in March 1918, and after three months' respite were almost continually involved in the 'Hundred Days' advance, being instrumental at Albert, Bapaume, Havrincourt, Epéhy, Cambrai and the Selle. In August alone, the division had lost "over 30 per cent of [its] officers and men",[112] and this almost continuous involvement in the front lines meant that opportunities for training were very limited.

> It had hoped for three weeks of open warfare practice in early August, but was instead called up as a possible reserve for the Amiens attack. Consequently, it was 'not up to that [standard] required for successful open warfare offensive operations. The main deficiencies were lack of tactical knowledge, which resulted in formations not being adapted to suit ground, and a lack of power to apply the principles of fire and movement, also a lack of intelligent patrolling'.[113]

Their commanding officer on 4 November was Major-General Philip Rynd Robertson, nicknamed 'Blobs'. He was commissioned in the Cameronians in 1886 and took the 1st Battalion of that regiment to war as Lieutenant-Colonel in 1914. In June 1915 he was promoted Brigadier-General and took command of 19 Brigade. Its only involvement in major offensive action during his tenure was at the Battle of Loos in September that year. It was here that he demonstrated his readiness to challenge higher authority, firstly requesting that the release of gas on his front be cancelled on account of unfavourable climatic conditions[114] and two days later calling off an infantry attack on his own authority after some of his officers had pointed out to him the futility of the exercise. As John Bourne has written, "Self confidence of this kind was unusual in brigade commanders at this stage of the war".[115] Robertson was promoted to command of 17th Division on 13 July 1916 at the age of 50. "He treated his new command as if it were a big battalion",[116] his style of command emphasising discipline and efficiency. This regular army approach did little to make him popular amongst the men of this New Army division, but he "had only contempt for popularity".[117] The 17th Division may have been efficient, but innovative and forward-looking it was not. Jonathan Boff asserts that "Divisions [...] began the [Hundred Days] campaign at different stages of readiness".[118] 17th Division may well have been rather low on that list:

---

112 Boff, *Winning and Losing*, p. 29.
113 Ibid, p. 64. Boff is quoting from TNA: PRO WO95/1985 17th Division General Staff War Diary. See also Chapter 5.
114 The request was denied and the gas attack went ahead.
115 John Bourne, Centre for First World War Studies, University of Birmingham. Profiles of Western Front Generals.www.birmingham.ac.uk/research/activity/warstudies/research/projects/ lionsdonkeys/n.aspx. (Accessed 31 December 2013).
116 Ibid.
117 Ibid.
118 Boff, *Winning and Losing*, p. 64.

German intelligence reports of 13 and 20 October 1918 concluded that 37th Division was "fully battle-worthy", with 38th Division "average", but 17th Division "creates no good impression".[119]

Why were these particular 13 divisions in the front line on the morning of 4 November 1918? In some cases, it was just 'their turn' – 17th Division and 21st Division had been 'leapfrogging' each other for most of the autumn and in that sector 21st Division had spearheaded the attack on 23-24 October that had pushed the front line to the edges of the Forêt de Mormal.[120] This pattern was repeated along most of the Third Army front: of the divisions involved in the attack on 24 October,[121] only the 19th was expected to be in the firing line on 4 November. On Fourth Army front, a different story emerges: on 24 October, 1st, 18th and 25th Divisions took part in the attacks. All three, plus 32nd and 50th Divisions, were to be first out of the blocks 11 days later. Byng, it would seem, was happy for his formations to be rotated; Rawlinson was more selective.

The decision to attack on or around the 4 November was of course Haig's. Definite orders were not issued until 29 October, but a glance at Rawlinson's papers reveals a longer process. On 25 October he writes: "I cannot force the passage of the canal here until Debeney[122] comes up on my right and he is very, very slow".[123]

Three days later it is clear that he had discussed the assault with Byng, saying that "He quite approved and will issue an order on the subject". He continues: "The plans for the next attack are quite good – Hope we shall be able to carry them out before the Armistice comes".[124]

He was able to approve his Corps Commanders' schemes at a Fourth Army conference held at Busigny the following day. The date for the attack was settled. After the conference, "after tea, [he] went out to III Army to arrange zero hour and the new boundary which shorten[ed his] front considerably".[125] Discussions with Third Army did not all go swimmingly: zero hour remained a sticking point and on 30 October Rawlinson wrote:

> All arrangements for the attack on the 4 are now practically settled except zero which Byng's people want to have at 5:30 in the dark.[126] I cannot agree for with Tanks this won't do. The 25 Dvn have a difficult task at Landrecies for the canal is 2000 yards from their starting line.[127]

Rawlinson told Byng the following day that he could not accept a zero hour earlier than 0615and in the end, zero hours were not uniform.[128]

---

119 Ibid, p. 160.
120 Following the Battle of the Sambre, it was again 21st Division that pushed forward from the eastern edge of the forest on 7 November.
121 These were 2nd, 3rd, 5th, 19th, 21st, 33rd and 42nd Divisions.
122 General Marie-Eugène Debeney, Commander of French First Army.
123 Churchill College Archives, Cambridge. Rawlinson Papers.
124 Ibid.
125 Ibid.
126 Sunrise on 4 November 1918 was 0637.
127 Churchill College Archives, Cambridge. Rawlinson Papers. Clearly, divisions have been allocated by this date.
128 Zero hour for XVII Corps was 0600. On VI Corps front, the Guards Division also had 0600 as zero, but 62nd Division were half an hour earlier. IV and V Corps moved off at 0530, except for 118 Bde

Rawlinson visited all his divisions on the morning of 3 November and "found everyone in good heart and confident of success". He added his own note of caution:

> He [the Germans] evidently means to put up a fight tomorrow – he has his best Divns here on my front including Cyclists, 8, 19 and some Jaeger. The canal is a big obstacle and I shall be very pleased if we force all the passages. XIII Corps is going at 0615 on account of using tanks and wanting the daylight.[129]

Once orders had been issued on 29 October, it was down to Army commanders to draw the initial overall objective lines on the map. From there, SS135 (January 1918) had a recommended ideal seven-point process:

1. Corps allots tasks to division and outlines broad artillery plan;
2. Divisional commander conducts reconnaissance and works up outline plan 'which will include the task to be carried out by each body of infantry, generally how each body is to be disposed prior to the assault, and his general intentions as to the action of his reserve';
3. Corps approves divisional plan;
4. Divisional plan issued to subordinates as 'Warning Order';
5. Divisional staff works out details necessary to give effect to plan and issues them in a series of 'Instructions';
6. Lower formations issue orders to their subordinates based on these 'Instructions';
7. Plan is summarised in an 'Operations Order' under a checklist of up to 14 headings, and issued to subordinates. 'If possible not less than 24 hours should elapse between the time the order leaves Divisional Headquarters and the hour fixed for the operation.[130]

In this case, all of the above was to happen within a very short timescale. In reality, of course, some formations, including Royal Engineer companies, had been working on the problem for some days prior to the 29 October Order. They knew that the assault was coming; only the actual date was unknown. Infantry units had been patrolling the ground in front of them and in places had been able to push their lines forward where German withdrawals allowed. Some limited 'raids' had taken place (not all successful) to improve the jumping off positions for the coming assault. The paper trail from GHQ down to individual battalion level can be traced in the following example:

Example Pathway:
GHQ → Third Army → V Corps → 17th Division → 51 Brigade → 7th Bn Lincolns.

(38th Division) on the right who jumped off at 0615 in order to conform with Fourth Army on their right. XIII Corps set off at 0615, though some of the tanks moved off at 0545. On IX Corps front, zero hour was 0545.
129 Rawlinson Papers, Churchill College Archives, Cambridge.
130 SS135, January 1918, pp. 12-14. Quoted in Boff, *Winning and Losing on the Western Front,* pp. 194-195.

Origin / Reference	Date / Time	Details
GHQ: OAD948	29 Oct	Order to resume advance on or after 3 November.
Third Army: GS 78/4	31 Oct	Third, Fourth & First Armies would continue the advance, on a date to be notified later, towards line Avesnes – Maubeuge – Mons. First bound would be to line Landrecies – Locquignol, high ground astride Avesnes to Valenciennes railway & Rhonelle river, E & NE of Jolimetz, spur between Wargnies-le-Grand & Eth. IV Corps would surround Le Quesnoy.
Third Army: GB 469 & GS 78/7	1 Nov	Tanks allocated to IV, V & VI Corps. 8 to V Corps, 5 to IV Corps, 12 (Whippets) to VI Corps.
GHQ: OAD 948/1	2 Nov	Date fixed for attack – 4 November
Third Army: GS 78/46	3 Nov / 1125	Zero hour fixed for 4 November.
Third Army: GS78.38	3 Nov	Long range gun programme for 0630 4 Nov to 0630 5 Nov.
V Corps: G541	1 Nov / 1100	Notification of conference at Corps HQ for GOCs, CRAs, GSOs 1 at 1430 hrs.
V Corps: G548	1 Nov / 1315	Relief orders – 21 Div to be relieved by 17 Div.
V Corps: G556	1 Nov / 1835	GOC 9th Tank Bde to report to 17 & 38 Divs between 0900 – 1000 on 2 Nov.
V Corps: Orders 239 & 240	1 Nov / 2245	Details of advance up to Blue, Red & Green Line Objectives, including allocation of divisions. Appendix A: Artillery, Appendix B: Engineers.
V Corps: Addendum to Order 239 (GS 518/24)	2 Nov	Tank allocations, objectives and cooperation orders.
V Corps: Addendum to Order 239 (GS 518/43)	2 Nov	Signals, Communications, etc. Use of wireless, runners.
V Corps: Addendum to Order 240 (GS 518/71)	3 Nov	Operations on Z+1 (5 Nov)
V Corps: GS 518/57	3 Nov	Details of Zero hours. (0545 except for right of V Corps – 0615)
17 Div: Div Order 27	1 Nov / 2000	Orders for relief of 21 Div by 17 Div.
17 Div: Div Order 28	2 Nov / 0230	Order for resumption of advance, date to be notified. Phases 1, 2 & 3 outlined, including artillery plan. Appendix A adds machine gun barrage plan.
17 Div: Addendum to Div Order 28	3 Nov / 1500	Tank operations & infantry unit movements to assembly positions.
17 Div: Div Order 29	4 Nov	Orders for continuation of attack on Z+1
51 Bde: Brigade Order 17	1 Nov	Orders for reliefs 2 – 3 Nov.
51 Bde: Brigade Order 18	3 Nov	Objectives for attack, including maps. Dispositions of attacking battalions, artillery barrage timings, notification of zero hour.

Origin / Reference	Date / Time	Details
51 Bde: Brigade Order 19	3 Nov	Assembly positions detailed.
17th Bn Lincolns:	2 Nov	Brigade Order 17 received with orders for attack. Commanding Officer attends Brigade HQ Conference at 1100 hrs. CO then meets with his officers and disseminates plan.
17th Bn Lincolns: 'Warning Order I' issued to Companies.	3 Nov	Details of boundaries, direction, objectives, formation, assembly & communication. Appendix B: artillery barrage details
17th Bn Lincolns:	3 Nov / 1530	Notified of Zero hour.

The amount of paper is not overwhelming, as it had been two years earlier for 1 July 1916, when a similar number of divisions had gone into the attack. By this stage of the hostilities, much more could be left to lower formations and instructions could be disseminated by word of mouth at conferences – by November 1918 the British Army was well practised in offensive actions, the average number of attacks made by each of these frontline divisions since August 1918 was 25.

Army commanders painted in the broadest of brush strokes: Byng

gave his Army, as an intermediate objective, the long straight road which runs through Pont-sur-Sambre and Bavai (the Bavai road)[131] which he expected would be reached on the 5th.[132] In the path of 4th Corps lay the ancient fortress of Le Quesnoy which he ordered to be surrounded but not stormed.[133]

Rawlinson pencilled in the two main objectives:

The first, or red line, extended approximately due north and south from east of Fesmy to east of Landrecies, and thence northwards through the Mormal Forest about 3000 yards from its western edge. [...] The second objective, or line of exploitation, ran east of Cartignies, Dompierre and St Remy Chaussée. This was some three miles short of the general objective defined by the Commander-in-Chief, namely the Avesnes – Maubeuge road, and was considered to be the limit of penetration that could be reached before a halt would be necessary in order to reorganise and complete the communications.[134]

Corps allocated divisions and devised the artillery plans. Thereafter, divisions, brigades and battalions filled in the necessary finer details. These details are contained in the following chapters as the actions of each of the six Corps involved are analysed.

---

131 See Map 1: the road itself is not marked, but the two towns are.
132 Byng was being optimistic: the troops reached the road on the 7 November.
133 J.Williams, *Byng of Vimy: General and Governor General* (London: Leo Cooper, 1983) p. 257.
134 Montgomery, *The Story of the Fourth Army in the Battles of the Hundred Days*, p. 243.

2

XVII Corps

Introduction

This chapter shows how XVII Corps was able to adapt a plan of attack to suit the dynamic situation along its front, the line of the original first objective becoming the jumping off positions at very late notice. With no tanks available the attack was of the (by then) standard pattern: infantry units leapfrogging each other under a creeping barrage that began at Zero Hour in order to maintain surprise. Command and control was such that a pause could be successfully improvised prior to an advance against two fortified villages under an extemporised artillery barrage, allowing units to reach their final day's objectives with relatively few casualties.

*   *   *

The style of the coming attack was set by a conference of battalion and company commanders at 56 Brigade Headquarters on 2 November: "it was the duty of every unit to push on in order to gain ground and tactical features irrespective of whatever might be happening on the flanks [and] advances were to comprise a series of bounds from one tactical feature to another and [...] the unit commander was to use his own discretion to make further bounds when he saw the opportunity to do so without waiting for orders. [...] [T]he policy was to be to create salients wherever possible. It was to be realised that we were now fighting against a beaten and partly demoralised enemy who was weak in effectives and therefore not likely to put in any strong or determined attack to regain ground lost".[1]

The Third Army front, which stretched from Jenlain in the north to just south of the village of Englefontaine, itself just west of the Forêt de Mormal, was divided between three Corps: XVII Corps (Fergusson), VI Corps (Haldane) and IV Corps (Harper).

Fergusson's XVII Corps had been active in support of First Army on the ground between the villages of Jenlain and Villers Pol for the previous three days and had already taken some of the objectives given it for 4 November.

---

1   TNA: PRO WO95/2077 War Diary 56 Brigade.

At 1310 [3 November] XVII Corps had issued orders for divisions in the line to keep in touch with the enemy and form a jumping off place for the attack on 4th November.

At 1530 hrs 24th Division reported their troops advancing to the BLUE objective (i.e. LE QUESNOY – JENLAIN road) and an hour later 19th Division reported their troops on this line and in touch with 11th Division [First Army] at L.11.c.3.4. XXII Corps had reached the line of RAILWAY, JENLAIN – CURGIES with patrols pushed to the Aunelle River.

By nightfall we held the LE QUESNOY – JENLAIN Road and the latter village. Hostile artillery fire became heavy from the region E of BRY – ETH. M.G. fire from G.8.a and c. The situation of the Corps on our right had not materially altered though hostile artillery which had heavily bombarded our positions in the early morning ceased about 0500 hrs.[2]

Lieutenant-General Fergusson added his own thoughts on the situation in his private diary entry for 3 November:

The Bosch started retiring this morning from east of Valenciennes down to our right. We followed up and made about 2,000 or 3,000 yards of ground. He may stand tomorrow, but I think we have only a rearguard in front of us. This rather spoils the battle which was to have taken place tomorrow.[3]

The artillery arrangements for the attack required a creeping barrage with lifts of 100 yards every four minutes (see Sketch Map 1), but these were timed to reach the Blue Line two hours after Zero. As this was now the jumping off line, hastily adjusted timings had to be sent out to the gunners.[4]

19th Division[5]

The 19th Division (Major-General G.D. Jeffreys) on the left of the Corps frontage had estab-lished themselves on the Blue Line by 1600 hours on 3 November, and "it was decided that the 'Jumping Off' Line for the attack next morning would be the line of the main LE QUESNOY – VALENCIENNES road with the opening barrage 5-600 yards beyond it. This necessitated withdrawing forward posts and patrols, but it was considered preferable to do this than attempt to assemble East of the village".[6]

The division lined up with 58 Brigade (Brigadier-General A.E. Glasgow) on the left, 56 Brigade (Brigadier-General R.M. Heath) on the right and 57 Brigade (Brigadier-General A.J.F. Eden) in reserve. 56 Brigade had decided at 1830 hours on 3 November that their troops

2   TNA: PRO WO95/2077 War Diary 56 Brigade.
3   TNA: PRO WO95/936 War Diary XVII Corps HQ, General Staff. "Extract from 1918 Private
     Diary of Lt-Gen Sir Charles Fergusson, Commanding XVII Corps, Third Army".
4   TNA: PRO WO95/943 War Diary XVII Corps.
5   See Map 2.
6   TNA: PRO WO95/2057 War Diary 19th Division HQ. General Staff.

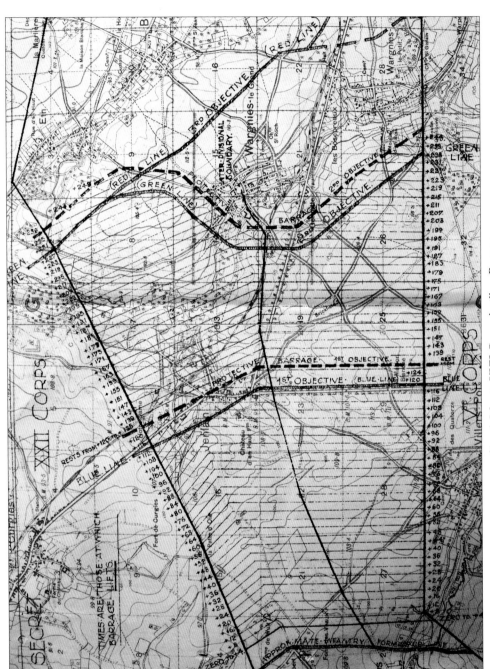

Sketch Map 1 XVII Corps Artillery Barrage.

on the picquet line along grid line L.18.a.0.0[7] were to withdraw to the line of the Courgies – Jenlain road, this running approximately north-west from the latter village, and that the barrage opening line would be the original 163 minute line (see Sketch Map 1), this being chosen in preference to the line of the Petit Aunelle River (another 500 yards to the east) as it was impossible to know whether the houses on the eastern edge of the village still concealed pockets of enemy troops. Orders were sent to the effect that the withdrawal of forward picquets should take place between 0430 and 0515 hours, and it was decided that 58 Brigade would take over their portion of the front during the night instead of during the attack as had previously been arranged. The 2nd Battalion Wiltshire Regiment [2/Wiltshire] took up their front line positions on the left, with 9th Battalion Welsh [9/Welsh] on their right and 9th Battalion Royal Welsh Fusiliers [9/RWF] in reserve near the Ferme de Wult, ready to move to square L 16.a at Zero. All this was contained in a third Addendum to the original orders,[8] which still at this late stage had Zero as 0530 hours. A signal was sent to brigades at 2015 hours (3 November) confirming the start line of the creeping barrage and changing Zero to 0600 hours.

The rearrangement and subsequent movements were carried out with "considerable difficulties";[9] it was an intensely dark, moonless night and it was raining heavily for most of it. There were no guides available and the movements were made over unreconnoitred ground. Luckily, enemy shelling was conspicuous only by its almost total absence. Nevertheless, the brigade was formed up ready to attack by 0115 hours.[10] Last in place was Brigade Headquarters, which was established at the Ferme de Wult at 0530.

The barrage opened at six o'clock, remaining on the new opening line for 10 minutes before moving forward at the previously agreed rate. The rain had stopped, but there was a heavy mist lying in the valleys that hung around stubbornly for several hours.

The 2/Wiltshire began the attack on a one-company front as the Brigade frontage was only 500 yards. This expanded rapidly to nearly 2000 yards on the Green Line Objective and necessitated the change to a two-company front as the Petit Aunelle River was crossed. The 9/Welsh were on a two-company front from the start.

The War Diary of the 2/Wiltshire records that "little opposition was encountered until the Petit Aunelle River was reached".[11] This was a "deep stream running between high banks"[12] around 10 yards wide and proved to be a "more serious obstacle than was expected".[13] Bridging it was the responsibility of one section of 94 Field Company R.E.: initially they were to use "trees felled at the site or material brought from Jenlain".[14] Subsequently, "every effort [was to be] made to render the crossings practicable for guns and limbers".[15]

The enemy artillery reply was not heavy and could best be described as patchy: the Brigade HQ at the Ferme de Wult suffered more than most, this area being "fairly heavily shelled"[16] for

---

7   See Appendix V: an explanation of contemporary map reference conventions.
8   TNA: PRO WO95/2089 War Diary 58 Brigade.
9   Ibid.
10   Ibid.
11   TNA: PRO WO95/2093 War Diary 2nd Battalion Wiltshire Regt.
12   TNA: PRO WO95/2089 War Diary 58 Brigade.
13   Ibid.
14   TNA: PRO WO95/2066 War Diary 19th Division CRE.
15   Ibid. 19th Division Order No.252.
16   TNA: PRO WO95/2089 War Diary 58 Brigade.

the half hour after Zero. Gas shells bursting in the air both east and west of Jenlain gave rise to some consternation amongst the men of the reserve battalion (9/RWF) "caus[ing] a good deal of coughing and some sickness, as the valleys very soon became full of gas, but no casualties".[17]

Once on the banks of the Petit Aunelle, main resistance came, unsurprisingly, from enemy machine gun fire. The diary of the 2/Wiltshire puts it simply: "This was overcome."[18] Once the first troops were across, resistance rapidly melted away, "the German gunners in most cases running away and abandoning their guns before the Infantry could get to close quarters. A number of machine guns were captured, but very few prisoners".[19] The Diary of 2/Wiltshire reports sadly that "2nd Lt. W. F. Virgin "B" Coy was killed in the advance to the first objective".[20]

The men of 2/Wiltshire and 9/Welsh were able to push on and reached the Green Line objective by 1015 hours. Second-Lieutenant French of 2/Wiltshire then took out a patrol and returned with nine prisoners from the outskirts of the village of Eth.[21]

56 Brigade formed up with 9th Battalion Cheshire Regiment [9/Cheshire] on the left, 1/4th Battalion King's Shropshire Light Infantry [1/4th KSLI] on the right and 8th Battalion The Prince of Wales's (North Staffordshire Regiment) [8/N.Staffs] in reserve. The brigade had moved into the area on 7 October and a programme of training had been devised. This was, however,

> somewhat broken up due to constant moves, brought about by the continual advancing of the battle front, but was devoted in the main part to practice of advance guards, the following up of a retiring enemy over long distances, the driving in of enemy rearguards, the practice of supply of ammunition, communications and the dealing with isolated MG pockets. [...] The use of forward sections of RFA, MGs and RE with an advanced guard battalion was practised, though unfortunately to no great extent.[22]

To the right of 56 Brigade front, 24th Division had commenced its opening barrage at 0530 and unfortunately the enemy reply strayed into the area west of Jenlain where 1/ 4th KSLI, on the right brigade front, were waiting until 0600 before they could move. The "heavy annihilating barrage [caused] a large number of casualties".[23] Our barrage came down at 0600 and the forward troops moved off, keeping as close to it as they dared. Their experience was very similar to that of 58 Brigade to their left: machine gun fire was encountered from the eastern bank of the Petit Aunelle River and from the high ground to the north and east of the village of Wargnies-le-Grand.[24] This was eventually suppressed by "covering fire from forward troops"[25] and the advance continued. The 1/4th KSLI had encountered severe opposition during this

---

17   TNA: PRO WO95/2092 War Diary 9th Battalion Royal Welsh Fusiliers.
18   TNA: PRO WO95/2093 War Diary 2nd Battalion Wiltshires.
19   TNA: PRO WO95/2089 War Diary 58 Brigade.
20   TNA: PRO WO95/2093 War Diary 2nd Battalion Wiltshires. Second Lieutenant William Job Farnham Virgin is buried in Cross Roads Cemetery, Fontaine-au-Bois, one of 19 fatalities suffered by the battalion that day.
21   Ibid.
22   TNA: PRO WO95/2077 War Diary 56 Brigade.
23   Ibid.
24   Ibid.
25   Ibid.

phase of the action, suffering, according to the Battalion War Diary, 110 casualties "on arriving E. of Jenlain".[26] They reached the Green Line by 0730 and "consolidated on a line running N[orth] from Wargnies-le-Grand Rly Station".[27]

The 9/Cheshire were able to keep up, although they too had encountered "considerable opposition [...] from the river eastwards".[28] Between the two battalions they had bagged 100 prisoners west of the river and the Cheshires had captured a German field gun which had still been in action. They then became victims of their own guns: "on the capture of the Green Line considerable trouble was caused by our own barrage falling very short. Some casualties occurred and the left company withdrew for a short time".[29] In fact, the Cheshires had got a little ahead of themselves and were probably caught up in the protective barrage, where it paused in its advance ahead of the second objective (Green Line) and possibly victim to some 60 pdr shells falling on the village of Wargnies-le-Grand "and its approaches".[30]

As soon as the protective barrage ceased, this company moved forward again, past its original objective and then swung south, moving down the Eth – Wargnies-le-Grand road, taking prisoners and capturing machine guns as it went. All this was done under its own covering rifle fire which was trying to suppress enemy fire emanating from the higher ground to the north-east of the village. (Square G15.d – see Map 2)

We return briefly to the 58 Brigade sector: at noon, the 2/Wiltshire, still on the Green Line to the south-west of Eth, sent out more "strong patrols [...] with a view to clearing the village".[31] They were met by considerable levels of retaliatory artillery and machine gun fire and had to return to their original positions. A glance at Sketch Map 1 will confirm that the German troops encountered here had not been subject to any artillery bombardment: the eastern limit of the initial barrage plan coincided with the Green Line. Similarly, patrols sent forward by the 9/Welsh were able to reach the outskirts of Bry, but "were heavily fired on and forced to withdraw".[32] At around the same time, the reserve battalion, 9/RWF, were ordered forward to occupy the ground in squares L12 a & c just to the west of the Petit Aunelle River. The move was completed within the hour.

It was becoming clear now that the villages of Eth and Bry, and more importantly the high ground to the east of them, were not going to be occupied without a coordinated assault with artillery support. An attack along the entire divisional front under a barrage was proposed for 1630.

The reserve battalion of 56 Brigade was the 8/N.Staffs. They had commenced their follow-up advance at 0540, this enabling them to cross the Blue Line at 0620. They were hampered slightly by thick mist but managed to maintain their direction of march and crossed the line only 10 minutes late. It was at this point that they ran into the enemy artillery barrage of high explosive and gas shells between Jenlain and the Petit Aunelle. They pushed on and reached

26   TNA: PRO WO95/2078 War Diary 1/4th Battalion King's Shropshire Light Infantry. It was at this stage of the assault that Captain Leonard Owen Jordan MC was killed, age 24. He is buried in Maresche Communal Cemetery.
27   Ibid.
28   TNA: PRO WO95/2079 War Diary 9th Cheshires.
29   Ibid.
30   TNA: PRO WO95/943 War Diary 19th Division CRA.
31   TNA: PRO WO95/2093 War Diary 2nd Wiltshires.
32   TNA: PRO WO95/2089 War Diary 58 Brigade.

the Green Line, but had suffered a number of casualties including four of their officers.[33] Their advance drew comment from other units: "The steadiness with which the 8/N.Staffs R. moved forward through [the barrage] was very praiseworthy and was commented upon by officers of other units who observed it".[34]

Indeed, Jenlain was evidently still not completely clear of German troops as one company of the 8/N.Staffs was obliged to mop up an enemy machine gun post, taking eight prisoners in the process.

Such tribulations meant that the battalion reached the Green Line 25 minutes late: their task was to leapfrog the 9/Cheshire and continue the advance to the Red Line. Such was the rigidity of the artillery timetable that their protective barrage had already ceased and the men had to go forward with no artillery support at all. In spite of enemy machine gun fire and "close 'Pip Squeak' fire from a Battery just behind Bry",[35] the leading companies were able to get forward, advancing by rushes under covering fire from rifles and Lewis guns across terrain offering "no cover of any description",[36] as far as the ridge to the north of the track running from Wargnies-le-Grand to Bry through square G15 a., north-north-east of the village. An attempt was made by two platoons under Lieutenant Harris to force their way around the left flank into Bry itself, but they were driven back, having suffered a number of casualties. These troops had been out on a limb, their left flank in the air as there was still at this time a 600 yard gap to the right flank unit of 58 Brigade which was still struggling up to the Green Line.

On the right of the 8/N.Staffs a platoon tried to force their way into the northern outskirts of Wargnies-le-Grand, but were halted by machine gun fire from the high ground east of the village. With the 24th Division to the south still held up at the river, it was deemed appropriate to form a defensive flank facing the village. When the author of the 8/N.Staffs' "Account of Operations" was able later to walk the ground over which his battalion had advanced, he "counted 7 M.G. positions close to the WARGNIES-LE-GRAND – BRY road alone, each with a large pile of empty cases".[37] Up to this point it was estimated that the battalion had suffered over 100 casualties, including two officers killed and two others wounded. The author takes up the story again:

> I got forward a section of Vickers Guns, but could not find the Advanced Field Guns who were unable to cross the river till later. The Coys dug in, and I asked for Artillery Support, without which, until the 24th Division came up, I saw it would be impossible to advance. The gas through which the men had passed earlier in JENLAIN was beginning to affect some of the Officers and NCOs who had been compelled to take off their masks from time to time. At 1530 orders were received that the advance would continue under a barrage.[38]

With the 24th Division held up, and the right flank of the 19th Division, that is the right of the 8/N.Staffs, exposed to machine gun fire from in and around Wargnies-le-Grand, it fell to the 9/

33   TNA: PRO WO95/2082 War Diary 8th Battalion North Staffordshire Regiment.
34   TNA: PRO WO95/2077 War Diary 56 Brigade.
35   TNA: PRO WO95/2082 War Diary 8th Battalion North Staffordshire Regiment.
36   Ibid.
37   Ibid.
38   Ibid.

Cheshire to remedy the somewhat precarious situation. An unidentified Company Commander "determined to mop up [...] the village of WARGNIES-LE-GRAND and to attack in the rear some hostile MGs located near G15.d.5.0. This was accomplished, the whole village being mopped up (a considerable number of prisoners taken) and platoon posts established at G15.d.75.25 [on the Wargnies-le-Grand to Bry road] and G15 d.05.50 by 1000 hours".[39] Orders were given to consolidate the positions held and await developments. It was not yet 1030. At around quarter to 11 two sections of Field Artillery came up onto the high ground in square G8 (just to the rear of the Green Line), were placed under the command of the 8/N.Staffs' Commanding Officer and were to be ready to act as anti-tank guns should the need arise.[40] Just before midday, the guns commenced the first of three artillery shoots on the high ground to the west and south of Bry. These were timed at 10 minute intervals and were designed to neutralise enemy machine gun posts in that area prior to the next assault.

The orders for the 1630 attack were received at 1420: the advance would recommence under a creeping barrage. The order read as follows:

1. 19th Division will continue the attack at 1630 hours today with the object of establishing the line of the road LA MARLIERE – BRY – WARGNIES-LE-GRAND.
2. 58th Brigade will attack through G3 to G4 and thence along the spur to the road LA MARLIERE – BRY.
3. 8/N.Staffs will attack due EAST to the road from G.16.a.0.0 to cross roads G10.d.3.7. 8/N.Staffs will exploit this attack if possible by sending patrols to occupy the spur in G16 central in order to make valley in G16.d and b untenable to the enemy.
4. Attack will take place under creeping barrage moving at rate of 100 yds in 4 minutes. Barrage will open on the line G15.b.9.0.to G9.d.7.0. to A27.c.3.0 and will rest on this initial line for 10 minutes.
5. Heavy artillery and MGs will barrage Eastern slopes of BRY and ETH and sunken road in G16 d and G22 b.
6. A battalion of 24th Division is passing through Southern portion of WARGNIES and endeavouring to establish a position in G15 d and G22 a this afternoon AAA 8 N/Staffs will take advantage of this battalion as a flank guard if in position if not in position Staffords will form a defensive flank.
7. Zero hour will be 1630 hours.
8. Very urgent. Acknowledge.[41]

It had been hoped that a smoke barrage would be put down on the slopes to the east of the two villages, but it turned out not to be possible in the time available.[42]

Brigade orders were then sent to reorganise the battalions for the attack: on the 56 Brigade front the 8/N.Staffs were to take over the whole of the Brigade front and spearhead the attack. The 1/4th KSLI became the support battalion on the Green Line and 9/Cheshire moved back

39   TNA: PRO WO95/2077 War Diary 56 Brigade.
40   The Germans had used captured British tanks in an abortive counter attack against 49th Division near Valenciennes on 1 November.
41   TNA: PRO WO95/2077 War Diary 56 Brigade.
42   TNA: PRO WO95/2089 War Diary 58 Brigade.

to reserve positions on the Petit Aunelle. The 58 Brigade battalions were to remain unchanged, 2/Wiltshire and 9/Welsh going into the attack. The rear companies of each battalion would pass through those currently holding the front line positions and lead the assault, the former leading companies following in support. The reserve battalion, 9/RWF, would occupy the vacated positions on the Green Line at Zero plus five minutes. The precipitate nature of the enemy withdrawal was noted by their diarist: as they established a forward battalion headquarters at around one o'clock in the afternoon, "there were evident signs that the enemy had hastily evacuated, leaving half-consumed meals behind them."[43]

The 1630 attack on the 56 Brigade front can be quickly told: the reserve and support companies of the 8/N.Staffs (A & D) leapfrogged their forward companies (B & C) and gained their objectives, an advance of 5-600 yards, with few casualties and were soon in touch with troops on both flanks. "The enemy apparently ran as soon as the barrage opened".[44] Captain A.H. Buch was wounded and Second-Lieutenant Platt missing.

58 Brigade did not have it so easy. The events are best told by the diarist of the brigade:

> The enemy reply to our barrage was heavy and very prompt, coming down on the ridge in G8 within two minutes of zero. The attack was also met by heavy machine gun fire the moment it started. Both Battalions however pushed on though suffering heavy casualties. The Support and Reserve Companies of the 9th Welsh Regt suffered most severely. The 2nd Wilts Regt also met with considerable opposition in the village of ETH itself, and also from machine gun fire from their left flank as the attack by the 11th Division [First Army] did not materialise. Eventually the Right Company of the 9th Welsh Regt established itself on the objective (the WARGNIES-LE-GRAND – LA MARLIERE Road) where touch was gained with 56th Brigade. The Left Company swung back to join 2nd Wilts Regt who had captured ETH and established a line on the slopes East of it, but were unable to gain the crest of the spur. The left of the 2nd Wilts Regt was unable to get touch with anyone as (owing apparently to their orders not reaching them in time) the 32nd Brigade of the 11th Division had not attacked at all. The Support Company therefore formed a defensive flank to protect the Left and Rear of the Battalion. About 50 prisoners were captured during this attack.[45]

The diary of 2/Wiltshire also adds that B Company under Second Lieutenant Auton had the job of mopping up the village after the leading companies had passed through: they captured 50 prisoners from the chateau, bringing their total up to 60 for the day, along with six machine guns.[46]

The 19th Division had effectively finished for the day. As darkness fell it held a line in advance of its Red Line objectives. On the right flank, a line on the road to the east of the spur of land north-east of Wargnies-le-Grand had been established where troops had strayed into 24th Division territory. The line followed the road northwards to the north-east of Bry, whence it continued in a north-westerly direction, more or less on the 100 metre contour line, just shy

43   TNA: PRO WO95/2092 War Diary 9th Royal Welsh Fusiliers
44   TNA: PRO WO95/2089 War Diary 58 Brigade.
45   TNA: PRO WO95/2089 War Diary 58 Brigade.
46   TNA: PRO WO95/2093 War Diary 2nd Wiltshires.

of the crest of the ridge to the north-east of Eth. The remains of the day's objectives, and indeed the town of Roisin beyond them, were taken without opposition the following morning.

Detailed casualty figures for 58 Brigade are not available, but fatal casualties for the battalions can be estimated as follows:

	Officers	Other Ranks
9th Royal Welsh Fusiliers	–	–
9th Welsh Regt.	–	23
2nd Wiltshire Regt.	1	16

Similarly, for 56 Brigade:

	Officers	Other Ranks
9th Cheshire Regt	–	11
1/4th King's Shropshire Light Infantry	1	11
8th North Staffordshire Regt.	3	19

Detailed figures are available for 56 Brigade for the period 2–9 November:

Unit	Officers			Other Ranks		
	K	W	M	K	W	M
9/ Cheshires	1	8	–	12	110	12
4/ KSLI	2	2	–	16	104	13
8 /N.Staffs	4	7	1	21	101	9
Total	7	17	1	49	315	34[47]

That these figures can be considered 'light' is backed up by a comment made by the diarist of the 9/RWF in their "Short Account of Operations": "The country in this area was wooded and full of steep valleys with small streams through them and would, had the enemy meant to fight seriously, have been most difficult and costly to capture".[48]

The 9/Cheshire diarist, summing up lessons learnt or emphasised in his after action report asserts that:

> The battalion profited greatly by the recent training. All Infantry and Machine Gun opposition was quickly dealt with by supporting sections pushing round the enemy's flank, whilst the sections held up gave covering fire. These tactics were invariably successful.[49]

47   TNA: PRO WO95/2077 War Diary 56 Brigade.
48   TNA: PRO WO95/2092 War Diary 9th Royal Welsh Fusiliers.
49   TNA: PRO WO95/2079 War Diary 9th Cheshire Regiment.

Interestingly, he also adds, as the final point of his report, that "A good supply of rum is essential."[50]

24th Division[51]

To the south, 24th Division (Major-General A.C. Daly) frontage was quite narrow; originally less than 1,000 yards, and it was planned that the attack would be made on a single battalion front with the 9th Battalion Royal Sussex Regiment [9/R.Sussex] leading the assault, the other battalions of 73 Brigade (Brigadier-General R.J. Collins) in close support. The frontage widened to 2,000 yards at the first objective (the Blue Line) and to approximately 3,000 yards by the time the Red Line, which ran north-west to south-east, was reached. The northern divisional boundary snaked in a more or less east-north-easterly direction to include most of the village of Wargnies-le-Grand, and the southern boundary followed the east-west grid line on the map that ran just to the south of Wargnies-le-Petit. (See Map 3) As we have already seen, troops from 19th Division had encroached into their neighbour's territory by attempting to clear the more northerly of the two Wargnies villages. The southern divisional / corps boundary was obviously purely artificial, not conforming to any geographical or strategic features and Operation Order No.39 issued by XVII Corps Heavy Artillery noted "the lines depicting objectives are purely diagrammatic, the tactical features in their neighbourhood form the real objectives, similarly, lines showing CORPS and divisional boundaries are only intended as a guide to frontages. They may always be crossed for tactical purposes by arrangement with neighbouring Divisions".[52]

Just as on the 19th Division frontage, 24th Division found themselves facing an enemy in retreat on 3 November: "Leading Brigade as advanced guard to push on and keep touch with enemy and if serious opposition is encountered an attack in strength supported by Artillery is to be carried out under Divisional arrangements".[53] The 13th Battalion Middlesex Regiment [13/Middlesex] pushed patrols forward in accordance with a XVII Corps General Staff order issued at 1310 hours requiring the advanced units eventually to "form a jumping off place"[54] for the forthcoming attack and "reached the Blue Line (1st Objective) with little opposition"[55] by three o'clock that afternoon. They were ordered "not to advance beyond this line",[56] thus removing the possibility of heavy action that day. At 1515 hours the 9/R.Sussex "were ordered to move forward and assemble 1,000 yards in the rear of 13/Middlesex and be prepared to attack through the latter at dawn on the 4th inst".[57] An order issued later in the day was perhaps too optimistic: "If touch with enemy is lost, Corps mounted troops moving forward at daylight will take up pursuit, passing through infantry and locate enemy."[58] The mounted troops would be frustrated for a day or so longer.

50   Ibid.
51   See Map 3
52   TNA: PRO WO95/944 War Diary XVII Corps Heavy Artillery.
53   TNA: PRO WO95/2192 War Diary 24th Division HQ.
54   TNA: PRO WO95/936 War Diary XVII Corps General Staff.
55   TNA: PRO WO95/2217 War Diary 73 Infantry Brigade.
56   Ibid.
57   Ibid.
58   TNA: PRO WO95/2192 War Diary 24th Division HQ.

At 1930 hours on 3 November the modified orders for the attack on the following morning were issued. The original, Order No.259, had stated that the "73rd Brigade will capture the BLUE and GREEN LINES, as explained to all concerned at yesterday's [1 November] Brigade Conference. 17th Infantry Brigade will then pass through the 73rd Infantry Brigade and will capture the RED LINE".[59] A further advance was a possibility, but this "will however only be carried out on the first day on the initiative of Battalion Commanders by patrols to maintain touch with the enemy".[60]

Even at this stage, the new orders were not definitive. Order No. 259/1 still envisaged 17 Brigade (Brigadier-General G. Thorpe) leapfrogging their comrades on the Green Line to take the two villages and the Red Line positions. The reality was fundamentally different: the advance all the way to the Red Line was to be the sole responsibility of 73 Brigade. The units of 17 Brigade got no further forward than the Blue Line on 4 November. Orders received at 2200 hours that day required them to pass through the 73 Brigade's positions and continue the advance the following morning. Even so, as the 1st Battalion Royal Fusiliers [1/R.Fus] (17 Brigade), having spent most of 4 November in support positions in the valley west of Jenlain and Villers Pol (that is, still west of the Blue Line), entered Jenlain to occupy their billets for the night, they encountered enemy shelling which went on sporadically through the night.[61] "Casualties were caused as follows: Killed 5 O[ther] R[anks] Wounded Lt. J.A. CASE and 20 OR".[62]

72 Infantry Brigade (Brigadier-General R.W. Morgan), in reserve, played no active role on the day. All three battalions were billeted on the night 4/5 November in the village of Sepmeries, some four miles south-west of Jenlain. The War Diary of the 1st Battalion North Staffordshire Regiment [1/N.Staffs] notes the great interest taken by members of the battalion in the 380 or so "Boche prisoners" taken and sent back by 73 Brigade.[63] Sepmeries was clearly very crowded that night, as the diarist of 8th Battalion Royal West Kent Regiment [8/W.Kent] felt it appropriate to comment on "very close billeting".[64]

The 9/R.Sussex moved forward to their jumping off positions from Sepmeries at 1600 hours on 3 November. "The march to the Assembly Positions was made through a good deal of enemy shelling particularly in the vicinity of VILLERS POL. Enemy machine guns were very active whilst Companies were actually getting into their positions. A number of casualties were sustained before ZERO by [sic] these MGs".[65] The battalion lined up with C Company on the left, A Company in the centre, B Company on the right and D Company in support. The battalion had seen no action since 17 October and their subsequent week's sojourn in Cauroir had seen a curious mixture of activities: the evenings had been taken up by concert parties, and daylight hours were filled by inter-battalion football matches, a Brigade Sports Day and a nail hunt that had harvested over 80 pounds of nails. Fortunately, time was also found for Lewis Gun training and a demonstration on how to envelop an enemy strongpoint which was holding

59   TNA: PRO WO95/2205 War Diary 17 Infantry Brigade.
60   Ibid.
61   TNA: PRO WO95/2205 War Diary 17 Brigade HQ.
62   TNA: PRO WO95/2207 War Diary 1st Battalion Royal Fusiliers.
63   TNA: PRO WO95/2213 War Diary 1st Battalion North Staffordshire Regiment.
64   TNA: PRO WO95/2213 War Diary 8th Battalion Royal West Kent Regiment.
65   TNA: PRO WO95/2219 War Diary 9th Battalion Royal Sussex Regiment.

up an advance. A practice Brigade attack on "high ground" was also organised on the last day of the month, added interest being assured by the inclusion of "imitation tanks".[66]

The advance commenced, in artillery formation, along with the artillery creeping barrage, at 0600 hours.[67] The barrage advanced at a rate of 100 yards every four minutes: the 18 pounders were firing 45 percent High Explosive, 45 percent Shrapnel and 10 percent Smoke at a rate of two rounds per minute, the 4.5" Howitzers managing half that rate.[68] The front line troops managed to evade the worst of the enemy counter barrage,[69] but encountered very heavy machine gun fire, particularly as they crested the ridge to the west of the Brickfields (see map, Square G19 d). Casualties were heavy. At 0630 hours "airmen reported enemy apparently on the line G20 a 8.2 – G26 a 9.9 with our troops advancing to this line in artillery formation".[70] A and B Companies on the right were held up by machine gun fire from their right flank, but A Company 24th Battalion Machine Gun Corps were able to bring their guns forward to Square G26 c, "facing South East to fire across the valley in front.[71] The 73rd Light Trench Mortar Battery were also able to lend support: they sent one "Minenwerfer" under Captain H.H. L'Estrange MC as far as the Jenlain – Villers Pol road and, "ascertaining that the 9th Royal Sussex Regiment were held up by hostile MG fire pushed forward to engage, picking up two 'minenwerfers' on the way – Guns came into action at 300 yds range + engaged the MG's [...] also 2 Heavy MGs later [...] came into action on the right of the 'minenwerfer' guns. The enemy retired over the river..."[72] By 0715 hours the troops were established on the Green Line, except on the extreme right where enemy machine gun fire was still a problem.

The 7th Battalion Northamptonshire Regiment [7/Northamptonshire] had been detailed to support the advance of the 9/R.Sussex. B and D Companies, under Captains B.Wright and J.A. Elliman respectively, had moved off at 0300 hours and by 0800 hours had joined the front line troops in their positions overlooking the Petit Aunelle River, B Company supporting the left flank, D Company the right. D Company had been "caught in the Hun counter-barrage and a number of casualties were caused".[73] Captain Elliman was one of the wounded. B Company had "successfully eluded the counter-barrage on the left (N) flank and succeeded in establishing themselves in a position which dominated the small bridge over the river AUNELLE. The bridge [G21 c 3.9] carried the main JENLAIN – BAVAY road which separated Wargnies-le-Grand and Wargnies-le-Petit and by concentrated Lewis Gun and rifle fire and by forward

66   Ibid.
67   The war diary of 9th Royal Sussex, possibly typed some days after the event, records this mistakenly as 0530 hours. The diarist may have taken this time from the original orders. The diary of 73rd Brigade makes the same error in its 'Summary of Operations' written on 13 November. The XVII Corps Diary confirms "The V, IV and VI Corps attacked at 0530 hours. [...] The XVII Corps attack at 0600 hours." See also *Official History 1918 Vol V*, p. 486, Harris & Barr, *Amiens to the Armistice* p. 277 and the War Diary of 7th Bn Northamptonshire Regiment. Oddly, the War Diaries of 13th Bn Middlesex Regt and 106th Brigade RFA both record the assault as commencing at 0630 hours.
68   TNA: PRO WO95/943 War Diary XVII Corps CRA.
69   TNA: PRO WO95/2291 War Diary 9th Battalion Royal Sussex Regiment.
70   TNA: PRO WO95/936 War Diary XVII Corps HQ.
71   TNA: PRO WO95/2201 War Diary 24th Battalion Machine Gun Corps.
72   TNA: PRO WO95/2219 War Diary 73rd Light Trench Mortar Battery.
73   TNA: PRO WO95/2218 War Diary 7th Battalion Northamptonshire Regiment.

patrols they managed to keep it whole".[74] The Germans were still shelling the roads and the ridge was being swept by machine gun fire. The advance had stalled.

At 1030 hours, Brigadier-General Collins, commanding 73 Brigade, issued verbal instructions to relieve the pressure by outflanking both villages: units of 13/Middlesex were to "move round [the] northern outskirts of Wargnies-le-Grand and establish themselves on the high ground east of the village in G15 d – 16 c and 22 b. 7th Bn Northamptonshire Regt to dribble troops forward between the railway and the river in G21 d and then move forward and occupy the high ground in G29 central",[75] thus regaining touch with the 13/Middlesex.

This assault was to be timed to coincide with the 19th Division attack at 1630 hours, but the 13/Middlesex had moved forward from Le Coron, where they had concentrated that morning, and were able to advance through Wargnies-le-Grand, reaching its northern and eastern outskirts by 1545 hours, in effect mopping up positions already overrun by the 9/Cheshire (19th Division) earlier in the day. Even so, the War Diary reports "considerable opposition being experience [sic] from machine guns. Capt. H.R. Mallett MC was wounded".[76] They established positions to the east of the village, as planned, by 1730 hours.

The outflanking of Wargnies-le-Petit was entrusted to A and C Companies of 7/Northamptonshire. They were to cross the Petit Aunelle by the very bridge kept intact by their comrades in B Company earlier that day, and "keeping their left on the main road" were to "push through the village and then onward to the high ground east of it".[77] They went forward with C Company in front under 2nd Lieutenant J.C. Pike and A Company (Captain C.A. Williamson MC) in support. "Machine gun fire was met with but overcome by grenades and rifle fire and both companies established themselves well forward of the village".[78]

Meanwhile, D Company of 9/R.Sussex had pushed patrols forward through Wargnies-le-Petit under Lieutenant P.R. Hill and 2nd Lieutenant W. Aldridge at 1600 hours only to find that, as in other sectors, opposition had melted away after the initial resistance had been overcome and they established touch with the 7/Northamptonshire to the east of the village by 1730 hours. The latter battalion was tasked with one more problem before their work was complete for the day. Some German machine guns were still active in the Bois de Ferrière. These outposts were successfully overrun during the night and by dawn on 5 November "our troops had established themselves on the Red Line along the whole of the Brigade front".[79]

The two liberated villages, it was noted by the diarist of 7/Northamptonshire, were "inhabited by a fair number of French civilians".[80] The 24th Division HQ Diary estimates the number at around 600. The same diarist lists 315 prisoners taken, 15 of whom were Officers.[81] The two 'minenwerfers' of 73rd Light Trench Mortar Battery earlier employed on the high ground west of the Green Line were sent forward at 1900 hours "through Wargnies-le-Grand and took up positions for the night covering the BAVAY road".[82]

74 Ibid.
75 TNA: PRO WO95/2217 War Diary 73 Infantry Brigade.
76 TNA: PRO WO95/2219 War Diary 13th Battalion Middlesex Regiment.
77 TNA: PRO WO95/2218 War Diary 7th Battalion Northamptonshire Regiment.
78 Ibid.
79 TNA: PRO WO95/2217 War Diary 73 Infantry Brigade.
80 TNA: PRO WO95/2218 War Diary 7th Battalion Northamptonshire Regiment.
81 TNA: PRO WO95/2192 War Diary 24th Division HQ.
82 TNA: PRO WO95/2219 War Diary 73rd Light Trench Mortar Battery.

Casualty figures for the units involved that day were not assiduously recorded by all. Only the 9/R.Sussex noted detailed figures for the 4 November. They were estimated at:

> One Officer (Lieutenant H.G.Welham, C Company) killed, and, amongst Other Ranks, 35 were killed, 95 wounded and 5 missing.[83]

The 9/R.Sussex also recorded gallantry awards for the operations commencing 4 November: 13 Military Medals were awarded to Other Ranks. (To two Sergeants, three Corporals, two Lance Corporals, two Signallers and four Privates).

Fatal casualties for the Division can be estimated as:

17 Brigade

1st Royal Fusiliers	5
8th Queens	–
3rd Rifle Brigade	–

73 Brigade

9th Royal Sussex	42
7th Northants	12
13th Middlesex	8

Total	**67** [84]

72 Brigade, in reserve the whole day, suffered no fatal casualties.

If the number of wounded were to be estimated at between two and three times the number of fatalities, the resulting figure would be between 134 and 201. Even if the upper figure were taken, the number of casualties for the day would still be classified as slight.

Conclusion

The tactics of fire and movement have been shown to be well understood and implemented successfully against some serious opposition, including machine gun nests and fortified villages. Such positions were outmanoeuvred and overrun, but commanders were mindful not to over-stretch their troops, and the pause in front of the ridge and the villages of Eth and Bry was instrumental in reducing casualties. The withdrawals of German units in the face of this final push demonstrated that they could not defend their positions in depth and would prove to be a common occurrence along the whole front.

---

83   TNA: PRO WO95/2291 War Diary 9th Battalion Royal Sussex Regiment.
84   Figures from 'Soldiers Died in the Great War' CD Rom and Commonwealth War Graves Commission.

3

VI Corps

Introduction

VI Corps was faced with a situation comparable to that of XVII Corps to the north. This chapter shows how a similar plan of attack proved more difficult to implement. Objectives were altered at the last minute, requiring some battalions to advance much further than originally envisaged. Mist and rain made it difficult for some units to maintain direction and the obstinate defence of woods and farms by German machine gunners and some effective artillery fire held up the advance for a time. Nevertheless, the pragmatism of lower-level command is seen to prevail, as rivers were crossed and three villages captured by units well-versed in platoon or company attack methods.

*   *   *

Order No. 401 was issued by VI Corps on 1 November, stating that the advance was to be continued "towards the line AVESNES – MAUBEUGE – MONS on a date and at an hour which have been notified separately to all concerned".[1] Once the Red Line was reached, the units of the Corps were ordered "to continue to press their advantage energetically" and to "be prepared to continue the operations on Z plus 1 and subsequent days".[2] The attack was to be carried out by the Guards Division on the left Corps front with 62nd Division on the right. The 3rd and 2nd Divisions were held in reserve. The latter were to be "moved forward behind the leading divisions as the advance progress[ed]" and were to be prepared to complete the task of the VI Corps, if required, in the Right and Left Sectors respectively".[3] It seems as if the commanders were anxious to complete the job as soon as possible: "The advance is to be pressed with the utmost urgency".[4]

The ground over which the Corps would advance is described in the Official History:

1   TNA: PRO WO95/775 War Diary VI Corps HQ General Staff.
2   Ibid.
3   Ibid.
4   TNA: PRO WO95/1214 War Diary 1 Guards Brigade.

The country to be traversed rose gently, and was cut into spurs by four small streams, which ran across the front. Of these the westernmost, the Rhonelle, was passable by vehicles only at the bridges, which were down, or at a ford south-west of Villers-Pol. The Petite Aunelle (which runs into the Aunelle below Eth), though deep cut, with 30-foot banks in places, had but little water in it. The other two streams were unimportant. The area contained a number of villages surrounded by orchards and fields enclosed by hedges or wire, but few woods. Most of the roads were sunken, and had as much as two feet of mud in them. The ground it would be thought favoured the defence; but in the event its difficulties aided the better soldiers, for the enclosures enabled the West Riding men [62nd Division] and the Guards to manoeuvre round and outflank the defenders.[5]

"Everything was ready for [the] next forward movement" wrote Bladenburg in his history of the Coldstream Guards, "which was to be an operation of great importance. [...] It was in fact to be a decisive attack [...] with the object of finally breaking up the crumbling defences of the Germans and of dealing them their death-blow".[6]

Zero hour was set at 0530 on 4 November. On 1 November C Company, 6th Tank Battalion, "consisting of 12 Whippet Tanks, was allotted to VI Corps, and I [Haldane] placed this company with the remainder of the Corps Cavalry and Cyclists under the command of the O.C. Oxfordshire Hussars".[7] The tanks and the cavalry were to play no part in the advance of 4 November: the decision as to their usefulness had already been taken: "Past experience had shown that there is little chance of using mounted troops in any numbers during the first day of operations, and I [Haldane again] therefore decided that the Corps Cavalry, Cyclists and Whippet Tanks [...] should be concentrated in Corps Reserve in the vicinity of PONT DE BUAT, so as to operate in the later stages of the advance. The task of the mobile force would be to exploit success in the direction of Maubeuge and to endeavour to seize the river crossings and railway before the enemy could destroy them".[8]

The pattern of artillery arrangements was similar to those of Corps to the north and south: prior to the assault there was to be "no marked increase in the normal daily volume of fire".[9] As was by now standard procedure, there was to be no preliminary bombardment: artillery action would begin as the infantry moved from their jumping off positions. According to the VI Corps 'Gun Statement', timed at noon on 4 November, the number of guns in action were as follows:

Field Artillery	Guards Div	62nd Div
	64 18 pdrs	86 18 pdrs
	23 4.5" Howitzers	29 4.5" Hows

5   J.E. Edmonds & R. Maxwell-Hyslop, *Military Operations France and Belgium 1918, Vol. V* (London: HMSO, 1947) pp. 484-485.
6   Sir J. Ross-of-Bladenburg, *The Coldstream Guards 1914-1918 Vol. II* (London: Humphrey Milford, 1928) p. 369.
7   TNA: PRO WO95/775 War Diary VI Corps HQ General Staff.
8   Ibid.
9   TNA: PRO WO95/783 War Diary VI Corps CRA.

Heavy Artillery	46 6" Hows
	5 8" Hows
	12 9.2" Hows
	21 60 pdrs
	4 Mk. VII 6" guns
	4 Mk.XIX 6" guns

Totals	Field Artillery: 202 guns
	Heavy Artillery: 94 guns[10]

Shells to be dumped at gun positions as follows:

18 pounders	400 rounds per gun
4.5" Howitzers	350 rounds per gun
6" Howitzers	300 rounds per gun
60 pounders	300 rounds per gun
8" Howitzers	200 rounds per gun
9.2" Howitzers	150 rounds per gun
6" Howitzers	150 rounds per gun.[11]

The creeping barrage laid down by 18 pounders and extended in depth by 4.5" Howitzers and by three 6" Howitzer batteries per division was to be "formed by H.E. and Shrapnel, with approximately 10 percent of Smoke".[12] The barrage would move forward at a rate of 100 yards in four minutes as far as the Blue Line (see Maps 4 & 5). At Zero plus 135 minutes it would move on from the Blue Line at the faster pace of 100 yards in three minutes until it reached the Green Line at about Zero plus 235 minutes. The right of the 62nd Division would pause for 20 minutes on the Blue Dotted Line (at Zero plus 185 minutes) before continuing the advance in conjunction with the New Zealand Division on their right. It was envisaged that the pause on the Green Line would be no more than 15 minutes: thereafter the infantry advance would supported only by mobile artillery units moving up from their original positions. "CRAs would detail one 18 pdr and one 4.5" Howitzer battery and B.G. Heavy Artillery one 6" How. Battery to be at the direct call of the Brigadier of each attacking Brigade beyond the BLUE objective".[13] More detailed instructions followed: "special features and lines of approach should be selected for bombardment by batteries as they come into action. The time at which firing must cease on any particular objective must be arranged by the Infantry Brigadier in conjunction with the Field Artillery Group Commander and the Heavy Artillery Brigade Commander".[14] Artillery commanders were to get in "personal touch"[15] with Infantry Brigade commanders prior to the assault to make the necessary arrangements. It was possible

10   Ibid.
11   Ibid.
12   Ibid.
13   TNA: PRO WO95/775 War Diary VI Corps HQ General Staff.
14   TNA: PRO WO95/785 War Diary VI Corps CRA.
15   Ibid.

for individual sections or even single guns to be used to deal with anti-tank guns, machine gun nests or other stubborn strongpoints.

The Heavy Artillery would be used for counter-battery work: this would include gas shells, though it was noted that these could not be dropped closer to the barrage than 800 yards (300 yards if the wind was within 20 degrees of due west). Selected objectives ahead of the barrage were also to be shelled at the discretion of the BGHA as guns dropped out of the counter-battery programme. On 4 November, VI Corps Heavy Artillery was able to engage and disrupt 34 enemy batteries. Aircraft from 12 Squadron RAF were in the air to work in conjunction with the artillery units, including one looking out for signs of German counter-attack preparations and 'contact' planes observing flares from infantry units at Zero plustwo, four and six hours, and thereafter as required by Divisions.[16] From daylight to Zero plus three hours, four aircraft were to be in the air, observing fall of shot for counter-battery units and communicating any corrections required.[17]

The artillery were also to use 'Thermit'[18] in the early stages of the attack on 62nd Division front, these shells being fired into the sunken road west of La Folie Farm and into the ravine running north to south to the east of the farm. The ravine running between the farm and Vieux Moulin and its extension southeast from the mill was to receive similar treatment. A general order was also issued to the effect that villages would be spared the destructive force of high explosives: "Howitzers will not barrage through villages. Through villages only shrapnel will be fired".[19]

The approximate number of shells fired on VI Corps front on 4 November was as follows:

18 pdr shrapnel	21,050
18 pdr HE	21,750
18 pdr smoke	2,199
4.5" How. HE	6,050
60 pdr Shrapnel	1,573
60 pdr HE	764
6" How. HE	4,223
6" How. Gas	184
6" Gun Shrapnel	127
6" Gun HE	257
8" How. HE	195
9.2" How. HE	608
Total	58,980[20]

The orders sent down from Corps repeatedly emphasise the need to keep the attack secret:

16   TNA: PRO WO95/775 War Diary VI Corps HQ General Staff.
17   Ibid.
18   'Thermit' was a type of incendiary shell.
19   TNA: PRO WO95/3073 War Diary 62nd Division HQ CRA.
20   Ibid.

Attention is called to the necessity of preserving the strictest secrecy as to the operations, especially:

The movement of troops only under cover of darkness.

No marked increase or decrease in artillery fire.

No marked increase in wireless activity or in the number of stations in action before zero.[21]

At the same time, the overall policy is stated explicitly to be "to keep the Germans on the run".[22] It was envisaged that patrols would be pushed forward to the Brown Line[23] by the evening of Z Day.

The Guards (Major-General T.G. Matheson) and 62nd Divisions (Major-General Sir R.D. Wigham) came into the line during the night 2 – 3 November, relieving 2nd Division. Neither of these Divisions had been in action since 22 October 1918.[24] Strong patrols were then sent forward to try and gain touch with enemy units that were reported to be withdrawing. "On the right of VI Corps front, the 62nd Division found no change in the enemy's positions. Machine gun fire was encountered from the copse in R.16.b, La Folie Farm; ORSINVAL appeared to be held in strength".[25]

Guards Division[26]

On the left, the 2nd Battalion Coldstream Guards [2/Coldstream Guards], 1 Guards Brigade, (Brigadier-General C.R. Champion de Crespigny) and 1st Battalion Coldstream Guards [1/Coldstream Guards], 2 Guards Brigade, (Brigadier-General B.N. Sergisson-Brooke) were sent forward to ascertain the situation on their fronts: reports were sent back to the effect that the enemy had withdrawn from the east bank of the Rhonelle River and in return orders were sent for two companies of 2/Coldstream Guards to be pushed across the river. The river was easily fordable[27] and patrols entered the village of Villers-Pol. They encountered some sniping[28] or machine gun fire[29] from the church but they were able to advance to within 400 yards of the Blue Line, where they dug in at 2330 hours, "the high ground immediately in front being strongly held by the enemy".[30]

21   Ibid.
22   Ibid.
23   This was approximately nine miles east of the Red Line. This line was not reached until 7 November.
24   The Guards Division had been in action 21–28 August, 3–27 September and 9–22 October. 62nd Division had been in action 25 August–2 September, 12–15 September, 28–30 September and 18–22 October: TNA: PRO WO95/775 War Diary VI Corps HQ General Staff.
25   Ibid. Report on Operations 27 October–11 November 1918. La Folie Farm had been raided on 1 November and nine German prisoners captured.
26   See Map 4.
27   TNA: PRO WO95/1218 War Diary 2 Guards Brigade HQ.
28   TNA: PRO WO95/1196 War Diary Guards Division HQ General Staff.
29   TNA: PRO WO95/1218 War Diary 2 Guards Brigade HQ.
30   TNA: PRO WO95/1215 War Diary 2nd Battalion Coldstream Guards.

The 1/Coldstream Guards received their orders at 1600 hours on 3 November to push forward and try to reach the high ground east of Villers-Pol. Patrols moved off accordingly at 1930. No.2 Company (Lieutenant R. Atkinson) encountered machine gun fire whilst attempting to cross the Rhonelle, but the machine gun post was taken by half of No.3 Company (Captain G.Barry) on their left who had crossed the river without opposition. More machine gun fire was encountered in the village, but this was dealt with after "some sharp hand to hand fighting".[31] At about one o'clock in the morning of 4 November the enemy put down an artillery barrage on the line of the river, and the leading companies had been held up on the eastern outskirts of the village. This situation was reported at 0200 hours in the hope that "a proper barrage could be arranged for the attack".[32] The original artillery barrage was, of course, meant to start well to the west of Villers-Pol.

At 2359 hours, 3 November, urgent orders were sent from Divisional Headquarters informing 1 and 2 Guards Brigades that Zero Hour would now be 0600. 62nd Division would advance at 0530, as per the original plan. The Guards Division artillery barrage would start on the Blue Line at 0600. A telephone message to Guards Divisional Headquarters timed at 0500 had placed troops along the line of the road R.5.b central to L34.b.2.6 (see Map 4) and "an attempt was made to arrange for the barrage to start at 0600 hours on a line NE of this road, but this had to be abandoned as wires were down to left group and there was no time to arrange by D.R.L.S. [Despatch Rider Letter Service]".[33]

On 1 Guards Brigade front, the 2/Coldstream Guards, in a change to the original plan, was now tasked in taking both the Blue and Green Lines. The 2nd Grenadier Guards [2/Grenadier Guards] would then pass through their positions and continue the advance to the Red Line. The 1st Irish Guards [1/Irish Guards] were to follow in support.

The barrage came down on the Blue Line at 0600: the high ground to the east of Villers-Pol was swathed in dense fog.[34] The leading companies of 2/Coldstream Guards headed for the Blue Line and were met with machine gun fire from the road and high ground to the east of it. "The resistance was overcome and about 200 of the enemy were taken prisoner"[35] states the War Diary of 1 Guards Brigade rather matter-of-factly. The diary of the battalion skips this episode entirely. They advanced with No. 1 Company on the right (Captain Wilkinson), No. 2 on the left (Captain Spencer), No. 4 in support (Captain Eccles) and No. 3 in reserve (Lieutenant R.V. Martin).[36] In the fog, the battalion veered to the right, mistaking the woods around La Flaque Farm (see Map 4, M.2.a & b) for those further to the north-east (G.32 & 33) and "the whole attack swung south-east".[37] "The objective was reached at 7 a.m." continues the battalion War Diary, and "during the last 700 yards of the advance severe fighting took place and very heavy casualties were inflicted on the enemy including several gun teams. The Battalion also captured 200 prisoners, and 8 Field Guns, many machine guns and a few trench mortars".[38] The diary

---

31   TNA: PRO WO95/1219 War Diary 1st Battalion Coldstream Guards.
32   Ibid.
33   TNA: PRO WO95/1196 War Diary Guards Division HQ General Staff.
34   TNA: PROP WO95/1214 War Diary 1 Guards Brigade Headquarters.
35   Ibid.
36   Bladenburg, *The Coldstream Guards*, p. 371.
37   TNA: PRO WO95/1214 War Diary 1 Guards Brigade Headquarters.
38   TNA: PRO WO95/1215 War Diary 2nd Battalion Coldstream Guards.

states that they "consolidated slightly south of their allocated positions".[39] In reality they had strayed far enough out of position for touch to be lost with the 2/Grenadier Guards following behind. The diary of the Guards Division views the situation even more seriously, stating that, at 1045 hours, "2nd Coldstream Guards [...] cannot be found".[40]

The battalion's casualties for the day were not that heavy: Lieutenant J.R. Saunders was killed, Lieutenant J.C. Hayes and Second-Lieutenants Vincent and V.W. Eardle-Beecham were wounded. Captain Eccles was also wounded, but remained at his post. Among Other Ranks, five were killed, 77 were wounded and three missing.

The 2/Grenadier Guards had formed up on the Blue Line at 0720, No. 4 Company (Lieutenant C.C. Cubitt) on the left, No. 3 Company (Lieutenant R.H.R. Palmer) on the right, with No. 2 Company (Lieutenant W.H.S. Dent) in support and No. 1 Company (Captain L. St.L. Hermon-Hodge) in reserve. "The rain stopped in the early morning, but a heavy thick mist hung over the ground, and when the battalion advanced from the BLUE LINE at 7:30 a.m. it was only possible to see about 200 yards ahead".[41] Half a mile or so into their advance they had met no opposition, but could see troops ahead of them, "moving along behind our barrage".[42] It was assumed that these were men of the 2/Coldstream Guards heading for the Green Line. Only later did they discover that they were retreating Germans. At 0940, Guard's Division Headquarters were able to ascertain from German prisoners that, as far as they knew, there were no Germans between the advancing Guards and the distant town of Maubeuge but for a few scattered outposts. The Battalion War Diary continues the story:

> As No.4 Coy passed over the high ground in G.32.b the mist lifted and they came under heavy machine gun fire from the sunken road in G.27.c. Lt. C.C. Cubitt was wounded and the Coy suffered a considerable number of casualties. 2/Lt B.R. Osborne led two platoons forward by short rushes to a line running from G.27.c.1.1 to G.33.a.4.8. From this position further advance was impossible owing to intensity and accuracy of the machine gun fire. Field guns also fired from north-east of the village [Wargnies-le-Petit] over open sights at any movement of our troops. 2/Lieut. B.R. Osborne went forward to make a personal reconnaissance of the enemy positions and was killed by a machine gun bullet while returning to report the situation. No.4 Coy was now without an officer and No.18523 Sgt. E. Carter took charge of the Coy.[43]

Meanwhile, No.3 Company advanced through the southern part of the wood in G.33.c and

> on debouching from the eastern edge came under severe machine gun and rifle fire from the enemy who were entrenched in slits 200 yds east of the wood. Lt. R.H.R. Palmer ordered his Coy to advance by short rushes covered by mutual supporting fire. By this method the enemy position was captured and the entire garrison was killed or taken prisoner. Three machine guns were captured and one minenwerfer. The Coy was unable to advance further

39   Ibid.
40   TNA: PRO WO95/1196 War Diary Guards Division HQ General Staff.
41   TNA: PRO WO95/1215 War Diary 2nd Battalion Grenadier Guards.
42   Ibid.
43   Ibid. Lt. Osborne is buried in Wargnies-le-Petit Communal Cemetery.

as the forward slope was swept by enemy machine gun fire from the southern edge of the village.[44]

Advances such as these were materially aided by guns of 74 Brigade RFA, which had advanced at Zero + 1 and was engaging enemy machine gun emplacements directly from positions north of La Flaque Farm.

Companies were dug in in positions in and around the wood by 1000 hours. Only on the right did Second-Lieutenant Harcourt-Vernon succeed in pushing his platoon forward to within 200 yards of the road in G.33.d, more or less coinciding with the Green Line. No.2 Company, coming up in support, came under machine gun fire from the wood as they neared its western point and as the fog lifted, they were able to deal with those machine guns and "proceeded to clear the rest of the wood".[45] They then became involved in the fighting to the east of the wood and were able to take a number of prisoners, capturing three field guns in the process. All companies were still taking casualties from machine gun and rifle fire from enemy positions on the Wargnies-le-Petit ridge (G.28.d & 29.c).

Only once artillery had been brought forward once more during the afternoon and these enemy positions in and to the south of Wargnies-le-Petit had been fired upon were Nos. 2 & 3 Companies able to advance and take up positions along a line from G.34.a.1.1 to M.4.a.6.7. The 1/Irish Guards passed through these positions at 1830 hours and the Grenadiers were subsequently assembled in the recently captured wood (G.33.a & c) and reorganised. Nos.3 & 4 Companies were amalgamated into a Composite Company under Lieutenant Palmer. Total casualties for the day were recorded as follows:

> 2/Lt B.R. Osborne killed (No.4 Coy)
> Lt. C.C. Cubitt wounded (No.4 Coy)
> 2/Lt. C.J.N. Adams wounded (No.2 Coy)
> Other Ranks: 10 killed, 89 wounded, 9 missing.[46]

The 1/Irish Guards had the job of advancing in support of the 2/Grenadier Guards. Their advance from their starting positions well in the rear of Villers-Pol was not straightforward. As they moved eastwards along the road in Square R.4 they became mixed up with the 1st Battalion Scots Guards [1/Scots Guards] of 2 Guards Brigade. On nearing the outskirts of the town they ascertained that the bridge over the Rhonelle was broken and they had to halt and take their Lewis Guns off their limbers as passage for wheeled transport was not possible. As they reached the bridge, the "last man of the 3rd Grenadier Guards [also 2 Guards Brigade] was just going over and the battalion was able to commence crossing straightaway. It was slow progress as only one man crossed at a time, being assisted up the bank by German prisoners".[47] The battalion then came under shell fire as they reached the crossroads at Les Quatre Vents, but "by marvellous luck"[48] suffered no casualties. They halted to reorganise into artillery formation

44   Ibid.
45   TNA: PRO WO95/1214 War Diary 1 Guards Brigade Headquarters.
46   TNA: PRO WO95/1215 War Diary 2nd Battalion Grenadier Guards.
47   TNA: PRO WO95/1216 War Diary 1st Battalion Irish Guards.
48   Ibid.

before going over the crest in L.36.c. About a mile further on they found the 2/Grenadier Guards held up by machine gun fire. The Irish decided to dig in where they were [square G.32.c] and await developments. They had been there about an hour when they came under enemy trench mortar fire "from somewhere about G.32.d.9.9".[49] They counted about a dozen rounds, these killing eight or nine horses belonging to Royal Engineer and Royal Field Artillery units in the vicinity. Sadly, they also caused a few casualties in the battalion, including Lieutenant A.L. Bain, who was killed.[50]

"The situation remained unchanged on our immediate front until late in the afternoon".[51] At around 1630 hours, the battalion was ordered to advance through the 2/Grenadier Guards, as 2 Guards Brigade was already across the stream on their right. Their diarist takes up the story:

> No.1 Coy was at once ordered forward preceded by a strong patrol – No.3 Coy followed in support. No.4 Coy about 400 yds behind No.3 Coy. No.2 Coy remained where it was. Skirting the S. Point of the wood in G.33.c, No.1 Coy crossed the stream at G.33.d.9.5. Bn HQ crossed just behind rear platoon of No.1 Coy. No.3 crossed a little N[orth] as they were ordered to follow No.1 Coy slightly echeloned to their left to protect that flank as the situation there was obscure. The stream was a slight obstacle as it was boggy at the bottom and had steep overhanging banks of about 4 foot. The men crossed on stretchers laid across. It was now almost dark and the undergrowth exceedingly thick. Nos. 1 & 3 Coys halted on the top of the very steep slope on the 100 contour [line]. No.4 Coy remained at the foot. There had been no opposition beyond a little shelling.[52]

It was becoming clear that enemy resistance was beginning to melt away and a patrol was sent out to see if they could gain touch with the 3/Grenadier Guards at the crossroads at M.5.a.5.9. This was achieved and No.1 Coy was sent forward to occupy the orchards north of Preux-au-Sart in G.35.a. No.3 Coy was sent across the Corps boundary into G.29.c and touch was eventually established with 24th Division troops there, whilst No.4 Coy established itself along the road running north-west from the southern edge of the orchards. All this manoeuvring was done in "pitch dark" and was "v. difficult owing to orchards and very high, thick hedges.[53]

The small village of Preux-au-Sart had fallen without much of a fight. There was some shelling of the forward Companies during the night and "No.1 Coy killed some Germans".[54]

No detailed casualty figures are available for the 1/Irish Guards, but fatalities for the day number only three. The diarist is content to record a happy event from the following day: "The inhabitants on coming out of their cellars in the morning were delighted to find British troops and showed the greatest cordiality".[55]

On 2 Guards Brigade front, the advance was begun by the 1/Coldstream Guards. The tone of the War Diary of this unit might suggest that the diarist was less than pleased by the events

---

49   Ibid.
50   Lieutenant Andrew Lusk Bain is buried in Wargnies-le-Petit Communal Cemetery.
51   TNA: PRO WO95/1216 War Diary 1st Battalion Irish Guards.
52   Ibid.
53   Ibid.
54   Ibid.
55   Ibid.

of the period: after recording the battalion's request for a "proper barrage"[56] and presumably having had the request denied (as had his colleagues to the north), he noted that "the troops on our right [62nd Div.] refused to attempt to move forward so that a very awkward exposed flank had to be watched by the support and reserve companies".[57] His mood did not improve as zero hour approached. The 62nd Division had advanced at 0530 as per the original orders and the 1/Coldstream Guards moved off under "a naturally rather ragged barrage".[58] They had No.2 Company (Captain G. Barry) on the right, No.3 Company (Lieutenant R. Atkinson) on the left, No.1 Company (Captain A.G. Salisbury-Jones) in support and No.4 Company (Lieutenant M.V. Buxton) in reserve.[59] They were subject to "heavy machine gun fire"[60] but pushed on, soon passing the Blue Line. The diarist of 2 Guards Brigade does not back up our diarist's view of the intensity of enemy fire, describing it as "slight",[61] allowing the 1/Coldstream Guards to "gain a line about 200 yds W of the Green Line".[62] During the advance, Captain A.G. Salisbury-Jones MC was hit in the arm and Second-Lieutenant C.W. Williams (No.4 Coy) was wounded in the leg. In the newly-won positions, the Coldstream came under "very heavy and accurate fire from enemy field guns which were firing over open sights".[63] During this period, Second-Lieutenant E.P.A. Moore (No.1 Coy) was killed.[64]

The 1/Coldstream Guards remained in these positions, still under heavy shelling, until permission was granted after dark to withdraw the leading companies into slit trenches near the La Buvette inn, where a "very cold night was spent".[65]

It now fell to the 3/Grenadier Guards to continue the assault.[66] They had breakfasted at 0300 hours, moving off an hour and 20 minutes later. They too became embroiled in the log-jam that was the single plank bridge over the Rhonelle on the approach to Villers-Pol, sustaining one Other Rank casualty wounded by shell fire in the process, and reached their assembly positions in the rear of La Flaque Farm Wood by 0800. Half an hour later they came under fire: they immediately advanced through the Coldstream Guards positions and "captured"[67] the Green Line. In doing so, No.2 Company captured four 77mm guns and four 4.2" Howitzers. "Touch was obtained with the 2nd Grenadier Guards"[68] and patrols were sent across the Aunelle River.

By 1000 hours leading companies were over the river and through into the orchards, though the high ground just beyond remained in enemy hands. The grenadiers were subject to heavy

56   TNA: PRO WO95/1219 War Diary 1st Battalion Coldstream Guards.
57   Ibid.
58   Ibid.
59   Sir J. Ross-of-Bladenburg, *The Coldstream Guards 1914-1918 Vol. II* (London: Humphrey Milford, 1928) p. 371
60   TNA: PRO WO95/1219 War Diary 1st Battalion Coldstream Guards.
61   TNA: PRO WO95/1218 War Diary 2 Guards Brigade.
62   Ibid.
63   TNA: PRO WO95/1219 War Diary 1st Battalion Coldstream Guards.
64   Second-Lieutenant Edward Patrick Aylett Moore is buried in Villers-Pol Cemetery Extension, grave G1.
65   TNA: PRO WO95/1219 War Diary 1st Battalion Coldstream Guards.
66   The mood of the 1st Coldstream Guards diarist (Captain A. De L. Cazenove) had not lightened by this stage. He states: "The 3rd Bn Grenadier Guards and 1st Bn Scots Guards passed in turn through us but never succeeded in getting much further." Ibid.
67   TNA: PRO WO95/1219 War Diary 3rd Battalion Grenadier Guards.
68   Ibid.

machine gun fire from that high ground, at a range of 3-500 yards.[69] Finding the left flank of the battalion completely in the air, No.3 Company was pushed up to defend this area. By 1500 hours the right company had worked around the flank of the enemy positions and attacked it under a smoke grenade barrage. The enemy gave up the high ground and the guardsmen were able to occupy the position. During this assault, Lieutenant C.C. Carstairs was wounded, and Second-Lieutenant G.R. Gunther was killed.[70]

Two hours later the battalion was able to capture Preux-au-Sart and take prisoners from an enemy defence line to the east of it. On the right the advance was pushed forward across the Gommegnies – Preux-au-Sart road and a line of enemy trenches occupied. Lieutenant K. Campbell was wounded during this action. At this stage, all the Officers in the Right Company had become casualties and Lieutenant F. Anson MC was "sent up to take command with orders to clear the M.G.'s out of houses on the St. Aubert–Gommegnies road.[71] It took two attempts, the second, at 2200 hours, being successful.

The battalion, which had 'never succeeded in getting much further', had in fact advanced over two miles, capturing three defensive lines, crossing a river and occupying a village and some enemy positions beyond it. It had cost them 2 Officers[72] and 15 Other Ranks killed, 4 Officers and 91 Other Ranks wounded and 3 Other Ranks missing.[73]

The 4th Battalion Guards Machine Gun Regiment had also played its part: Nos. III & I Companies supplied two sections to 2 and 1 Guards Brigades respectively. The attack on Preux-au-Sart was to be assisted by machine guns from No. III Company, but by the time the gunners got into the vicinity, the village had already been taken, so guns were deployed to the east and north of it. No. I Company had earlier sent one gun from No.3 Section forward to suppress enemy machine gun fire from the wood in G.33 and had fired 350 rounds. On going forward to recce the wood, the CO of No. 4 Section, Second-Lieutenant A.G. Hunt, was killed. Two of No.3 Section's guns were then sent to the north of the wood and "did good work in silencing and inflicting casualties on the teams of the two German machine guns which were firing from the sunk road in G.27.c. central".[74]

The reserve battalion, the 1/Scots Guards, played a limited rôle on the day: Battalion HQ made it as far forward as the southern edge of La Flaque Farm Wood, and C Company was called upon in the evening to move forward in support of the 3/Grenadier Guards. Nevertheless, 30 wounded and three killed was the price paid. Guardsmen 16876 James Banks, 5821 John Reilly and 8786 Archibald White lie in Villers-Pol Cemetery Extension. The final positions reached on the day can be seen on the map.

---

69   Ibid.
70   Second-Lieutenant Geoffrey Robert Gunther is buried in Villers-Pol Cemetery Extension, grave E1.
71   TNA: PRO WO95/1219 War Diary 3rd Battalion Grenadier Guards.
72   The other Officer is Second-Lieutenant A.E. Filmer-Strangeways-Rogers, who is also buried in Villers-Pol Cemetery Extension, Grave G2.
73   TNA: PRO WO95/1219 War Diary 3rd Battalion Grenadier Guards. Total fatalities, according to the Commonwealth War Graves Commission and 'Soldiers Died in the Great War' amount to 21.
74   TNA: PRO WO95/1206 War Diary 4th Battalion Guards Machine Gun Regiment.

62nd Division[75]

The 62nd Division had not been in action since 22 October. They had taken part in the attack on Havrincourt on 12 September, the town being part of the 'Hindenburg Line' defence system, during which action Sergeant Lawrence Calvert (2/5th KOYLI) won a Victoria Cross for single-handedly capturing two machine gun posts and killing their crews. Casualties had been heavy: 8 Officers and 199 Other Ranks killed, 34 Officers and 1,068 Other Ranks wounded, 228 Other Ranks missing. On 19 and 20 October they attacked the village of Solesmes, crossing the River Selle. Acting-Sergeant John Bruyton Daykins (2/4th York & Lancs) won his VC here – another two machine gun posts put out of action. Casualties here amounted to 57 Other Ranks killed, 10 Officers and 370 Other Ranks wounded.[76]

The much depleted Division was brought back up to strength by a large number of drafts during October: the 5th Duke of Wellington's [5/ Duke of Wellington's] received 11 Officers and 248 Other Ranks, the 2/4th Duke of Wellington's 16 and 326 respectively, the 2/4th Hampshires 9 and 184. (A total of 794 for 186 Brigade.) 187 Infantry Brigade received a total of 743, distributed as follows: 5th KOYLI [5/KOYLI] 12 Officers and 336 Other Ranks; 2/4th KOYLI 10 and 135; 2/4th York & Lancs 3 and 247. 185 Brigade received a total of 883 men. Including Royal Engineers, Machine Gun Corps and other units, the total reinforcements for the Division amounted to 103 Officers and 2,631 Other Ranks. To absorb these numbers in such a short space of time and yet remain a cohesive fighting force was a remarkable achievement.[77]

For the assault, the Division lined up with 187 Brigade (Brigadier-General A.J. Reddie) on the left, 186 Brigade (Brigadier-General J.L.G. Burnett) on the right and 185 Brigade (Brigadier-General Viscount Hampden) in reserve. It was decided that each front line brigade would attack on a one battalion frontage. The front battalion would take the Blue Line and the second and third battalions would leapfrog through onto the Green and Red Lines respectively. "All battalions of the 186th and 187th Infantry Brigades reached their assembly positions without incident, a double Brigade Headquarters being established at RUESNES.[78] Patrols had been sent out at dusk on 3 November in order to determine if the enemy had withdrawn as they had on the Guards Division front to the north. It proved not to be the case: "patrols [...] found touch immediately. On the front of this Division La Folie Farm and the Copse in R.16.b were reported held. [...] The 62nd Divn was to advance as previously arranged at 0530 hours so as to be in touch with the Guards Divn on the Blue Line. No alteration was made in the barrage of the 62nd Divn except that the heavy artillery and the 4.5 Hows. were ordered to keep well within the Divisional Boundary".[79]

187 Brigade had 2/5th KOYLI in the front line. Their jumping off positions were in the orchard in square R.9. B and D Companies were in front with A and C Companies on the line

---

75   See Map 5
76   L.Magnus, *The West Riding Territorials in the Great War* (London: Kegan Paul, Trench, Trubner & Co., 1920) pp. 213-218.
77   There is no reason to assume that this was a one-off. Reinforcements for the division for November 1918 numbered 62 Officers and 1,344 Other Ranks. Nor should one assume that this was peculiar to 62nd Division.
78   TNA: PRO WO95/3071 War Diary 62nd Division HQ General Staff.
79   Ibid.

of the railway running along the south-western edge of the trees. "Directly after Zero hr a heavy mist fell and this coupled with smoke which crept across from the front of the New Zealand Division was a source of great inconvenience and direction was difficult to maintain".[80]

Their first problem was the German garrison in La Folie Farm (R.10.b.7.5). They put up some "serious resistance",[81] but the farm was in British hands by 0600, resulting from "tact on the part of the Officers & N.C.O.'s in handling their men and the excellent dash of [the] men themselves".[82] A prisoner from the *1st Bn, 23rd R.I.R., 12th Reserve Dn* captured at the farm revealed that his Division, coming down from Belgium, had relieved the *21st Reserve Dn* at the farm during the night of 3–4 November.[83] It is interesting to note that these troops had no knowledge of the retirement of their compatriots to the north and that "their orders were to fight where they stood".[84]

The next obstacle was the Rhonelle River: the first two companies waded across, but those in the second wave had time to use improvised bridges of planks and tree trunks. In order to help those units moving up later, these crossings were marked by means of tape by Regimental Scouts.[85] The Germans put up stiff resistance in the Vieux Moulin (an old mill) on the river at R.11.c.2.4 and particularly in the northern part of the village of Orsinval, but with some help from trench Mortar fire, the positions were overcome and the village was taken by 0700.

By 0745 hours, the 62nd Division headquarters had still not received confirmation of this, "owing to communications being out",[86] but the Guards Division had reported 187 Brigade troops crossing the Blue Line at 0600 hours.[87] During these operations the 2/5th KOYLI claimed to have taken over 200 prisoners.[88] The KOYLIs were to spend the night reasonably comfortably in billets in Orsinval. The attack had cost them only four fatal casualties.

They were leapfrogged on the Blue Line by their sister battalion, the 2/4th KOYLI. They had formed up on a 1,500 yard frontage, but this was to narrow to half that distance on their objective. They advanced on a three company front, with B Company (Captain Clarke) on the left, C Company (Captain A. Fox) in the centre and D Company (Captain C. Fox) on the right. A Company (Captain Rooke) was in support. Each company placed two platoons in the front line and two in the second. As the front narrowed, B Company was "squeezed out"[89] and continued the advance in support of C Company. They moved off in the rear of 2/5th KOYLI at Zero plus 25 minutes in artillery formation and arrived on time at the Blue Line. They staggered their move off from this line from right to left, "owing to the barrage being curved",[90] companies moving at Zero plus 144, 156 and 135 minutes. The diarist also states, however,

80   TNA: PRO WO95/3091 War Diary 2/5th Battalion King's Own Yorkshire Light Infantry.
81   Ibid.
82   Ibid.
83   TNA: PRO WO95/3071 War Diary 62nd Division HQ General Staff.
84   Ibid.
85   TNA: PRO WO95/3091 War Diary 2/5th Battalion King's Own Yorkshire Light Infantry.
86   TNA: PRO WO95/3071 War Diary 62nd Division HQ General Staff.
87   Ibid.
88   TNA: PRO WO95/3091 War Diary 2/5th Battalion King's Own Yorkshire Light Infantry.
89   Ibid.
90   Ibid.

that "considerable opposition was encountered in Orsinval village, the mopping up having been neglected and 'B' Coy sustained rather heavy casualties"[91] as they cleared the area.

Enemy shelling at this stage was "negligible",[92] but resistance stiffened as the battalion tried to advance further. This was chiefly in the form of machine gun fire from the copse in the centre of square M.9. Lewis Gun fire was returned and the position was taken along with 20 prisoners. The two leading companies then pressed on to the Green Line. At this point they had reached the western outskirts of the village of Frasnoy and were greeted by a "considerable amount of machine gun fire".[93] This was "quickly silenced"[94] and troops were able to get into the outskirts and mop up the first few houses. These dispositions were quite quickly judged to be somewhat restrictive and it was decided to "withdr[a]w to a line slightly in the rear of the Green Line, owing to there being a better field of fire".[95] The diarist logs one fatal officer casualty: Second-Lieutenant Campbell,[96] along with 71 Other Ranks. The Other Ranks figure must include wounded and missing, as the battalion suffered 16 fatalities that day.

The baton now passed to the 2/4th York & Lancs. They had moved off from their shelters at 0620 under command of Major J.E.D. Stickney MC. They moved on from La Folie Farm, moving directly eastwards, at 0800, C and B Companies in front, A and D in support, Lewis Guns carried on pack mules. "No information was known of the results of the attack of the two Bns in front".[97] As they crossed the Blue Dotted Line, B Company experienced some machine gun fire from their right flank where 186 Brigade "had not succeeded in keeping sufficiently far forward",[98] and C Company on the left came under artillery fire at around M.8.a.4.4. They pressed on and the leading companies reached the Green Line and immediately attacked the village of Frasnoy. Enfilade fire from the right continued to be a problem, but the attack was pressed home and "street fighting ensued",[99] but resistance was overcome, "killing or making prisoners of the enemy and capturing several guns, including an 8" howitzer".[100] The capture of the village was confirmed to Divisional Headquarters at 1145 by an aerial reconnaissance report timed at 1055. C and B companies reached their objectives beyond the village along the line of the foot of the escarpment running northwest-southeast through squares M.10.b and M.11.c. A Company leapfrogged through C Company and pushed on the short distance to the main road in M.11.c. They got no further: their "flank [was] so exposed as to make further advance impossible".[101] A final outpost line was established from M.11.b.3.0 to M.11.b.3.7 and from M.6.c.2.0 to M.12.a.2.6., the latter point being just over the Red Line objective (see Map 5).

---

91   Ibid.
92   Ibid.
93   Ibid.
94   Ibid.
95   Ibid.
96   This must be Second-Lieutenant Willie Campbell, aged 21, from Halifax, Yorkshire. He must have been attached to the 2/4th KOYLI as the CWGC have him in the 2/4th York & Lancs Regiment. He is buried under the York & Lancs regimental badge in Ruesnes Communal Cemetery, grave I.B.8.
97   TNA: PRO WO95/3090 War Diary 2/4th Battalion York & Lancaster Regiment.
98   Ibid.
99   Ibid.
100 Ibid.
101 Ibid.

Meanwhile, D Company, under Second-Lieutenant Perkins, pushed out patrols towards the railway only to come up against artillery fire from the embankment. Two mounted German officers were spotted at this point and fired upon: the diarist claims that one of them was hit. Lewis Gun and rifle fire was directed "with good effect"[102] at the artillery positions. The Germans were in the process of withdrawing the guns and such was their haste, that with both gunners and horses becoming casualties, they abandoned several guns. D Company was unable to follow up owing to heavy machine gun fire from their right flank and ended the day just short of the Red Line in M.11.d. Fatal casualties that day for the battalion numbered 13. Brigade casualties were estimated at 7 Officers and 295 Other Ranks.[103]

On 186 Brigade front, comprising the southern sector of 62nd divisional frontage, the first objective, the Blue Line, ran along the Orsinval to Le Quesnoy road and its capture was entrusted to the 2/4th Battalion Hampshire Regiment. Again, a one battalion frontage was preferred, with the 2/4th Duke of Wellington's taking the Green Line and the 5/Duke of Wellington's the Red. The early stages of the attack were also to be covered by an overhead machine gun barrage. Two sections of D Company, 62nd Battalion MGC were to advance and be ready to give covering fire from the high ground in squares M.15.d and M.17.a. to the later stages of the assault as the Red Line was approached. Support would also be available at this stage from the 186th Trench Mortar Brigade who were to take two mortars and 100 rounds forward on pack animals and were to be used "as the occasion demanded".[104]

The 2/4th Hampshire were in their jumping off positions along the railway line in square R.16 by 2330 hours on 3 November.[105] They lined up, ready for the off: B and A Companies in the front line, left and right respectively, D and C likewise in support. The front companies' objective was the ravine running from the Vieux Moulin down into square R.17.d. The support companies were to pass through and secure the Blue Line on the high ground along the Orsinval to Le Quesnoy road. As Zero Hour struck, the Germans put down an artillery barrage on the railway line. "Fairly heavy casualties"[106] were inflicted before the men had even moved.

A Company met with considerable opposition from machine gun fire as they set off for the ravine, and their Company Commander, Captain W. Brierley, was wounded. They were nevertheless able to take their objective "with fine dash"[107] and captured three machine guns and 55 prisoners in the process. B Company also met with immediate opposition from an enemy strongpoint in the copse in square R.16.b. "After a sharp fight, the Enemy Machine Guns were silenced, the crews either killed or captured, and the advance continued".[108] They had found the ravine strongly held, but "the resolute bearing of the Company beat down the opposition",[109] taking one Officer and 80 Other Ranks prisoner.

D and C Companies leapfrogged through as the barrage lifted at around Zero plus 30 minutes and continued the advance up the steep slope. "The enemy held a very strong position with many

102 Ibid.
103 TNA: PRO WO95/3089 War Diary 187 Brigade HQ.
104 TNA: PRO WO95/3080 War Diary 186 Brigade HQ.
105 This was according to the War Diary of 186 Brigade. The Battalion War Diary puts it at 0230 on the 4th.
106 TNA: PRO WO95/3080 War Diary 186 Brigade HQ.
107 TNA: PRO WO95/3087 War Diary 2/4th Battalion Hampshire Regiment.
108 Ibid.
109 Ibid.

machine guns, but the men were keen for the fight and the platoons were handled so skilfully that the position was carried. Sergt. Hamilton greatly distinguished himself at this stage. At various positions on this company front, the enemy fought well, but the opposition was soon overcome".[110] The machine gun posts had been subdued largely by Lewis Gun fire. Connection was established with the New Zealand troops on their right and also with those of 187 Infantry Brigade on the left, the Battalion was reorganised and the position consolidated. Their day's work was done, but fatal casualties had numbered 15. The War Diary details casualties for the month of November as 19 Other Ranks killed, 2 Officers and 70 Other Ranks wounded, 2 Other Ranks missing.[111]

The 2/4th Duke of Wellington's moved forward from their assembly positions in a sunken road, but as they approached the railway they were forced to deploy into artillery formation as the German guns were still putting down a barrage on this line. They reached their jumping off positions behind the 2/4th Hampshire well before the allotted time. They passed through these positions at exactly 0751 hours, advancing on a two-company front. The right company came under harassing fire almost immediately from enemy machine guns, but "gradually worked forward",[112] capturing the guns and killing the crews. The left company came up against the strongly-held eastern bank of the Rhonelle River: by now 'standard' tactics were employed. The enemy positions were engaged by Lewis Gun fire as platoons waded through the 30 inch deep water. Two platoons outflanked the position and a third mopped up.

The Belle Maison Farm on the slopes of the far bank was the next stumbling block. The attackers came under direct fire from machine guns and trench mortars, but the centre company was able to move forward using the farm walls as cover and forced their way into the farmhouse where they captured four machine guns and killed a number of Germans.

Following the barrage closely they then took the sunken road in M.14.a & b and one platoon, working its way up the road into M.8.d, captured two field guns.

At this point, the rear companies passed through their comrades' positions and set out for the Green Line. They advanced with little opposition for some distance. The right company was held up around M.15.c (at the road junction) for a while, but were able to overcome the enemy resistance, capturing 3 Officers, 73 Other Ranks and 10 machine guns, and reached the Green Line at 1015 hours. The left support company arrived on the Green Line at much the same time, only encountering enemy fire once they had reached it. Battalion casualties for the month were recorded as 2 Officers and 17 Other Ranks killed, 3 Officers and 94 Other Ranks wounded, with 21 Other Ranks missing.[113] On 4 November they had suffered 22 fatalities, none of them an Officer.

It was down to the 5th Duke of Wellington's to complete the day's work: they had left their assembly positions at 0630 hours. On reaching the railway line they too, rather annoyingly, were confronted by the continuing German barrage, though they were able to push through with "comparatively few casualties".[114] The battalion paused to reorganise in the sunken road in R.17.a

110 Ibid.
111 Ibid.
112 TNA: PRO WO95/3086 War Diary 2/4th Battalion Duke of Wellington's Regiment.
113 Ibid.
114 TNA: PRO WO95/3086 War Diary 5th Battalion Duke of Wellington's Regiment.

& c and then moved eastwards in "artillery formation of platoons",[115] D and B Companies (left and right respectively) in the lead positions. They were forced to deploy into a more extended formation as they came under machine gun fire on crossing the grid line between squares M.14 & 15. The German positions were in the orchards along the Green Line and were still holding up the 2/4th Duke of Wellington's just short of their objective.

The leading companies of 5th Duke of Wellington's decided to leapfrog through their sister battalion and take the fight to the Germans. D Company were able to deal with the machine guns in the orchard to their front, but were held up briefly by others in R.16 a & b. These were "successfully dealt with by Lewis Gunners and two machine guns fell into our hands".[116] They were then able to establish a line on the high ground in M.17.a. "This company captured 90 prisoners, eight 4.2" Howitzers, three machine guns and a considerable amount of shells and other stores".[117]

B Company, on the right, found two companies of 2/4th Duke of Wellington's held up at around 0930 by machine guns firing from an orchard in M.15.c. The company Commander decided to take the matter into his own hands and press on: one platoon advanced on the German position frontally while another worked around the left flank. This latter manoeuvre precipitated a German withdrawal, but not before 20 prisoners had fallen into British hands. B Company were able to continue their advance at 1130, this time meeting "very little further resistance",[118] and were able to establish a liaison post with the New Zealand Division at the Pont de l'Alouette. (M.23.a.5.6).

A Company were advancing in support of D Company on the left of the battalion frontage and eventually passed through the latter's positions in M.17.a, but then lost direction, veering drastically to the right. Attempts to readjust were thwarted by machine gun fire from a house at the railway bridge at M.17.b.6.0 and from the adjacent railway cutting,[119] and with their Company Commander becoming a casualty, the manoeuvre was not accomplished. Two attempts to capture the house and the bridge were unsuccessful.

C Company, advancing behind B Company, leapfrogged through them in M.16.d, but were held up by a machine gun in Gommegnies Church and by those in the house near the railway bridge. A further troublesome strongpoint was spotted in a house at M.18.c.7.0. An attempt was made to take this house by one platoon, but the building "proved to be held in strength and had machine guns on either flank as well as in the upper rooms and the platoon, after losing its commander and several men, had to fall back. The O.C. Company then decided to take up a line west of the Sunken Road running from Les Tous Verts [M.18.c.6.0] to Petit Marais [M.11.c.8.2]. A further attempt to take this house with three platoons of the NZ Division failed",[120] although the enemy were observed at one point to be waving a white flag from the skylight of the house.[121]

At dusk, the battalion line was reorganised, with D Company on the left, C Comapny on the right, with A Company holding a line of strongpoints linking the two (see map). B Company

115 Ibid.
116 Ibid.
117 Ibid.
118 Ibid.
119 TNA: PRO WO95/3071 War Diary 62nd Division HQ General Staff.
120 Ibid.
121 TNA: PRO WO95/3086 War Diary 5th Battalion Duke of Wellington's Regiment.

were in reserve in M.17.c. The diarist of the 5th Duke of Wellington's summarises the day and its denouement:

> The day's fighting had been hard, after a very long march up to the point where resistance was met. Direction was very difficult to keep owing to the numerous hedges which were very strong, and enclosed country, and in many cases platoons had to work around. Immediately after dusk the enemy came nearer and commenced digging in opposite our whole front, but on the New Zealand Division attacking Le Carnoy at 2130 hrs opposition ceased and no further machine gun fire was heard after 2300 hours. The casualties of the battalion during the day amounted to 6 Officers and 80 Other Ranks. 13 guns were captured, 220 prisoners were captured and 15 machine guns, besides large quantities of munitions, etc.[122]

The original plan had envisaged 185 Brigade advancing eastwards from the Red Line that day, and they had followed the advance with this task in mind: at 2045 hours orders were issued delaying this move until 0600 hours on the following morning.[123] 5 November was a "miserable, wet day",[124] and the 185 Brigade "attacked, [...] and, encountering no opposition, made a rapid advance".[125] The Red Line may not have been reached along the VI Corps front on 4 November, but in the end it did not matter: the damage had been done. The advance was turning into a pursuit.

Conclusion

Despite not quite reaching the day's final objectives before darkness forced a halt to the advance, VI Corps had been able to use well-practised small-unit tactics, including the effective use of Lewis Guns, trench mortars, rifle grenades and advanced RFA guns to deal with both stubborn resistance and difficult topographical and meteorological conditions. Once more, the assertions that German defence relied on natural features such as watercourses, woods and farms and that they could not defend in depth were proved right.

122 Ibid.
123 TNA: PRO WO95/3080 War Diary 186 Brigade HQ.
124 TNA: PRO WO95/3086 War Diary 5th Battalion Duke of Wellington's Regiment.
125 Ibid.

4

IV Corps

Introduction

IV Corps orders reflect the complexity of the task facing it. On the left flank, the encirclement of Le Quesnoy by the New Zealand Division and the subsequent advance into the Forêt
de Mormal required a complicated artillery fire plan and a five-phase infantry assault. On the
right, an attack initially supported by tanks would capture two villages surrounded by the ubiquitous orchards and hedges and then continue into the forest. The unreliability of the tanks
was factored into divisional planning: 37th Division presumed that armoured support might
not materialise and were proved right. They were able to fall back on standard infantry/artillery
tactics and once more German resistance cracked and then disintegrated in the face of superior
numbers, tactics and weaponry, but not before some fierce hand-to-hand fighting had taken
place.

* * *

IV Corps (Lieutenant-General Sir Montague Harper), which had had a difficult autumn,
having suffered over 13,000 casualties since the middle of September, was responsible for just
over four miles of front, stretching from the railway line north of the town of Le Quesnoy to
the relatively open country south of the villages of Ghissignies and Louvignies. Ghissignies was
in British hands, Louvignies was not. The left, or northern, Corps front was the responsibility
of the New Zealand Division (Major-General Sir A.H. Russell).[1] Twelve field and five heavy
brigades of artillery under Brigadier-General J.G. Geddes were in support. To the south was
the 37th Division.

---

1   These were the only non-British troops engaged on 4 November 1918, except for a small number of
     Australians from the 1st Australian Tunnelling Company attached to 1st Division.

New Zealand Division[2]

The jumping off line for the New Zealand Division (Major-General Sir A.H. Russell) units ran north-south, less than a mile to the west of the fortified town of Le Quesnoy. According to the Official History, "The town was enclosed by a seven-sided bastion enceinte, with a covered way tenaille (a continuous rampart of salients and re-entrants) outside it, the space between the two lines forming a dry ditch with mounds of earth, with trees growing on them, scattered over it".[3] These fortifications had long been obsolete in the face of modern heavy artillery and high explosive, but it was decided that the town would not be assaulted frontally,[4] for three reasons: such an assault would be costly in terms of military casualties; the required bombardment would effectively destroy a picturesque medieval town's architecture and, perhaps most importantly, the town was full of French civilians. It made military and moral sense to precipitate the German garrison's surrender by encirclement. Once

Major-General Sir A.H. Russell,
Commander New Zealand Division.
(Australian War Memorial)

this phase of the operation was completed, the advance eastwards into the Forêt de Mormal would continue.

The initial stages of the encirclement were entrusted to 3 New Zealand Rifle Brigade (Brigadier-General H.E. Hart), who had in the front line, north to south, its 2nd, 4th and 1st Battalions. This brigade was 7 officers and 969 other ranks under strength: all companies had been organised into three platoons, each averaging 28 men each.[5] 1 New Zealand Infantry Brigade (Brigadier-General C.W. Melvill) would complete the encirclement from the north and then assume total responsibility for the advance from the Green Line to the Red Line objectives.[6]

---

2   See Maps 6 and 7.

3   J.E. Edmonds & R. Maxwell-Hyslop, *Military Operations France and Belgium 1918, Vol. V* (London: HMSO, 1947) p. 482. In simpler terms, a typical Vauban-inspired star-shaped fortress with ramparts (see photograph overleaf).

4   This clear instruction appears in IV Corps orders issued 1 November, and is repeated in orders distributed down to battalion level.

5   TNA: PRO WO95/719 War Diary IV Corps HQ.

6   See Map 6.

Le Quesnoy from the air, 30 October 1918. (TNA)

New Zealand Division Order No. 214, issued on 2 November, divided the assault into five phases: the first was the gaining of the Blue Line. This entailed the capture of the railway line to the west of Le Quesnoy, the railway triangle to the north and the large orchards to the south. The elaborate artillery barrage plan meant that the infantry were allowed two hours to complete this task.[7] Phase two required the 3rd Battalion New Zealand Rifle Brigade [3/N.Z. Rifle Battalion] to leapfrog its sister battalion in the south and take the Blue Dotted Line. Twenty minutes or so later the 1st Auckland Battalion [1/Aukland] (1 New Zealand Infantry Brigade) would skirt the northern suburbs of the town, trespassing briefly into 62nd Division territory, and pass through the 2nd Rifles and onto the Blue Dotted Line, capturing the suburb of Ramponneau in the process.

The third phase saw the 3rd Rifles and the Auckland Battalion meeting at the crossroads at M26. d. 1.9. The units of 1 New Zealand Infantry Brigade would then extend their line southwards to the Divisional Boundary, thus occupying the whole of the Green Line.

Phase four: "The 1st New Zealand Infantry Brigade Group will, at ZERO plus 290 minutes, continue the advance from the GREEN LINE to the RED LINE, under a barrage of all

7   See Artillery Barrage Sketch Map 2.

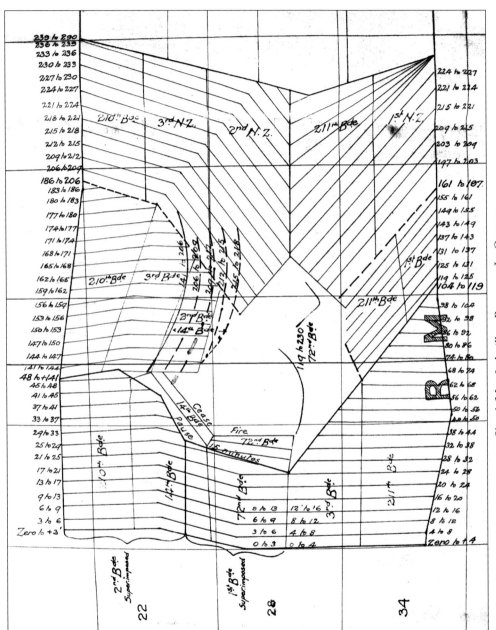

Sketch Map 2 Artillery Barrage at Le Quesnoy.

available artillery. [...] This barrage will die out on reaching the limit of the range of the guns and the advance will be continued without a barrage, supported by Forward Sections or batteries".[8]

The first sentence of the orders for phase five began: "Should the enemy weaken, ..."[9] Were this the case, units were to be pushed forward to the Red Dotted Line. The orders continued: "Should opposition be met with, a definite line will be established [...] and Artillery brought forward preparatory to an attack by the 2nd New Zealand Infantry Brigade Group during the afternoon".[10] As implied above, the final stages of the advance were to take the infantry beyond the range of their 18 pounder gun support. Order No. 108, issued on 2 November by the New Zealand CRA, stated:

> Immediately on the Blue Line being captured, the following Brigades will be prepared to advance by Batteries to the areas indicated, in order to carry the barrage on from the GREEN to the RED LINE. Continuity of fire on the Brigade task will be maintained, the remaining batteries being distributed over the Brigade front and increasing the rate of fire to compensate for the battery on the move; and each battery as it arrives resuming its task from its new position:

211th Brigade RFA	R.35. c
72nd (Army) Bde RFA	R28. d & 34 b (Eastern Edge)
210th Bde RFA	R22 b & d (Eastern Edge)
14th (Army) Bde RFA	R16 d (Eastern Edge)[11]

As will be seen from Map 7, this brings most of these batteries into positions just shy of the original outpost line, with 211th Brigade east of the railway, a passage through the embankment having been dug by the Royal Engineers.

The New Zealand Machine Gun Battalion (specifically the Auckland and Otago Machine Gun Companies) were detailed to the "special tasks of enfilading the streets and RAMPARTS of LE QUESNOY"[12] and "Q" Special Company Royal Engineers were to project 300 drums of burning oil[13] onto the ramparts at Zero. The western ramparts were also to be subjected to a dense smoke barrage. On both the northern and western ramparts the Germans had installed 77mm guns (Minenwerfer) and a large number of machine guns. The attack across the railway line was also "covered by the two medium trench mortar batteries and by two batteries of light trench mortars, whose barrages would conform with and advance 300 and 100 yards respectively in front of the field artillery barrage".[14] All of the above might serve to convince the German garrison that the town itself was under threat, whereas the reality was that the main thrusts would be to the north and south of the town.

8   TNA: PRO WO95/3661 War Diary New Zealand Division HQ General Staff.
9   Ibid.
10   Ibid.
11   TNA: PRO WO95/3665 War Diary New Zealand Division CRA.
12   TNA: PRO WO95/3661 War Diary New Zealand Division HQ General Staff.
13   Ibid.
14   H. Stewart, *The New Zealand Division 1916-1919* (Uckfield: Naval & Military Press, n.d.), p. 572.

New Zealand Support Line near Le Quesnoy. (National Library of New Zealand)

The 2nd Battalion New Zealand Rifle Brigade [2/N.Z. Rifle battalion] took over the left brigade frontage (about 1000 yards) from the 4th Battalion, having marched out from their billets in Beaudignies at 1700 on 3 November. The relief was complete by 1830, although on the way one German shell landing right in the sunken road in R. 22. b. caused 11 casualties in one platoon of C Company. By midnight, Battalion Headquarters was established in the sunken road at R16. d. 6.0. Almost immediately (at 0001 hrs) a patrol of four men under Rifleman Blaskett was sent out to "ascertain if the enemy was still in his forward positions".[15] A second patrol of one NCO (Lance Corporal Ollerenshaw) and three men went out at 0320 with an identical mission. Both patrols were able to report that the "enemy [was] still in his positions".[16] During the night there was some heavy shelling from enemy artillery, but it fell harmlessly behind the assembly positions.

At Zero hour, 0530, "all guns opened out together, creating an awful din"[17] and the men set off towards the railway triangle and their objective beyond it, C Company on the left, A Company in the centre, D Company on the right, with B Company in reserve. Almost immediately, A Company "met with considerable resistance on the high ground in R23. a.",[18] reporting heavy casualties, having been held up by fire from a machine gun just north of the railway junction at R17. c. 3.3. This machine gun was directly opposite a gap between A and C Companies

15   TNA: PRO WO95/3709 War Diary 2nd Battalion New Zealand Rifle Brigade.
16   Ibid.
17   Ibid.
18   Ibid.

and the confusion it caused resulted in some men of A Company advancing too quickly, passing through their own barrage. The machine gun was finally stormed by a party from A Company, but the company then encountered serious opposition in the railway triangle. The right platoon was particularly badly hit and it was up to Sergeant J.Grubb in the platoon on its left to cover the frontage with his own men. He cleared two machine gun posts and then overcame a nest of three more with the help of a light trench mortar.[19] Seeing the disarray in front of him, Lieutenant L.H. Denniston, commanding B Company, brought his men forward to strengthen the line and "their timely assistance facilitated the capture of the objective".[20]

C Company, on the left, had it slightly easier: they were held up briefly by close-range machine gun fire, but Rifleman C. Birch, "a member of a light trench mortar team attached to the battalion, promptly volunteered to go forward and locate the machine gun. This he did with great coolness, and his comrades destroyed it with their mortar bombs. Birch thereupon, completing his recon-naissance of the locality, captured a German officer and 27 men".[21] C Company was thus able to reach the Blue Line at 0620 without any further serious resistance.[22]

D Company fought its way across the southern part of the railway triangle, meeting "considerable resistance",[23] but reached their objectives. They then sent patrols forward to the sunken road in R23. d. Met here by fire from another German machine gun, Sergeant W.P. McGillen "got his Lewis Gun into action, silenced the enemy gun and compelled the crew to retire to a house in rear of the German position. Quickly following up, McGillen personally rushed the house, killing 5 of the enemy with a bomb and capturing 14 more".[24]

Not content with occupying their assigned objec-tive, B Company sent forward a patrol of one NCO and three men toward the ramparts. They managed to get across the moat (at approximately R23. d. 8.6) and capture a machine gun, throwing it into the moat. They were driven back out by superior forces, however. No.7 Platoon of B Company made another attempt to get across the moat with support from a platoon of D Company. Some of the men made it into the moat (dry

Rifleman C. Birch, attached 2nd Battalion New Zealand Rifle Brigade, won his DCM on 4 November 1918. (National Library of New Zealand)

at this point), but the supporting platoon was driven back and they were compelled to stay where

---

19   Stewart, *The New Zealand Division*, p. 575.
20   Ibid. p. 575.
21   Ibid. pp. 575-576.
22   TNA: PRO WO95/3709 War Diary 2nd Battalion New Zealand Rifle Brigade.
23   Ibid.
24   Stewart, *The New Zealand Division*, p. 576.

The Walls of Le Quesnoy. (National Library of New Zealand)

they were, able "neither to get forward or to get out"[25] until late that afternoon. The Blue Line was therefore gained along the whole of the battalion front, even if a machine gun nest in the triangle at Factory Corner was not overcome for a further three hours. One casualty sustained at this point was particularly unfortunate. "Our barrage was reported by all Coys to be very good. There were very few shorts until the objective was taken. After that, shells fell short in considerable numbers, particularly on the eastern end of the railway triangle. 2nd Lt. Bate DCM was killed at the assembly point by a short and several men were wounded".[26]

The 4th Battalion New Zealand Rifle Brigade [4/N.Z. Rifle Battalion] went into the line with a strength of 28 officers and 726 other ranks. Battalion Headquarters was in cellars in Chapel Farm, 1,200 yards west of Le Quesnoy on the Ruesnes road. A Company, on the right, was in position along the hedge to the east of the Ferme de Béart. B Company, in the centre, was on the higher ground, and C Company, on the left, was astride the Le Quesnoy – Ruesnes road, about 300 yards east of Battalion Headquarters. D Company was in reserve. The 18 pounder barrage opened "good and even"[27] at 0530, while Stokes and Trench mortars drenched the railway line. This was the battalion's only real objective of the day and it was taken exactly to schedule: Order No. 214 (2 November) then required "patrols [to] be pushed forward to ascertain if the town is still occupied".[28] All three forward companies did as they were asked: on

25   TNA: PRO WO95/3709 War Diary 2nd Battalion New Zealand Rifle Brigade.
26   Ibid. Second-Lieutenant George Ronald Bate is buried in Le Quesnoy Communal Cemetery Extension, Grave I.A.22.
27   TNA: PRO WO95/3711 War Diary 4th Battalion New Zealand Rifle Brigade.
28   TNA: PRO WO95/3661 War Diary New Zealand Division HQ General Staff.

the left, C Company under Lieutenant C.N. Rathbone pushed forward to the southern section of the sunken road reached by 2nd Rifles further to the north. Here they were pinned down by very accurate machine gun and mortar fire from the ramparts. Their situation is summed up rather poetically by the Official Historian:

> Even apart from this fire the way here was barred by a 40-feet broad expanse of deep water which reflected in an unbroken mirror the rich red of the brick rampart and the russets, browns and yellows of the trees. Here the company could make no progress, and here it remained practically isolated for the rest of the day.[29]

A and B Companies, under Lieutenants H.S. Kenrick and V.F. Maxwell respectively, made similar aggressive forays into the maze of moat, re-entrant, bastion, tree-topped islet and grassy bank. The nature of the ground allowed them freer movement than was possible further north. "The space between the outer and inner ramparts was dotted with a series of lofty islets crowned with trees and thick undergrowth. The sides of these islands were steep, faced with brick or stone and all of them about 20 to 30 feet in height. Boche snipers and machine gunners were very persistent in firing from these excellent positions".[30]

One platoon under Second-Lieutenant Evans "made a very daring advance"[31] and after bombarding one of the 'islands' with rifle grenades, used a scaling ladder to clamber onto and occupy it. Evans went forward with four men and a Lewis Gun and made it onto one of the inner bastions. There, at around 0900, they were seen by an enemy machine gun crew on top of the ramparts and pinned down in a hole by very accurate fire. "After a moment, on the machine gun's ceasing fire, Evans tried to scale the steep side of the inner bastion. He was immediately shot through the brain and rolled back dead into the hole".[32] A similar fate was met by his batman who tried to bring the Lewis Gun into action. The three remaining members of the patrol remained where they were, unable to escape, for six hours. The 4th Rifles paused for breath.

The 1st Battalion New Zealand Rifle Brigade [1/N.Z. Rifle Battalion] (Captain E.A. Harding MC)[33] occupied the right brigade frontage: they had a ration strength on 1 November of 26 officers and 544 other ranks. They attacked with three companies in the front line: their objective line (see Map 6) ran north-west to south-east. The right company (D Company) faced an advance of 1500 yards to their target, the Landrecies road running south through squares 31 b & d. The left company had around a third of that distance to make. On the left, B Company's objective was the northern edge of the orchard largely in square 35. A Company, in the centre, was to gain the line between the orchard and the Ghissignies road. All companies initially faced the well-defended railway line and embankment. They were in position by 0525 and the barrage opened 10 minutes later. Its first lift was at Zero plus three minutes and it crept forward at a rate of 100 yards every three minutes, the New Zealanders on its heels. "Several machine

29 Stewart, *The New Zealand Division*, p. 586.
30 TNA: PRO WO95/3711 War Diary 4th Battalion New Zealand Rifle Brigade.
31 Ibid.
32 Stewart, *The New Zealand Division 1916-1919*, p. 588. Second-Lieutenant Francis Meredith Evans (age 24) is buried in Romeries Communal Cemetery Extension, Grave X.A.6.
33 Lieutenant-Colonel R. C. Allen had been wounded on 3 November. Captain Harding had previously commanded 'B' Company.

guns on [this] line pinned the attackers for some minutes to the ground".[34] Infantry tactics learned at platoon level served them well: machine gunners were pinned down by Lewis Gun fire, suppressed by rifle grenades and then outflanked and / or rushed. Sergeant R. L. Ferguson, Corporal M.J. Mulvaney DCM, Rifleman E.W. Hallett and CSM M.E. Olsen are all named in the *Official History* as having captured machine gun posts, some of them single-handed.[35] Once across this obstacle, the companies were able to advance quickly to their respective objectives, B Company by 0640, A Company by 0645 and D Company by 0825. C Company, in reserve, had, by just after 0610, moved forward to positions just east of the railway. There, it was "given the most piquant adventure that befell the battalion during the day".[36]

A group of Germans counter-attacking the 37th Division troops to the south feared encirclement and decided to withdraw. They attempted to get back to Le Quesnoy by following the railway line, clearly unaware of how far the New Zealanders had already advanced. As these troops appeared through the lingering fog, C Company detached a section under Corporal C. Taylor to deal with them. The Germans were so surprised to see their way blocked that the five officers and 150 men "threw up the sponge"[37] and surrendered to Taylor and his men. 1st Rifles casualties for the day totalled 82.

With the Blue Line securely held, it was time for the next phase of the attack to begin. It was the job of 3/N.Z. Rifle Battalion to advance through the 1st Battalion positions in the south and gain the Blue Dotted and Green Lines.

The 3/N.Z. Rifle Battalion had started its move forward from its assembly positions at 0540 and, as it crested the ridge line just to the west of the original front line position, just as dawn was breaking, German artillery fire cost the battalion its only fatal casualties of the day: three other ranks from B Company and Second-Lieutenant P.M. Beattie of C Company.[38]

By 0615 the battalion had crossed the railway line and was advancing with A Company on the right, D Company on the left, with C and B Companies in support. By 0710 they were poised behind the Blue Line positions. At 0729 the advance commenced, sections going ahead under the barrage in artillery formation. The diarist noted that a heavy mist had come down by this time and visibility was down to 20 yards in places.[39] German resistance would appear to have been minimal, as the Blue Dotted Line was gained at 0800, that is, ahead of time. The Official History states that "no other noteworthy incident marked the 3rd Rifles' progress to the Blue Dotted Line".[40]

At 0729, just as the battalion attack went in, Major Cockroft and his Intelligence Officer Second-Lieutenant E.C. Drummond, were some distance back, awaiting word from Advanced Battalion Headquarters to follow on, when they noticed a large number of men approaching from the south. Their first thought was that they were troops from 37th Division who had lost direction, but the truth quickly dawned. They were Germans. Their presence threatened

---

34   Stewart, *The New Zealand Division*, p. 573.
35   Ibid. See p. 574.
36   Ibid. p. 574.
37   TNA: PRO WO95/3708 War Diary 1st Battalion New Zealand Rifle Brigade.
38   Second-Lieutenant Percival Moore Beattie is buried in Cross Roads Cemetery, Fontaine-au-Bois, Grave I.E.14.
39   TNA: PRO WO95/3710 War Diary 3rd Battalion New Zealand Rifle Brigade.
40   Stewart, *The New Zealand Division*, p. 577.

to separate the advancing companies from their supports, and just as they were preparing to set up their machine guns, Drummond charged forward and fired his revolver at them. The four officers and 70 men immediately surrendered to him.

The Blue Dotted Line positions to the north-east of Le Quesnoy were to be taken by the 1/Auckland of 1 New Zealand Infantry Brigade. They had moved from their assembly positions just north of Beaudignies at Zero plus 15 minutes. As they crossed the Ruesnes to Le Quesnoy road (running east to west through square R21 b) an enemy plane was noticed overhead. "Immediately after, his artillery opened up and heavily shelled the line of advance, but very few casualties were caused".[41]

The first companies (6th Hauraki and 15th North Auckland) reached the Le Quesnoy to Orsinval road (running north-south through squares 17b & 18d) at 0618, starting forward from there under cover of the artillery barrage on time at 0751. The battalion had been careful in its approach to leave at least 500 yards between it and the railway so as to avoid any enfilade fire. They were also shrouded by the mist and the smoke barrage on the ramparts. The suburb of Ramponneau was in their hands by 0836 for less than 50 casualties.[42] Their companies swung to the right, linking up with the 2nd Rifles on the right and reaching as far as the railway station on the left. The encirclement of Le Quesnoy was almost complete. The second phase of the attack had been successfully accomplished: the move onto the Green Line would now follow.

To the south of the town, it was down to the two forward companies (A & D) of the 3rd Rifles to move forward from their positions on the Blue Dotted Line onto the Green Line. The author of the New Zealand Official History sets

26/45 Corporal Frederick J. Alexander, 3 New Zealand Rifle Brigade, killed in action 4 November 1918. (Author)

Captain James McCarthy, 1st Aukland Battalion, 1 New Zealand Infantry Brigade, Romeries Communal Cemetery Extension. (Author)

41 TNA: PRO WO95/3688 War Diary 1st Auckland Battalion.
42 These included one officer killed: Captain James Charles McCarthy (age 35) is buried in Romeries Communal Cemetery Extension, Grave IV.B.16.

the scene in his customary style: "The sun was now well up in the east, the mist had dispersed and the day was bright and warm".[43] B Company passed through D Company on the left flank and took up precautionary positions, establishing posts along the southern edge of the lakes, the *Etang Neuf* and *Etang du Mayeur,* which flanked the main causeway leading south-east from the Porte de Fauroeulx. This was to cover the increasingly unlikely event of a German counter attack emanating from Le Quesnoy itself. No such attack materialised.

The advance of D and A Companies to the Green Line is described very briefly in the battalion war diary: "At 8:47 a.m. the advance was again continued to the Green Line and although opposition was met with from enemy posts and machine guns the advance was only temporarily checked and the Green Line was gained on schedule time".[44]

The Official History goes into more detail where the 'opposition met' is concerned: the New Zealanders were moving in more open country in the by now "clearer light"[45] and presented much better targets to the German machine gunners. These machine gun posts proved difficult to locate and threatened to hold up the attack. "Rfmn N. Coop, a No. 1 of a Lewis Gun team, worked forward into the open to draw the fire of these guns and thus induce them to betray their exact positions. His fearless behaviour had the desired effect, and the No. 2 was enabled to bring his gun forward and put the enemy guns out of action".[46]

It was A Company, on the right, under Captain F.E. Greenish, that faced the fiercest opposition. Moving forward from the vicinity of the Château de Montout (see map – M32 d), once they had crossed the Le Quesnoy to Jolimetz road they entered more open country "devoid of cover and swept by machine guns from a commanding ridge directly in front of the Chateau".[47] For once, the fabled determination of German machine gun teams was left wanting, it would seem: they either withdrew from the ridge or surrendered in the face of the determined, unfaltering and fearless[48] advance of Greenish's men. "The ridge was gained with surprising ease".[49]

The task of completing the total encircle-ment of Le Quesnoy fell to the 1st and 2nd Wellington Battalions [1/Wellington & 2/Wellington] of 1 New Zealand Infantry Brigade

Captain Arthur Blennerhassett, 1st Wellington Battalion, 1 New Zealand Infantry Brigade. Le Quesnoy Communal Cemetery. (Author)

---

43   Stewart, *The New Zealand Division*, p. 578.
44   TNA: PRO WO95/3710 War Diary 3rd Battalion New Zealand Rifle Brigade.
45   Stewart, *The New Zealand Division*, p. 579.
46   Ibid. p. 579.
47   Ibid. p. 579.
48   Ibid. p. 579.
49   Ibid. p. 579.

(Lieutenant-Colonel F.K. Turnbull & Major H.E. McKinnon respectively). Their initial engagements met with very limited opposition: the 1/Wellington had reached their assembly positions in the sunken road in squares R17 a & c by 0800. Here they came under fire from enemy artillery and their Adjutant, Lieutenant A.R. Blennerhassett, was killed[50] and Second-Lieutenant P.H.G. Bennett wounded.

They left their assembly positions at 0802 with their sister battalion, 2/Wellington, on their left, passing through the 1/Aukland men at 0856, West Coast Company on the right, Ruahine Company on the left. Apart from a "short fight"[51] on the Villereau road, where one machine gun post was rushed and captured single-handed by Sergeant Charteris, they met with little or no trouble and were on the Green Line by 0925.[52] The 2/Wellington arrived with them, having been held up by nothing more than the woods on the steep banks of the Rhonelle river.

The 1/Wellington then extended their lines to the south, the Taranaki Company (Captain E. White) on the right and the Hawkes Bay Company on the left pushing through, the former "taking over the frontage captured by the 3rd N.Z. (R) B".[53] Thus, 1 New Zealand Infantry Brigade was in position to begin the fourth phase of the attack. Le Quesnoy, now fully surrounded and bypassed, became, arguably, though still in German hands, a tactical nuisance but an operational irrelevance.

As the final manoeuvres of 'Phase 3' were being launched, the advancing troops witnessed an impressive moment in the scheduled artillery barrage's advance: the two leading edges of the enveloping wings of the creeping barrage met, precisely and on time at the crossroads to the east of the *Etang du Mayeur* (M26 d 1.9), coalesced and continued as one onto the Green Line.

The two Wellington Battalions resumed the advance towards the Red Line at 1020:[54] four British artillery brigades, firing from the Ferme de Béart Wood, would supply the creeping barrage, advancing at a rate of 100 yards every three minutes. This barrage would, as mentioned earlier, peter out as the troops moved beyond the guns' maximum range. The 1st New Zealand Artillery Brigade, under Lieutenant-Colonel Symon, was to advance around the northern outskirts of Le Quesnoy, but the intensity of the machine gun fire from the ramparts forced them abandon this route and go around the southern side of the town – quite a detour!

The 2nd NZ Artillery Brigade suffered similar harassment, but merely edged further to the north and were able to take up positions at St Sepulchre, east of Villereau (M21.d.9.9) by 1330. The 1st and 3rd Brigades arrived at positions in the vicinity some time later.

The 2/Wellington, on the left frontage of the advance, reported the Germans as "being more content to withdraw more quickly than our troops could advance".[55] The 1/Wellington on the right encountered similarly demoralised resistance: "The enemy was in considerable strength on our front and fought well at some places, but in many instances seemed only too pleased to surrender".[56]

50   Captain (?) Adjutant Arthur Reginald Blennerhassett, age 28, is buried in Le Quesnoy Communal Cemetery Extension, Grave I.B.22.
51   Stewart, *The New Zealand Division*, p. 580.
52   Sergeant R. Charteris was subsequently awarded the Military Medal.
53   TNA: PRO WO95/3689 War Diary 1st Wellington Battalion.
54   See Map 7.
55   TNA: PRO WO95/3690 War Diary 2nd Wellington Battalion.
56   TNA: PRO WO95/3689 War Diary 1st Wellington Battalion.

The 2/Wellington reached the Red Line more or less on schedule and began to reorganise their companies. On the way, a party of signallers under Lance-Corporal J.H. Griffiths, busy laying a telephone wire, happened upon three enemy 77mm guns still in action. Griffiths ordered his men to "drop their wire and charge the guns".[57] They captured the guns, along with two prisoners who had briefly attempted to keep the New Zealanders at bay with rifle fire. The other eight artillery men had fled at once. The signallers then resumed their wire-laying.

Patrols were sent forward from the Red Line, but were unable to get any further than 200 yards on the left owing to flanking machine gun fire. The right flank proved more fruitful, patrols reaching the western edge of the Forêt de Mormal. At 1800, orders were received to advance to the Red Dotted Line: under a light barrage at 2130, the West Coast & Ruahine Companies pushed forward, the Hawke Company in support. "The stunt was a complete success as the enemy had withdrawn at 1500 the same day".[58] A Forward Battalion Headquarters was established at M24.d.8.4 and it was whilst going forward to that location that the Battalion commander, Major McKinnon and his Adjutant, Lieutenant S. A. Murrell, were killed by an enemy shell.[59] Captain D. S. Columb, commanding Taranaki Company, was sent for to take over the battalion.

Final dispositions for the day show the companies in positions in the northern part of the Forêt de Mormal.[60] Casualties for the day numbered 8 officers and 58 other ranks.

The 1/Wellington were on the Red Line by 1156 and patrols took the road running along the eastern edge of the forest. At 1415 they pushed on through the forest and met only a cavalry patrol, this being fired upon, resulting in four dead horses and two human prisoners. "The inhabitants of the villages through which the battalion passed welcomed us with joy and pressed coffee and fruit and milk on our men".[61] The Red Dotted Line was reached at 2330: only one enemy post had been encountered and "dealt with".[62] By 0130 on 5 November they had edged forward as far as the Sarioton road.

Casualties for the day had been:

	Officers	Other Ranks
Killed	1	7
Wounded	2	20

They had captured: 45 field guns, 7 trench mortars, 60 machine guns, 100 rifles, 11 limbers, 2 wagons, 1 water cart, 2 small carts, 14 horses and 1,000 prisoners.

The 2/Wellingtons' haul was: 29 field guns, 4 8" Howitzers, 5 trench mortars, 33 machine guns and 400 prisoners.[63]

The advance, impressive as it was, could have been pushed even further: at 1530 the 2/Wellington reported the enemy retreating east of the Red Dotted Line and requested permission

---

57   TNA: PRO WO95/3690 War Diary 2nd Wellington Battalion.
58   Ibid.
59   Major Hugh Edgar McKinnon, age 30, and Captain (?) Sydney Allan Murrell, age 26, are buried in Le Quesnoy Communal Cemetery Extension next to each other in graves I.B.24 & 23 respectively.
60   See Map 7.
61   TNA: PRO WO95/3689 War Diary 1st Wellington Battalion.
62   Ibid.
63   Ibid.

to push on to the village of Le Sart. It took two hours for the message to reach Brigade HQ, however, and by the time the affirmative reply came back to the Wellingtons, the Germans had reoccupied the village. Back at Le Quesnoy, stalemate persisted, Stewart stating that "the persistent and obstinate efforts of the Rifle Brigade to clear Le Quesnoy had been for many hours frustrated by a tenacious defence and by the strength of the position".[64]

Each battalion of the New Zealand Rifle Brigade was vying for the honour of being the one to precipitate the surrender of the German garrison still ensconced behind the town ramparts. The 3/N.Z. Rifle Battalion had been able to withdraw their men from their forward positions on the Blue Dotted Line south of Le Quesnoy at around 1020 as the Wellington battalions of 1st NZ Infantry Brigade moved off from the Green Line. They were soon in positions facing the south-eastern sector of the town, the two lakes now directly in front of them. At 1100 they pushed patrols forward along the causeway between the two 'Etangs', but were immediately checked by heavy machine gun fire which caused several casualties and "as instructions had been issued to avoid casualties once the town was surrounded no offensive action was adopted".[65] Soon after, three captured Germans were sent in through the Porte de Fauroeulx to explain to their comrades that the town was surrounded, that the battle had passed well to the east of them and that surrender would now be the sensible option. No reply came back: indeed, for the next three hours the defenders sniped at the New Zealanders from the walls of the town. "At 3 p.m. two more German messengers were sent into the town with instructions to inform the Commander of the garrison that he could surrender his garrison by 5 p.m. if he wished and the garrison would be treated as ordinary prisoners. In the event of his not doing so by that hour, on his surrender later the whole garrison would be treated according as we see fit".[66] Half an hour later, the "emissaries returned".[67] The men were willing to throw in the towel. The officers were not and so the stalemate in the south-east persisted. It was around this time that an RE.8 (Aircraft No. 2869) from 59 Squadron RAF flew over Le Quesnoy, Lieutenants Dexter (pilot) and Rowley (observer) on board, at a height of only 200 feet, from where they dropped leaflets into the town. The leaflets read:

AN DEN KOMMANDANTEN DER GARNISON VON LE QUESNOY.
Die Stellung Le Quesnoy ist jetzt völlig eingeschlossen. Unsere Truppen sind weit östlich von der Stadt. Daher werden Sie aufgefordert, sich mit Ihrer Garnison zu ergeben. Die Garnison wird als ehrliche Kriegsgefangene behandelt werden.[68]

but produced no answer.

---

64 Stewart, *The New Zealand Division*, p. 584. For a detailed account of the fall of the town see pp. 584-593.
65 TNA: PRO WO95/3710 War Diary 3rd Battalion New Zealand Rifle Brigade.
66 Ibid. The finer points of this second option were not detailed in the diary.
67 Ibid.
68 TNA: PRO WO95/3710 War Diary 3rd Battalion New Zealand Rifle Brigade. This leaflet had presumably been made ready several days in advance. It reads: "To the commanders of the Le Quesnoy Garrison. The fortress of Le Quesnoy is now completely surrounded. Our troops are well to the east of the town. You are therefore invited to surrender yourselves and your garrison. The garrison will be treated as honourable prisoners of war." The 59 Squadron Record Book details the mission as follows: "1 bag and 1 roll of leaflets dropped in the square and 4 bags and 1 roll in other parts of Le Quesnoy, from 200'. Heavily machine gunned from the Town." TNA: PRO AIR 1/1783/204/150/20.

The Scaling of the Walls of Le Quesnoy by George Edmund Butler 1920.
(National Library of New Zealand)

The 2/N.Z. Rifle Battalion was still in positions facing the Porte de Valenciennes in the northern sector of the town. A party under Second-Lieutenant Kingdon had worked their way around to the bridge over the railway line in square R9 d and had found it still intact. They also sent an enemy prisoner across to negotiate a surrender, but they too received no reply. As if to emphasise their non-compliance, the Germans blew the span of the bridge nearest the town at 1345. New Zealand engineers spanned the gap with timber and "a dash was made to get into the town by some officers and men and one Pioneer. The latter actually did get into the town [...] and shot one Hun".[69] The party was driven off by machine gun fire. A Stokes Mortar was brought up into position behind the crossroads in square R24 c at around 1500, but it took another hour for the appropriate ammunition to arrive. For half an hour subsequently, they shelled the ramparts.

It was to the 4/N.Z. Rifle Battalion that fell the honour of precipitating the collapse of German resistance. Patrols skirmishing amongst the islets, bastions and re-entrants to the west of the town had gradually driven the defenders back behind the main inner ramparts. These being close to 60 feet high, how the 30 foot scaling ladders that had been supplied were to be used was not immediately evident. Second-Lieutenants L.C.L. Averill MC (Battalion Intelligence Officer) and H.W. Kerr (14 Platoon, 'D' Company) eventually found a narrow bridge near a sluice gate between the two south-westerly protuberances of the ramparts,[70] high enough and just wide enough to accommodate their ladder. The adjacent ramparts were shelled by trench mortars and swept by Lewis Gun fire to allow the two officers and their patrol to get to the inner wall unmolested. They raised their ladder: it just reached the top with a foot to spare, its top resting on the grassy bank that crowned the ramparts. It was around 1600. Averill and Kerr climbed the ladder. Averill reached the top and crawled onto the grass bank. He sent a revolver bullet after two retreating Germans and was soon joined by Kerr. The latter fired a shot at another group of Germans who immediately disappeared into an underground cavern under the ramparts. Resistance crumbled with almost indecent haste. By now the rest of the battalion were swarming up the ladder, led by their commanding officer, Lieutenant-Colonel Barrowclough. "A few shots were fired and the Boche rapidly surrendered. The whole Battalion mopped up the town, all prisoners being collected in the PLACE D'ARMES. The whole Battalion climbed up that single ladder".[71]

Fifteen minutes later, the 2/N.Z. Rifle Battalion was marching through the Porte de Valenciennes and within the hour "the cookers were in the town and the men got a good meal".[72] Around 700 prisoners were taken.

69   TNA: PRO WO95/3709 War Diary 2nd Battalion New Zealand Rifle Brigade.
70   See aerial photo of Le Quesnoy on page 82.
71   TNA: PRO WO95/3711 War Diary 4th Battalion New Zealand Rifle Brigade. A plaque now adorns the ramparts of Le Quesnoy where the ascent took place.
72   Ibid.

The plaque commemorating the scaling of the walls of Le Quesnoy. (Author)

New Zealand Officers entering Le Quesnoy, 5 November 1918. (National Library of New Zealand)

New Zealand Soldiers assembled in Le Quesnoy market square following its recapture.
(National Library of New Zealand)

A New Zealand regimental band playing in Le Quesnoy the day following its capture.
(National Library of New Zealand)

Battalion diaries summarise the day's casualties as follows:

	Officers			Other Ranks			Total
	K	W	M	K	W	M	
3 NZ Rifle Bde							
1st Battalion	–	9	–	15	53	5	
2nd Battalion	3	4	–	15	92	4	
3rd Battalion	1	–	–	3	45	–	
4th Battalion	2	–	–	11	42	2	
1 NZ Infantry Bde							
1st Auckland	1	1	–	9	37	–	
1st Wellington	1	2	–	7	20	–	
2nd Wellington	2	6	–	13	45	–[73]	
1st Machine Gun Bn	–	2	–	6	20	–	
Total	10	24	–	79	354	11	478

37th Division[74]

The 37th Division (Major-General H. Bruce-Williams) frontage straddled the village of Ghissignies, being approximately 2500 yards in length, north to south. The attack would proceed due east and would entail, initially, the capture of the villages of Louvignies and Jolimetz. Beyond there, the western edge of the Forêt de Mormal crossed the axis of the assault at an angle of 45 degrees, running south-west to north-east, though the Germans had felled the trees over quite a large area: this included most of the area up to the Red Line objective. (See map). Proper woodland would only be encountered on the approach to the Red Dotted Line, some 9,000 yards from the jumping off positions.

The infantry would advance behind the ubiquitous creeping barrage: 18 pounders from five RFA Brigades would supply this, supplemented by a line of 4.5" shells landing 150 yards ahead of the main belt. To add even more depth, one 18 pounder battery per brigade would fire 250 yards in advance of the other batteries.[75] Again, as usual, only shrapnel and smoke would be fired on villages.[76] Heavy artillery would bombard certain areas of tactical importance ahead of the barrage (See Sketch Map 3) and would be employed in counter-battery work: "heavy artillery brought neutralising fire to bear on 24 suspected hostile battery positions from zero onwards. […] Estimate of hostile strength on evening of 3rd instant was about 35 batteries or say 100 guns and from guns captured, and evidence since obtained this estimate would appear

---

73   2nd Wellington casualties have been extrapolated from numbers from the Battalion War Diary and the Commonwealth War Graves Commission.
74   See Map 8
75   TNA: PRO WO95/2517 War Diary 37 Division CRA
76   Ibid.

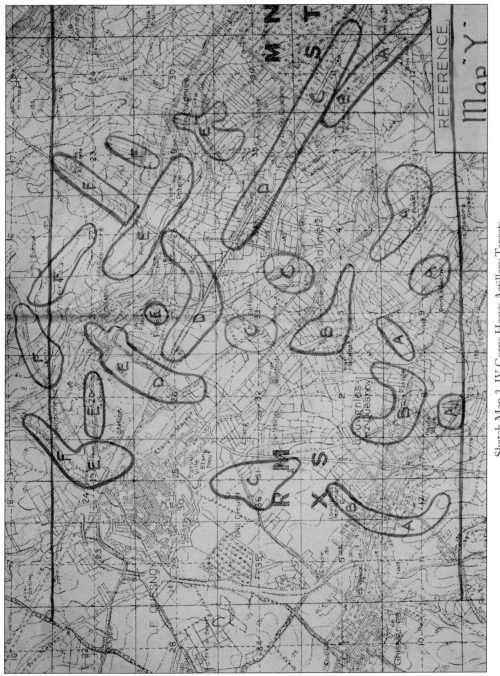

Sketch Map 3 IV Corps Heavy Artillery Targets.

to have been fairly correct".[77] Ammunition expended by the heavy artillery batteries during the 24 period from 1200 3 November to 1200 4 November was recorded as follows:

60 pounders	2,000 rounds
6" Howitzers	4,519 rounds
8" Howitzers	228 rounds
9.2" Guns	174 rounds
6" Guns	244 rounds
5.9 German guns	18 rounds
Total	7,183 rounds

The barrage would open at zero hour and would move forward from its initial line (See Map 8) at zero plus 4 minutes. It would advance as follows:

Leave Opening Line	zero + 4 minutes	(0534 hrs)
Arrive Blue Line	zero + 104 minutes	(0714 hrs)
Leave Blue Line	zero + 119 minutes	(0729 hrs)
Arrive Blue Dotted Line	zero + 167 minutes	(0817 hrs)
Leave Blue Dotted Line	zero + 197 minutes	(0847 hrs)
Pause on Green Line	12 minutes on left	
	120 minutes on right	
Leave Green Line	zero + 342 minutes on left	(1117 hrs)
	zero + 449 minutes on right	(1259 hrs)

The rates of advance of the barrage were: the first 700 yards, 100 yards every 4 minutes. From this point on, 100 yards every 6 minutes as far as the Green Line. It would revert to 100 yards every 4 minutes thereafter.[78]

Planning of the barrage was a collaborative process. Orders issued on 1 November stated that "37th & New Zealand Divisions will submit their plans for the barrage and notify any points they wish bombarded by the Heavy Artillery as soon as possible".[79]

The initial advance would fall to 111 Infantry Brigade (Brigadier-General S.G. Francis), with 13th Battalion Rifle Brigade [13/Rifle Brigade] in the van on the left and 13th Battalion King's Royal Rifle Corps [13/KRRC] on the right. The 10th Royal Fusiliers [10/Royal Fusiliers] would be in support on the right brigade frontage. The 13/Rifle Brigade would advance to the Blue Line and the Blue Dotted Line. On the right, the 13/KRRC would go as far as the Blue Line, with one company also responsible for the mopping up of the village of Louvignies, where the 10/Royal Fusiliers would leapfrog them and continue the attack as far as the Blue Dotted Line.

---

77 TNA: PRO WO95/719 War Diary IV Corps HQ. This is taken from a report written on 8 November.
78 TNA: PRO WO95/2531 War Diary 111 Infantry Brigade & WO95/2519 War Diary 37 Division CRE. The time of arrival on the Green Line varied due to this line not being perpendicular to the axis of attack (See Map 8).
79 TNA: PRO WO95/719 War Diary IV Corps HQ.

112 Infantry Brigade (Brigadier-General W.N. Herbert) would carry on the assault from there, with the 8th Battalion Somerset Light Infantry [8/Somerset L.I.] attached from 63 Brigade.

The attack plan included five tanks. The original plan envisaged 55 tanks (Mark V), 12 Whippets (Light Tanks) and 9 Armoured Cars being used on the whole 4 November attack frontage. Tank Corps losses through the summer, including a substantial number of mechanical breakdowns, meant that only 2nd Tank Brigade were able by this stage of the conflict to supply machines. To begin with, these were all allocated to Fourth Army, the distance required to reach the assembly positions on Third Army sector being deemed prohibitive. This decision was eventually reversed and 11 tanks were allocated to Third Army: 14th Tank Battalion would supply five tanks to IV Corps and 9th Tank Battalion would supply six tanks to V Corps.[80] The tanks were to move up into their positions (about 1000 yards behind the infantry jumping off line) on the night of 3 / 4 November, the noise of their engines being masked from 0100 by low-flying aircraft. This was clearly not going to be a massed tank attack as had been seen at Cambrai or Amiens, and on 25 October, in a document entitled "Notes on Recent Operations by the IV Corps", Lieutenant-General G.M. Harper included a paragraph on co-operation with tanks:

> Mark IV tank commanders must realise that they are the 'hand maidens' of the Infantry. They therefore must work in conformity with the Infantry. This implies that they must ascertain what the Infantry are expected to do and they must conform and not go off on independent missions.[81]

Co-operation and liaison being the key, therefore, and with time for combined training non-existent, the plans for the use of tanks were relatively straight forward and yet rather lacking in detail: they would

> (a) assist 111th Inf. Bde. In the capture of Louvignies
> assist 112th Inf. Bde. In the capture of Jolimetz and the RED LINE.
> Tanks will move into assembly positions in rear of the attacking troops of 111th Bde on the night 3/4th Nov and will so time their advance that they can assist that Bde in the capture of Louvignies.[82]

111 Brigade were under no illusions as to the level of assistance the tanks might provide:

> Attacking Battalions will not wait for these tanks, but it is hoped that they will be in time to assist in clearing the orchards and enclosures West of Louvignies. They will not actually pass through the village.[83]

80 TNA: PRO WO95/95 War Diary Tank Corps HQ & WO95/102 War Diary 2nd Tank Brigade.
81 TNA: PRO WO95/719 War Diary IV Corps HQ.
82 TNA: PRO WO95/2519 War Diary 37th Division CRE.
83 TNA: PRO WO95/2531 War Diary 111 Infantry Brigade HQ. In the end, only one tank ('Job' No. 9043 Commanded by Second-Lieutenant A. Harris) was to make any substantial contribution.

Both front-line battalions were billeted in the village of Salesches the day before the attack. 13/Rifle Brigade moved out at 0030 on 4 November, 13/KRRC an hour and a half later. Both were on the start line by zero minus 30 minutes.

Aware that the Germans had withdrawn from their forward positions in some places north of Le Quesnoy, 37th Division GSO2 visited 111 Bde HQ at 2030 3 November bringing orders from Divisional HQ. 63 Infantry Brigade, who were currently holding the front line east of Ghissignies, were to carry out "active patrolling" during that night to "ensure that touch with the enemy was not lost".[84]

Reports were to be wired to 37th Division HQ hourly. Should no contact be made with the enemy by 0300, the Brigade would advance across the original start line at 0530, but with no artillery barrage, the guns being ready to provide one on "any line west of the Green Line" should it be deemed necessary.[85] As it turned out, the hourly reports revealed an enemy still in place and "intend[ing] to make a stand".[86] Enemy machine guns were also reported to be firing intermittently all night from the vicinity of the chapel in square X5 a. The Germans were clearly nervous and perhaps aware of the preparations to their front as their trench mortars were active through the night and a large number of Very lights were sent up into the night sky.[87]

The 13/Rifle Brigade, on the left of the brigade frontage, had C, A, and D Companies on the jumping off line, left to right, with B Company in reserve in cellars in Ghissignies. The barrage opened at 0530 and remained on the line of the railway for four minutes: it moved forward, as did the men, at 0534, whereupon 500 drums of oil were launched from positions in the Ghissignies orchards into the Chapel area. The German positions on the railway line were taken "after a fierce struggle and much hand to hand fighting"[88] by D Company, supported by two platoons from A Company, resulting in the capture of around 50 prisoners and a dozen machine guns. Two platoons comprising C Company's right flank were held up at the railway line, but the other two platoons, plus one from A Company were able to continue the push forward and arrived on the Blue Line along with D Company "well up to schedule time".[89] The hold up in the left centre was caused by the machine guns securely dug in around the afore-mentioned chapel at X5 a 4.5. 'B' Company moved out from their cellars at 0800 and approached the railway. The Company Commander, correctly assessing the situation, organised a two-platoon attack of the position from the south, helped by a tank and a trench mortar section and had "thus cleared up the pocket of Germans by 09.15 hours. Several Machine Guns and 70 prisoners were [captured] in these pockets".[90] B Company and the remaining units of A and C Companies were then able to advance to the Blue Line, thus catching up with their colleagues.

84   Ibid.
85   Ibid.
86   Ibid.
87   Ibid.
88   TNA: PRO WO95/2534 War Diary 13th Battalion Rifle Brigade.
89   Ibid.
90   Ibid. The tank in question was 'Job' No. 9043, commanded by Second-Lieutenant A. Harris. This
     machine had developed mechanical trouble prior to crossing the railway line, and the subsequent
     delay in rejoining the advance had placed it in the perfect position to offer assistance to 'B' Company.
     There is some uncertainty as to which units finally cleared the machine gun nests at the chapel: the
     diary of 37th Division HQ (TNA: PRO WO95/2515) gives the honour to their Pioneer Battalion
     (9th Battalion North Staffordshire Regiment) who, following the advance in order to repair roads,

It transpired that the fiercest opposition had already been met: "In the attack on the Railway Line the casualties sustained were considerable, including two Company Commanders and several Platoon Commanders".[91] Thereafter, shell fire was the only serious problem up to the Blue Dotted Line. The advance from the Blue Line commenced at 0800 (Louvignies village being reported clear of the enemy at 0815).[92] It is a recurring theme across the whole attack frontage of 4 November that the Germans held their front line positions strongly, but once these had been overrun, they were prone to either retreat or surrender.

> The enemy opposition was now broken, and prisoners were giving themselves up freely: only one or two isolated posts offered resistance, and these were quickly mopped up by Platoons or Sections being detailed to deal with them. The Blue Dotted Line was reached by 08.50 hours, and by 10.20 hours Companies had been reorganised and the line consolidated.[93]

Enemy shell fire in reply to the British barrage had come initially just to the east of Ghissignies and this had lifted back to Louvignies at 0800. This was too far to the west to cause many casualties to the advancing infantry, but it played havoc with attempts to lay wire to the Brigade Advanced Report Centre: this was not accomplished until 1115 and "made communication with Battalions extremely difficult throughout the morning".[94] Alternatives proved equally problematic: "Visual signalling was rendered quite impossible due to the mist. In addition the country between Battalion Headquarters and the line until a late hour, was heavily shelled, so that several runners became casualties and messages subsequently lost".[95] The problem of battlefield communication was never satisfactorily solved during the First World War. This aspect's 'learning curve' was probably one of the shallowest. Even by 4 November 1918, communication between soldier and tank on the battlefield, for example, consisted of the former waving his helmet on the end of his rifle to the latter. The latter hoisted flags of varying colour combinations to signal his intent to the former.[96]

The Battalion War Diary summarises the 13/Rifle Bde casualties for the day as follows:

came across a small pocket of 2 officers and 20 men and rushed them at about 0715. The War Diary of the Pioneers (TNA: PRO WO95/2524) places this action, led by a party under 'A' Company Commander Captain Caddick-Adams, at X35. c. 0.0., some 500 yards to the north-west. A number of Germans were driven northwards from the Chapel position: these were probably the men taken prisoner by Major Cockroft and Second-Lieutenant Drummond of the 3rd Battalion New Zealand Rifle Brigade earlier in this chapter.

91 Ibid. The 13th Battalion Rifle Brigade suffered 37 fatal casualties on 4 November, including Second-Lieutenant James Macaulay, age 20, Second-Lieutenant Alexander Park, Captain Robert Colvill-Jones MC, age 22, and Temporary Second-Lieutenant / Acting Captain Philip Francis Davy MC, all buried in Ghissignies British Cemetery, in graves B23, B24, B25 & B26 respectively. Captain Colvill-Jones' brother, Captain T. Colvill-Jones, 48th Squadron RAF, had been killed on 24 May 1918, age 20.
92 TNA: PRO WO95/2531 War Diary 111 Infantry Brigade HQ.
93 TNA: PRO WO95/2534 War Diary 13th Battalion Rifle Brigade.
94 TNA: PRO WO95/2531 War Diary 111Infantry Brigade HQ.
95 TNA: PRO WO95/2534 War Diary 13th Battalion Rifle Brigade.
96 For details see the War Diary of 13th Battalion King's Royal Rifle Corps, "Instructions No. 1" issued 3 November 1918, TNA: PRO WO95/2533.

	Officers	Other Ranks
Killed	2	27
Wounded	5	90
Missing	–	14

The 13/KRRC had received their Operation Orders on 3 November: the battalion was tasked with advancing to the Blue Line, capturing the village of Louvignies on the way. The former was in reality the road running north-south in square S8 (the Le Quesnoy to Englefontaine road) and it would be assaulted by A Company (Captain E.J. Putman MC) on the left and C Company (Captain T.B. Craig MC) on the right. B and D Companies (Captains J.N. Evans-Jackson MC and H.A.C. Williams MC respectively) in support with the specific duties of mopping up the village behind their own advanced companies and those of 13/Rifle Brigade. Their task was made easier by aerial reconnaissance: "Enlargements of air photos of the village were made and special areas were allotted to each platoon of the two supporting companies, so that each section could immediately make its own route direct to the scene of its operations".[97] The diarist adds a further detail, a mixture of pragmatism and logistical legerdemain:

> As electric torches will be very necessary for this operation and none were [sic] provided by Ordnance, Sgt Hugkulstone set out for DOULLENS on Saturday morning [2 November]. He was unexpectedly successful in lorry jumping and returned to the Bn by mid-day on Sunday with his purchases having covered a distance of over 150 miles.[98]

Three tanks were detailed to follow the infantry advance and assist in the mopping up of the orchards near Louvignies. Their help was not taken for granted, however, as we have already seen.[99] The diarist adds that "The tanks detailed to operate behind the Battalion were not seen and fortunately their services were not required". The five tanks of C Company, 2nd Tank Brigade allocated to 37th Division were: 9117 (Second-Lieutenant W.D.B. Miller); 9043 (Second-Lieutenant A. Harris); 9050 (Sergeant H.W. Thompson); 9389 (Second-Lieutenant E.A. Hayes) & 9047 (Second-Lieutenant K.C. Skuce). The details of their involvement are less than impressive: 9050 broke a track on the approach and took no part in the operations.

9117 advanced with 9043 to the north of Ghissignies and went into action west of the railway line, helping to clear German machine gun posts from the embankment. Here, it took an armour-piercing round to the auto-vac and was put out of action. 9047 moved off from its starting position to the south of Ghissignies at zero hour but became ditched and developed engine trouble at X 11. C. 3.2 and took no part in operations. 9389, suffering chronic mechanical trouble, never caught up with the infantry and, despite reaching the Blue Line, never came into action.

---

97   TNA: PRO WO95/2533 War Diary 13th Battalion King's Royal Rifle Corps.
98   Ibid. Brothers John and William Hugkulstone of Westminster, Middlesex both enlisted in the 13/KRRC on 13 September 1914, acquiring the sequential regimental numbers 4272 and 4273 respectively. Both were deprived of four days' pay for being absent without leave on 15March 1915 and both were Sergeants and battalion cooks by November 1918. As no initial is mentioned in the battalion War Diary, it is impossible to say which of the brothers took the trip to Doullens. Both brothers survived the war.
99   Ibid.

As the men of 13/KRRC approached their assembly positions just before 0330, the enemy put down a counter-preparation barrage and Second-Lieutenant Meikle of 111th Trench Mortar Battery was killed,[100] and his whole section put out of action for some time. The advanced companies moved off close behind the barrage and almost immediately the commander of D Company, Captain Williams, was wounded. The men immediately came under heavy machine gun fire from the orchards and hedges in front of the village, but the attack "Was strongly pushed and the enemy severely handled".[101] The stream running across the axis of the advance proved not to be a serious obstacle and a message was received from B Company at 0715 (message sent at 0640) that A and C Companies had both crossed the main road in Louvignies and that "the attack was going well".[102] The diarist continues:

Second-Lieutenant James Meikle, 13th King's Royal Rifle Corps, attached 111th Trench Mortar Brigade. Beaurain British Cemetery. (Author)

"At 09.10 hrs messages were received from 'C' and 'A' Coys that they were on their objectives to time and in touch with both flanks".[103]

Opposition had been mixed: "In many cases, as soon as our men were within hand-to-hand fighting distance, the enemy surrendered, but here and there more determined resistance was met with and considerable bayonet work took place. The Field Ambulance informed our M.O. that an unusually large number of enemy wounded passed through suffering from severe bayonet wounds".[104] The gruesome nature of the diary intensifies as the business of 'mopping up' is described. For the most part, it would appear again that the German garrison was eager to surrender to B and D Companies once they realised that the front-line action has passed well beyond them. However, "several gory individual contests took place in cellars. One N.C.O. of 'B' Coy fought with 3 Huns in a cellar and killed the lot. His weapon was a small hand axe which he was carrying for cutting his way through hedges, and so the good work went on!"[105] The 'good work' had cost the 13/KRRC 26 fatal casualties, and just under 100 wounded, but they had fought their last action of the war.

100 Second-Lieutenant James Drysdale Meikle 13th KRRC attached 111th TMB, age 30, is buried in Beaurain British Cemetery, grave B3.
101 TNA: PRO WO95/2533 War Diary 13th Battalion King's Royal Rifle Corps.
102 Ibid.
103 Ibid.
104 Ibid. The tone of the diary suggests a certain pride in the amount of cold steel used!
105 Ibid.

The baton now passed to the 10/Royal Fusiliers, 112 Infantry Brigade. Their War Diary gives us a glance at the processes by which orders were disseminated down the chain of command: there had been a Brigade Conference at 1800 on 31 October where Commanding Officers were informed of the forthcoming attack and of 37th Division's role within it. On the following day, a Divisional Conference was held at Brigade HQ at Neuville: Brigadiers and Battalion Commanders were present to discuss the plans. The 2 & 3 November were taken up by reconnaissance, the study of aerial photographs and organising their own smaller unit conferences. Order No. 274 was issued by 111 Infantry Brigade, setting out artillery arrangements, battalion movements and deployments, tank cooperation and battlefield objectives at 2100, 2 November.

On the night 3 / 4 November, the battalion assembled on the railway line in X 10 d. and X 11 a. (See map). All units were in place by zero minus 30 minutes, after having had a hot meal in Salesches at midnight. They came under intermittent shell fire through the night and suffered a number of casualties, including Lieutenant A.N. Usher MC,[106] commanding officer of A Company, killed around 0500 as he was "Supervising the assembling of the company in the Railway Embankment".[107]

They moved off at 0530, C and B Companies (left and right) in the lead, D and A Companies 50 yards behind. "Each company will advance on a 2-Platoon frontage with the third platoon in close support, Platoons advancing in Section 'blobs'".[108] A Stokes Mortar detachment advanced behind D Company and took up position in the sunken road at S 8 b. 10.45., ready to deal with "any determined resistance".[109] The narrative of the attack is brief in all the relevant War Diaries:[110] the troops leapfrogged the 13/KRRC on the Blue Line and reached their objectives on the Blue Dotted Line on time at 0815. D Company "killed and captured a large number of the enemy" as they passed through the village of Louvignies, and Lieutenant-Colonel Waters, writing the after action report simply records that "some hostile machine gun posts were met and dealt with".[111] B Company occupied the right hand section of the objective, C Company in the centre and D Company on the left. One platoon

Lieutenant Arthur Usher, MC & Bar, 10th Battalion Royal Fusiliers. Beaurain British Cemetery. (Author)

---

106 Lieutenant Arthur Norman Usher MC & Bar, age 21, was buried in Beaurain British Cemetery on 7 November 1918, along with four Other Ranks.
107 TNA: PRO WO95/2532 War Diary 10th Battalion Royal Fusiliers.
108 Ibid.
109 Ibid.
110 TNA: PRO WO95/2532 War Diary 10th Battalion Royal Fusiliers; TNA: PRO WO95/2531 War Diary 111 Infantry Brigade; TNA: PRO WO95/2515 War Diary 37th Division HQ.
111 Ibid.

of A Company was ready to fill in any gaps on D Company's frontage (which was the longest), the other two being ready to form a defensive flank on the right should it be necessary. The assault cost the battalion 7 fatal casualties and fewer than 50 wounded. The Brigade casualties were assessed as:

	Officers	Other Ranks
Killed	8	49
Wounded	11	199
Unaccounted for	–	26

The advance would now be continued by units of 112 Infantry Brigade: 1st Battalion Essex Regiment [1/Essex] would take the lead on the left brigade front, with 1st Battalion Hertfordshire Regiment [1/Hertfordshire] on the right. Their objective was the Red Line (see map), pausing on the Green Line "to enable guns to be brought up".[112] From there, if the opportunity presented itself, the 13/Royal Fusiliers and 8/Somerset L.I. (attached from 63 Infantry Brigade), would advance into the still wooded area of the Forêt de Mormal and push on to the Red Dotted Line.[113]

1/Essex on the left were delayed in reaching their jumping off positions on the Blue Dotted Line by the persistent enemy resistance in X 5 a (Chapel) and at one point found themselves behind their supporting battalion, 13/Royal Fusiliers. They eventually managed to cross the Blue Dotted Line at 1035, some 90 minutes behind schedule, having lost the barrage. They advanced on a three company front, X Company on the left (Captain Calverley MC), Y Company in the centre (Captain Attfield), Z Company on the right (Captain Walker) with W Company in reserve (Captain Gillett), the latter with orders to "mop up the village of Jolimetz and leave a garrison in same".[114]

X Company were able to advance quickly, and by 1050 they were well to the east of the cemetery in M 33 d. "The enemy appeared to be recovering from the effects of our barrage and were manning the orchards and houses and also the roads leading from Jolimetz".[115] Their flank was turned by the speed of the left Company's advance, however, and "many prisoners and guns were taken".[116] The remainder took refuge in the village and were overrun by the centre company now arriving on the scene. The enemy were being pushed toward the south-east and were seen to be reorganising in square S 4 d., the area "being full of them".[117] Enfilade fire from the left and rear as the left companies pressed on toward the Green Line and then frontal fire from Z Company forced the issue and after the Germans had suffered a number of casualties they began to realise the hopelessness of their situation and "surrendered freely".[118]

The three front-line companies pressed on to the Green Line leaving W Company to its mopping up duties. They met with more resistance than they might have expected, but

---

112 TNA: PRO WO95/2537 War Diary 1st Battalion Hertfordshire Regiment.
113 TNA: PRO WO95/2515 War Diary 37th Division HQ.
114 TNA: PRO WO95/2537 War Diary 1st Battalion Essex Regiment.
115 Ibid.
116 Ibid.
117 Ibid.
118 Ibid.

Lieutenant Harris' tank, 'Job', arrived at the opportune moment and "worked down the main street mopping up any opposition that was encountered".[119] The village was "cleared of the enemy in a remarkably short and thoroughly workmanlike style. Those who came out at once were taken prisoners, those who did not were shot or bayoneted".[120] The reserve company claimed to have bagged 400 prisoners.

At 1112, the battalion advanced from the Green Line "and reached the RED LINE with little difficulty, the enemy being completely bewildered as to the direction of our attack after the capture of Jolimetz, and surrendering freely the whole way across the Divisional front. Excellent targets were obtained by Lewis Gunners who pushed boldly forward".[121]

The battalion's commanding officer, Lieutenant-Colonel T.J.E. Blake, in writing the after action report, had no doubt as to the reasons for the success of the day's action: "The success of the operation was due to a thorough and complete understanding on the part of all ranks of the object and intention in view. All orders were, even under most difficult circumstances, readily assimilated and carried out and the battalion, despite the initial start arrived on its objective in the proper place at the right time. Company Commanders appreciated the various tactical situations with commendable accuracy and their many reports proved invaluable to the Battalion Commander. Platoon Commanders fought their platoons well and displayed the greatest keenness and it was due to them that each man went into action knowing well where he had to go and what was expected from him at different places".[122]

On the right divisional front the 1/Hertfordshire and 8/Somerset L.I. reached their assembly positions on the Blue Dotted Line with no dramas or difficulties. The 1/Hertfordshire commenced their advance at 0917. The attack was going well until they reached the stream and orchards in S 9 b. & S 10 c. "At this juncture [...] Nos 2 & 3 Companies were held up by heavy MG fire. The nature of the country greatly favoured the defence, being very close, and therefore it was very difficult to locate the enemy".[123] The left companies were encountering machine gun fire coming "straight up the valley from approximately S 3. Central",[124] and the assault stalled. The men were unable to advance any further until the machine gun posts were overrun by the right company of 1/Essex, who captured 16 machine guns and 40 prisoners in the area. The battalion then records that no further trouble was encountered until the men reached the area of the Forêt de Mormal where the trees had been felled (see Map 8), and ran into an "extremely thin enemy barrage put down in S11 b. & d".[125] This coincided with machine gun fire, but the latter lasted "only 20 minutes, at the end of which period the enemy retired".[126] The enemy retirement allowed the battalion to reach their final objective by 1500.

119 Ibid.
120 Ibid.
121 TNA: PRO WO95/2515 War Diary 37th Division HQ.
122 TNA: PRO WO95/2537 War Diary 1st Battalion Essex Regiment.
123 TNA: PRO WO95/2537 War Diary 1st Battalion Hertfordshire Regiment.
124 TNA: PRO WO95/2515 War Diary 37th Division HQ.
125 TNA: PRO WO95/2537 War Diary 1st Battalion Hertfordshire Regiment.
126 Ibid. The area labelled "Trees Felled" on the map is described in the 'Annexe to 37th Division Intelligence Summary No.5' (TNA: PRO WO95/2515 War Diary 37th Division) under 'Notes on the Forest of Mormal' thus: "The stumps of felled trees are still left standing about 2'–2' 6" above the ground. Space between stumps said to be 4 – 5 metres."

The advance from the Red Line was delegated to the 13/Royal Fusiliers on the left and to the 8/Somerset L.I. on the right. This movement took the men into the forest proper: tall, mature trees, thick undergrowth intersected by paths, or 'rides', these classified in three categories: 13 feet wide metalled roads; 13 feet broad unmetalled lanes and 3 feet broad footpaths, with wired ditches marking the edge of the forest and clearings, and tree stumps also wired,[127] the British troops could well have been forgiven for expecting another 'High Wood' or 'Delville Wood' experience.[128] The reality turned out to be very different.

The 13/Royal Fusiliers went into the attack well under strength: "owing to the extreme weakness of the battalion since operations of 24th Oct. Battn. was reorganised on a two company basis – 'A' & 'B' Coys. – under command of Capt. G.G. Ziegler & Capt. M.O. Lewis respectively. Coys. about 100 strong each on new organisation".[129] Captain & Adjutant G. Chapman's after action report dated 8 November bemoans the lack of men: "It was found quite impossible to maintain constant touch on the flanks and even between companies during the whole operation. This was due (a) to the enclosed nature of the country (b) to the extreme weakness of the battalion. The Battalion was covering a frontage of 1000 yards, with 2 Coys, each approximately 100 strong. This necessitated a platoon covering a frontage of 250, i.e. about 12-14 yards per man. There is no doubt that had any serious resistance been made by the enemy it would have been quite impossible to reach the final objective. It is suggested that at least one man to every 3 yards is a sine qua non in operations in enclosed country such as the Forest of Mormal".[130] Movement proved difficult, but not due to enemy action: "Owing to the extremely thick undergrowth and trees, and to the rides being deep in mud, progress was very slow. […] Darkness falling at about 17.00 hours naturally increased the difficulties".[131] Isolated pockets of resistance were overcome, the main body of the German units having long since melted away to the east. One platoon under Sergeant 8021 W. Green proved far from "sticky": it was Green, "who with great daring pushed […] right through the Forêt de Mormal in complete darkness, arriving on the final objective [Red Dotted Line] at 18.20 hours. No other patrols were able to come up with him during the night. However, he and his platoon remained on the objective & patrolled the ground for about 1,000 yards Eastwards until morning, when the 5th Division pushed through".[132]

The 'capture' of the forest had cost the battalion only one fatal casualty.[133]

127 Ibid.
128 High Wood and Delville Wood were taken only after prolonged struggles and at huge cost during the Battle of the Somme in 1916.
129 TNA: PRO WO95/2538 War Diary 13th Battalion Royal Fusiliers.
130 Ibid.
131 TNA: PRO WO95/2515 War Diary 37th Division HQ. See also Jonathan Boff *Winning and Losing on the Western Front*. Cambridge (Cambridge University Press, 2012), pp. 211-214. Boff suggests various reasons for a lack of vigour in Third Army's 'pursuit' of a beaten German Army in November 1918.
132 TNA: PRO WO95/2538 War Diary 13th Battalion Royal Fusiliers.
133 Private 77704 Fausto Maria Ibanez De Aldecoa, age 19. Hailing from London, he is buried in Romeries Communal Cemetery Extension, grave V. A. 3.

The 8/Somerset L.I. lost two company commanders during their advance to their assembly positions: A/Captain Briggs and Second-Lieutenant Brooks "lost their lives reconnoitring forward with a view to merging with 1st/1st Herts Regt in order to make a further attack".[134]

Advancing into the forest, the battalion encountered isolated pockets of resistance: rifle and Lewis Gun fire forced the enemy to retire, but the thickness of the forest, the darkness and their "ignorance of the way"[135] prevented any swift pursuits. It was decided to push patrols, each one or two platoons strong, out eastwards along the rides.[136] As on the 13/Royal Fusilier's front, the enemy had gone. A line of outposts was set up to the west of the Red Dotted Line and forward patrols were pushed on from there, reaching the eastern edge of the forest before dawn. Lieutenant-Colonel Sheringham, commanding 8/Somerset L.I., was able to advise 5th Division that adopting attack formation on the western edge of the forest was a waste of time, the forest being clear of Germans. The 8/Somerset L.I. assault had cost them 8 fatal casualties and 25 wounded.

Private Fausto Maria Ibanez de Aldecoa, 13th Battalion Royal Fusiliers. Romeries Communal Cemetery Extension. (Author)

The timely advance of the support and reserve units of 37th Division had been facilitated by the creation of five cross-country tracks. Praise for the work of the 152nd Field Company Royal Engineers was fulsome:

The very enclosed nature of the country over which the operations of the last 24 hours had been carried out, traversed as it was by thick hedges running diagonally to the line of advance, would have seriously hampered the forward movement of all troops following up the attack and would probably have caused them to lose direction, had not the 152nd Field Co. R.E. been employed on the construction and marking of Infantry and Artillery tracks. Commencing at 05.30 hours on the 4th Nov., this company worked until 03.00 hours on the 5th Nov.[137]

---

134 TNA: PRO WO95/2529 War Diary 8th Battalion Somerset Light Infantry. Lieutenant/Acting Captain Orriell Briggs, age 30, is buried in Romeries Communal Cemetery Extension, grave V. C. 2. Second-Lieutenant Horace William Briggs MC, age 24, is buried in Cross Roads Cemetery, Fontaine-au-Bois, grave III. B. 20.
135 Ibid.
136 See Map 8.
137 TNA: PRO WO95/2515 War Diary 37th Division HQ.

The diary of the R.E. Company was more matter-of-fact: "Attack 5.30 a.m. 5 Infantry tracks made from front line to final objectives. 3 men wounded".[138]

The 37th Division had captured two defended villages and then followed a retreating army through the Forêt de Mormal, advancing 9,000 yards. The total fighting strength of the seven battalions involved that day numbered 128 officers and 2,936 other ranks.[139] They had encountered German units from *4th, 14th, 22nd & 239th Divisions* and reported their enemy's average company strength to be 45.[140]

37th Divisional casualties were:

	Officers	Other Ranks
Killed	9	60
Wounded	15	257
Missing	–	27
Total	24	344

These figures equate to a casualty rate of 18.75 percent for officers, and 11.71 percent for other ranks.

Since 21 August, (77 days), the Corps had advanced 48 miles, with 37th Division responsible for 33 of those in 50 days in the front line.

Conclusion

The New Zealand Division proved more than capable of executing a complicated plan of attack. Whether the eventual capture of Le Quesnoy was brave and audacious or foolhardy under the circumstances remains a moot point. It was certainly contrary to orders.

37th Division, despite isolated incidents of obstinate defence, was able, without the help of the tanks, to push on against an enemy who was increasingly inclined to surrender. Although confronted with the difficult task of moving through the forest in pitch darkness, the withdrawal of German units allowed patrols to reach the day's objective line unopposed.

138 TNA: PRO WO95/2522/1 War Diary 152nd Field Company Royal Engineers.
139 TNA: PRO WO95/2515 War Diary 37th Division HQ. This is an average of 18 officers and 419 other ranks per battalion.
140 Ibid. "The German Divisional boundaries at zero ran E.N.E. and running E gave our attack the additional advantage of a flank attack. Thus, at the beginning, the *22nd* and *4th Divs* were met whilst later on the *239th Div* and *14th Div* predominated." 26 officers and 1184 other ranks were taken prisoner.

5

V Corps

Introduction

V Corps' attack was to take the men deep into the Forêt de Mormal. This chapter highlights the differing fortunes of the two divisions involved. The under strength 17th Division, short on training and perhaps lacking in innovative leadership, was unable to apply the tactics of fire, manoeuvre and infiltration and failed to reach their objectives on the day. This was in total contrast to 38th Division, themselves down on numbers, who showed dash and initiative in using the nature of the terrain to their advantage and eschewing frontal assaults, particularly in the latter stages of the advance, in order to gain their final objectives.

*   *   *

During the second half of October, V Corps (Lieutenant-General C.D. Shute) had been advancing in a north-easterly direction from the River Selle near Neuvilly, capturing the villages of Ovillers, Vendegies-au-Bois and, most recently, Poix-du-Nord, the latter occupied on 24 October by 21st Division, the 33rd Division on their right coming up just short of Englefontaine.[1]

The allied armies paused for breath in the face of the Forêt de Mormal and the Sambre-Oise Canal and consolidated their lines in preparation for the next effort. The northern sector of V Corps' line ran north-west to south-east for almost 3,000 yards from the Salesches to Louvignies road just south of the village of Ghissignies to the Englefontaine to Futoy road. This section was to be entrusted to the 17th Division. The line then turned more or less due south and extended a further 2,000 yards, just brushing the eastern outskirts of Englefontaine. 38th Division was to advance from these positions.

The planned assault would take both divisions deep into the Forêt de Mormal. This

---

1   For details of the advance see Derek Clayton, *From Pontefract to Picardy* (Stroud: Tempus Publishing), 2004. Englefontaine was finally taken by 33rd Division during the night of 25-26 October.

...is a forest of oak and beeches, about nine miles in length from north to south and from three to four miles broad. The woodland roadways through it were mostly narrow tracks, unmetalled or at the best with a light layer of unrolled stones or gravel. These tracks generally crossed each other on lines from north-east to south-west and north-west to south-east, marking off the forest into large diamond-shaped blocks. [...] Before the war the forest had been well cared for by the woodmen of Locquignol, [...] but during the years in which it had been in possession of the invaders they had made, here and there, extensive clearings by felling trees to provide timber for their entrenchments, huts, bridges and other work. [...] In many of the clearings large quantities of timber were stacked ready for removal. [...] In the uncleared parts of the wood little or nothing had been done to check the undergrowth, and in some places it had grown up into dense thickets. But there were fewer of these obstacles than expected.[2]

The edge of the forest ran south-west to north-east along the dead-straight Englefontaine to Bavai road, and therefore lay at almost 90 degrees to the assembly positions of the 17th Division units.[3]

The overall plan for 4 November required the capture of four successive objective lines, Blue, Red, Brown and Green.[4] Each division would attack on a single brigade front, and brigades would leapfrog: the front-line brigade would take the Blue Line, the next would move the assault onto the Red Line and the third-line brigade would take both the Brown and Green Lines. This was, in effect, a three-stage 'bite and hold' operation that would take the line almost to the eastern edge of the forest.[5]

The artillery barrage would be supplied by 10 brigades of the Royal Field Artillery[6] and five brigades of Royal Garrison Artillery[7] and was composed as follows: two-fifths of the 18 pounders would fire shrapnel 300 yards ahead of the advancing infantry, one round in every six being smoke. This line was to be supplemented by all available 6" Trench Mortars. One hundred yards ahead would fall shells from the 4.5" Howitzers and a further 200 yards ahead the remaining 18 pounders would fire High Explosive with 50 per cent Thermite. "60 pounders firing shrapnel and 6" Howitzers with 106 fuzes were to fire on tactical points not closer than 700 yards ahead of the rear line of the barrage".[8] Counter battery work had begun on 1 November, with a total of 32 guns[9] doing their best to neutralise enemy batteries.

2   A.Hilliard Atteridge, *History of the 17th (Northern) Division* (Glasgow: Maclehose, 1929), pp. 451-452.
3   See Map 9.
4   See Map 9.
5   This was the 'First Phase' of a three-phase plan. The second phase would see 33rd and 21st Divisions continue the advance on 'Z' Day plus 1 as far as the Avesnes-Bavay road, with 38th and 17th Divisions joining in again on 'Z' plus 2 to push on towards Maubeuge and Mons. TNA: PRO WO95/752 War Diary V Corps HQ & WO95/1985 War Diary 17th Division HQ.
6   In the 17th Division area by 78, 79, 94, 95 & 34 Brigades RFA and in 38th Division area by 121, 122, 48, 162 & 169 Brigades RFA.
7   In the 17th Division area by 17, 22, 54 & 58 Brigades RFA and in 38th Division area by 13 Brigade RFA.
8   TNA: PRO WO95/752 War Diary V Corps HQ.
9   Ten 6" Howitzers, ten 8" Howitzers, ten 9.2" Howitzers & two 12" Howitzers. The strength of the German artillery response would suggest that the counter battery work was not particularly effective.

The regular creeping barrage would only be available as far as the Red Line. Thereafter, the strength and efficacy of any artillery support would depend on how many guns could be pushed forward in time. "After the capture of the second objective, Divisions were to act independently with no set barrage. Artillery support was then to take the form of short rapid concentrations of all natures on edges of woods, ditches, etc. [...] One Brigade RFA on each Divn front was to be specially allotted to the leading Bde of infantry for close support".[10]

The nature of the artillery barrage had been the subject of much discussion: "There was considerable danger to our infantry from bursts in the trees bordering the roads and in the Forest of Mormal owing to their being some 80 feet high, if the infantry attempted to follow the barrage closely. [...] Eventually it was decided to adhere to the normal shrapnel barrage and to warn the infantry not to try and get too close to it".[11] The plan went on: "In order further to reduce danger and to get a greater volume of fire effect on open spaces, barrages were not to creep through the wooded belts in the forest".[12] This was directly linked to a directive given to all 'Subordinate Commanders' who were "warned of the impracticability of attempting to traverse densely wooded belts in extended order. Movement when the forest is reached should be by Platoon along the edges of wooded belts or of rides and tracks on which Artillery is being directed to concentrate its fire". [13]

It was destined to be a mainly infantry/artillery operation, but other branches of the services were involved: the infantry would be followed "at one hour's distance"[14] by two Royal Engineer Companies and the Pioneer Battalions, whose job it would be to clear felled trees and other obstacles from roads and then to open up the main routes through the forest for motorised transport. 15th Squadron RAF was to send out a contact patrol as soon after dawn as was practical and at "odd hours",[15] that is 0900, 1100, and so on. Infantry were required "on demand from contact aeroplanes"[16] to light two red flares per company frontage. Counter attack patrols were also to be flown, and if such a development was detected, the aircraft was to drop a red smoke bomb "over the place where the enemy was seen".[17]

Attached from IV Corps as from midday 2 November was one squadron of 3rd Hussars. They were "employed primarily in conducting prisoners of war from Division to Corps prisoner of war cages. They may also be employed, should the situation allow, in mounted reconnaissance duty, but will not be used for dismounted action".[18]

It was initially planned for six tanks of 9th Tank Battalion to be attached to V Corps, three each being given to 17th and 38th Divisions. Divisional and Brigade commanders were determined not to build up their men's hopes in this area, however, as an addendum to 17th Division Order No.28, issued on 3 November demonstrates: "It will be impressed on the attacking infantry that ON NO ACCOUNT WILL THEY WAIT FOR THE TANKS whose role

10   TNA: PRO WO95/752 War Diary V Corps HQ.
11   TNA: PRO WO95/1985 War Diary 17th Division HQ.
12   Ibid.
13   Ibid.
14   Ibid.
15   TNA: PRO WO95/752 War Diary V Corps HQ.
16   TNA: PRO WO95/1985 War Diary 17th Division HQ.
17   Ibid.
18   TNA: PRO WO95/752 War Diary V Corps HQ.

is entirely separate yet supplementary to that of the infantry".[19] The actual involvement of the tanks will be dealt with later.

17th Division[20]

The 17th Division was "warned to take part in the next attack" on 31 October and were "to be ready to relieve 21st Division on night 2/3rd November".[21] The following day, the Corps and Divisional objectives were allotted and the Divisional Commander, Major-General P.R. Robertson, held a conference at 1700 hours and "explained the roles of all formations and units. G.Os C. Brigades, C.R.A., C.R.E., Signals Q., M.G.Bn, and as many Bn. Commanders as possible attending".[22] Divisional Orders for the attack were then issued on 2 November. 52 Brigade (Major/Temp. Brigadier-General W.Allason DSO) would lead the attack, 51 Brigade (Major/Temp. Brigadier-General R.M. Dudgeon DSO, MC) would be in close support, tasked with the Red Line objective, and 50 Brigade (Major/Temp. Brigadier-General J.F.R. Hope DSO) would complete the picture by taking the Brown and Green Lines.

The strengths of units in 17th Division were as follows:[23]

	Officers	Other Ranks	Total	Officers	Other Ranks	Total
50 Brigade						
10 West Yorks	21	826	847			
7 E. Yorks	25	843	868	74	2,195	2,269
6 Dorsets	28	521	549			
51 Brigade						
7 Lincolns	27	693	720			
7 Borders	24	625	649	78	2,014	2,092
10 Sher Fores.	27	696	723			
52 Brigade						
10 Lancs Fus.	28	604	632			
9 Duke of Well.	25	740	765	74	1,954	2,058
12 Manchesters	21	610	631			
Pioneers						
7 York & Lancs	32	706	738			
Total				**258**	**6,869**	**7,127**

---

19   TNA: PRO WO95/1985 War Diary 17th Division HQ.
20   See Maps 9 and 9a.
21   Ibid.
22   Ibid.
23   This puts the division at only two thirds of its full strength. Table quoted in Atteridge, *History of the 17th (Northern) Division*, p. 453.

Zero hour was 0530, at which point an artillery barrage would open up on a line 300 yards ahead of the waiting infantry. It would remain there for four minutes before advancing "by lifts"[24] at a rate of 100 yards every four minutes. Both 51 and 52 Brigade troops would advance at this time, both brigades under orders to "clear the starting line as quickly as possible"[25] in the hope that both units could avoid the worst of any enemy retaliatory barrage that might fall on the jumping off positions. This proved to be a vain hope.

The line would, in effect, pivot on the right wing of the right hand battalion until the Englefontaine – Futoy road was reached, thus aligning themselves north-south. There, they and the artillery barrage would pause until Z + 45 minutes before an advance behind artillery lifts of 100 yards every six minutes would be resumed. This pause was dual-purpose: it allowed the 17th Division the tricky manoeuvre of swinging 45 degrees to the right and then reorganise if required, and also conformed with the 38th Division on their right, whose 0615 zero hour had been set to match that of Fourth Army troops on their right. Unfortunately it also meant that the front line troops came under fire from enemy artillery for some considerable time.

The nature of the country across which the 17th Division was to advance was described in their 'Narrative of Operations':

> As far as the Louvignies road the country was comparatively open – Between the road and the MORMAL FOREST were a series of orchards enclosed by thick and high hedges very difficult to negotiate and obstructing view, several isolated farms, and the straggling village of FUTOY. Air photos disclosed a great many of the enemy's defences and enabled a shrewd guess to be made as to the whereabouts of his various lines of resistance, but the orchards and hedges afforded splendid cover for Machine Guns and machine gun defence so established was impossible to locate.[26]

52 Brigade consisted of 10th Battalion Lancashire Fusiliers [10/Lancashire Fusiliers] (Lieutenant-Colonel G.L. Torrens), 9th Battalion Duke of Wellington's [9/Duke of Wellington's] (West Riding Regiment) (Lieutenant-Colonel A. Driver) and 12th Battalion Manchester Regiment [12/Manchester] (Lieutenant-Colonel S. Danby). All three battalions were to be in their assembly trenches "immediately after dark 3rd November, and cover themselves with outposts until zero minus 15 minutes, when outposts will be withdrawn".[27] They would advance with two companies in front and two in support between 25 and 50 yards behind.[28] Once they arrived on their objective (Blue Line) they were to push patrols forward "to the limit of the protective barrage"[29] and be prepared to support the attack of 51 Brigade on the Red Line. At this point, two 'Golden Rain' rockets per company would be sent up to signal their success to the watching RAF contact patrol aircraft. The momentum of the assault was emphasised in Brigade Orders:

24   TNA: PRO WO95/752 War Diary V Corps HQ.
25   TNA: PRO WO95/1985 War Diary 17th Division HQ.
26   TNA: PRO WO95/1985 War Diary 17th Division HQ. 'Narrative of Operations Part V. October 31st – November 11th.'
27   TNA: PRO WO95/2011 War Diary 52 Infantry Brigade HQ. Outposts were withdrawn to avoid casualties from their own opening barrage.
28   Ibid.
29   Ibid.

Mark V Tank. (Australian War Memorial)

"Throughout, the barrage will be followed closely and points of resistance will be passed round and mopped up from the flank or rear".[30]

An addendum to Brigade Orders issued on 3 November announced that three tanks would assist in the attack: one would advance "simultaneously with the leading infantry, breaking down hedges en route to facilitate the passage of the infantry and will assist in the clearance of enemy defences at road junction S.20 d. 1.0. This tank will then follow the leading infantry at a distance of 300 yards and assist in dealing with any strongpoints holding up the advance".[31] The other two tanks would also follow 300 yards behind the advancing infantry. In the event, of the six tanks allotted to V Corps, "three were unable to start owing to mechanical trouble". With two allocated to 38th Division, this left one for the 17th Division. This tank "left its starting point at zero, but at an early stage in the attack received a direct hit and was put out of action".[32]

The brigade was drawn up with the Lancashire Fusiliers on the left, the Duke of Wellington's in the centre, and the Manchesters on the right. The depth of the initial advance varied, north to south, from 2,500 to 1,000 yards. "On the left, the country was quite open, with the exception

---

30   Ibid.
31   Ibid.
32   TNA: PRO WO95/102 War Diary 2 Tank Brigade HQ. 17th Division turns out to be less than enamoured by tanks. In their after-action report, their experiences with tanks is summed up as follows: "This being the last big attack made by the Division it may be mentioned that in no previous attack made by the Division had tanks proved of service. It is questionable whether employed in two's or three's with Divisions they are employed usefully. Their fewness makes them an easy target for enemy guns. Two or three Supply Tanks to carry up supplies and stores during or after an attack would on the other hand be of value to a Division." TNA: PRO WO95/1985 War Diary 17th Division HQ.

of a hedged field, until the Louvignies Road was reached. From there onward lay a series of orchards enclosed by thick hedges, several isolated farms, and the straggling village of Futoy. The whole of the ground was carefully prepared for defence, machine guns being located in the most unlikely positions, under trees in the centre of fields, enfilading hedgerows, and in houses".[33]

The 10/Lancashire Fusiliers, on the left, advanced on a two-company front, D and C Companies (left and right) in front, A and B Companies, respectively, in support. The initial moves were made in the dark, daybreak not coming until around 0845, and under cover of an "extremely heavy ground mist".[34] The first real opposition was encountered in the copses in X18 a & c and S13 d, resulting in the capture of two Officers and 31 Other Ranks, and in orchards in S14 d. D Company "charged"[35] and captured the former, whilst the leading platoon of C Company dealt similarly with the latter before pushing on towards Futoy, these manoeuvres undoubtedly being helped by the mist. The orchard, where a number of prisoners had been captured in rifle pits, had been overrun by "using rifle grenades freely".[36] They reached the Louvignies road at 0606, D Company bypassing La Motte Farm, leaving it for A Company to mop up. This they did against "heavy MG fire" from a hole in the wall of the farm buildings complex. One platoon rushed the German post under covering Lewis Gun fire. "The remainder of the company moved to the east side of the buildings and were in time to capture several of the enemy emerging from an outhouse".[37]

The advance continued, close behind the barrage,[38] and opposition on the western edges of Futoy was quickly overcome by the leading companies. The rest of the village was mopped up once the artillery barrage had lifted from the road running north-south in squares S14 a & c and was reported as captured by 0705. Hostile artillery had, until now, been concentrated on the original jumping off positions, but switched between 0700 and 0800 to the tracks and rides in the area now occupied by the Lancashire Fusiliers. They were also under "desultory"[39] fire from machine guns near Pont à Vache in the 37th Division area to the north, but these were eventually neutralised by our own guns of the 17th Machine Gun Company and a liberal sprinkling of rifle brigades. The battalion's final objective (Blue Line) was reached at 0800 and positions were established east of the line, though the digging in was done under severe shelling. The War Diary quotes casualties for the month of November 1918 as 9 killed, 78 wounded and 8 missing. Commonwealth War Graves Commission records show 13 fatalities for 4 November, including one officer.[40] The 10/Lancashire Fusiliers were in billets in Futoy by the evening.

33   TNA: PRO WO95/2011 War Diary 52 Infantry Brigade HQ. 'Report on Operations of the 52nd Infantry Brigade'.
34   TNA: PRO WO95/2012 War Diary 10th Battalion Lancashire Fusiliers.
35   TNA: PRO WO95/2011 War Diary 52 Infantry Brigade HQ.
36   Ibid.
37   Ibid.
38   One company commander reported that the mist was so thick that it was "only possible to follow the barrage by sound." Thermit shells also proved valuable in keeping direction. TNA: PRO WO95/2011 War Diary 52 Infantry Brigade HQ.
39   TNA: PRO WO95/2012 War Diary 10th Battalion Lancashire Fusiliers.
40   Temp. Second-Lieutenant Robert Carswell Lee, age 20, native of Liverpool, (18th Battalion The King's (Liverpool Regiment), attached 10th Lancashire Fusiliers, is buried in Romeries Communal Cemetery Extension, grave VI D 3.

The centre battalion, the 9/Duke of Wellington's (Lieutenant-Colonel A. Driver MC), had moved up from the village of Poix-du-Nord at 1930 on 3 November and were in their jumping off positions by 2300. On the way, D Company had been caught by enemy shellfire and suffered over 40 casualties.[41] They moved forward at 0530 on 4 November, the War Diary recording that "from the quickness of the enemy's reply to our barrage it is evident that the enemy expected our attack".[42] They also encountered very heavy machine gun fire from the Louvignies – Englefontaine road (S13 d), losing four officers killed with two others wounded, and "many other ranks [were] casualties".[43] They pushed on into the orchards, these being "carefully organised for machine gun defence, but, thanks to the mist and the extensive use of rifle grenades, the attack progressed, many prisoners being taken and a considerable number of Germans killed".[44]

At this point, units must have become mixed up with those of the Lancashire Fusiliers, as two companies of the Duke of Wellington's went to the north of Futoy, the other two to the south of the village. The diary records the support companies mopping up the village while the forward companies pushed on to their final objective. The companies were then reorganised, gaining touch with units on both flanks. The attack, though ultimately 'successful', was far from straightforward and was very costly: the battalion had attacked with 15 officers and 584 other ranks. "Of these, 13 officers and 226 other ranks became casualties during the advance".[45] After deducting prisoner escorts, stretcher bearers, signallers and runners, the "fighting strength of the battalion was reduced to 2 company officers and 200 men. That they were able, with these […] numbers to make good their final objective speaks highly of the determination of all ranks. Lieut-Col. Driver MC was up personally directing the attack and the success may be attributed largely to his leadership".[46] The Battalion War Diary records five officers killed and eight wounded,[47] adding that two companies were "entirely without officers one hour after the attack started, and the remaining Coys had only one officer each".[48]

52 Infantry Brigade 'Report on Operations' catalogues additional difficulties:

> The barrage was a very difficult one to follow as there were no natural features, such as parallel roads, on which it dwelt.[49] The road in S20 a and S14 c had to be crossed by the right flank at 0554 and by the left flank at 0632. The advance had to be made for the first 1,000 yards with the left flank thrown back at an angle of 45 degrees from the line of

41   TNA: PRO WO95/2014 War Diary 9th Battalion Duke of Wellington's (West Riding Regiment).
42   Ibid.
43   TNA: PRO WO95/2011 War Diary 52 Infantry Brigade HQ.
44   Ibid.
45   Ibid.
46   TNA: PRO WO95/2014 War Diary 9th Battalion Duke of Wellington's (West Riding Regiment).
47   Ibid. Commonwealth War Grave Commission records show a total of 40 fatalities for 4 November, the five officers being: Captain George Douglas Gelder, age 24; Second-Lieutenant Claude Arthur Bouchier, age 36; Second-Lieutenant Edwin Wilson, age 21; Second-Lieutenant Henry Woodhouse, age 19, all buried in Romeries Communal Cemetery Extension, graves VII A 2, VII A 5, VII B 13 & VII A 4 respectively, and Lieutenant William Charles Roche Rowland, age 23, buried in Ruesnes Communal Cemetery, grave I B 5.
48   Ibid.
49   TNA: PRO WO95/2011 War Diary 52 Infantry Brigade HQ. This was not strictly true: the barrage paused on the road running north-south through S14 c & S20 a & c until zero + 45 minutes in order to synchronise the advance with that of 38th Division to the south.

advance. This was further complicated by the enclosed nature of the country and necessitated constant reference to the compass bearing. The mist increased the difficulty of recognising the line the barrage had reached and it appears to have been a little thin. There was undoubtedly a certain amount of short shooting: Lieutenant-Colonel Driver reported at 1000 hours that he was at S21 a. Central and that 4.5" shells were falling in S20 b.[50]

The 12/Manchester were on the brigade right. "Their task was a comparatively small one".[51] Their initial move to the 'pause line' meant an advance of 500 yards for their left flank, and only 100 yards for their right. They were to halt just after the Englefontaine – Futoy road and advance at 0620 in conjunction with the 38th Division on their right.

> The country on the right was very enclosed and had proved impassable during a previous attack by the 38th Division. This was on account of the hedges being strongly staked and reinforced with plain wire the thickness of a slate pencil. This resisted any ordinary wire cutter. These hedges were flanked by a large number of carefully concealed machine guns. […] Special efforts were made to obtain 'bulldog' wire cutters and additional cutting tools.[52]

D and B Companies lined up on the road running diagonally through square 19 d, with A and C companies in close support. The attack went in on time, "assisted by [an] excellent artillery barrage, supplemented at intervals by M.G. barrage".[53] The left flank was forced to move faster than the right, the latter being initially almost stationary, "in order to bring the line of the attack N-S".[54] An enemy barrage came down on the jumping off positions almost immediately and remained there for some time, as did some of the unfortunate infantry. The left companies "got away from under it", but the right companies "suffered considerably".[55] As the advance moved on at 0620, the "enemy put up a determined resistance […] and his morale appeared good".[56] The hedges were a formidable obstacle, as feared, but some of the 'bulldog' wire cutters had been acquired and "proved invaluable".[57]

The mist persisted for a good two hours after Zero and this "somewhat assisted the attack […] as our front line troops were better able to surprise the Bosche in the closely wooded Forest of Mormal through which we were attacking".[58] During the advance, the right company's commander (probably Second-Lieutenant (Acting Captain) J.W. Barton MC) was wounded

50   TNA: PRO WO95/2011 War Diary 52 Infantry Brigade HQ. 'Report on Operations of the 52nd Infantry Brigade'. Whether the Colonel's 4.5s in S20 b were in fact German shells is up for discussion, but the lack of company officers so soon after the start of the assault may explain some of the misfortune which befell the battalion. Forty fatal casualties puts the 9th Duke of Wellington's third in the Battalion 'League Table' for the day, surpassed only by the 9th Battalion Royal Sussex Regiment (42) and the 16th Battalion Lancashire Fusiliers (52).
51   Ibid.
52   Ibid. These wire obstacles would have been tackled by the tank, had it crossed the start line.
53   TNA: PRO WO95/2012 War Diary 12th Battalion Manchester Regiment.
54   Ibid.
55   TNA: PRO WO95/2011 War Diary 52 Infantry Brigade HQ. 'Report on Operations of the 52nd Infantry Brigade'.
56   Ibid.
57   Ibid.
58   TNA: PRO WO95/2012 War Diary 12th Battalion Manchester Regiment.

and captured, but the support company drove on and overran the position where he had been held prisoner and were able to release him. "The left Coys were able to advance from hedgerow to hedgerow making use of rifle grenades to deal with MG's and taking a considerable number of prisoners".[59]

The Blue Line was gained on time, for an estimated casualty total of 6 officers and 100 other ranks. The battalion suffered 32 fatalities that day, all 'other ranks'. The whole brigade was thus on the Blue Line, ready for the 51 Brigade to move through their positions and assault the Red Line. Brigadier-General W. Allason, commanding 52 Brigade, made a number of important observations in his after-action report. He mentioned telephone lines and power buzzers being set up between the 12/Manchester and 52 Brigade HQ, but had to affirm that these were interrupted immediately at Zero hour by the enemy bombardment, adding that the first message to come through to Brigade HQ, other than by runner, was a wireless message timed at 1100 hours. Visual signalling was severely hampered by the mist; none of the 'golden rain' rockets sent up were seen. The use of Thermit to mark the limits of the barrage was seen as a positive, particularly in view of the weather. It had been arranged that each man in the attack would carry five rifle grenades: a large proportion of these were fired and proved invaluable in getting forward through the enclosed country to the west of the forest. He pessimistically concludes, however, that "an attack in daylight would probably have failed with heavy casualties owing to the number of German machine guns well dug in and protected by strong fences".[60] His brigade had made their objectives, but had suffered the highest number of brigade fatalities recorded for 4 November: 85, including six officers.[61] 52 Brigade losses from 4–11 November were as follows:

	Officers			Other Ranks			Total
	K	W	M	K	W	M	
10th Lancashire Fusiliers	1	3	–	8	76	2	90
9th Duke of Wellington's	5	8	–	30	193	3	239
12th Manchester Regt.	–	6	–	23	104	9	142
Total	6	17	–	61	373	13	471

The units of 51 Brigade were tasked with the capture of the Red Line. This followed the line of the road running north-south through squares S17 and S23 and was between 1500 and 2000 yards east of the Blue Line. The battalions moved into their assembly trenches on the evening of 3 November, trenches "which had been dug by 21st Division running parallel to and immediately behind the front line trenches".[62] They were arranged with 10th Battalion

59   TNA: PRO WO95/2011 War Diary 52 Infantry Brigade HQ, 'Report on Operations of the 52nd Infantry Brigade'.
60   Ibid.
61   This is calculated from Commonwealth War Grave Commission records and 'Soldiers Died in the Great War' CD ROM. The second worst brigade fatality figure is for 96 Brigade (32nd Division), whose attempts to cross the Sambre Canal south-west of Landrecies *failed*. (See Chapter 7).
62   TNA: PRO WO95/2006 War Diary 51 Infantry Brigade HQ.

Sherwood Foresters (Nottinghamshire & Derbyshire Regiment) [10/Sherwood Foresters] on the left, 7th Battalion Lincolnshire Regiment [7/Lincolnshire] in the centre and 7th Battalion Border Regiment [7/Border] on the right. The flanking battalions adopted a three-company frontage, and the Lincolns in the centre a two-company frontage. As planned, the 51 Brigade units moved off at Zero, clearing the start line as soon as possible. In the event, this was an important decision, as the enemy barrage "came down very quickly and was the best that he had done since August 23rd".[63] The 10/Sherwood Foresters had spent an uncomfortable night in the assembly trenches: enemy shellfire accounted for 14 casualties, including Second-Lieutenant Taylor and the Regimental Sergeant-Major wounded, and the deaths of Captain A.Kerr and one other rank.

They moved off from these trenches at 0520 in platoon columns and advanced 500 yards behind the 10/Lancashire Fusiliers. B Company, (Lieutenant Holding MC) was on the left, A Company (Captain Brandt MC) in the centre, C Company (Lieutenant Lynch) on the right, with D Company (Second-Lieutenant Foster) in support. Movement was difficult: "the country was covered with thickly fenced orchards to the north of Futoy & the Battn had great difficulty in getting forward – particularly because the enemy very heavily shelled the village for some long time. Companies moved by platoons in fours and in following up 2Lt. Wilson was killed, Lts. Holding & Lynch & 2Lt. Street were wounded".[64] Nevertheless, the battalion was formed up on the first objective by 0835. Twelve minutes later both they and the resumed creeping barrage set off for the Red Line. They reached their objective "without meeting much opposition",[65] capturing it "in magnificent style".[66] Lieutenant Winkley, the battalion Signalling Officer is singled out for particular praise, having done "exceptionally good work during the attack, and maintained touch with Bde HQ by telephone throughout".[67] A Company had managed to capture two field guns, complete with horse teams and officers, along with five machine guns, though their commanding officer, Captain Brandt, was wounded just as the objective was reached. Despite meeting "very little opposition", indeed the battalion diary states that "throughout this attack there was very little MG or rifle fire",[68] the battalion suffered 102 casualties (4 officers and 98 other ranks). Such was the damage that C and D companies were amalgamated with Second-Lieutenant Foster in command, Second-Lieutenant Ross taking over A Company from the unfortunate Brandt. Fatal casualties for the day can be confirmed at 17.

In the centre of the brigade front, the 7/Lincolnshire had reached their assembly trenches on 3 November by 2100 hours, after setting off from Poix-du-Nord at 1930 on a "dark and rainy night".[69] The diarist describes "heavy crashes of 5.9's and .77 HE" around the trenches during

---

63   TNA: PRO WO95/2008 War Diary 10th Battalion Sherwood Foresters (Nottinghamshire & Derbyshire Regiment).
64   Ibid. Lieutenant Lynch was sent back to the Casualty Clearing Station suffering from shell shock. Second-Lieutenant E.E. Wilson, age 33, is buried in Englefontaine British Cemetery, grave B 1.
65   Ibid.
66   Ibid. Narrative: "The Battle of the Forest of Mormal".
67   TNA: PRO WO95/2006 War Diary 51 Infantry Brigade.
68   TNA: PRO WO95/2008 War Diary 10th Battalion Sherwood Foresters (Nottinghamshire & Derbyshire Regiment).
69   TNA: PRO WO95/2007 War Diary 7th Battalion Lincolnshire Regiment.

the night, but adds that these did "no damage" and that "the men got some sleep in spite of the rain and cold".[70]

The rain had given way to mist by Zero Hour and the battalion moved off, C Company on the left, A Company on the right, B Company in support and D company in reserve. They crossed the Englefontaine – Le Quesnoy road "close on the heels"[71] of the 9/Duke of Wellington's, but then halted for 15 minutes in the orchards 200 yards beyond the road to "give the [Dukes] time to get forward".[72] The battalion then "moved forward in a fog so dense that it was impossible to see a man 20 paces off. 'B' Company moved away to its right in this and got lost".[73] Reorganisation took place as the battalion crossed the road (S14 c and S20 a) and was here joined by a company of the 9/Duke of Wellington's that had somehow detached itself from its own battalion, and took B Company's place in support. Moving forward from there, the mist and the oblique lines of hedges "deflected"[74] the whole battalion to the left and they found themselves at Futoy village: "2 Coys moved down each side of the village keeping clear of the road which was at the time being shelled by our own heavy artillery with great accuracy and effect".[75] Despite their detour, the 7/Lincolnshire (or at least three-quarters of them!), were on the Blue Line at 0835, ready to advance as per the timetable. A Company, with D Company in support, moved across the open[76] in square 22 c until they reached the Route St Hubert (S22 d. 1.3), whereupon they followed it as far as the Red Line. C Company advanced through S16 c[77] and then in a south-easterly direction along the Laie Hequet, rejoining the rest of the battalion on the Red Line (the Route Duhamel). During these manoeuvres, "very little opposition was met with, a little desultory rifle and machine gun fire".[78] The objective was reached at 1041. One hundred and 20 prisoners were sent back and 10 field guns had been captured, along with eight machine guns. B Company had "meantime rejoined".[79] A message sent from the Red Line reported casualty figures: Second-Lieutenants W.T Epton, A. Cliff and S. Sheckell were wounded, and it was estimated that 96 other ranks were also casualties. Battalion strength was estimated at 16 officers and 394 other ranks.[80]

The 7/Border had had a bad October. They had been in action in a night attack on the 20th and had lost nine officers, including their commanding officer Lieutenant-Colonel W.E. Thomas DSO MC, killed in a German counter attack. Overall casualties for the month numbered 247. On the morning of 4 November they moved forward, as per plan, at 0530, 500 yards behind the 12/Manchester. "During this move, however, our 'B' Coy found a gap

70 Ibid.
71 Ibid.
72 Ibid.
73 Ibid.
74 Ibid.
75 Ibid. Perhaps Lieutenant-Colonel. Driver of 9th Duke of Wellington's was right to claim that his own heavy artillery was shooting *behind* his advanced position. (See fn. 50).
76 Ibid. In order to avoid the thicker parts of the forest.
77 The main units had become separated by a distance of approximately 1000 yards, though the 51 Brigade HQ narrative relates that "skirmishers worked through the thick wood in S22." TNA: PRO WO95/2006 War Diary 51 Infantry Brigade.
78 TNA: PRO WO95/2007 War Diary 7th Battalion Lincolnshire Regiment.
79 Ibid.
80 Ibid. Fatal casualties for the day totalled 10. Simple arithmetic would suggest that the battalion attacked with a strength of 19 officers and 490 other ranks.

between the Manchester Regt. and the 38th Division on the right. The Officer commanding 'B' Company got into the gap and succeeded in capturing 35 prisoners".[81] All companies were on the Blue Line ready for the advance at 0847: A, B and C Companies were in front, with D Company in reserve. They followed the creeping barrage and found it "pretty easy going"[82] until they were within 100 yards of their objective. Here, they came under "fairly heavy"[83] machine gun and rifle fire. One machine gun team, at S23 c 25.65 (directly on the road that marked the objective), was "very persistent".[84] Four of the team were killed and one wounded in the bayonet charge that finally put the gun out of action. This, it appears, was their only serious opposition and the Red Line was gained with no further alarms by 1040. At 1417 they were ordered forward onto final positions just short of the Brown Line (between S23 b 80.35 & S24 c 3.3) where they spent a "very quiet"[85] night. During the operation they had captured 127 prisoners, eight machine guns, one trench mortar and four field guns. "There were many dead Bosche to be seen in the wood".[86] The 7/Border's casualties were three officers[87] and 55 other ranks. Fatalities for the day were 18.

The 51 Brigade diary summarises the Brigade's casualties for 4 November as follows:

	Officers	Other Ranks
7th Lincolns	3	96
7th Border Regt.	3	55
10th Sherwood Foresters	6	98
Total	12	249

Of these, 45 were fatalities.

The capture of the Brown and Green Lines fell to the units of 50 Infantry Brigade (Brigadier-General J.F.R. Hope). This, after a pause of over two hours, during which artillery was brought up to support the operation, would take place almost entirely within the area of the Forêt de Mormal. On the afternoon of 1 November, Hope had given a lecture to all officers and NCOs in the Brigade on 'Wood Fighting'.[88] The units of 50 Brigade, arranged north to south, were 7th Battalion East Yorkshire Regiment [7/East Yorks], 6th Battalion Dorsetshire Regiment [6/Dorsetshire] and 10th Battalion The Prince of Wales's Own (West Yorkshire Regiment) [10/West Yorks]. Their assembly for the attack was carried out in stages: they moved off from the area around the village of Poix-du-Nord at 0130 on 4 November and arrived at their first assembly point on the Englefontaine – Arbre de la Croix road (south-east – north-west in squares X28 & 29) at 0430. By 0930 they were on the Englefontaine – Louvignies road (north – south in squares X24 & S13). "There was considerable hostile shelling at this time and some casualties were incurred, including Captain F.C. Tonkin DSO MC, Adjutant, 7th East Yorkshire

81 TNA: PRO WO95/2008 War Diary 7th Battalion Border Regiment. 'Attack on Mormal Forest'.
82 Ibid.
83 Ibid.
84 Ibid.
85 Ibid.
86 Ibid.
87 Second-Lieutenants H.Hutchins, H.C. Sykes & J. Gibson were wounded.
88 TNA: PRO WO95/1999 War Diary 50 Infantry Brigade HQ.

Regiment, who was fatally wounded".[89] The final stage, the assembly behind 51 Brigade on the Red Line, was completed by 1130. "This assembly was somewhat impeded by a barrage fired by our own guns apparently in answer to a RED Smoke bomb dropped by an aeroplane in S16 d. The barrage continued on Squares S22 b & d from 1200 to 1230 hours; it was luckily mostly behind our assembly position but caused some casualties to the 6th Dorsetshire Regiment and the 51st Infantry Brigade".[90]

The brigade began its advance proper at 1300. The artillery support was less than satisfactory: it was, on the right, "as well carried out as could be expected under the circumstances, which rendered a barrage extremely difficult".[91] In the centre and on the left "it was not possible to recognise a barrage line. One or two batteries on the left fired consistently short from 01.00 hours to 2.30 hours [1300–1430]. This caused some 20 casualties to the 7th East Yorkshire Regiment and considerably hindered their advance. In the centre, no barrage opened at 01.00 hours but at 02.00 hours, Artillery commenced to fire roughly on an area along the grid line between S18 and 24 squares as far east as the ROUTE FLAQUETTE. The 6th Dorsetshire Regt lost two killed and 14 wounded as the result of this shoot, which made touch difficult to maintain in the advance".[92]

The 7/East Yorks, on the left, conformed only roughly to the Brigade assembly orders: they were gathered at 0300 to the north of Poix-du-Nord and moved to the first assembly position. There, at 0600, "all ranks were served with a hot breakfast"[93] before moving off at 0715 to their second assembly position, their arrival there being reported to brigade HQ at 0850. They moved on from there at 1015, but came under machine gun and artillery fire "whilst passing through the orchards of Futoy in S14 a & b from the enemy who appeared to be still holding Louvignies. In order to avoid this fire I [Lieutenant-Colonel East King] took the main body through S15 c & d, with one Company detailed to watch the left flank but not to become involved outside our area".[94] The author will quote extensively from this document. It is written from a very personal viewpoint – that of Battalion Commander, by Lieutenant-Colonel East King – and allows us insight into the thinking of such a commander as he reacts to developing situations and guides his men to their objectives. A cynic may suggest that he puts himself in a favourable light. On arrival at the Red Line, East King found the left of the 10/Sherwood Foresters in the air at S17 a 7.2, the 37th Division on their left being nowhere to be seen. The enemy were still holding positions in square S10, that is, behind the 17th Division's left flank, so he formed a defensive flank at around midday. Half an hour later he sent out two platoons to extend the line to the left and occupy the crossroads at S17 a 6.8.

At 1259, the battalion began its move forward "despite the fact that the enemy was on and in rear of our left flank".[95] With this in mind, East King ordered his support company to advance

---

89   Ibid. Captain Frederick Cuthbert Tonkin, age 24, is buried in Forest Communal Cemetery, Grave C 34.
90   Ibid.
91   Ibid.
92   Ibid.
93   TNA: PRO WO95/2005 War Diary 7th Battalion East Yorkshire Regiment. 'Narrative of Operations in the Forêt de Mormal'.
94   Ibid.
95   Ibid.

on that flank "echeloned in rear of the leading company".[96] Almost immediately he received a message from the left company of the 6/Dorsetshire on his right to the effect that their right was "held up and that they were not moving forward without further orders".[97] East King "immediately sent a written order ordering them to move forward at once on [his] right flank failing direct orders from their CO to the contrary. This was done".[98]

By 1500, the leading troops of 7/East Yorks were in squares S18 a & c, though East King was complaining bitterly that the "Barrage from our guns was most ragged, many shells falling were in rear of our Assembly Positions, [...] shells falling on my Reserve Company when in S17 b as late as 1500 hours".[99] They were in touch with the Dorsets on the right, but the left flank remained a problem. "Here we were held up by heavy enemy machine gun fire from direction of wood in T13 a & c and some advanced posts in S18 b & d. [...] By outflanking the advanced posts and attacking them from the flank and rear, we had completely mopped these up by 1630 hrs, capturing 12 prisoners and 6 machine guns & killing 14 of the enemy machine gunners. These captured guns were then turned upon the enemy positions in the wood [...] and we continued the advance by short rushes".[100] One platoon was ordered to work its way forward to the crossroads at S18 b 5.9 in order to establish a liaison post with the Somerset Light Infantry of 37th Division, but there was no sign of them until eight o'clock that evening, when a post was finally created at S12 d 9.3. By that time, the 7/East Yorks line ran from that point southwards to the road at T13 a 0.4, and from there south-eastwards along the road to approximately T13 c 4.9. With the Dorsets still not up, East King was forced to throw back a one company defensive flank from there to about S18 d .6.[101] "This line was reported to Brigade with a

Second-Lieutenant Frederick W. Selch, attached 7th Battalion East Yorkshire Regiment. Romeries Communal Cemetery Extension. (Author)

96   Ibid.
97   Ibid.
98   Ibid.
99   Ibid.
100 Ibid. The Narrative of 50 Brigade gives Lt-Col. East King credit for his part in this action: "... these posts were successfully dealt with largely owing to the personal gallantry and leadership of Lt-Colonel G.EAST KING DSO." TNA: PRO WO95/1999 War Diary 50 Infantry Brigade HQ. He was clearly not solely responsible: "2nd Lt. H.A. Disney MC DCM, 17th Bn MGC fought his guns with great skill and turned the enemy's guns against them. In all, about 12 enemy M.G.'s were used in this manner by the MG Section, and proved of great use in keeping down the enemy's fire whilst the posts were outflanked." Ibid. Luckily, a "good supply of cartridges" had been captured along with the guns. See Atteridge, *History of the 17th (Northern) Division*, p. 459.
101 See Map 9a.

disposition map at 2100 hrs together with estimated casualties given as 2 Officers killed[102] [...] 2 Officers wounded[103] & 100 ORs."[104]

Battalion HQ was visited at 2230 by the Brigade Major, Captain Barbour, who "gave instructions that no further advance would take place so that 21st Division would have a definite line to advance from the next morning".[105] These orders were cancelled at around 0200 on 5 November: it had become clear that the Germans in front of 7/East Yorks had melted away in the darkness and that the advance could resume unopposed. East King completes the story: "I was ordered to establish the Line of Final Objective viz road running N & S through T18 a & d. [The Green Line] I took up three platoons at once and by 5.30 hrs we had gained final objective without further opposition".[106] The casualty figures recorded by 50 Brigade HQ for 7/East Yorks were: Officers – two killed, two wounded. Other Ranks – 13 killed, 86 wounded, nine missing.[107] Battalion fatalities can be confirmed at 22.[108]

The 6/Dorsetshire (Lieutenant-Colonel E.S. Weldon), in the centre of the Brigade front, left Vendegies at 0210 and suffered eight casualties from enemy shell fire even before they reached their assembly positions at 0400. They crossed the Englefontaine – Louvignies road at around 0920 and the diarist adds at this point: "Enemy on the run" and with "very little enemy shelling"[109] to contend with, they were at their jumping off positions on the Red Line by 1230. They went into action with four Lewis Guns per company, 12 magazines per gun being taken into the line,[110] but with "very little barrage from our own artillery".[111] Just over an hour later, at 1410, they had reached the north-eastern sector of square 24 b when "our 18 pounders put down a heavy barrage on our leading Coys, causing a number of casualties".[112] By half past three, the Dorsets' rather lacklustre assault was being held up by machine gun fire from the far side of the Route de la Flaquette (north-west to south-east through squares S18 d & T19 a) and from the village of Locquignol. One episode may show that the Dorsets were not totally devoid of fighting spirit: a patrol from A Company, led by C.S.M. Britt, "rushed an enemy MG post to their front holding five MG's and a post 200 yards to their left flank holding two MG's. Seven of the enemy machine gunners were killed and seven MG's captured. This operation was successful chiefly owing to the cool, clear fire orders and gallant leadership of CSM Britt".[113] The Dorsets were able to take up positions facing the Route de la Flaquette, D and A Companies in front, C in support and B in reserve with Battalion HQ, but were "unable to

102 The second officer killed was Second-Lieutenant Frederick William Selch (9th Yorkshire Regt, attached 7th East Yorks) who is buried in Romeries Communal Cemetery Extension, Grave VIII B 18. The Commonwealth War Graves Commission incorrectly records his date of death as 14 November 1918.
103 Lieutenant K. Middlemiss MC and Second-Lieutenant E.L. Stead.
104 TNA: PRO WO95/2005 War Diary 7th Battalion East Yorkshire Regiment.
105 Ibid.
106 Ibid.
107 TNA: PRO WO95/1999 War Diary 50 Infantry Brigade HQ.
108 Commonwealth War Graves Commission & Soldiers Died in the Great War CD ROM.
109 TNA: PRO WO95/2001 War Diary 6th Battalion Dorsetshire Regiment.
110 This is stipulated in Battalion Operation Orders No. XI, dated 3.11.18.
111 TNA: PRO WO95/2001 War Diary 6th Battalion Dorsetshire Regiment.
112 Ibid.
113 TNA: PRO WO95/1999 War Diary 50 Infantry Brigade HQ. One can assume that Lewis Guns played a major role here.

Present-day Locquignol Church. (Author)

continue the advance".[114] Following the retreat of the Germans during the night, orders came at 0500 and a platoon from each company was sent forward to the Green Line objective, this being reached at 0700 on 5 November. The 6/Dorsetshire had suffered eight fatalities and 24 wounded, including two wounded officers.[115]

The 10/West Yorks (Lieutenant-Colonel W. Gibson) breakfasted at 0700 on the morning of 4 November. Their subsequent approach to their jumping off positions on the Red Line were without incident and they moved off into the attack on time, "keeping close to the barrage",[116] D Company on the left, A on the right, B Company in support and C in reserve. Half an hour later, around 1330, they had reached the north-south grid line S24 a 0.0 – S30 a 0.0 having met "little or no resistance".[117] By quarter past two, D Company had reached the *Institut Forestier* (S24 d. 4.4) and cleared this building within 25 minutes, having killed the enemy garrison within. They then placed a Vickers Machine Gun on the roof to give covering fire to their next move forward. By 1500, however, both lead companies were held up by heavy machine gun fire from both flanks and from the village of Locquignol, where the Germans had a machine gun firing from the church tower. D Company was in disarray, having suffered around 35 casualties, and were ordered to stand fast while A Company were moved north and then east around the *Institut Forestier,* passing through D Company to continue the advance towards the village. Meanwhile, B Company were to push forward through A Company's previous position and continue the advance south of, and parallel to, the road leading to Locquignol. It was dark by now, and both companies were eventually halted short of the village.[118] At 1710, Captain Lawson and two other ranks of B Company patrolled to within 200 yards of Locquignol church, encountering two enemy soldiers whom they killed. They were fired upon by two machine guns south of the church and were forced to retire. A Company's Captain C. Archer MC was also able to push a patrol out a little way forward, but by then it had been decided that no further attack on the village would be made until artillery from 95th Bde RFA and trench mortars could be brought up. Locquignol was to be assaulted from the north at 2200. It had not been possible to arrange the attack for any earlier, as communication with the artillery units had proved difficult.[119]

During this halt in proceedings, the Brigade Major, Captain P.S. Barber, paid a visit to Battalion HQ (by now in the *Institut Forestier*) with orders issued at 1930 "stating that a definite line must be reported to Division before 2200 hours. This line was therefore reported as it stood and attack cancelled."[120] D Company were then moved forward and north in order to fill the gap between A Company and the 6/Dorsetshire, "whose position on the left was uncertain".[121]

---

114 TNA: PRO WO95/2001 War Diary 6th Battalion Dorsetshire Regiment.
115 TNA: PRO WO95/1999 War Diary 50 Infantry Brigade HQ. The 6th Dorsetshire War Diary names only one wounded officer: Second-Lieutenant D.F.Mills.
116 TNA: PRO WO95/2004 War Diary 10th Battalion Prince of Wales's Own (West Yorkshire Regiment).
117 Ibid.
118 See Map 9a.
119 TNA: PRO WO95/1985 War Diary 17th Division HQ & TNA: PRO WO95/1999 War Diary 50 Infantry Brigade HQ.
120 TNA: PRO WO95/2004 War Diary 10th Battalion Prince of Wales's Own (West Yorkshire Regiment).
121 Ibid.

At 2300, two patrols were sent out, one to reconnoitre the village and another to try to establish a post at the major crossroads east of it. (T25 b 0.8). The former was able, by midnight, to report that Locquignol had been vacated by the enemy. The latter had established a post just west of the crossroads, one platoon strong, but in close touch with an enemy post just to the east of it. C Company was accordingly ordered forward to occupy the village and to establish posts to the east and south-east. By 0500, the enemy was seen retiring through the thicker parts of the wood east of the Green Line and B Company was ordered forward to establish platoons on the battalion's final objective. This was complete by 0630 on 5 November. 10/West Yorks casualties numbered one officer wounded, 10 other ranks killed, 35 wounded and five missing. Fatalities can be fixed at 12.[122]

50 Brigade War Diary gives total casualties for the day as: 30 killed, 150 wounded and 17 missing, a total of 197. [123] The diary also estimates the number of Germans killed on the Brigade front to be 100, with 74 machine guns captured.

Total fatalities for the 17th Division on 4 November amount to 172, and wounded can be estimated at 710. This is a casualty rate of almost 14 per cent amongst the engaged infantry battalions. The 17th Division War Diary concludes its account of 4 November with a section entitled "Remarks on the Attack." It begins: "The attack worked to plan in the early stages, but not in the later stages".[124] The early stages, although 'successful', had been the most costly. The report continues:

> The mist undoubtedly assisted the attack in the earlier stages by obstructing the view of the enemy Machine Gunners, but it made the Artillery barrage difficult to follow and there is no doubt that the most advanced troops, who had the difficult task of a change of direction to carry out during the attack, ran into our barrage and incurred casualties from it.[125]

The next section dwells on the "failure of 50th Brigade to gain its objectives rapidly".[126] It suggests that a daylight advance against a large number of machine guns in relatively open ground can only be successful if the attack is on a wide front and has "effective" artillery support. The implication is that the Artillery messed up: "The artillery barrage in support of 50th Brigade was not a success: on the right the barrage was reported good – in the centre an hour late, and on the left several batteries to be shooting consistently short".[127] The idea of rushing sections of 18 pounders forward so quickly along a small number of available routes and expecting a viable barrage at the end of it is described as "questionable".[128] The fact that this later barrage was not

122 According to Commonwealth War Graves Commission records and 'Soldiers Died in the Great War'
       CD ROM.
123 TNA: PRO WO95/1999 War Diary 50 Infantry Brigade HQ. CWGC & SDGW records show
       final Brigade fatalities to be 42.
124 TNA: PRO WO95/1985 War Diary 17th Division HQ.
125 Ibid.
126 Ibid.
127 Ibid.
128 Ibid.

to move through the denser parts of the forest, but was to concentrate on the rides, tracks and borders of the cleared areas, made it an almost impossible task for the gunners.[129]

The success of the attack (based purely on objectives gained) came at a price: the 17th Division's casualties were the heaviest divisional casualties of the day.[130]

Far from being an all-arms attack, on this divisional sector, and particularly in the 50 Brigade sector, it descended into an infantry versus infantry fight where the fire power of the platoon and the drive, skill and courage of individual commanders became deciding factors. These factors, evident to some extent in both flanking battalions of 50 Brigade, though apparently largely lacking in the centre, were not enough to ensure the timely execution of the plan. Its ultimate completion was down to the withdrawal of German troops during the night, this allowing a final unopposed advance of some 2,000 yards. The author of 17th Division's diary seems to be at odds with the reality of the situation when he writes that "The Forest of Mormal was believed to be a much more serious obstacle than proved to be the case. Except in patches it was found during the attack to be no obstacle at all, owing to extensive clearings which had been made."[131] It was in precisely these clearings that 50 Brigade troops were held up, with commanders unwilling to take the bold option to bypass the centres of resistance as orders had required. The author then goes on to suggest a different reason for the hold-up: "The cause of the failure of 50th Brigade to gain its objective rapidly was not new – it was demonstrated once again that in face of numerous machine guns infantry can in open ground only be got forward during daylight by effective artillery and MG support and if attack is to be made on a wide front."[132] The 38th Division, on their right, albeit with better artillery provision, was about to prove this assertion wrong.

38th Division[133]

The task of the 38th Division (Major-General T.A. Cubitt) was very similar to that of the 17th: the three infantry brigades, 115, 113 and 114 were allocated, respectively, the Blue, Red and Green objective lines. The attack would involve an advance of between 6,000 and 7,000 yards, largely through the Forêt de Mormal, on a frontage of approximately 2,000 to 2,500 yards. There were no settlements or villages of any size in this sector of the forest, but the criss-cross pattern of rides and tracks was repeated, and these were to be used to great advantage by the troops of this division.

---

129   The artillery barrage trace/overlay map makes no allowance for these complications. It merely shows a normal linear timed advance across the area to be attacked by 50 Brigade, with lifts of 100 yards every 6 minutes from Z+449 to Z+675, this divided between five RFA Brigades, with no regard for battalion boundaries. Ibid.
130   See Appendix III.
131   TNA: PRO WO95/1985 War Diary 17th Division HQ.
132   Ibid.
133   See Map 10.

"The plan was perfectly straightforward".[134] The author goes on: "Owing to the very enclosed nature of the country the execution of the plan was not so simple".[135] Even so, their experience was to be very different from that of the 17th Division.

The timetable for the attack was as follows: 115 Infantry Brigade (Brigadier-General H.D. De Pree) would begin their advance at Zero + 45, that is 0615, in order to conform with the 18th Division on their right.[136] They would arrive on the Blue Line an hour later on the left flank, but not until 0800 on the right. The 113 Infantry Brigade (Brigadier-General H.E. ap Rhys-Price) was scheduled to complete the assault on the Red Line by 1030, and 114 Infantry Brigade (Brigadier-General T.R.C. Price), after a pause of between 90 and 110 minutes, would continue the advance, arriving on the final First Phase objective, the Green Line, at 1540 on the right and 1710 on the left.

The artillery would supply a creeping barrage, advancing 100 yards every six minutes "to give the infantry plenty of time to work their way through the enclosed country and forest".[137] This would continue as far as the Red Line. Thereafter, the efficacy of the barrage available to the advancing troops would depend on RFA Brigades being able to move their guns forward in time to lay down a barrage conforming to the final stages of the assault. 156 and 162 Brigades RFA would begin their moves forward as soon as the Blue Line was captured, taking up new positions east of Englefontaine in squares A.2 and S.26 respectively. 121 Brigade RFA would move its guns to squares A.3 and A.9 once the Red Line was in allied hands. 122 Brigade RFA would perform a similarly-timed move to squares S.27 and A.3.[138] "In this ingenious and skilful manner, Brigadier-General Topping, CRA 38th Division, arranged a powerful barrage to break the crust at the opening of the attack, and the infantry were provided with a reasonable barrage continually in front of them afterwards".[139] By sacrificing intensity, Topping had ensured continuity of the barrage, keeping enforced halts on the objective lines to a minimum. As we have seen earlier in this chapter, the 17th Division's attempts to provide a barrage for the latter stages of their attack had met with mixed fortune.

The 38th Division barrage was supplemented initially by Stokes Mortars, which subsequently moved forward with their respective Infantry Brigades, and by the 38th Machine Gun Battalion who fired over the village of Englefontaine onto the western edge of the forest and onto the Blue Line. They too then moved forward in order to protect lines occupied during the advance before finally coming under command of Brigadier-General H.E. ap Rhys-Price of 114 Infantry Brigade, in support of the final move onto the Green Line.

A section of four tanks of the 9th Tank Battalion was allocated to 38th Division, and were to act under the orders of Brigadier-General H.D. De Pree, commanding 115 Infantry Brigade. "They were to advance with the infantry and assist them by breaking down hedges and by engaging any hostile posts holding up the advance among the orchards, on the edge of the forest

134 H.D. De Pree, *A History of the 38th (Welsh) and 33rd Divisions in the Last Five Weeks of the Great War* (Reprinted from *Royal Artillery Journal*, 1933), p. 173.
135 Ibid. p. 173.
136 By 0615 the 17th Division's initial 'line straightening' manoeuvre would also be complete.
137 Ibid. p. 174.
138 See Map 10. Also, TNA: PRO WO95/2558 War Diary 114 Infantry Brigade HQ, 38th Division Artillery Order No.123, issued 2 November 1918.
139 De Pree, *The 38th (Welsh) Division*, p. 175.

or in the houses in A.2.c and S.26.a. As soon as the infantry had entered the forest, they were to withdraw to their rendezvous of the night before [West of Englefontaine]".[140]

On 2 November, a conference took place at Divisional Headquarters at 1700 hrs, when future operations were discussed, brigade commanders being present.[141] Earlier that day, tactical training had taken place in Vendegies Wood, involving troops of 115 Brigade, whilst those of 113 Brigade were practising "wood fighting".[142] The following morning, at 1030, the War Diary of 114 Brigade records a conference at their HQ where "CO's of all units concerned"[143] were made party to the details of the forthcoming attack. Detailed orders (Order No. 250) came down from Division on that day, accompanied, tellingly, by 'Tactical Instructions'. Troops were warned not to follow the barrage too closely in the wooded areas, being liable to injury from shells bursting in the tops of trees, and to expect hostile gas bombardments. Most importantly, however, point 7 details the method of advance to be adopted:

"It is to be impressed upon all down to Company Commanders that in thick woods loss of direction and control is to be expected, therefore extensions are quite out of place and advances are to be made on narrow fronts by Companies under the personal command and control of the Company Commander and if necessary the Battalion Commander with one Company as advanced guard." This was reinforced by Order No. S.S. 149/12, issued on 3 November:

Brigadiers should impress upon all Battalion Commanders the importance of getting forward, in tomorrow's attack, as rapidly as possible and as fast as the barrage permits. It is quite possible that, as we are attacking more by blocks of platoon or companies, as opposed to widely extended order, we shall leave pockets of enemy in places in the woods. **This does not matter,** [my emphasis] many other troops will be continually passing through from rear to front and the surrender of such pockets is ensured. The most important point is to get on and get on quickly, deliberately leaving gaps and keeping our own men together and in hand.[144]

Also on 3 November, Major-General Cubitt, commanding 38th Division, was able to visit most of the battalions under his command.[145]

"The attack was a splendid success"[146] states the War Diary of 115 Infantry Brigade. The brigade had lined up on their jumping off positions, just to the east of the village of Englefontaine, on a three battalion front, 17th Royal Welsh Fusiliers [17/RWF] on the left, 10th South Wales Borderers [10/SWB] in the centre, and 2nd Royal Welsh Fusiliers [2/RWF] on the right. Each battalion placed two companies in the front line, whose objective was the western edge of the forest. The two rear companies of each battalion would then "leapfrog on this line and move

140 De Pree, *The 38th (Welsh) Division*, p. 177.
141 TNA: PRO WO95/2558 War Diary 114 Infantry Brigade HQ.
142 TNA: PRO WO95/2560 War Diary 115 Infantry Brigade HQ & TNA: PRO WO95/2554 War Diary 113 Infantry Brigade HQ.
143 TNA: PRO WO95/2558 War Diary 114 Infantry Brigade HQ.
144 TNA: PRO WO95/2558 War Diary 114 Infantry Brigade HQ. S.S. 149/12 was issued by 38th Division GSO1, Lieutenant-Colonel J.E. Munby on 2 November 1918 and copies were distributed to all units down to battalion level.
145 TNA: PRO WO95/2540 War Diary 38th Division HQ.
146 TNA: PRO WO95/2560 War Diary 115 Infantry Brigade HQ.

direct to the final objective, the Blue Line".[147] It was the job of the original front companies to mop up any enemy defensive positions left in action along the edge of the forest, and then to reform and move forward in support of their comrades. They would fill in any gaps between units on the Blue Line: each battalion was operating on a frontage of around 700 yards, but companies were ordered "not to move on a greater front than 200 yards"[148] each, thus making gaps in the line inevitable. They were to move, in general terms, on a bearing 090 degrees. For the less technically minded, 38th Division orders also included the advice that this was "a little to the left of the sun."[149] Considering the hour of the assault and the prevailing weather conditions, this could be considered unhelpful.

The 17/RWF (Lieutenant-Colonel R.L. Beasley) on the left of the Brigade front, after practising 'wood fighting' on 1 November, had taken over positions from 14th Bn Welsh Regt. [14/Welsh] in the Englefontaine line on the following day. They passed "a quiet day" on the 3rd, before attacking at 0615 on the 4th.[150] All accounts[151] of this advance are brief, but agree that it was very successful: both objectives were taken "well up to time"[152] and casualties were light, totalling one officer and seven other ranks killed,[153] three officers and 41 other ranks wounded.

In the centre, the 10/SWB (Lieutenant-Colonel A.L Bowen) had also gone into the line on 3 November, but had been subjected to enemy artillery fire, suffering some casualties,[154] but no fatalities. They attacked in a dense fog with B and A Companies in front (left and right respectively), with D and C Companies in support. They were assisted by two tanks of 9th Tank Battalion, one of which appears to have "strayed"[155] slightly to the north from the 2/RWF area. One tank "proceeded to S.26.a.6.7 and cleared up machine gun positions, then continuing to the NW edge of the MORMAL forest, where it again dealt with several m.g. posts and broke down hedges to make passages for the infantry".[156] It subsequently developed engine trouble. The other headed straight for the edge of the forest, flattening hedges and neutralising machine gun posts as it went. It then entered the forest, strictly against orders, and became "bellied on a tree stump. The infantry commanders on the spot expressed themselves as particularly well pleased with the action of this tank".[157]

147 De Pree, *The 38th (Welsh) Division*, p. 178.
148 Ibid. p. 178.
149 TNA: PRO WO95/2540 War Diary 38th Division HQ.
150 TNA: PRO WO95/2561 War Diary 17th Battalion Royal Welsh Fusiliers.
151 See De Pree *A History of the 38th (Welsh)* p. 181; TNA: PRO WO95/2560 War Diary 115 Infantry Brigade HQ; TNAA:PRO WO95/2561 War Diary 17th Battalion Royal Welsh Fusiliers.
152 De Pree, *The 38th (Welsh) Division*, p. 181.
153 Temporary Second-Lieutenant Norman Edward Evans, age 20, of Liverpool and formerly RFC, is buried in Englefontaine British Cemetery, grave C 21. The fatalities, according to Commonwealth War Graves Commission records and Soldiers Died in the Great War CD ROM, totalled 16 other ranks.
154 The War Diary of 10th Battalion South Wales Borderers (TNA: PRO WO95/2562) puts the number at two other ranks wounded. C.T. Atkinson, in *The History of the South Wales Borderers 1914-1918* (London, Medici Society 1933) cites "nearly a dozen casualties including Second-Lieutenant Shawson wounded." p. 476.
155 De Pree, *The 38th (Welsh) Division*, p. 181.
156 TNA: PRO WO95/102 War Diary 2nd Tank Brigade.
157 Ibid.

The battalion's final objective, some 800 yards inside the forest, was reached by 0715. Opposition from elements of the *16th* and *58th German Infantry Divisions* was described as "very weak and easily overcome".[158] The "junior officers and NCO's had ample opportunities for showing their capacity to use ground and take advantage of the cover which hedges and enclosures offered".[159] Special praise goes to "Corporals Dover and Parker and [...] Lance Corporal Apps who were prominent in dealing with the machine gun posts".[160] The attack had cost the battalion 42 casualties, 10 of which were fatal, including Second-Lieutenant H. Jones[161] and the battalion Medical Officer, Lieutenant Cassell of the USA Medical Corps. By nightfall, they were in billets in Englefontaine.

On the right of the brigade front, the 2/RWF (Lieutenant-Colonel G.E.R. de Miremont) was formed up in their jumping off positions by 0500 on 4 November, D and C Companies in front, (left and right respectively), with A and B companies in support. Their advance was complicated by having the Ruisseau des Eclusettes on its right boundary. This stream "twists a great deal in its course",[162] meaning that the jumping off positions were on a frontage of only 500 yards, but their Blue Line objective was 1200 yards wide. This meant that once the leapfrog line (edge of the forest) had been reached, a third company had to push forward into the front line. A Company would push through D Company on the left, but B company would become the new right front company, extending the battalion line southwards, leaving C Company in the centre front line. With only D Company now left in support, it was deemed that they were insufficient in number to complete the mopping up operations required behind the Blue Line, and Battalion HQ was made responsible for mopping up the houses bypassed at the start of the attack in square A.2.c.

The attack commenced on time behind a "very heavy and accurate barrage".[163] The mist hampered the battalion, making it difficult to keep direction, but it "hampered the enemy's movements considerably and was helpful to the Battalion in overcoming opposition, which was particularly heavy in MG and TM fire".[164] The tank allocated to the 2/RWF failed to materialise, but one from the 18th Division area that had lost its way was commandeered and gave valuable assistance: a gap of some 400 yards appeared between the right of the battalion and the left of 18th Division, and the Germans were able to enfilade the Fusiliers' attack with machine gun and trench mortar fire from this area. The tank helped to neutralise the menace, but B Company suffered particularly and it was only through the "skilful handling"[165] of Captain Butler that the company made it to its objective. Once the Blue Line had been secured, D Company, from its position in support, crossed the Ruisseau des Esclusettes and cleared the enemy from their positions, pushing as far back as the outskirts of the village of Hecq, dropping posts as they went to form a defensive flank.

---

158 TNA: PRO WO95/2562 War Diary 10th Battalion South Wales Borderers.
159 C.T. Atkinson, in *The History of the South Wales Borderers 1914-1918* (London, Medici Society 1933), p. 477.
160 Ibid. p. 477.
161 Second-Lieutenant Herbert Thomas Jones, age 28, is buried in Terlincthun British Cemetery, grave VIII AC 10.
162 TNA: PRO WO95/2561 War Diary 2nd Battalion Royal Welsh Fusiliers.
163 Ibid.
164 Ibid.
165 De Pree, *The 38th (Welsh) Division*, p. 181.

The battalion had killed around 50 of the enemy and had captured four officers and 120 other ranks. Their own casualties were reported as one officer[166] and 10 other ranks killed, with 65 other ranks wounded or missing.[167]

Brigade casualties for the day can be estimated at:

	Officers		Other Ranks		Total
	K	W	K	W & M	
17th Royal Welsh Fus.	1	3	16	41	
10th South Wales Borderers	2	1	8	32	
2nd Royal Welsh Fus.	1	–	10	65	
Total	4	4	34	138	180

The task of taking the Red Line fell, as noted earlier, to 113 Infantry Brigade (Brigadier-General H.E. ap Rhys-Price). They were to move off from the Blue Line at 0830, 16th Royal Welsh Fusiliers [16/RWF} on the left, 14th Royal Welsh Fusiliers [14/RWF] in the centre and 13th Royal Welsh Fusiliers [13/RWF] on the right.

They had all reached their jumping off positions, some 200 yards behind the men of the 115 Brigade, by 0500.[168] They were instructed to dig in on these positions as protection against any German counter barrage, but only had half an hour to do so.

The 16 & 14/RWF were to make a "straightforward" attack.[169] With two companies in the front line, and two behind, the leading units were to capture the line of high ground between A.4.a.0.0 and S.28.a.0.2 and the road running northwest from the latter point.[170] The support companies would then leapfrog through and gain the final objective. They were expecting most resistance from the edges of the blocks of trees remaining in this sector of the forest and were advised to move along their edges and "clear them up from a flank".[171]

The instructions for the 13/RWF on the right were very different: one company was to take the high ground in A.10.a. The other three companies would move in column along the path of the stream in squares A.3.d, A.4. c & d and link up with the 8th Royal Berkshires [8/R. Berkshire] (18th Division) just south of the big six-way road junction in A.10.b., thus pinching out the open ground to the south of the stream.[172]

166 Second-Lieutenant William Robert Cyril Keepfer, age 24, formerly 3rd Dragoon Guards, is buried in Montay-Neuvilly Road Cemetery, grave II D 24.
167 Fatal casualties for the day proved to be one officer and nine other ranks. (Commonwealth War Graves Commission records and Soldiers Died in the Great War CD ROM). Only one has no known grave: Private 94469 William Henry Roberts is commemorated on the Vis-en-Artois Memorial, panel 6.
168 The assembly positions had been altered on 3 November in order to put the 113 Brigade troops nearer to the 115 Brigade jumping off positions.
169 De Pree, The 38th (Welsh) Division, p. 182.
170 See Map 10.
171 TNA: PRO WO95/2554 War Diary 113 Infantry Brigade HQ.
172 This type of infiltration tactic will be seen on a larger scale when the attack of the 114 Brigade is examined later in the chapter.

The men going into the attack would wear packs instead of haversacks and would carry one day's preserved meats and biscuits. They would have 30 sets of wire cutters per battalion as well as billhooks and axes divided up amongst platoons.[173] Leaving their assembly positions respectively at 0845, 0700 and 0715, the 16th, 14th and 13th Battalions moved off in artillery formation in good time to form up on the Blue Line, ready to attack at 0830.

The 16/RWF (Lieutenant-Colonel C.E. Davies) had suffered "heavy casualties"[174] at their assembly positions, but "very few casualties in the Forest".[175] The battalion War Diary is very matter of fact, stating simply "All objectives gained".[176] They suffered over 100 casualties on the day, including 30 killed. Three officers were recorded as wounded: Second-Lieutenants Gwilym Rees and Hugh Skyrme and the Reverend Irwin MC. The battalion spent the night of 4 and 5 November in their positions on the Red Line.

The 14/RWF moved into the attack at 0845. Their Commanding Officer, Lieutenant-Colonel B.W. Collier, had gone on leave on 3 November, but his stand-in, Major W.P. Wheldon DSO, was wounded as he left Battalion HQ early on the morning of the attack. Two other officers were killed by the same shell.[177] Major Wheldon managed to carry on until Lieutenant-Colonel Collier was recalled and was able to take over around one o'clock in the afternoon.

C Company, (Captain C.J.S. Nicholls), and D Company, (Lieutenant C.C. Danes) attacked first and captured the high ground in squares A.4.a and S.28.c before A Company (A/Captain W.D. Roderick MC) and B Company (Second-Lieutenant R.C. Seel) leapfrogged and reached the Red Line "without serious opposition".[178] The only officer casualty was Captain Roderick who received a slight wound. They had suffered 8 other ranks killed during the day.

The 13/RWF (Lieutenant-Colonel J.F. Leman), on the right wing of the brigade attack, had also suffered a few casualties in the assembly positions from the German barrage, but were able to move off at 0615. They were harassed by machine gun fire from the south as they advanced through the orchards in square A.2 to the Blue Line, but were able to deploy on time and move off into the attack. The isolated "batches of enemy who were still hiding in the undergrowth"[179] cared little for the fight and proved no obstacle to the advance. Once early opposition had been overrun, the Fusiliers were able to "swe[ep] onto their objectives well up to time".[180] Most casualties had occurred in the earlier stages of the assault and amounted to 10 killed and 65 wounded.[181]

The 113 Brigade War Diary only contains casualty figures for the period 4 – 10 November 1918. They are as follows:

173 TNA: PRO WO95/2554 War Diary 113 Infantry Brigade HQ.
174 TNA: PRO WO95/2556 War Diary 16th Battalion Royal Welsh Fusiliers. It is likely that the German retaliatory barrage prompted by the 17th Division's attack at 0530 was responsible for this.
175 Ibid.
176 TNA: PRO WO95/2556 War Diary 16th Battalion Royal Welsh Fusiliers.
177 Lieutenant William Burrows Clement Hunkin, age 22, and Second-Lieutenant Vivian Llewellyn, age 20, are buried in the same plot, C39, in Forest Communal Cemetery.
178 De Pree, *The 38th (Welsh) Division*, p. 184.
179 TNA: PRO: WO95/2555 War Diary 13th Battalion Royal Welsh Fusiliers.
180 De Pree, *The 38th (Welsh) Division*, p. 184.
181 The one officer killed was Captain Francis Jones-Bateman, age 22, who is buried in Cross Roads Cemetery, Fontaine-au-Bois, grave III D 22.

Lieutenant William Hunkin, 14th Battalion Royal Welsh Fusiliers. Forest Communal Cemetery. (Author)

Second-Lieutenant Vivian Llewellyn, 14th Battalion Royal Welsh Fusilers. Forest Communal Cemetery. Hunkin & Llewellyn were killed by the same shell. (Author)

Officers			Other Ranks		
K	W	M	K	W	M
3	8	–	39	272	20

Brigade fatalities for 4 November can be confirmed at 50.[182]

114 Infantry Brigade (Brigadier-General T.R.C. Price), tasked with the final objective of the day, the Green Line, consisted of the 13th, 14th and 15th Battalions Welsh Regiment, commanded respectively by Lieutenant-Colonels H.F. Hobbs, G.F. Brookes and E. Helme. The method of advance proposed was unique amongst units of Third Army that day: all three battalions would assemble on the far right sector of the Red Line positions (squares A.9.b and A.10.b) and would advance by companies in artillery formation along the rides through the forest, gradually fanning out to occupy previously-designated localities on the Brown and Green Lines.[183]

It is interesting to note the strengths of the three battalions and the numbers that actually went into battle:

---

182 Figure calculated from Commonwealth War Graves Commission records and Soldiers Died in the Great War CDRom.
183 See Map 10.

	13/Welsh		14/Welsh		15/Welsh	
	Off.	OR	Off.	OR	Off.	OR
Battalion Strength	29	837	27	775	30	855
Battle numbers	14	543	17	558	16	537[184]

Original orders envisaged the Brigade moving off from its assembly positions in the forest at 0930, but "the situation in front being somewhat obscure",[185] orders were received to hold fast await further instructions. Unfortunately, it was during this waiting period that the troops suffered "a certain amount of shelling".[186] Indeed, it was here that most of the day's casualties were incurred.[187] Orders for an immediate move came at 1100. By midday the 14/Welsh were in their jumping off positions on the Route du Chene Cuplet. The 13th and 15th Battalions were in their positions 1000 yards to the rear along the track running north-south through A.9.b 15 minutes later.

At 1220, the Brigade attacked behind a creeping barrage, the 15/Welsh on the right moving on a two-company front, (A & C Companies left and right in front, D & B Companies in support),[188] astride the Route d'Hecq, accompanied by two sections of the 38th Machine Gun Battalion and two Stokes Mortars. They were followed initially at a distance of 500 yards by the 13/Welsh. The 14/Welsh, advancing at 1300, became the left front battalion with twin spearheads moving north-east along parallel tracks. Opposition proved to be slight, though the 14/Welsh on the left encountered problems when confronted by machine gun fire across the open space in A.5.d. Retaliation from the machine gun section attached to the 15/Welsh soon neutralised the threat and the advance was able to continue to their objectives on the Brown Line (Route de Raucourt) relatively unchallenged. Once on the Brown Line, the 14/Welsh had completed their day's work. Subsequent advances by the other two battalions of the brigade left them in position as Brigade Support. They did later push patrols into the orchards on the south-western outskirts of Locquignol, where they encountered some desultory but ineffective small-arms fire from houses in the village. Casualties for the day totalled one officer (Lieutenant V.G. Gundrey MC) and 58 other ranks wounded. Only eight fatalities were suffered, and both leading battalions were on the Brown Line by 1415, slightly ahead of schedule. The 15/Welsh had captured 10 enemy guns on the way, and these were handed over to the artillery, who turned them on the German positions.

At 1440, the two support companies of 15/Welsh (D & B Companies) passed through the leading companies and headed for the Green Line. Simultaneously, the 13/Welsh advanced across the Brown Line on a one-company front on the north side of the Route d'Hecq. "Enemy resistance was of similar character as that encountered during the BROWN LINE advance".[189] That is to say, minimal.

The 15/Welsh were established on the Green Line by 1540. By 1715, three companies of 13/Welsh had positioned themselves along the portion of the Route d'Hecq that ran to the

184 TNA: PRO WO95/2558 War Diary 114th Infantry Brigade HQ.
185 TNA: PRO WO95/2559 War Diary 13th Battalion Welsh Regiment.
186 Ibid.
187 De Pree, *The 38th (Welsh) Division*, p. 185.
188 TNA: PRO WO95/2559 War Diary 15th Battalion Welsh Regiment.
189 TNA: PRO WO95/2558 War Diary 114th Infantry Brigade HQ Narrative of Operations.

south-east of Locquignol and established them-selves as the northern sector of the brigade's Green Line target, having encountered their only real resistance from a machine gun firing from the crossroads at B.1.d.4.9. A fourth company branched off to the north and made tentative moves towards the southern outskirts of Locquignol. One patrol made it as far as the church, but found the village unoccupied. "They fired a few shots to attract attention, but with no results".[190]

Infiltration tactics had worked splendidly, albeit against less than tenacious defenders. Casualties in the 13th Battalion amounted to two fatalities and around a dozen wounded. They had captured 137 prisoners. The 15/Welsh fatal casualties come to five, the one officer concerned dying of wounds later in the day.[191] Around 50 were wounded, including Lieutenant-Colonel Helme DSO.

At around 2230, the 13/Welsh reported that their patrols could find no enemy troops within 2000 yards of the crossroads in T.26.b, which marked their left flank. A and B Companies were ordered to advance at 0220 on 5 November and

Lieutenant Arthur Roberts, 15th Battalion Welsh Regiment. Forest Communal Cemetery. (Author)

were able to push east as far as the villages of Croix Daniel and Sarbaras, a further two miles. On the way, they managed to capture 40 prisoners along with a German Field Ambulance with 32 wounded Germans and one wounded soldier of the 14/RWF and 10 staff. Prisoners of 22 different German battalions from 10 regiments of five divisions had entered the 38th Divisional cage by the close of play on the 4th, but mainly from the *14th Division* and *58th Saxon Division*. A prisoner from the former was part of a draft of 100 men sent from Germany in late October: 40 of them had deserted en route in Luxembourg.[192]

Major De Pree sums up the Brigade performance thus:

> Three companies were on the move from 0700 on the 4th November till the same hour on the 5th, during which time they had covered a distance of 11½ miles, the first half of which was traversed under shell fire, and the second in continuous contact with the enemy. As a result of their efforts, troops of the 38th Division had penetrated to a depth of about 4 miles further than the divisions on the right and left, and had overrun the first objectives of the next day's attack.

190 Ibid.
191 Lieutenant Arthur H.S. Roberts is buried in Forest Communal Cemetery, grave B11.
192 TNA: PRO WO95/2540 War Diary 38th Division HQ.

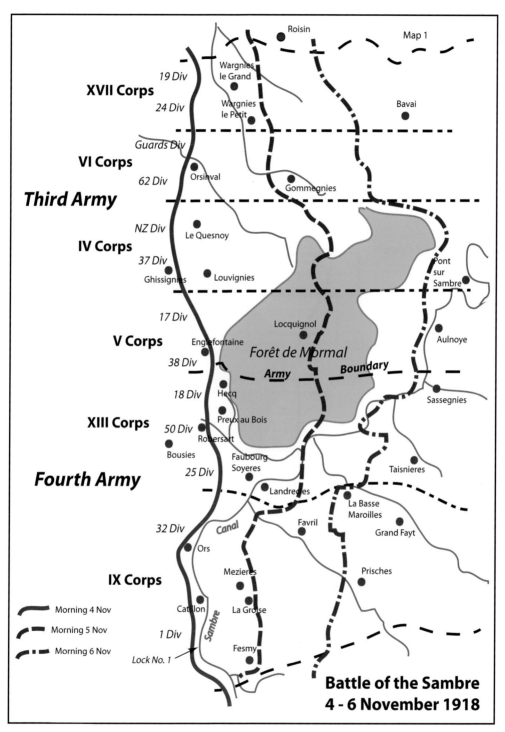

Map 1

Roisin

XVII Corps

19 Div

Wargnies
le Grand

24 Div

Wargnies
le Petit

Bavai

Guards Div

VI Corps

62 Div   Orsinval

Gommegnies

Third Army

NZ Div   Le Quesnoy

IV Corps

37 Div

Ghissignies   Louvignies

Pont
sur
Sambre

17 Div

Locquignol

V Corps   Englefontaine

Aulnoye

Forêt de Mormal

38 Div

Army   **Boundary**

18 Div   Hecq

Sassegnies

XIII Corps

50 Div   Preux au Bois

Robersart

Bousies   Faubourg
Soyeres

Taisnieres

Fourth Army

25 Div

Landrecies

La Basse
Maroilles

32 Div   *Canal*

Favril

Grand Fayt

Ors

Prisches

Mezieres

IX Corps

Catillon   La Groise

━━━ Morning 4 Nov

┅┅┅ Morning 5 Nov   *Sambre*

1 Div

▬·▬·▬ Morning 6 Nov

Fesmy

Lock No. 1

**Battle of the Sambre
4 - 6 November 1918**

Map 1 Battlefield.

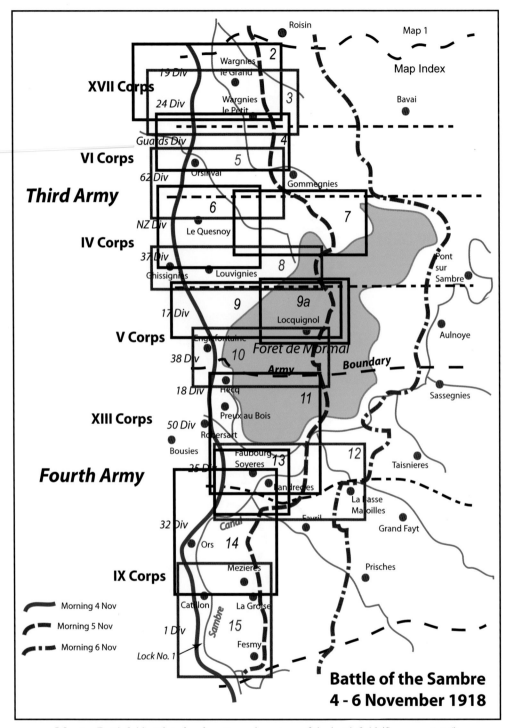

Map 1a Battlefield with index denoting sub-sectors of the battlefield (See maps 1-15).

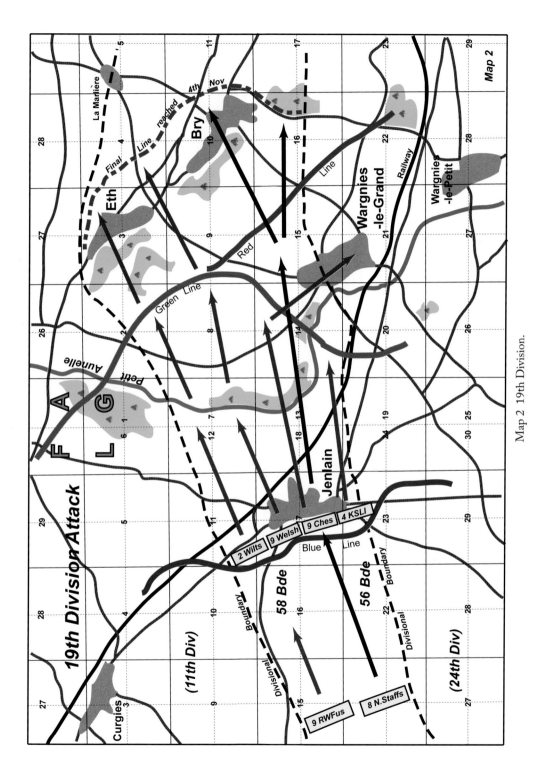

Map 2 19th Division.

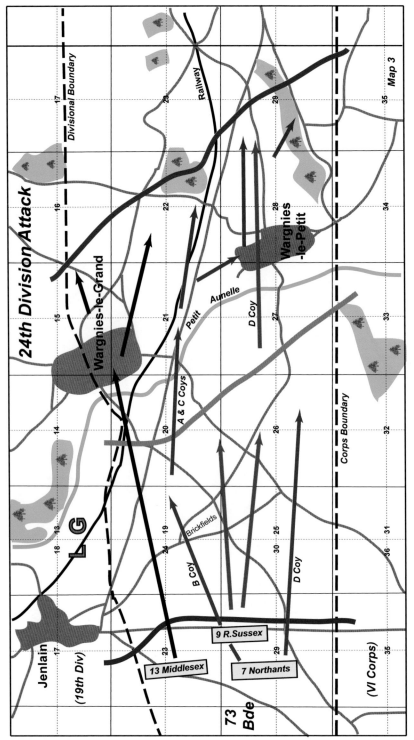

Map 3 24th Division.

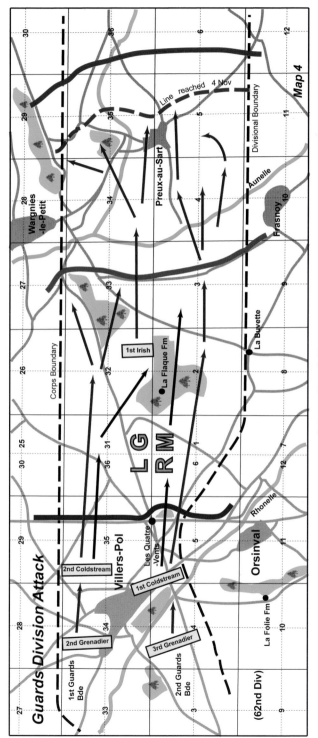

Map 4 Guards Division.

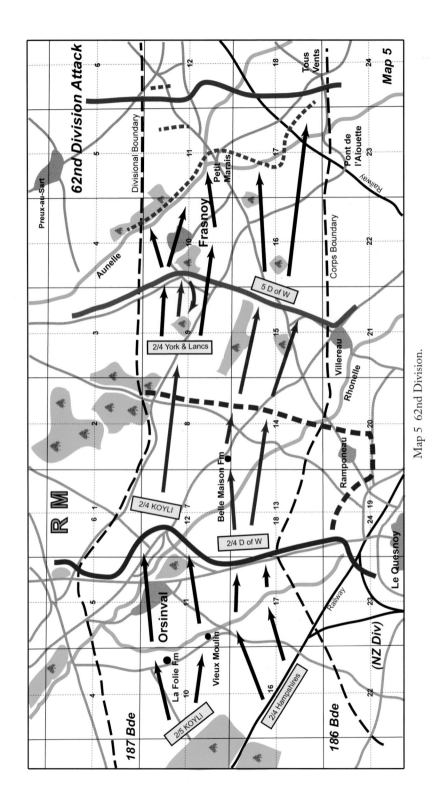

Map 5 62nd Division.

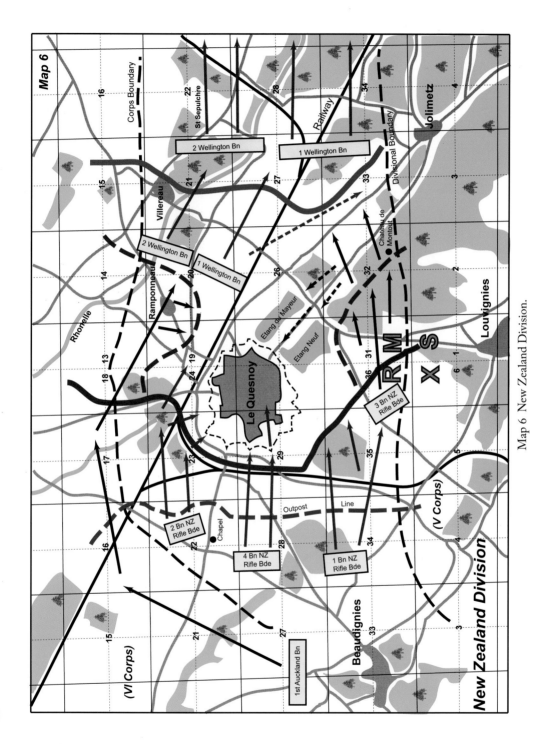

Map 6 New Zealand Division.

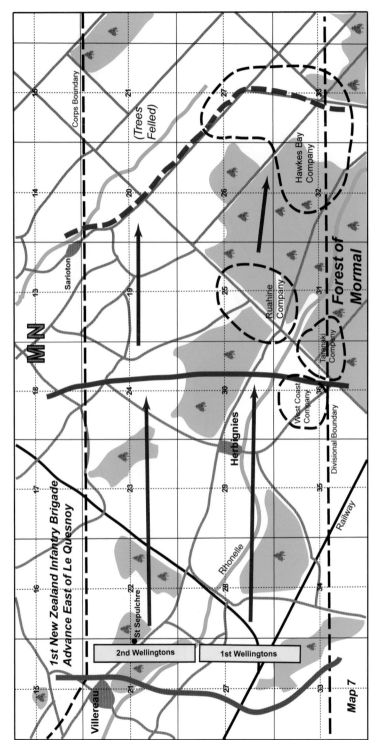

Map 7 New Zealand Division.

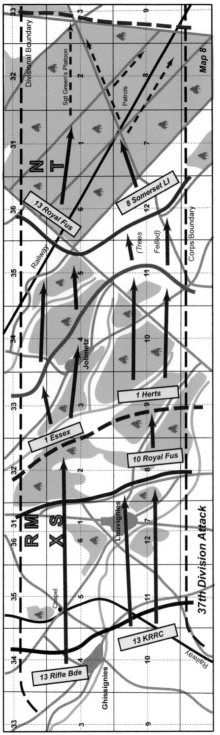

Map 8 37th Division.

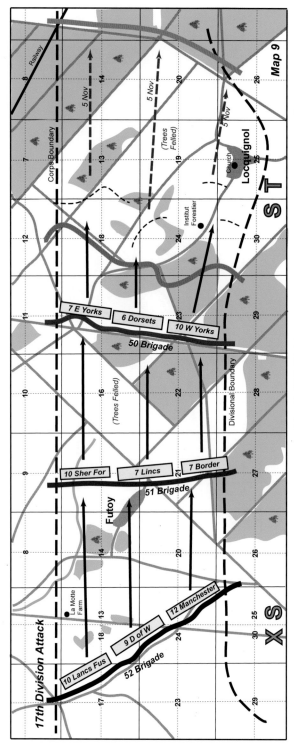

Map 9 17th Division.

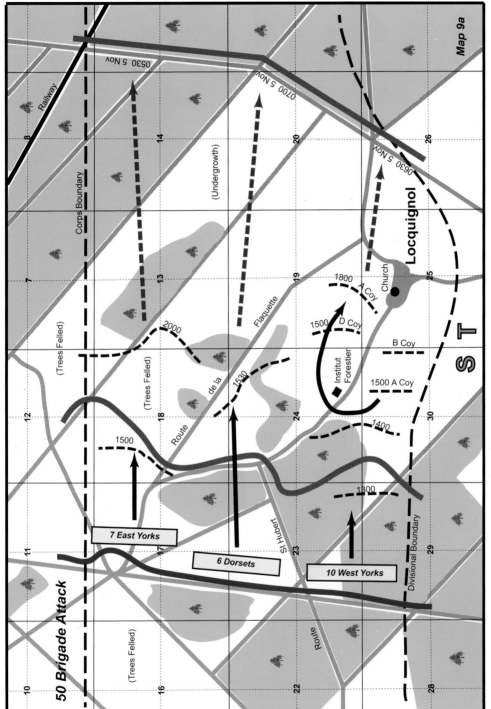

Map 9a 50 Brigade Attack.

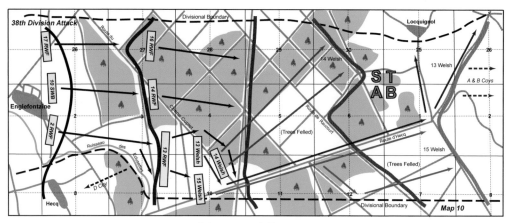

Map 10 38th Division.

Map 11 18th & 50th Divisions.

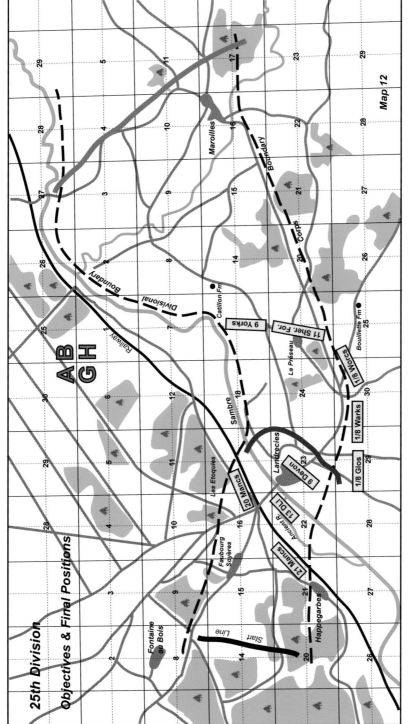

Map 12 25th Division.

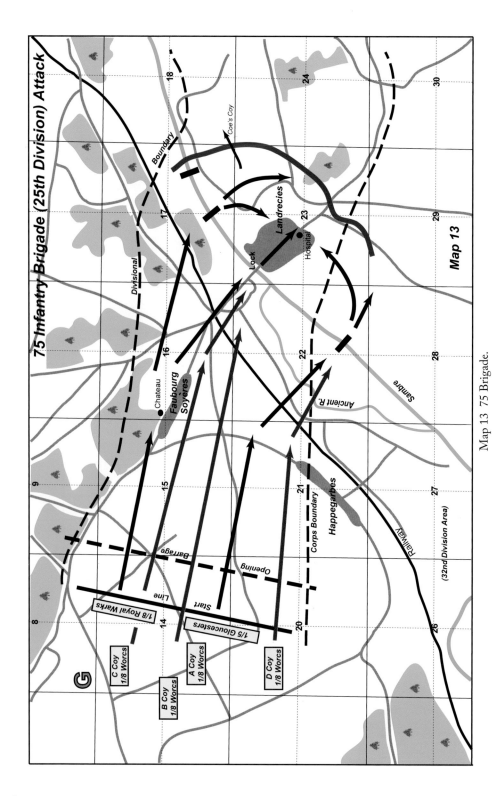

Map 13 75 Brigade.

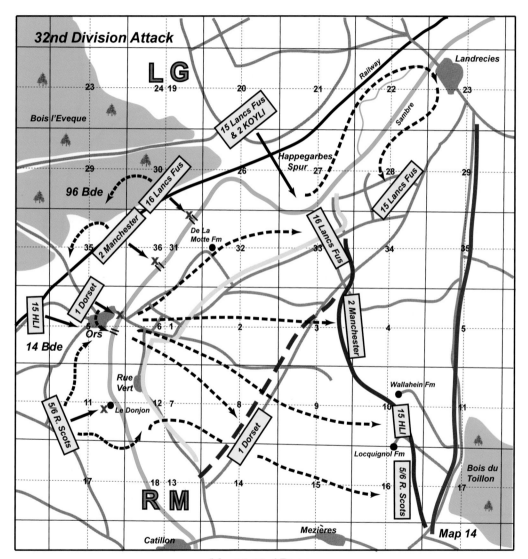

32nd Division Attack

Bois l'Eveque

Landrecies

Railway

Sambre

LG

23   24 19   20   21   22   23

15 Lancs Fus & 2 KOYLI

Happegarbes Spur

29   30   26   27   28   29

96 Bde

16 Lancs Fus

2 Manchester

15 Lancs Fus

De La Motte Fm

35   36 31   32   33   34   35

16 Lancs Fus

15 HLI

1 Dorset

Ors

2 Manchester

5   6 1   2   3   4   5

14 Bde

Rue Vert

Wallahein Fm

5/6 R. Scots

11   12 7   8   9   10   11

Le Donjon

1 Dorset

15 HLI

Locquignol Fm

5/6 R. Scots

Bois du Toillon

RM

17   18 13   14   15   16   17

Catillon

Mezières

Map 14

Map 14 32nd Division.

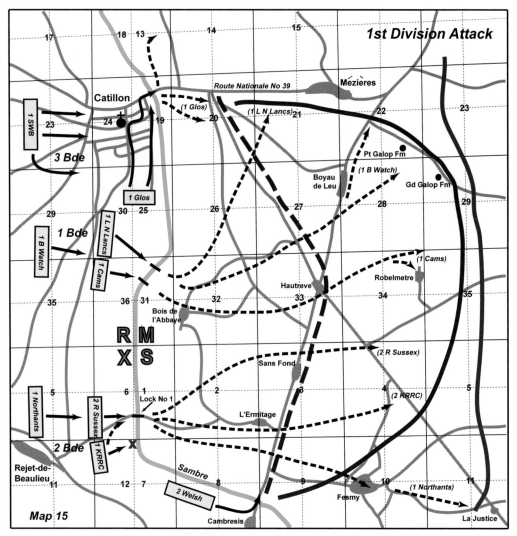

Map 15 1st Division.

The final advance of 'A' and 'B' Companies, 13th Welsh was a very good example of a commander promptly seizing an opportunity as soon as it presented itself.[193]

The Brigade's approximate casualties for the day can be put at: 15 killed (one officer) and 120 wounded.

This brings the 38th Division totals to:

	Killed	Wounded	Missing	Total
Officers	8	14	–	
Other Ranks	87	529	23	
Total	95	543	23	661

A report on the exploits of 13/RWF reached General Sir Julian Byng, commanding Third Army, and he sent a congratulatory note back down to 38th Division Headquarters, dated 11 November 1918:

> This report illustrates the proper application of the methods of open warfare. The determination to get on and not to stop and consolidate a line which would never be attacked resulted in the capture of 137 prisoners with practically no casualties.
>
> The action of the Company Commanders is most commendable and I hope will be copied by leaders in other units.[194]

The attacks made by both divisions in V Corps were ultimately successful, but close scrutiny reveals the difference in methods applied and the resultant difference in casualties suffered. 17th Division seemed unable or unwilling to embrace the tactics of infiltration, preferring to advance in line, and always aware and therefore restricted by the success, or lack of it, of units on companies' flanks. They allowed themselves to be pinned down by machine gun fire, eschewing the opportunities to outflank positions by use of the rides and tracks that criss-crossed the forest. Too much respect was paid to a defensive force that needed little in the way of encouragement to surrender or retire.

38th Division were happy to employ tactics appropriate to both the topography and the strength of enemy defences. "The chief feature of the attack was that the movement forward took place in columns moving on small frontages and leaving considerable lateral gaps. The problem of keeping direction in the wood was thus solved and many of the enemy were captured from behind."[195]

The artillery movement orders were effective and a good creeping barrage had been available for the latter stages of the attack. Battalions and Companies were allocated objectives and their commanders were allowed to get on as best they could, making decisions on the spot, largely unaffected by the fortunes of flanking units. Daring and dash had maximised the acreage captured and minimised the casualties sustained, but the remaining unanswerable

193 De Pree, *The 38th (Welsh) Division*, p. 188.
194 TNA: PRO WO95/2558 War Diary 114th Infantry Brigade HQ.
195 TNA: PRO WO95/2540 War Diary 38th Division HQ.

question is that of how two divisions, in receipt of the same basic orders from Corps, were able to interpret them so differently.

Conclusion

17th and 38th Divisions occupy very different places on the 'learning curve'. V Corps orders had required units to advance rapidly along the tracks and rides through the forest, but only 38th Division showed the confidence to do so. Even allowing for the more effective artillery provision during the latter stages of 38th Division's advance, it must be said that 17th Division, and particularly 50 Brigade, proved tentative. This chapter illustrates and confirms Jonathan Boff's assertion that training and performance was uneven amongst the units of the BEF.

6

XIII Corps

Introduction

This chapter highlights the flexibility in both stages of an assault – the planning and the execution. The basic formula for the advance demonstrated by most of the units of Third Army was altered almost beyond recognition, resulting in the most complicated plan of the entire attack frontage. The basic infantry / artillery combination would be supplemented successfully by the use of armoured support and the Royal Engineers would play a central role in the success of the attack. The ability of the artillery to provide an enfilade barrage within an otherwise standard pattern, the infantry tactics of envelopment as opposed to linear progression, and the ingenuity of the engineering companies in assuring dry passage across watercourses all demonstrate a very capable, dynamic and confident command hierarchy, able to tackle any problem that either the enemy or battlefield topography could pose.

*   *   *

The Fourth Army front at the beginning of November 1918 stretched from its junction with Third Army just south of the village of Englefontaine to include the section of the Sambre-Oise Canal just north of Oisy. Its two Corps, XIII and IX, held a front of approximately 15 miles, XIII Corps (Lieutenant-General Sir T.L.N. Morland) on the northern sector of six miles, and IX Corps (Lieutenant-General Sir W.P. Braithwaite) on the nine mile wide southern sector. The country that faced Fourth Army, and therefore the obstacles that it was tasked to overcome, was very varied. In the north, units faced the southern part of the Forêt de Mormal with the ubiquitous orchard-surrounded and closely-hedged villages at or near its western edge. The countryside then opened out somewhat before the town of Landrecies, which straddled the canalised River Sambre. The challenge here, as further south, was the crossing of this 70 feet wide waterway. The German defences lay, for the most part, on the eastern banks of this canal, and the British infantry, relying to a large extent on the inventiveness of their Royal Engineer colleagues, would be required to fight their way across, in the open, using improvised bridges and pontoons. At the locks at Landrecies, Ors, Catillon and 'Lock No.1',[1] the canal narrowed

---

1   See Map 1.

to only 17 feet, making them obvious places to attempt large-scale crossings. The German defenders were only too well aware of this, of course, and had reinforced those localities appropriately. They also held ground to the west of the canal at Landrecies, the Happegarbes Spur, Ors, Le Donjon and Catillon. By 2 November, the village of Ors had been cleared of the enemy. The other locations remained in German hands.[2]

The day's objectives would take XIII Corps about 3,000 yards into the Forêt de Mormal and to its eastern edge further south, and IX Corps, once over the canal, to a line well to the east of it in countryside devoid of any major settlements, but which "bore a striking resemblance to that of a dairy-farming county in England. There is little or no cultivation, the fields being pasture land; scattered farmsteads were frequent, and the villages, for the most part tucked away in the valleys, were of a very much better type than those to be found in the Somme area before the war wrought its devastation".[3]

Lieutenant-General Sir Thomas Morland, commanding XIII Corps, aware of the depleted strengths of his units,[4] decided to use three of his divisions in the initial assault. These were, north to south, 18th Division (Major-General R.P. Lee), 50th Division (Major-General H.C. Jackson) and 25th Division (Major-General J.R.E. Charles).[5] The 18th and 50th Divisions would advance into the Forêt de Mormal and 25th Division would be given the task of capturing Landrecies.

The standard field-artillery barrage would cover the first half of the advance.[6] It would commence at Zero Hour and, after remaining on the start line for four minutes, would creep forward at a rate of 100 yards every six minutes. It would pause on the Red Dotted Line, putting down a protective barrage. A cessation of fire for five minutes followed by four minutes of intense fire on that line would "indicate to the infantry the hour for the next advance".[7] The original procedure would then be repeated up to the Red Line. From there, "Divisions will arrange for the rapid advance of an adequate proportion of Field Artillery to support the attack between the Red and Green objectives".[8]

Various roads and areas would be targeted by the Heavy Artillery[9] and strict instructions were given that the guns must lift from these areas 400 yards in advance of the 18 pounder barrage, that is some 6-800 yards ahead of the advancing infantry.

Counter battery fire began on the evening of 3 November, 50 rounds per target being fired by 0300 the following morning. British commanders could thereafter order specific targets to be treated to five minutes 'rapid' and five minutes 'normal' fire should the enemy artillery prove troublesome. The total number of guns available to XIII Corps was as follows:

---

2   Montgomery, *The Story of the Fourth Army in the Battles of the Hundred Days*, p. 240. See also p. 241 for an account of the ultimately unsuccessful attempts by 15th & 16th Battalions Lancashire Fusiliers (96 Brigade, 32nd Division) to capture the Happegarbes Spur prior to the main assault.
3   Ibid pp. 242-243. Montgomery does not explain in what way he judged these villages to be 'better'. This is perhaps because he is here simply copying the words of the War Diary of XIII Corps HQ, Narrative of Operations TNA: PRO WO95/897.
4   For example: 25th Division: 4190 rifles; 18th Division, 53 Brigade 858 rifles, 54 Brigade 1059 rifles.
5   The 66th Division would remain in reserve at Le Cateau.
6   See Sketch Map 4.
7   TNA: PRO WO95/897 War Diary XIII Corps HQ.
8   Ibid.
9   Marked in Green on Map 11a.

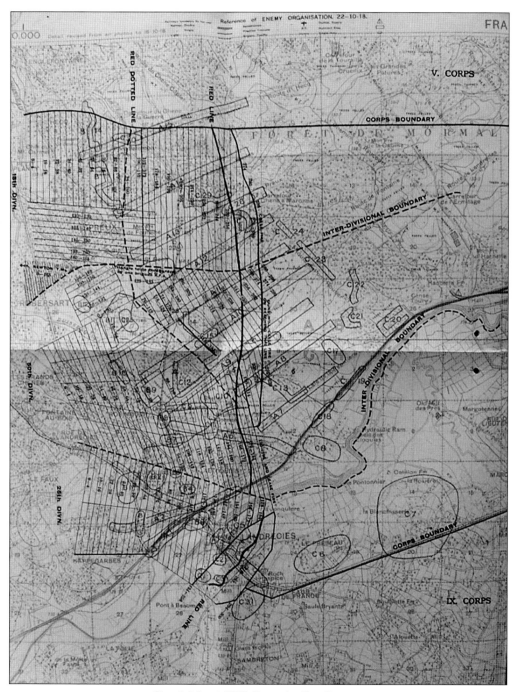

Sketch Map 4 XIII Corps Artillery Barrage.

Field Artillery	40	18-pdr batteries
	12	4.5" Howitzer batteries
Heavy Artillery	6	60-pdr batteries
	12	6" Howitzer batteries
	3	8" Howitzer batteries
	3	9.2" Howitzer batteries
	5	6" gun batteries.

This does not include the 10 batteries of Heavy Artillery available for the counter-battery work.[10]

Each division was allocated a number of tanks: 10 Mk.V tanks from 14th Tank Battalion were attached to 18th Division; the 9th Tank Battalion were able to muster 14 Mk.V tanks, 10 of which went to 50th Division, the remaining four to 25th Division. One supply tank[11] each was given to 50th and 18th Divisions. 25th Division received four, so that they could bring bridging materials forward to the canal at Landrecies.

The 18th and 50th Divisions were also allotted two armoured cars each from 17th Armoured Car Battalion.[12] Only the armoured cars would be allowed to advance beyond the edge of the forest: the tanks were restricted to clearing enemy machine guns in the villages to the west of the forest and on the edge of the forest itself. The armoured cars were free to roam along the main roads in the forest and cause as much mischief as they could.

18th Division[13]

Orders for the assault were issued by Corps on 30 October: they included the requirement that 18th and 50th Divisions perform an enveloping manoeuvre. The village of Preux-au-Bois was not to be attacked frontally: 18th Division would take on the lion's share of the task, assaulting it from the north, with units of 50th Division swinging to the north to help mop up the southern outskirts. It was decided that the thick hedges running north-south through the orchards to the west of the village would be better taken in the flanks, as this would allow the infantry to advance more easily and would restrict the fields of fire of the German machine guns hidden within them. Captain G.H.F. Nicholls, in his history of the 18th Division, deems this aspect of the attack worthy of mention:

> For the first time the 18th Division was to carry out an enveloping manoeuvre by order of a Corps. All previous enveloping movements, for which the Division so justly had become

10   TNA: PRO WO95/902 War Diary XIII Corps CRA. Between 1 and 11 November, XIII Corps artillery would fire 124,852 rounds.
11   Supply tanks were used to carry materiel forward and in order to maximise the load space they were largely stripped of armament.
12   Austin 2nd Series (or 'Model 1915'). They had an Austin Chassis, twin turret bodies with Hotchkiss machine guns and a 35 hp four-cylinder engine.
13   See Map 11.

noted, were initiated and carried through by General Lee in spite of, rather than by order of the Corps in which the Division happened to be serving.[14]

Major-General Lee imparted details of the operation to his subordinates on 30 October and Brigade Conferences took place the following day.

The 18th Division lined up on an initial frontage of 3,000 yards, with 53 Brigade (Brigadier-General M.G.H Barker) on the left, 54 Brigade (Lieutenant-Colonel K.C. Weldon) on the right, with 55 Brigade (Lieutenant-Colonel A.P.B. Irwin) in support. The jumping off positions were parallel to, and a little to the east of, the Englefontaine to Robersart road and zero hour was set for 0615. The weather was clear at that time, but a thick fog came down 20 minutes later and did not clear until around 0900. "Our infantry turned it to account".[15]

53 Brigade was to capture the "straggling"[16] village of Hecq, the responsibility for this falling on one battalion, the 7th Royal West Kents [7/R.W. Kents]. The carrying of the assault to the Red Line objective was job of the 8th Berkshires [8/Berkshire] and the 10th Essex [10/Essex]: to arrive at their jumping off positions required a tricky preliminary manoeuvre, however. These positions ran north-south, but were to the *east* of the village of Preux-au-Bois,[17] which was, as previously mentioned, being attacked in the flank, north to south, by 54 Brigade. Any delay in the 54 Brigade advance would require the Berkshires and Essex battalions to move along the northern edge of the village, possibly under enfilade fire, and then deploy to their right in the rear of positions still held by the enemy. The move would require nerve and determination. 55 Brigade would then leapfrog through the advanced units of 53 Brigade on the Red Line and continue the attack through the forest as far as the Green Line, the day's ultimate objective. The three battalions of 53 Brigade were far from being at full strength, their total numbers adding up to 858 officers and men.[18]

The 7/R.W. Kents (Lieutenant-Colonel L.H. Hickson) formed up along the road running north-south in squares A7 b & d. Each company was allocated an objective: C and D Companies were to reach the road on the eastern outskirts of Hecq (running north-south through squares A8 b & A9 c), left and right respectively. B and A Companies (again left and right respectively) were to advance a further 600 yards to the road running through squares A9 b & A9 d. Their advance was to be assisted by three tanks of 14th Tank Battalion.[19] These tanks were seen going into action at 0610 and C and D Companies advanced five minutes later as the artillery barrage began. The first resistance they met was after 600 yards or so in trying to cross the road running along the western outskirts of the village, but two platoons of each company were able to estab-

---

14   G.H.F. Nichols, *The 18th Division in the Great War* (London: Blackwood, 1922) p. 455.

15   Ibid. p. 457.

16   TNA: PRO WO95/2036 War Diary 53 Brigade HQ 'Narrative of Operations'.

17   See Map 11.

18   Fighting strengths were recorded as follows by Brigade HQ:

	Officers	Other Ranks
10th Battalion Essex Regt	12	270
8th Battalion R.Berks. Regt	15	243
7th Battalion R.W.Kent Regt	18	300

TNA: PRO WO95/2036 War Diary 53 Brigade HQ.

19   These formed Lieutenant C. Lockwood's section: 9557 Second-Lieutenant R. Robinson; 9590 Second-Lieutenant W.White; 9877 Second-Lieutenant D.W. Ormsby.

lish positions along the road and mop up enemy posts in the vicinity. The other two platoons advanced to their final objectives "but met with considerable opposition in the village of Hecq and "D" Coy had particularly bitter fighting".[20]

The three tanks that had advanced with the battalion were out of action by this time: Second-Lieutenant Robinson, commanding Tank 9557, had helped to knock out two enemy machine gun posts, one at the crossroads in A8 a, the other 200 yards further east. "He then traversed the orchards on the west side of this road and fired into the houses along the roads, causing many of the enemy to surrender".[21] At this point, Robinson somehow lost the Royal West Kents and ended up helping the Royal Welsh Fusiliers to clear a machine gun nest to the south of Englefontaine. On his way back to Hecq, he cleared two machine guns near the Ruisseau des Eclusettes before meeting up with Second-Lieutenant Chittenden (Tank 9185 – see below) who, with a party of Royal West Kents, was being held up by an enemy strongpoint consisting of two machine guns and two trench mortars. He managed to neutralise one machine gun before his tank took a bullet in the radiator. With this pierced, the engine stopped, and with "hostile fire being so heavy, he decided to evacuate his tank (taking two machine guns with him) and withdraw to a cottage with the Royal West Kents, then went in turn to look for assistance in taking the strongpoint".[22] During this action, the strongpoint eventually falling by 1500, Robinson and his 1st Driver took over a captured German machine gun, turned it on the enemy and captured 28 prisoners.[23] Robinson was then able to return to his tank and replace the machine guns.

Second-Lieutenant White's tank (9590) managed to advance about 400 yards before receiving a direct hit which wounded him and one of the drivers, Private Brown. Sergeant Button remained in charge of the tank while the wounded were escorted back. Although the tank was "not fit for action",[24] nine Germans came over to it and surrendered.

The third tank, (9877), commanded by Second-Lieutenant Ormsby, was able to knock out German machine guns in a farmyard in Hecq before three of his crew were rendered unconscious by fumes. He and his driver were also affected and Ormsby took over the driving as the former also succumbed. Ormsby stalled the engine, however, and was found immobile by the section commander, Lieutenant Lockwood. "He […] borrowed a driver from another tank and made four German prisoners help him to crank up and start it again. However, engine trouble developed and a track broke".[25] The machine played no further part in the action.

A and B Companies of the Royal West Kents advanced from their jumping off positions at 0625. They passed through D Company, "caught up with the barrage, and attacked the western edge of the Foret de Mormal, puching [sic] through to their final objective which they reached to time. A considerable number of the enemy were killed and many prisoners taken".[26]

Hecq was reported clear of the enemy by 0945, but later that morning a party of about 30 Germans, led by two officers, who had avoided the mopping up operations, attacked A Company

20   TNA: PRO WO95/2040 War Diary 7th Royal West Kents. 'Battle Narrative'.
21   TNA: PRO WO95/103 War Diary 14th Tank Battalion.
22   Ibid.
23   TNA: PRO WO95/102 War Diary 2 Tank Brigade.
24   TNA: PRO WO95/103 War Diary 14th Tank Battalion.
25   Ibid.
26   TNA: PRO WO95/2040 War Diary 7th Royal West Kents.

in the rear. "By a cleverly executed flank movement, O.C. 'A' Coy completely rounded up this party, who, when their officers had become casualties, surrendered".[27]

Other than a slight adjustment to their line, these companies remained in position until relieved the following morning, whereupon the battalion was able to gather in Hecq. Casualties had been light. Two officers were killed[28] and two wounded.[29] Seven other ranks were killed, with 33 wounded and five reported missing. 53 Brigade War Diary praises the battalion's efforts: "Men of this Battalion deserve great praise for the method in which they carried out this attack. Their task was a difficult one, and it was entirely due to the fighting spirit displayed by all ranks that the operation was so completely successful".[30]

The next phase of the attack was down to the 10/Essex (Lieutenant-Colonel R. Forbes) and 8/Berkshire (Lieutenant-Colonel N.B. Hudson). They moved off in artillery formation, 10/Essex first at 0725, the 8/Berkshire 10 minutes behind them, and headed for their jumping off positions to the east of Preux-au-Bois. The fighting in Preux delayed the advance of the 10/Essex and the two right companies of the 8/Berkshire: C Company, on the left, was however able to follow the 18-pounder barrage as it set off from the Red Dotted Line at 0907, advancing along the Route d'Hecq. It met no opposition for some 400 yards, but the firing from the left was soon suppressed and they reached the stream in square A10a just as the enemy blew up the bridge, wounding a few of the men in the leading platoon. They were able to keep moving, however, and reached the high ground in A10 b, where they came under fire from field guns in the wood to their left. They "gallantly pushed on",[31] reaching their Red Line objective by 1037, "after having rushed a strong enemy post by the building at A10 b 9.2".[32] This last effort had cost the battalion five other ranks wounded and the death of Second-Lieutenant L.J. Field.[33]

Second-Lieutenant F.J. Powell DCM MM, commanding C Company, sent a message back to Battalion HQ announcing his arrival on the objective, and his intention to stay there, despite having both flanks in the air. D Company had advanced to their rear, as ordered, and established posts along the Route d'Hecq, the furthest forward being at A10 central. Small arms ammunition and Lewis Gun drums were successfully taken forward by a tank of 14th Tank Battalion, under command of Second-Lieutenant Borrow, now playing the role of 'supply tank', all of his guns having been put out of action.

A and B Companies of the 8/Berkshire, following units of the 10/Essex, encountered problems in squares A14 a & b, coming under fire from enemy positions to the south that should, by that time, have been cleared by troops of 54 Brigade. Orders to detour to the north were issued to both battalions, but were cancelled when "Forbes, [...] in command of the 10th Essex, brought off a swift and brilliant manoeuvre".[34]

27   Ibid.

28   Second-Lieutenants Bernard Fuller, age 25, and Harry Sidney Peglar are buried together in Honnechy British Cemetery, in graves II B 38 and II B 37 respectively.

29   One of the officers wounded was Second-Lieutenant Percy James Bolton. Bolton, age 37, died of his wounds the following day and was buried in Busigny Communal Cemetery Extension, grave VIII A 11.

30   TNA: PRO WO95/2036 War Diary 53 Brigade HQ.

31   TNA: PRO WO95/2037 War Diary 8th Royal Berkshires.

32   Ibid.

33   Second-Lieutenant Leslie Jack Field, age 23, is buried in Montay-Neuville Road Cemetery, Montay, grave III B 16.

34   Nichols, *The 18th Division in the Great War*, p. 461.

The account continues:

> Reconnoitring in the labyrinth of orchards and plantations that reached the edge of Preux, Forbes discovered an opening, some 200 yards wide, in the enemy line. He determined to push the 10th Essex through this gap. He led them in person through a gate within the German posts, […] pushed on, formed up the battalion behind the enemy's front line, and advanced to the attack […] while the German's forward posts were still in action. This surprise manoeuvre had an immediate effect. The young lads of the 8th Berks operated in the same way on the left of the 10th Essex; the advance completed the enveloping movement; the enemy's escape from Preux was rendered impossible.[35]

The War Diary of the 8/Berkshire narrates a sequence of events more harrowing than Nicholls would have us believe:

> Time being now short, and the barrage being now lost, the Company Commander [Captain T.K. Pickard MC] determined to fight his way to the second assembly position […] and thence on to his final objective on the Red Line. The next three hours (11.00 to 14.00) were spent in working round hostile machine guns, in rushing posts and in neutralising the enemy fire, which was considerable. The casualties of 'A' Company during this period were comparatively heavy and the behaviour of section commanders and individual private soldiers was from every point of view beyond praise.[36]

It is probable that the extensive training undertaken during the October by the battalion, concentrating on the tactical use of the Lewis Gun in the attack, had proved useful.

The leading company was then able to work forward from the jumping off positions "without much opposition",[37] reaching its final objective at 1505, where they were able to gain touch with C Company on their left. B Company, following in its wake, had established posts along the left battalion boundary, but was not involved in any fighting. The attack had cost the Berkshires two officers killed,[38] 10 other ranks killed, 30 wounded and seven missing.

The 10/Essex had been able to move forward from their jumping off positions some time before the 8/Berkshire, and after some hard fighting along the Route Duhamel, were able to reach their objective at 1430. By this time, any resistance had disappeared and they pushed forward a further 400 yards on the right to the Route du Pont Routier in order to keep touch with troops (1st K.O.Y.L.I.) of 50th Division on their right. Three companies held this line, with the other in close support. At 1520, "two armoured cars passed through the battalion"[39] and headed up the Route de Preux deeper into the wood. Ten minutes later, troops of 55 Brigade passed through in order to continue the advance.

35   Ibid. p. 461.
36   TNA: PRO WO95/2037 War Diary 8th Royal Berkshires.
37   Ibid.
38   The other officer killed was Second-Lieutenant John Long, age 23, is buried in Preux-au-Bois Communal Cemetery, grave A 44.
39   TNA: PRO WO95/2038 War Diary 10th Essex.

Austin Armoured Car. (Australian War Memorial)

The two armoured cars of 17th Armoured Car Battalion under Lieutenant J.A.E. May had advanced along the Route de Preux, "passing through our attacking infantry at the entrance of the forest".[40] They proved to be "of great assistance in putting such pockets of the enemy as remained in the 55th Brigade area to flight".[41] They did not escape unscathed, however, as one car ditched at B13 a 2.8 and the crew were forced to evacuate the vehicle, taking the machine guns with them. They were able to find cover and "remained there until our Infantry passed them. Both cars had considerable amount of shooting and fired 1200 rounds S.A.A. at enemy infantry in the wood".[42]

The day had been relatively kind to the 10/Essex, their casualties amounting to two officers wounded, four other ranks killed, with 18 wounded and six missing, and 53 Brigade casualties for the day can be calculated at:

	Killed	Wounded	Missing	Total
Officers	4	4	–	
Other Ranks	21	81	18	
Total	25	85	18	128

The overall total amounts to almost 15 percent of those engaged.

40   TNA: PRO WO95/116 War Diary 17th Armoured Car Battalion.
41   TNA: PRO WO95/2048 War Diary 55 Brigade HQ 'Narrative No.7'.
42   TNA: PRO WO95/116 War Diary 17th Armoured Car Battalion.

The task of 54 Brigade (Lieutenant-Colonel K.C. Weldon[43]) looked fairly straightforward on paper: to clear the village of Preux-au-Bois. On a map, the complicated nature of the assault is evident: as mentioned above, the direction of the attack was to be north to south, that is, at right angles to the day's general advance. A conference was held at 54 Brigade headquarters on 31 October where details of the plan were disseminated to unit commanders.[44]

It fell to the 6th Battalion Northamptonshire Regiment [6/Northamptonshire], on the left, to clear the orchards to the north of Preux Village, in squares A14 a & b and A15 a, so that these areas could serve as assembly positions for the troops designated to clear the village itself. Two companies of 6/Northamptonshire would then swing to their right and consolidate positions to the north-east of Preux.

The main assault on the village was entrusted to the 2/Bedfordshire: the men would follow the advance of the 6/Northamptonshire, form up to the north of the village, facing south, and then follow a creeping barrage through the village until they met the 2nd Munsters [2/Munster] (50th Division) coming up from the south. On the right, a composite company of the 11th Royal Fusiliers [11/Royal Fusiliers] would also work their way south, this time on the western edge of Preux, whilst the other companies would stand fast in their original positions, facing east, but tasked only with "demonstrat[ing] from the west".[45] They would "open fire with L.G. [Lewis Guns], rifles and rifle grenades along the whole front in order to deceive the enemy as to the point of attack".[46]

The creeping artillery barrage would commence at Zero plus 113, remaining on the opening line for five minutes before moving south at a rate of 100 yards every five minutes. It would reach its southern limit at Zero plus 158.[47] One 18-pounder, firing over open sights, would shell the house on the main road at A20 a 0.8 as soon as it was light enough to see it, this therefore being "denied to the enemy" before it then accompanied the infantry down the road in A20 central "to deal with targets as they occur." Thirty-two machine guns of 18th Battalion MGC would be "employed on indirect fire to enfilade the streets of Preux-au-Bois".[48]

43   Lieutenant-Colonel Weldon was acting Brigade Commander in place of Brigadier-General O.C. Borrett, who had been gassed on 24 October 1918. Borrett returned to command on 6 November 1918. 'Parapet strength' on 4 November was as follows:

	Officers	Other Ranks
11th Royal Fusiliers	9	230
2nd Bedfordshires	17	360
6th Northamptons	18	425
Total	44	1,015

44   Present were: Brigade Commander, Lieutenant-Colonel K.C. Weldon; Brigade Major; Staff Captain; Commanding Officers of 11th Royal Fusiliers, 2nd Bedfords, 6th Northants, 54th Trench Mortar Battery, "B" Coy 14th Tank Battalion and representatives of 54th Field Ambulance, 80th Field Company Royal Engineers and 65th Brigade Royal Field Artillery. A Divisional Conference had been held the previous day at Le Cateau.
45   H.C. O'Neill, *The Royal Fusiliers in the Great War* (London: Heinemann, 1922) p. 334.
46   TNA: PRO WO95/2042 War Diary 54 Brigade HQ. Order No.200, 2 November 1918.
47   Ibid. This was different to the information given out at the conference, where a rate of advance of 100 yards every 6 minutes and a finish at Zero plus 180 were announced. The infantry were expected to advance quicker than initially planned.
48   Ibid.

Four tanks from 14th Tank Battalion were attached to 54 Brigade to assist in the mopping up of Preux-au-Bois, one each to the 6/Northamptonshire and 11/Royal Fusiliers, two to the 2/Bedfordshire. "Tanks will accompany the Infantry, but will not precede them".[49]

The thrust made by 6/Northamptonshire (Lieutenant-Colonel R. Turner) was to prove relatively costly: they were at their forming up positions two hours before zero. At 0615 "'D' Coy attacked due EAST with Royal West Kents on left and no-one on right".[50] This meant that the right flank of the company was enfiladed "quite hotly"[51] by German machine gun fire. Nevertheless, with A Company following 100 yards behind, D Company made it to a north-south line running through A14 b 8.0 by 0730, an advance of 1500 yards. A Company leap-frogged them and then swung to the south, arriving on an east-west line just inside the eastern fringes of the forest by 0815. C Company then appeared in worm formation, "two lines of platoons",[52] and they arrived at "the point of the wood at A15 a 4.0"[53] and then worked their way down the edge of the forest in a south-easterly direction until they reached the stream. Their job was done: their only subsequent encounter with the enemy was to beat off a one-company-strength counter-attack at around 0915. Although it is not mentioned in the Battalion War Diary, it seems that one tank, ditched at A15 a 7.5 was able to help break up this counter-attack. This was tank 9267, commanded by Lieutenant D.J. Gillies. He had advanced through the southern part of Hecq with the 10/Essex before turning south into Preux-au-Bois. There he had attempted to deal with a number of German machine gun positions by firing his 6-pounder gun. This and four of his Hotchkiss machine guns were subsequently damaged, so he with-drew to effect repairs before returning to finish the job. He then steered to the apex of the forest, before following its south-western edge, seemingly in conjunction with C Company of 6/Northamptonshire, as his intervention, prior to ditching, "enabled the infantry to continue their advance".[54] In attempting to unditch his machine, the left track broke.[55] The day's action cost the 6/Northamptonshire 3 officers wounded, 20 other ranks killed, with 96 wounded and one missing.

The men of the 2/Bedfordshire (Lieutenant-Colonel A.E. Percival) moved off from their assembly positions at 0650 "in rear of the 6th Northamptonshire Regt, who made an excellent and spirited attack and cleared the whole area over which the Battalion had to advance".[56]

The front-line companies, A Company on the left and C Company on the right, lined up to the north of the stream in square A14 d and waited for the barrage to begin. "A very heavy enfilade

49   TNA: PRO WO95/2042 War Diary 54 Brigade HQ, Appendix 'A' Notes of Conference at 54th Infantry Brigade HQ 31 October 1918.
50   TNA: PRO WO95/2044 War Diary 6th Battalion Northamptonshire Regiment.
51   Nichols, *The 18th Division in the Great War*, p. 457.
52   TNA: PRO WO95/2044 War Diary 6th Battalion Northamptonshire Regiment.
53   Ibid. See Map 11.
54   TNA: PRO WO95/103 War Diary 14th Tank Battalion.
55   The story of the tank officially attached to 6th Northants, commanded by Second-Lieutenant E.A. Hayes, is rather vague. The 2nd Tank Brigade War Diary records that this tank "got a direct hit and had its female sponson blown away, but in spite of this it continued the action." The diary of 14th Tank Battalion records him as losing his way going south "at the start", but also puts Hayes in command of a different tank, this one attached to 37th Division. It is possible that the original tank in question was actually commanded by F.Keeves, but the anomaly remains unsolved at the time of writing.
56   TNA: PRO WO95/2042 War Diary 2nd Battalion Bedfordshire Regiment.

barrage, with 4.5" howitzers beyond, came down on the brook"[57] at 0807 and commenced its forward creep four minutes later. C Company (Captain R.L.V. Doake MC), closely followed by D Company (Second-Lieutenant W. Pennington) encountered opposition from enemy posts in the orchards, but was able to overcome them, "many small, local attacks and enveloping movements being organised on the spur of the moment and successfully carried out".[58]

C Company made it to its objective in square A20 b. just after the scheduled time, allowed D Company to leapfrog them and then supported their comrades' advance through the village as far as the church, where they were able to get in touch with the 2/Munster arriving from the south. Lieutenant-Colonel Percival, writing the after-battle narrative, puts the success of the right wing of the attack down to "the splendid leading of the Officers", singling out Captain Doake, Second-Lieutenant Vaughan and Second-Lieutenant Ashton of C Company, and Second-Lieutenants Pennington and Whittingham of D Company.[59]

Doake also merits a mention in Nichols' 18th Division history:

> He was creeping through the orchards towards the village, his batman with him, when through a hedge not 20 yards away he saw four Germans and a machine gun. Captain Doake and his batman opened fire so rapidly and with such accuracy that it required only four rounds to bring all four Boche down. Doake got his DSO in this battle.[60]

On the left of the attack, A Company (Lieutenant A.F. Aldridge) was held up almost as soon as it had started forward by machine gun fire from the road junction at A15 c 0.5 where the Germans had laid a tree trunk across the road. They were quickly in danger of losing the barrage. A tank (probably the one commanded by Second-Lieutenant H.K. Blaker) made attempts to deal with this strongpoint, but was unable to put it out of action. Lieutenant W.J. Holbrook MC was able to lead the two right platoons of A Company in a flanking manoeuvre to the west of the strongpoint and "after a spirited struggle"[61] cleared the enemy from the cemetery. This enabled the two right platoons of B Company (Second-Lieutenant H.B. Lang) to "move forward and clear the main street as far as the road junction at A21 c 3.8".[62] An isolated machine gun nest about 250 yards to the north-east of this position was also mopped up by a party led by Second-Lieutenant Lang.

Meanwhile, the two left platoons of A and B Companies (Lieutenant A.E. Aldridge and Second-Lieutenant S. Goble respectively) had outflanked the original troublesome German strongpoint to its eastern side and began to clear the houses and cellars along the lane running north-west to south-east in square A15 c. By this time, the Germans in the strongpoint, having been outflanked on both sides and now being attacked in the rear, gave in. It was discovered that the stubborn machine gun crew had been firing through two well-camouflaged holes in the wall of a house.

57   Ibid.
58   Ibid. 'Narrative of Operations'.
59   Ibid.
60   Nichols, *The 18th Division in the Great War*, p. 459.
61   TNA: PRO WO95/2042 War Diary 2nd Battalion Bedfordshire Regiment.
62   Ibid.

The aforementioned failure of the tank to deal with the German strongpoint is the only point at which tanks feature at all in the 2/Bedfordshire's own narrative. Their involvement deserves more detailed treatment, however, their contribution being described as "awe-inspiring" by Nichols.[63] Indeed, the 14th Tank Battalion's account of the action begins: "The infantry they [the tanks] were working with were weak in numbers and the capture of PREUX must be largely ascribed to the tanks".[64] The three tanks in question were commanded by Second-Lieutenant H.K. Blaker, Second-Lieutenant J.T. Borrow and Second-Lieutenant H.I. Isaacs.[65]

Isaacs' tank, on the right of the attack, managed to overcome a handful of machine gun posts before becoming ditched at A20 a 8.7. A temporary withdrawal of the accompanying infantry meant that the machine was almost surrounded by German soldiers, prompting the crew to make a fighting withdrawal of their own, abandoning the tank. "They returned to the tank immediately the Infantry again came on, but were unsuccessful in their attempts to unditch. No blame can be ascribed for the ditching, as the ground was extremely treacherous and its marshy character was not apparent".[66] The storyline inspires little in the way of awe so far…

Blaker and Borrow, it is true, fared rather better:

> 2nd Lieut. H.K. Blaker's tank advanced in front of the infantry, who were digging in,[67] and after hard fighting to which the condition of the tank testifies, 2nd Lieut. H.K. Blaker broke down the opposition, went back and brought the infantry on. He continued clearing the east side of PREUX, and completed his task. His resource and determination in the action called for special mention.[68]

Second-Lieutenant Borrow's tank became "separated from the infantry in the mist",[69] and his position became critical for a while. He was "surrounded by the enemy. Three of his M.G.'s were out of action and his 6-pdr gun was badly jammed through enemy fire. He fought the tank with revolvers, as the enemy pushed up his remaining M.G.'s and even climbed on the top of the tank to bomb him".[70] Borrow and his crew emerged victorious in this squabble and were able to continue, completing his task of clearing the west side of Preux-au-Bois village. It would appear that both the infantry and the tanks tended to underestimate the contributions of their sister arm.

The 2/Bedfordshire's action on 4 November cost them one officer killed[71] and three wounded. Twelve other ranks were killed, along with 33 wounded and three missing. They had liberated some 1400 French civilians in Preux-au-Bois.

The 11/Royal Fusiliers, (Lieutenant-Colonel K.D.H. Gwynn), on the right of the brigade frontage, attacked with a composite company, commanded by Captain P. Hope, and formed

63   Nicholls, *The 18th Division in the Great War*, p. 459.
64   TNA: PRO WO95/103 War Diary 14th Tank Battalion.
65   Isaacs' tank was attached to the 11th Royal Fusiliers.
66   TNA: PRO WO95/103 War Diary 14th Tank Battalion.
67   Possibly in front of the German strongpoint at A15 c 0.5.
68   TNA: PRO WO95/103 War Diary 14th Tank Battalion.
69   Ibid. The 54 Brigade 'Narrative of Operations' (WO95/2042) claims that the tanks "by this time had lost their way".
70   Ibid.
71   Second-Lieutenant Sidney Herbert Abbott is buried in Cross Roads Cemetery, Fontaine-au-Bois, grave IV C 14.

from their original C and D Companies. They formed up in the sunken road in square A13 d two hours before Zero and then moved to their jumping off positions at Zero plus 30 minutes, platoons in extended order, facing south, almost along the east-west line separating squares A14 a and A14 c. The artillery barrage opened at Zero plus 113. "rather wide of the mark and we suffered a few casualties".[72] They moved off, accompanied by Second-Lieutenant Isaac's tank five minutes later. The tank broke down two hedges for the advancing infantry, but, once across the stream, it veered off to the left and broke down. "Beyond engaging the enemy with the 6-pdr gun it was of no further use to us".[73]

The infantry now found it difficult to negotiate the many hedges in their way, but battled on, encountering little in the way of enemy artillery fire. Machine gun fire from strongpoints along the road in A20 a halted their progress, casualties began to mount and "the position became serious".[74] One platoon had already been sent to the crossroads at A20 a 0.9 with orders to outflank the machine guns, but they were making little progress. It fell to Private D. Sale to rescue the situation: He "pushed straight forward, regardless of all danger, with his Lewis Gun and knocked out the enemy MG at A20 a 2.8".[75] He was immediately followed by his colleagues who promptly captured 30 prisoners. The momentum was now with them, despite their numbers having been reduced to 20 effectives, and they pressed on down the main road, through orchards on its left hand side, collecting prisoners from the houses as they went, that number rising to over 100, including five officers. They finally halted, with posts at A26 a 6.7, where they established touch with the Inniskillings,[76] and at A20 c 8.3.

By midday, Preux-au-Bois was cleared of the enemy and Captain Hope had earned himself a DSO. The 11/Royal Fusiliers' War Diary does not detail casualties for that day, but 54 Brigade HQ estimated them at one officer and 29 other ranks. Fatalities for the action can be confirmed at six other ranks.[77]

The 54 Brigade had attacked with a total strength of just over 1,000 men, that is, equal to one full-strength battalion, but managed to take an enemy-held village, capturing around 770 prisoners, six trench mortars, three anti-tank rifles, one field gun and 70 machine guns. It had cost them 202 casualties,[78] including 39 fatalities:

	Officers			Other Ranks		
	K	W	M	K	W	M
11th Royal Fusiliers	–	1	–	6	23	–
2nd Bedfords	1	3	–	12	33	3
6th Northants	–	3	–	20	96	1
Total	1	7	–	38	152	4

72   TNA: PRO WO95/2045 War Diary 11th Royal Fusiliers.
73   Ibid.
74   Ibid.
75   Ibid.
76   6th Battalion Royal Inniskilling Fusiliers, 151 Brigade, 50th Division.
77   According to Commonwealth War Graves Commission data and figures from 'Soldiers Died in the Great War' CDRom.
78   This gives a casualty rate of 19.25 percent.

The advance to the Green Line, the day's final objective, on a front narrowing to around 1,500 yards, was down to 55 Brigade (Lieutenant-Colonel A.P.B. Irwin).[79] The original timing had assumed an advance from the Red Line at 1131. Delays meant, however, that battalions were not able to move off from their assembly positions near Petit Planty until after 1230.

The plan of advance was to see the 7th Queen's (Royal West Surrey Regiment) [7/Queen's], (Major H.J. Tortise) on the left and 7th Buffs (East Kent Regiment) [7/Buffs], (Major W.H. Stronge) on the right, moving forward through the forest. The 55 Brigade HQ diarist likened it to a pheasant shoot: "[a] bold approach covered by powerful rifle, Lewis Gun and Machine Gun fire was to be made along the roads and rides running in an E.N.E. direction through the forest, whilst specially detailed parties "beat" the successive rectangular patches of wood".[80]

These battalions would establish themselves along a line 1,200 yards short of the Green Line, whereupon the 8th East Surrey Regiment [8/E.Surrey] (Major W.H. Baddeley) would leapfrog onto the final objective.

The 7/Queen's,[81] with D and B Companies in front, left and right respectively, were moving up to their jumping off positions on the Red Line when they came under hostile machine gun fire unexpectedly at A16 c 9.7. They had assumed that this ground had already been swept by the 8/Berkshire, but these had veered to the left during their advance, leaving a narrow section of enemy line unchallenged. No.5 Platoon, B Company, was sent forward to deal with the enemy posts and "all these hostile guns were knocked out by this platoon's fire".[82] The units were now able to re-organise along the Route Duhamel (in A16 b), capturing a field gun as they did so, before moving forward once more "on each side of the track in sectional rushes, sections giving covering fire as far as crossroads at A17 a 7.8. During the advance ['B'] Company captured a complete battery of field guns, at least two machine guns and their teams being knocked out, as well as various transport wagons, etc. A German runner on a bicycle was also shot here".[83]

On arriving at their original jumping off positions on the Red Line, the two forward companies swapped sectors, B Company now being on the left, D on the right. A and C Companies were in support. They attacked "in one wave",[84] D Company going forward with the Route de Preux as their right hand boundary, and reached their objectives without encountering any serious opposition. They were then given permission to move forward again, but they finished some 500 yards short of the Green Line, deciding to dig in as darkness began to fall along a line stretching through squares B7 b & d.

The 7/Buffs were finally let off the leash at 1250, with orders to "start moving forward gradually, and at 1330 hours to rush on at once with all speed".[85] They had reached their jumping off positions without incident by 1540. The Battalion's "Report on Operations 4th-6th November 1918" sums up the rest of their day:

79   Lieutenant-Colonel Irwin was standing in for Brigadier-General E.A. Wood who went sick on 24 October 1918. Irwin remained in command until 19 November 1918.
80   TNA: PRO WO95/2048 War Diary 55 Brigade HQ 'Narrative No.7'.
81   Total effective strength of the battalion on 1 November 1918 was 33 Officers and 622 Other Ranks. TNA: PRO WO95/2040 War Diary 7th Queen's (Royal West Surrey Regiment).
82   Ibid.
83   Ibid.
84   Ibid.
85   TNA: PRO WO95/2049 War Diary 7th Buffs (East Kent Regiment).

After the first stubborn resistance offered in the morning, the enemy had retired hurriedly through the FORET DE MORMAL and put up no fight in face of our advance. The battalion reached its objectives […] without opposition at 17.15.[86]

The 8/E.Surrey received information at around 1400 that the 7/Buffs and 7/Queen's were advancing to their objectives against very little resistance and so proceeded in columns through Preux-au-Bois and thence along the Route de Preux as far as Mon Fre de la Cabine (B7 d 4.4). By 1800, A and B Companies were establishing themselves on the Green Line, capturing four enemy field guns along the Chemin de Raucourt as they did so. Only C Company on the right met with any opposition, machine gun fire from their right from the Carrefour de l'Ermitage holding them up but briefly.

At 0230, 5 November, the positions of D Company were counter-attacked by a "strong enemy patrol",[87] but rifle and Lewis Gun fire saw the enemy retreat after sustaining a number of casualties. The troops of 55 Brigade were destined not to have a peaceful night:

"A few enemy aeroplanes came over in the early night and dropped bombs in the area occupied by the Brigade. These, however, inflicted no casualties on us".[88]

The 55 Brigade accounts are littered with phrases such as "slight opposition". Their advance was made against a retreating and demoralised enemy whose resolve had vanished once the village of Preux-au-Bois had fallen. The Battalion War Diaries do not bother to list casualty figures for 4 November 1918. The fatalities can be confirmed, however: the 8/E.Surrey suffered none; the 7/Buffs incurred three, and the 7/Queen's two, including one officer.[89]

Nichols sums up the 18th Division's passage through the Forêt de Mormal:

As has been shown, much of the progress through the great Forest, 'this formidable obstacle,' as Lord Haig called it in his Victory Despatch, had been swift and apparently fairly easy, thanks to the growing demoralisation of the enemy. Yet it has also been made clear that in the early part of the advance the fighting was stiff and the enemy resolute.[90]

50th Division[91]

After the Battle of the Aisne, 27-30 May 1918, the 50th Division had been reduced to 700 effectives. A month later it was reduced, this time by orders, to cadre strength and on 15 July it was decided that the three brigades would be re-constituted. In the end, however, not one of the original battalions remained, the only trace of the men from the old division being found in the

---

86   Ibid.
87   TNA: PRO WO95/2050 War Diary 8th East Surrey Regiment.
88   :PRO WO95/2048 War Diary 55 Brigade HQ 'Narrative No.7'.
89   Second-Lieutenant Norman Henry Towes, age 19, is buried in Poix-du-Nord Cemetery Extension, grave I A 17.
90   Nichols, *The 18th Division in the Great War*, p. 464.
91   See Map 11.

Sappers and Field Ambulance.[92] A considerable number of the new men had been withdrawn from Salonika and a significant proportion of them were suffering from malaria. Their continuing medical treatment only allowed for four hours training per day. This routine continued for several weeks and after joining Fourth Army the 'new' division saw its first action at the Battle of Beaurevoir, 3-5 October, commanded by Major-General H.C. Jackson.

Prior to assembly for the Battle of the Sambre, the 50th Division units had only spent 14 days in the line together.[93]

50th Division Instruction No.1 was issued on 2 November 1918. The first objective, the Red Line, was to be captured by 150 Brigade on the left and 149 Brigade on the right. The latter would make "every endeavour"[94] to push on to the spur in squares G 12 d and H 7 c[95] and thus be in a position overlooking the town of Landrecies, 25th Division's target, and be able to "enfilade the Canal from both directions".[96]

The advance to the Red Line would be supported by 10 tanks of 9th Tank Battalion, four allocated to 150 Brigade and six to 149 Brigade. The tanks would move off at 0545, half an hour before the infantry, their job being to "advance in touch with the infantry […] to W. Edge of FORET DE MORMAL, with the object of overcoming Machine Gun resistance and making tracks through the hedges for the infantry".[97]

At Zero plus 300 minutes, 151 Brigade would continue the advance from the Red Line.

The assault was to be supported by six brigades of artillery: the creeping barrage would begin at Zero, resting on the start line for four minutes before advancing at a rate of 100 yards every six minutes. The 250th Brigade RFA would be attached to 151 Brigade in order to support its advance to the Green Line. The 4.5" howitzers would bombard the Landrecies-Englefontaine road, the Ruisseau de l'Hirondelle and the western edge of the forest and would then keep 200 yards ahead of the 18-pounder barrage. The 60-pounders were to enfilade the roads running east-north-east through the forest whilst the 6" howitzers concentrated on important crossroads.[98] To the south of Preux-au-Bois, an enfilade barrage, including smoke shells, would protect the left flank of 150 Brigade for the first two hours of the attack, whence it would begin its creep northwards in conjunction with the 2/Munster's attack.

On the morning of the attack, all units were reported to be in their assembly positions by 0545. 150 Brigade on the left, had been able to confirm all their troops in position at 0351, but also that one tank had already "ditched itself on the way up".[99]

By 0615, zero hour, the tanks had already been on the move for half an hour. One of them was hit by an enemy gas shell whilst still behind the infantry start line, its entire crew *hors de combat*. The Section Commander gathered together a scratch crew from members of the 2nd Royal Dublin Fusiliers [2/R.Dublin Fusiliers] and was able to move off again at 0750, catching up with the infantry an hour later. "In spite of the fact that the crew of the tank (with the exception

92   See E. Wyrall, *The 50th Division 1914-19* (Chippenham: A. Rowe Ltd., 1939), pp. 350-356.
93   Montgomery, *Fourth Army* p. 263.
94   TNA: PRO WO95/2812 War Diary 50th Division HQ Instructions No.1.
95   See Map 11.
96   Ibid.
97   Ibid.
98   TNA: PRO WO95/2812 War Diary 50th Division HQ.
99   TNA: PRO WO95/2833 War Diary 150 Brigade HQ.

of the Tank Commander and 1 other rank) was entirely new to tank work, it was able to do excellent work and was responsible for the destruction of a great many m.g.'s".[100]

The 150 Brigade diarist begins with a weather report, announcing a misty but dry start to the day. This "prevented observation and greatly added to the difficulties of the attack".[101]

On the left Brigade front were the 2/R.Munster Fusiliers, "prepared to take on a special task previously allocated to them".[102] They were to mop up an area to the south of Preux-au-Bois and east of Robersart and then turn north to meet the troops of 18th Division coming in the opposite direction through Preux.

The battalion had moved to Fontaine-au-Bois at 0130 that morning, only to be heavily shelled, suffering three casualties in A Company. B Company advanced at zero, 10 minutes behind the left wing of the 2nd Northumberland Fusiliers [2/Northumberland Fusiliers] and began their mopping up operation in what turned out to be a rather thickly-wooded sector of the forest, a task they accomplished by 1300.

Meanwhile, at Zero plus 120, A Company (Captain Livingston) with C Company on its left, met up with the three tanks that had made it across the start line and set off toward Preux-au-Bois, "mopping up the open country to the west of the forest".[103] The area had been subject to heavy shelling, but one or two enemy strongpoints still held out and needed to be neutralised. "During this minor operation great confusion was caused in the enemy ranks who broke and fled in a North-westerly direction, at least 120 prisoners being taken in the vicinity of Preux".[104] Their advance northwards continued and "Capt Livingston met an officer of the 2/Bedfords close to the village of PREUX at 13.15 soon after the meeting of the two Barrages which had been advancing towards each other. At 14.30 Capt Livingston reported his task accomplished and all the enemy mopped up and liaison posts established. Part of C Company lost their way in the mist in the morning and didn't join up till next day".[105] The battalion was able to spend the night bivouacked in the western sector of the forest. Casualties for the day were one Officer[106] and eight other ranks killed, two officers and 59 other ranks wounded.

To the 2/Northumberland Fusiliers (Major A.W. Muir)[107] fell the responsibility of gaining the Red Line objective on the left Brigade front. They paraded at 0100 on the morning of the attack and advanced to their assembly area in squares G 2 a and c., completing the move by 0345. They moved off at 0615, C and D Companies in front, (Lieutenant Snailham and Captain Price), with B Company (Lieutenant W.H. Barrass) in support and A Company (Lieutenant

100 TNA: PRO WO95/102 War Diary 2nd Tank Brigade. See also Montgomery, *Fourth Army*, p. 253, fn. 2 and *Military Operations France & Belgium Vol. V*, p. 474, fn. 1. The identities of the tank and of the Section Commander remain unknown at the time of writing. There is no mention of the episode in the War Diary of the 2nd Royal Dublin Fusiliers.
101 TNA: PRO WO95/2812 War Diary 50th Division HQ. It no doubt also restricted the activities of German machine gunners.
102 TNA: PRO WO95/2833 War Diary 150 Brigade HQ.
103 TNA: PRO WO95/2837 War Diary 2nd Battalion Royal Munster Fusiliers.
104 TNA: PRO WO95/2812 War Diary 50th Division HQ.
105 TNA: PRO WO95/2837 War Diary 2nd Battalion Royal Munster Fusiliers.
106 Second-Lieutenant William Stone, commanding A Company, having died of his wounds, is buried in Le Cateau Military Cemetery, grave II B 2.
107 Former commander of C Company, promoted to Major on 23 October 1918. See H.R. Sandilands, *The Fifth in the Great War: A History of the 1st and 2nd Battalions, Northumberland Fusiliers, 1914-1918* (Dover: Grigg & Sons, 1938) p. 293.

Redwood) in reserve, preceded by their tank,[108] behind a barrage that "proved very effective".[109] The German counter barrage, "although very heavy, was wild and scattered and did very little damage".[110] By 1000, with the help of the tank, they had reached the western outskirts of the forest. Twenty minutes later 150 Brigade HQ received a report to that effect, the main body of the battalion being on the Hirondelle River, with detachments already advancing into the forest.[111] The advance was steady thereafter, the intermediate objective being reached by 1200, with "no part of the attack being held up",[112] and the final line reached by 1530. A number of enemy machine guns had been captured, along with 150 prisoners. D Company had gained the additional prize of a field gun. Casualties amounted to three officers wounded, Lieutenants Barrass, Snailham and Mouat,[113] with 85 other ranks killed or wounded. The day's fatalities can be confirmed at 23, including nine NCOs.

On the right of the brigade frontage were the 7th Wiltshires [7/Wiltshire] (Lieutenant-Colonel H.J. Hodgson), D and C Companies in front, left and right, A in support 150 yards behind and B in reserve a further 300 yards back. The move to the edge of the forest was made in artillery formation, with the creeping barrage scheduled to reach there at Zero plus 82 on the right and Zero plus 75 on the left. From there, there would be no creeping barrage as such, due to the density of the trees in that area, and artillery would confine itself to enfilading the roads and tracks 500 yards ahead of the troops. The men themselves would move in file down the sides of the roads with an "advanced guard thrown out in front".[114] The final push to the Red Line was across a cleared area, so the creeping barrage was able to resume there from Zero plus 172. Each front company would have its own tank: D Company had a female tank (I.36) and C Company a male (T.39).[115] They were to precede the infantry but were strictly forbidden from going any further than the edge of the forest. Infantry could communicate with the tanks in two ways: "if a tank is required for a special task a smoke bomb will be lighted by the infantry requiring assistance and fired in the direction in which the tank is required to go".[116] Should more detailed information need to be imparted to a tank commander, "messages can be handed in through a trap door in rear of the tank".[117]

It appears that the attack went largely to plan, the only real stubborn resistance being encountered early on at the Landrecies-Englefontaine road. In the end, the line gained and consolidated at around 1145 was just yards short of the Red Line, although they had outposts thrown out ahead directly on the objective. Casualties had totalled five officers and 67 other ranks. Twenty-six prisoners and 20 machine guns had been captured. Fatalities for the day were *one* other rank.[118]

---

108 Sandilands, *The Fifth in the Great War*, p. 293.
109 TNA: PRO WO95/2836 War Diary 2nd Northumberland Fusiliers.
110 Ibid.
111 TNA: PRO WO95/2833 War Diary 150 Brigade HQ.
112 TNA: PRO WO95/2836 War Diary 2nd Northumberland Fusiliers.
113 Sandilands, *The Fifth in the Great War*, p. 294.
114 TNA: PRO WO95/2836 War Diary 7th Battalion Wiltshire Regiment.
115 Male tanks were equipped with two 6-pounder guns. Female tanks had machine guns as their main armament.
116 TNA: PRO WO95/2836 War Diary 7th Battalion Wiltshire Regiment.
117 Ibid.
118 12457 Corporal Richard Samuel Suter, age 25, is buried in Busigny Communal Cemetery Extension, grave II C 2.

150 Brigade total casualties for the engagement can be calculated as follows:

	Officers			Other Ranks		
	K	W	M	K	W	M
2nd Royal Munster Fusiliers	1	2	–	8	59	–
2nd Northumberland Fusiliers	–	3	–	23	62	–
7th Wiltshires	–	5	–	1	67	–
Total	1	10	–	32	188	–

149 Brigade (Brigadier-General P.M. Robinson) were responsible for the right wing of the division front. They attacked with 13th Black Watch (Royal Highlanders) [13/Black Watch][119] on the left, 3rd Royal Fusiliers [3/Royal Fusiliers] on the right, and 2nd Royal Dublin Fusiliers [2/R.Dublin Fusiliers] in support. The Red Line was the goal of the front two battalions, the Dublin Fusiliers having been given a special task. Conditional on their sister battalions' success, and as mentioned earlier, they were to advance and take the spur of land in squares H 13 a and H 7 c., effectively outflanking the town of Landrecies to the north, which may have proved useful to the 25th Division, who were assaulting the town itself and needed to force a crossing of the canal in doing so.

The 13/Black Watch (Lieutenant-Colonel P.J. Blair), on the left, already had C Company holding the line on the night of 3-4 November. A, B and D Companies moved up during the hours of darkness into previously prepared trenches to the rear of their comrades. Just before zero, C Company withdrew to their support position behind B and A Companies, (front line, left and right respectively), D Company being in reserve. Each company would advance on a frontage of 150 yards, each on a one-platoon front, this widening to two platoons as the attack progressed. C Company would remain 200 yards in the rear, in Diamond Artillery formation. Even before they moved off at zero, they were subject to heavy shelling. The 149 Brigade diarist attributes this to the 0545 start of IX Corps on their right and the German artillery response to this: "Enemy's reply was heavy on our forming up line and casualties were sustained especially by the reserve battalion".[120]

Moving off at 0615, the Black Watch's initial progress was slow, hampered by the mist, the enemy barrage and heavy machine gun fire. Their left company reached 'Drill Ground Corner'[121] at around 0945, and it was about then that the German resistance "which was entirely MG apart from the artillery fire",[122] slackened and the mist lifted. The "operation became much easier"[123] and with the tanks "g[iving] great assistance",[124] the Red Line was reached about noon.

119 Also known as "Scottish Horse" and referred to as such in 149 Brigade Diary.
120 TNA: PRO WO95/2827 War Diary 149 Brigade HQ.
121 See Map 11. (G10 a 5.6).
122 TNA: PRO WO95/2831 War Diary 13th Black Watch.
123 Ibid.
124 TNA: PRO WO95/2827 War Diary 149 Brigade HQ.

Casualties were documented as follows: one officer killed,[125] with two wounded. Twenty-eight other ranks killed and 99 wounded. Other ranks fatalities can be confirmed at 35 for the day's fighting. The battalion was able to billet at Hachette Farm in the forest that night, only just behind the Green Line objective, but due to the bad state of the roads and the volume of traffic on them, it was very difficult to get rations up to them. The hungry men were eventually supplied by pack animal during the night.

On the brigade right were the 3rd Royal Fusiliers [3/Royal Fusiliers] (Lieutenant-Colonel M.O. Clarke), formed up with No.4 Company (Lieutenant D.S. Corlett) and No.1 Company (Captain R.M. Large) in front, left and right, No.3 Company (Lieutenant R.E. Pudney) in support and No.2 Company (Lieutenant B.W. Tanner) in reserve. They had three tanks of A Company, 9th Tank Battalion, 400 yards behind them, Tanks Nos. 13, 14 and 18. "Their objective [was] the line of trees in G 11 b and G 12 a & d and thence working southwards to the canal bank to establish posts in H 7 c".[126]

No. 1 Company was reported in position by 0525 on 4 November, but they became victims of the German barrage before they had a chance to move: "Captain MURRAY LARGE[127] reported killed by shell fire, and half of No. 1 Platoon casualties on tape line".[128] When our own barrage did come down at 0615, it "caused a thick fog, preventing one from seeing more than 20 or 30 yards".[129]

All communication was cut at the moment of zero hour, "all lines being down",[130] and the only information getting back to Battalion Headquarters was going to be by runner, it seemed. Two officers, Lieutenant Balding and Second-Lieutenant Bean were despatched at 0815 to get in touch with the advancing troops, but it was Private Town who arrived back at headquarters with nine prisoners at 0830 who was able to shed the first light on the rate of progress. He was able to confirm that the "Tanks were […] doing good work" and that "troops were about 500 yards across the road in G9 a central. […] Casualties were reported not very heavy after moving off and hostile artillery fire light, […] our men had not reached G 9 d by 0800".[131]

Bean and Balding had run into shell fire around 0930 and had been forced to "scatter", according to Balding's servant. Balding returned, a shrapnel wound in his stomach, at 1000. Bean managed to get a message back at 1045 to the effect that " 'B' Company of the R. Fus were held up in square G10 a and were being reinforced by 'C' Company".[132] A telephone message to Battalion Headquarters from the Brigade Major, timed at 1150, was cause for optimism: "The Bosche are on the run and Units are to push on".[133]

This series of messages and the ones that follow illustrate the communication difficulties typically encountered once an advance had begun, and the impossibility of reacting appropriately and

125 Second-Lieutenant James Robertson Gibb (6th Battalion Argyll & Sutherland Highlanders, attached 13th Black Watch), is buried in Cross Roads Cemetery, Fontaine-au-Bois, grave I A 10.
126 TNA: PRO WO95/2831 War Diary 3rd Royal Fusiliers.
127 Lieutenant / Acting Captain Ronald Murray Large, age 21, (7th Royal Fusiliers, attached 3rd Battalion) is buried in Cross Roads Cemetery, Fontaine-au-Bois, grave I B 18.
128 TNA: PRO WO95/2831 War Diary 3rd Royal Fusiliers.
129 Ibid.
130 Ibid.
131 Ibid.
132 It is unclear why the diarist has now reverted to designating companies by letter rather than number.
133 TNA: PRO WO95/2831 War Diary 3rd Royal Fusiliers.

in time: 10 minutes after the Brigade Major's telephone call, a message from Second-Lieutenant Savours, now commanding No.1 Company, timed at 1120, arrived at Battalion Headquarters reporting "objectives gained and consolidation being carried out on RED LINE. In touch with No.4 Company on left".[134] Also at noon, a message timed at 1130 from Lieutenant Tanner, (No.2 Company), reported the arrival on the Red Line of his company, along with No.3 and No.1 on left and right respectively.

The confusion was then compounded: "Later a message was received from OC No.3 Company (Lieut[enant] Pudney) timed at 1345 hours stated 'The battalion reached its objectives at 1010 hours – we are consolidating – in touch with SCOTTISH HORSE on our left and the WARWICKS on our right – we have captured a battery of Field Artillery complete with horses and limbers.' The message was not understood owing to the difference in timing (1 hr 20 minutes) with the other companies".[135]

Whatever the true sequence of events, the end result seems clear: the Red Line was reached and consolidated by midday. An after-battle report compiled by Company Commanders did eventually agree on 1130 as the time of arrival on the Red Line. No.2 Company was later sent forward to occupy the line of trees in G 12 a. No.3 Company later came up to support them, installing themselves on the high ground in G 12 c.

The tanks, it seemed, had played an important role in the initial phase of the action:

In this portion of the front [...], the enemy appears to have had a very complete system of m.g. defence, and the infantry ascribed their success in overcoming these and being able to continue the advance, largely to the co-operation of Tanks. The value of the training carried out with the infantry before the battle was many times demonstrated, the position of many machine guns being indicated to the tanks by the infantry". Co-operation had mutual benefits: "On one occasion a Tank was warned of an anti-Tank gun by an officer.[136]

This battalion also had difficulties getting rations up to the men:

Hot soup was taken up to the Battalion on pack mules at 1900 hours and rations which had been delayed owing to the late arrival of the Supply Train, were taken up on limbers at about 0100 hours, together with water. Owing to the bad state of the roads and blocks caused by Artillery which was moving up, each journey took about 6 or 7 hours.[137]

Casualties were estimated at the time to be one officer and seven other ranks killed, three officers and 102 other ranks wounded, with seven other ranks missing. Fatalities can be confirmed at one officer and 20 other ranks.

The 2/Royal Dublin Fusiliers (Lieutenant-Colonel W.A. Trasenster), in Brigade reserve, moved forward to Fontaine-au-Bois at Zero hour, some 800 yards behind the attacking battalions. "The Battalion almost immediately came under a heavy barrage and suffered heavy

134 Ibid.
135 Ibid.
136 TNA: PRO WO95/102 War Diary 2nd Tank Brigade.
137 TNA: PRO WO95/2831 War Diary 3rd Royal Fusiliers.

casualties".[138] They moved off "immediately after zero hour to avoid the heavy shelling".[139] At 1500,[140] they received orders to take the spur in squares H7 c and H13 a and d. It was taken by D Company under Captain J.N. Barry and about 10 men from C Company under Second-Lieutenant S.A. Morris. In doing so, they also captured "a battery of enemy field guns attempting to come into action near the canal bank".[141] The horses and drivers were shot and the Battery Commander captured. The diary of 149 Brigade asserts however that the spur was taken "without opposition".[142]

Casualties were estimated to be one officer killed,[143] along with 10 other ranks; three officers and around 100 other ranks were wounded, with three other ranks reported missing. Fatalities for the day can be finalised at one officer and 13 other ranks.

Brigade casualties can be estimated at:

	Officers			Other Ranks		
	K	W	M	K	W	M
13th Black Watch	1	2	–	35	92	–
3rd Royal Fusiliers	1	3	–	20	90	7
2nd Royal Dublin Fusiliers	1	3	–	13	100	3
Total	3	8	–	68	282	10

The reasons for the success of the Brigade's recent attacks were summed up by the diarist of 13/ Black Watch:

> On all occasions the tactics of our troops, which proved successful, were mutual support between sections, platoons and companies, with covering rifle and L.G.[144] fire and a gradual working forward by sections and platoons here and there, wherever the opportunity offered. The value of well-trained scouts was emphasised on all occasions. The necessity for full-sized tools was always brought out – the Entrenching Implement was found to be of little value. Air photographs were most useful. An understanding of the situation by NCOs and men and their capacity to use their own initiative was at times an outstanding feature. On all occasions the consciousness of their superiority over the enemy was a great factor towards success.[145]

138 TNA: PRO WO95/2831 War Diary 2nd Royal Dublin Fusiliers.
139 TNA: PRO WO95/2827 War Diary 149 Brigade HQ.
140 This timing is according to the diary of 149 Brigade HQ. The 2nd Royal Dublin Fusiliers' diary says that the spur had been taken by 1230. This is evidently wrong, as the 3rd Royal Fusiliers' diary has the Dubliners preparing to push on to the spur at 1500.
141 TNA: PRO WO95/2831 War Diary 2nd Royal Dublin Fusiliers.
142 TNA: PRO WO95/2827 War Diary 149 Brigade HQ.
143 Second-Lieutenant Hubert John McBrien is buried in Cross Roads Cemetery, Fontaine-au-Bois, grave I A 35.
144 Lewis Gun.
145 TNA: PRO WO95/2831 War Diary 13th Black Watch.

The capture of the day's final objective, the Green Line, on 50th Division front, was down to 151 Brigade (Brigadier-General R.E. Sugden). Of the three brigades in 50th Division, this one was nearest to being at full strength. Figures for 2 November 1918 were as follows:

	Officers	Other Ranks
6th Royal Inniskilling Fusiliers	20	718
1st King's Own Yorkshire Light Infantry	24	943
4th King's Royal Rifle Corps	31	617
Total	75	2,278

The original orders, issued 1 November, were for an advance on a two battalion front, with 1st K.O.Y.L.I. [1/KOYLI] on the left and 4th K.R.R.C. [4/KRRC] on the right. One company of the 6th Royal Inniskilling Fusiliers [6/R.Inniskilling Fusiliers], "to which a specific task is allocated",[146] was to be under command of the 4/KRRC, the rest of this battalion being in reserve. This was to change as the situation developed.

The 1/KOYLI (Lieutenant-Colonel H.Mallinson) was to assemble near Drill Hall Corner at Zero plus 120 and then form up for the attack at Zero plus four and a half hours on the Red Line astride the Route de Fontaine, with its right-hand company on the Laie du Mont Carmel. The 4/KRRC (Major G.A. Tryon MC)[147] followed a similar route and timetable before deploying to the right of 1/KOYLI astride the track running north-east from the rifle range through square B25 central.[148]

The 6/R.Inniskilling Fusiliers (Lieutenant-Colonel G.G.F.F. Greville), less one company, were to form up 500 yards behind 1/KOYLI, astride the Route de Landrecies. The detached company, (D Company), would move to the extreme right of the brigade front and advance along the railway line running parallel to and to the north of the River Sambre, establishing a series of posts as it went, these being supported by machine guns, their purpose being to "assist the RE in throwing bridges over the Sambre at these points if the situation demands".[149]

There would, of course, be no proper 18-pounder creeping barrage to support this stage of the attack: 60-pounders would "barrage all routes in the FORET DE MORMAL in enfilade" and 6" Howitzers "will bombard cross roads and other selected targets".[150] 250 Brigade RFA under Lieutenant-Colonel F.G.D. Johnston DSO would be rushed forward to support 151 Brigade, with officers meeting at Drill Ground Corner to liaise at Zero plus three hours. Two 18-pounder guns each would be allotted to 1/KOYLI and 4/KRRC "to be used by the Battalion Commander as he may direct".[151]

Orders for the advance were issued at 1115 on 4 November, and the two lead battalions crossed the Red Line at about 1330. "The advance progressed well, the resistance offered by

---

146   TNA: PRO WO95/2839 War Diary 151 Brigade HQ. Brigade Instructions No.1. 1 November 1918.
147   Lieutenant-Colonel George Arthur Tryon was killed in action on 7 November 1918, age 32.
148   See Map 11.
149   TNA: PRO WO95/2839 War Diary 151 Brigade HQ. Brigade Instructions No.1. 1 November 1918.
150   Ibid. Instructions No.2 Series 'B'. 2 November 1918.
151   Ibid.

hostile Machine Gunners being effectively overcome by rifle and lewis gun fire".[152] The 1/ KOYLI diarist describes the action in the briefest of terms:

> The Bn moved by the ROUTE DE FONTAINE through the forest, meeting a consider- able amount of opposition from enemy machine gun [illegible]. The Enemy retired in front of the Bn until dark".[153]

They dug in just short of the Green Line and, having veered slightly to the north, were partly outside the northern divisional boundary. The attack had cost them nine fatalities, including one officer.[154]

The 4/KRRC went forward astride the Route de Landrecies, B Company (Captain G.K. Wells) as the advanced guard, A Company (Captain Buller) as right flank guard, with C and D Companies (Captain Truter and Second-Lieutenant Methven) forming the main body. HQ Company (Lieutenant Burgoyne) brought up the rear.

First contact with the enemy was made at A 29 c 4.4 as they ran into machine gun and rifle fire. "A number of casualties were incurred in dislodging the enemy from the position. Considerable assistance was received here from an armoured car moving along the Route de Landrecies".[155]

The artillery was also able to play a vital supporting role:

> The 18-pdrs working with the Battalion were of great assistance where any organised resistance was met with; one instance of their value is worthy of special mention here.
>
> The 4th K.R.R.C. were being held up on their whole front by nests of hostile machine guns in A 29 b.; at the time the 18-pdrs supporting this Battalion were at G4 b 6.8. On receipt of instructions from O.C. 4th K.R.R.C., Lt. Garry got his guns into action with marked rapidity and shelled the above area with some 60 rounds after which the advance was resumed and continued almost uninterruptedly.[156]

The 4/KRRC diarist continues the story:

> From this point onwards more or less continuous touch was maintained with the enemy who appeared to be fighting a rear guard action with Cavalry Machine Gunners. The ground afforded ample cover for this procedure & made a rapid advance difficult. It was not until 15.45 that our advanced guard reached the E. Edge of the wood in B19 b. On debouching from the wood it was found that the enemy was making a determined stand on the high ground in B14 c, the Advanced Guard coming under heavy MG fire. It was found impossible to get forward under the fire so 'D' Company were ordered to work round on our right flank, through the wood in B20 and to dislodge the enemy by working up the ridge

---

152 Ibid. 'Narrative of Operations.'
153 TNA: PRO WO95/2843 War Diary 1st King's Own Yorkshire Light Infantry.
154 Second-Lieutenant Thomas Richard Allott is buried in Romeries Communal Cemetery Extension, grave IV B 9.
155 TNA: PRO WO95/2843 War Diary 4th King's Royal Rifle Corps. 'Narrative'.
156 TNA: PRO WO95/2839 War Diary 151 Brigade HQ. 'Narrative of Operations'.

on his flank. This manoeuvre was entirely successful and the crest of the ridge was captured just as dusk was falling at about 1700 hours.[157]

The battalion was then ordered to move to the right before consolidating their position after capturing the Green Line, but it was now dark and the Commanding Officer decided to stay put and consolidate the ridge. He placed C and D Companies in the old German trench just on the reverse slope of the crest, with B Company 200 yards behind in support, and A Company in reserve. They sat out the night there, under intermittent shelling and "occasional bursts of harassing MG fire".[158] Casualties were estimated at three officers and 30 other ranks. Five other ranks had been killed. Neither battalion had quite made it to the Green Line, but they had been ordered in any case "to dig in before dusk whether they had gained the objective or not".[159]

Even before the main assault, the 6/R.Inniskilling Fusiliers had been in action on 4 November. B and C Companies had been given the task of mopping up some buildings on the Englefontaine-Landrecies road at A26 a 7.4. They had completed this by 0840 and the battalion was at their assembly point at Drill Ground Corner by 1215.

At 1310 they leapfrogged the 13/Black Watch and advanced through the forest in Artillery formation, left flank on the Route de Landrecies, right flank on the railway, with C Company on the left, A Company in the centre, B on the right and D in support. Only slight opposition was encountered from machine guns and "snipers".[160] By 1530 they had received orders to establish a line extending southwards to the canal from B21 d 2.4. They consolidated this as darkness fell. During the night, Second-Lieutenant L. Briggs-Lawrence was "evacuated to Hospital [...] suffering from Shell-shock".[161]

The advance was to be continued the next day, and a conference of commanding officers took place at 2000 to decide on plans. The 151 Brigade diarist concludes his narrative by highlighting the role of the non-commissioned officers in the November fighting:

> It is impossible to close this Narrative without making special mention of the magnificent leadership displayed by N.C.O.'s of all Battalions in the Brigade. This was most significant in the case of the 6th R.Innis. Fus. Who had only 8 officers going into action with Companies on the 3rd instant and the 1st K.O.Y.L.I. who had 10. Of these the former lost 5 and the latter 7 but in spite of this these Battalions never failed to capture their objectives.[162]

The battle plan had worked well. The initial artillery barrage proved effective and the reduced and improvised nature of artillery support beyond the Red Line was sufficient (and, as seen above, sometimes crucial), as it coincided with the collapse of determined enemy resistance: a full creeping barrage was no longer necessary by that stage of proceedings. Tanks and armoured cars were able to work in concert with the infantry where terrain allowed for it, and leeway

---

157 Ibid.
158 Ibid.
159 TNA: PRO WO95/2839 War Diary 151 Brigade HQ.
160 TNA: PRO WO95/2843 War Diary 6th Royal Inniskilling Fusiliers. 'Narrative'.
161 Ibid.
162 TNA: PRO WO95/2839 War Diary 151 Brigade HQ. 'Narrative of Operations'.

within planning and tactics meant that battalions were able (and willing) to take independent action where necessary, with infantry pushing on through the forest, along the roads and tracks, feeling confident enough to abandon linear advances in favour of infiltration and outflanking manoeuvres, points of resistance being either bypassed and mopped up later, or taken by bold manoeuvre with mobile machine gun and artillery support. After the November fighting, the diary of 50th Division listed a number of 'lessons learnt', including the statement "it is essential that the principles laid down in SS.135 Section IV be in no way modified".[163] The recently re-formed division had learnt its lessons quickly and well.

25th Division[164]

25th Division (Major-General J.R.E. Charles) was to assault the German positions on a front of around 2,000 yards: their first, and main objective was the capture of the town of Landrecies, but this first entailed an advance of about one and a half miles across the familiar enclosed terrain of orchards, fields, hedges and, on the northern flank, the straggling suburb of Faubourg-Soyères. Then came the crossing of the Sambre-Oise Canal. The Red Line objective was to the south and east of the town, and the Green Line was a further two miles to the east.[165] The move to this second objective "was, however, contingent on the successful advance on the right by the 32nd Division".[166]

The most formidable obstacle was, of course, the canal, and it fell to the Royal Engineers to devise ways of getting the infantry across the water. On 31 October, Lieutenant-Colonel Done, CRE 25th Division, visited his counterpart at 46th Division to find out how they had crossed the St Quentin Canal at Bellenglise five weeks earlier. Done afterwards muses on the problems facing his men:

> To begin with, the CANAL itself was known to be 53' to 55' wide, with a depth of 6' or 7'. The infantry would have to fight their way through a very enclosed country, a distance on the right of 2,300 yards; and on the extreme left a distance of 3,200 yards, before reaching the CANAL. Swimming was ruled out by the G.O.C. as a feasible manner of crossing. At this time of year the water was too cold to expect the men to swim a canal and to advance and fight, and remain holding the line during the night in wet clothes. Further more after the men had fought their way for an average distance of 2,700 yards, on arriving at the CANAL, unless means were provided for them to get across, they might think that they had done all they could reasonably be expected to do; and there was some likelihood that the advance would come to a stop on the CANAL bank. The G.O.C. desired the R.E. to have ready on the CANAL bank with the first Infantry, some means of passing the Infantry over dry.

163 TNA: PRO WO95/2812 War Diary 50th Division HQ.
164 See Maps 12 and 13.
165 See Map 12.
166 M. Kincaid-Smith, *The 25th Division in France and Flanders* (London: Harrison & Son, 1920) p. 366. The advance to the Green Line did not take place on 4 November. (For an account of 32nd Division's action see Chapter 7).

Since the Bridging Material was required on the CANAL with the leading infantry; and because it is possible neither to drive up Bridging Wagons and Teams by day in face of shell and M.G. fire; nor to carry Pontoons over 1½ miles, the regular Bridging Equipment would not be suitable for the passage of the Infantry. Besides, to attempt to cross a wide Canal by Bridging it at one, or possible two places, is to ask for trouble, and to court failure. An unlucky shell, or the fire from one MG may stop the whole operations. There is only one sound way to attempt such a crossing; which is, to continue to advance on a wide front.[167]

Done's visit to 46th Division had confirmed his aversion to using cork floats: they would be far too heavy to be carried the required distance to the canal. He was, however, buoyed by the idea of using rafts with empty petrol tins as floats, and, once he had Major-General Charles' approval, he promptly put in a requisition for 3,000 tins.

The responsibility for designing and building the rafts was given to Major Richards, 105th Field Company, RE. By the afternoon of 31 October, Richards had designed and built a proto-type. This was tested "by being dropped some feet on to the ground, two or three times. It stood the test well. [...] The raft was then carried to HONNECHY pond and tried. It was found to be sufficiently buoyant and quite handy".[168] Time was short, however: all the rafts had to be built in three days and men in 105th Field Company RE had been falling ill with influenza, so they were supplemented by men from 106th Field Company. Indeed, on 3 November, Major Richards himself "was obliged to go sick".[169] All the rafts were completed by midday on 2 November. Each raft was made from 16 petrol tins, weighed 95 pounds,[170] and with a buoyancy of 220 pounds, could take the weight of one fully-equipped soldier, even if one or two tins were perforated by bullet or shrapnel.

That afternoon, a demonstration was organised on the River Selle, using six rafts:

The Selle River was about 32' wide, but served for our purpose. A platoon of infantry[171] made a demonstration attack on it followed by Sappers carrying rafts and superstructures. On reaching the River, the Sappers duly paddled across, the platoon of Infantry was ferried across and the rafts were made into a bridge. The realistic nature of the operation was somewhat marred by the enormous crowd of spectators; who found amusement in the efforts of one or two of the Infantry to balance themselves on the rafts. There was some general feeling of doubt, I think, as to whether the operation would be feasible under fire. One C.O. gave it as his opinion, that it would be a "Sporting Event."[172]

The Engineers had not put all their eggs in one basket, however: intelligence received from civilian residents in Landrecies told that the main bridge over the canal was still intact, though mined. To the north-east, the Germans had built a wooden bridge suitable for horse transport

---

167 TNA: PRO WO95/2232 War Diary 25th Division CRE. The spelling and punctuation are as in the original.
168 Ibid.
169 Ibid.
170 The cork floats weighed 300 pounds each.
171 The platoon came from D Company, 1/8th Battalion Worcestershire Regiment, 75 Brigade.
172 TNA: PRO WO95/2232 War Diary 25th Division CRE.

and to the south-west there were three single-plank footbridges. All this was confirmed by aerial photographic reconnaissance. The capture of any of these bridges would provide alternatives to the rafts, but just in case the main bridge should be blown up by the Germans, Done arranged for two light footbridges, capable of spanning the 17 foot-wide Lock, to be carried forward.

There was one more water hazard to be negotiated: to the west of Landrecies, and north of the Canal, was the 'Ancient River',[173] the path taken by the River Sambre prior to its canalisation in 1818, 20 feet wide in places and four to five feet deep. There were, therefore, in the end, three Bridging Parties:

> No.1 Party To bridge the Ancient River. It was decided to put three floating bridges across it. This would require 15 rafts and 18 pieces of superstructure.[174]

> No. 2 Party To bridge the CANAL between the Lock and the right Divisional Boundary. This party would have 30 rafts.

> No. 3 Party To bridge the CANAL between the Lock and the left Divisional Boundary. This party would have 35 rafts.[175]

A procedure for their delivery to the canal and their deployment was worked out.

Each raft would have three men: two Pioneers would carry it and a Sapper with a hand-axe would either help to carry it, or cut a pathway through hedges as required. Then, "on reaching the CANAL the groups were to spread out, so that the rafts would be about 20 yards apart along the whole front of the CANAL. The rafts would be launched, the Sapper on each raft would paddle himself across on it, a line being paid out by the Pioneers. On reaching the far bank, the Sapper would take the 2nd line, which was fast to the front of the raft, and securing it to the bank, the raft would then be pulled backwards and forwards by the Sapper and the Pioneers, an Infantry Soldier being put across on each trip. As soon as the first wave was across the rafts were to be collected and formed into permanent floating bridges. [...] All the Infantry destined to cross on rafts were provided with lifebelts in case they should get wounded while actually crossing".[176]

The three bridging parties would total 311 men, 110 of whom were Royal Engineers. No. 1 Party would be under command of Second-Lieutenant A.L. Armstrong, No. 2 Party was commanded by Second-Lieutenant Wells, and No. 3 Party by Second-Lieutenant J.M Petty. Three Supply Tanks were allocated to the Royal Engineers: fearful that a breakdown or enemy shell fire could put a tank out of action and therefore jeopardise the whole operation, Lieutenant-Colonel Done decided that he would entrust the transportation of only the bridge superstructures to the tanks.[177]

---

173 See Map 13. The 'ancient river' is largely in square G22.
174 The 'superstructure' referred to consisted of decking pieces to be used once a bridge was formed.
175 TNA: PRO WO95/2232 War Diary 25th Division CRE.
176 Ibid.
177 In the event, one tank broke down, but its load was transferred to the other two and the equipment was delivered to the rendezvous point (G 16 d 0.4) on time, at Zero plus 3 hours.

Finally, a section of the 182nd Tunnelling Company RE was attached to Done's force: they were to be used in an attempt to capture the existing bridges over the canal. "Two parties of 3 Sappers each were to rush the H[orse] T[ransport] bridge and the footbridges NE and SW of LANDRECIES respectively; and 1 N.C.O. and 10 Sappers were to rush the main bridge at Landrecies.[178] Once there, they were to remove any explosive devices.

The Bridging Parties formed up behind the Infantry Battalions: No.3 Party would advance with the 1/8th Royal Warwickshire Regiment [1/8th R.Warwickshire], Nos. 1 & 2 Parties would be with the 1/5th Gloucestershire Regiment [1/5th Gloucestershire].

The infantry assault was to take place on a single-brigade front, and the honour fell to 75 Brigade (Brigadier-General C.W. Frizell). It lined up with 1/8th R.Warwickshire (Lieutenant-Colonel P.H. Whitehouse) on the left, 1/5th Gloucestershire (Lieutenant-Colonel D. Lewis) on the right, and four Companies of 1/8th Worcestershire Regiment [1/8th Worcestershire] (Lieutenant-Colonel H.T. Clarke) spread out behind them across the whole brigade frontage.[179] Two companies of 21st Battalion Manchester Regiment [21/Manchester] (7 Brigade) would mop up the area north of the canal on the extreme right flank near the hamlet of Happegarbes.

74 Brigade (Brigadier-General H.M. Craigie-Halkett) would follow up the advance of 75 Brigade and be ready to continue the advance to the Green Line objective, whereas 7 Brigade (Brigadier-General C.J. Hickie) were held in reserve, near Pommereuil on the far side of the Bois L'Eveque, but ready to move at 15 minutes' notice. "The fighting strength of the infantry of the Division was now 4,190 rifles".[180]

All battalions were in position on the morning of 4 November by 0415 and a "noise barrage"[181] was opened by our machine guns at 0545 to coincide with Zero Hour of IX Corps on 25th Division's right. By way of reply, a German counter barrage fell, causing 10 casualties amongst the Gloucesters.

At Zero Hour, 0615, our main barrage opened and solicited a short-range reply from German positions just across the canal. A German despatch captured later that morning seemed to indicate the German Officers had assumed, until the 25th Division troops arrived at their positions, that the assault would be confined to the 32nd Division front, as it had been the previous morning.[182]

On the left, the 1/8th Warwickshire had the furthest to go, and this across "very difficult country",[183] and were soon well behind the barrage.[184] They had encountered their first opposi-

---

178 TNA: PRO WO95/2232 War Diary 25th Division CRE.
179 See Map 13. All ranks of the 1/8th Worcesters were to be equipped "as lightly as possible – puttees will not be worn".TNA: PRO WO95/2249 War Diary 75 Brigade HQ.
180 Kincaid-Smith, *25th Division*, p. 366.
181 TNA: PRO WO95/2249 War Diary 75 Brigade HQ 'Narrative'.
182 Ibid.
183 TNA: PRO WO95/2232 War Diary 25th Division CRE.
184 The War Diary of 1/8th Royal Warwickshires, TNA: PRO WO95/2251, is of little use to the chronicler: the whole day's action is summed up in three and a half lines of narrative, almost totally devoid of any detail. The story of the Warwickshires is therefore collected from other sources:
     Montgomery, *Fourth Army* pp. 252-253
     Kincaid-Smith, *25th Division*, pp. 366-370
     TNA: PRO WO95/2227 War Dairy 25th Division HQ
     TNA: PRO WO95/2249 War Diary 75 Brigade HQ
     TNA: PRO WO95/2235 War Diary 105th Field Company RE

tion from enemy machine gun posts at the crossroads at G 9 a 6.1, but these were quickly dealt with by one of the two tanks that made it any distance over the jumping off line[185] and by Lewis Gun fire. They had reached the line of a light railway in squares G 15 b & d by around 0730.

Half an hour later, the Warwicks were held up by machine gun and 'minenwerfer'[186] fire from Faubourg-Soyères, and there began a "fight for fire supremacy".[187] Again, with the help of tank No. 9107, (Second-Lieutenant Knowles), but chiefly due to the action of Lance-Corporal W. Amey and his section,[188] the German resistance in this area was overwhelmed, three 'minenwerfers' being captured, and the advance was able to continue. Amey and his section overran a German strongpoint containing several machine guns, capturing 50 prisoners. Then, after finishing off another machine gun post, Amey single-handedly captured the Chateau in the village, along with its garrison of about 20 German soldiers.

During the fighting, Lieutenant J.G. Eccles became separated from his Company quite early on and was captured, only to turn up at battalion headquarters three hours later with eight prisoners of his own. Eccles was in command of B Company, 1/8th R.Warwickshire. A Company was commanded by Second-Lieutenant H. Fawke, C Company by Captain E.S.C. Vaughan and D Company by Lieutenant A.P. Hack.

By 1030, the 1/8th R.Warwickshire were at the canal, some in Landrecies itself, some to the north-east, the former just in time to see the main bridge over the canal blown up by the Germans. On the right, the 1/5th Gloucestershire lined up with C and A companies in front, left and right, (Lieutenant G.H West and Second-Lieutenant W.H. Robbins), with D Company (Captain G.E. Ratcliffe) as "moppers up"[189] and B Company (Captain V.B. Bingham-Hall) in reserve. They set off in the mist and before long A Company had become "somewhat split up"[190] amongst the hedges and orchards, but B Company were pushed forward into the gap that had appeared and the momentum of the attack was maintained. C Company had, meanwhile, come up against a machine gun post at G 16 a 1.1, but was able to overrun it with the help of a tank and A and B Companies of the Worcesters.

By 0730, B Company had reached the crossroads at G 15 d 9.1: they then turned south and arrived at the railway line. "Here, much opposition was met with",[191] but enemy fire slackened as our barrage advanced and with the help of two tanks, the Gloucesters were able to reach the 'Ancient River'. The bridge over it, earlier pinpointed by aerial photography, was found "intact, though mined".[192] Sergeant Wood and Sapper Barbour, both of 105th Field Company RE, were first there and were able to withdraw the charges. B Company 1/8th Gloucestershire and

TNA: PRO WO95/2232 War Dairy 25th Division CRE.

185 Of the four tanks allocated, one developed mechanical trouble before leaving the Tankodrome and another suffered a direct hit and was put out of action "at an early stage. The other two did very useful work with the Infantry units […] and it is estimated that between 20 and 30 m.g.'s were destroyed by this section". (TNA: PRO WO95/102 War Diary 2nd Tank Brigade).

186 A type of German mortar: literally 'mine thrower'.

187 TNA: PRO WO95/2249 War Diary 75 Brigade HQ 'Narrative'.

188 Lance-Corporal Amey was awarded the Victoria Cross for his actions. See Appendix IV for full citation.

189 TNA: PRO WO95/2251 War Diary 1/5th Battalion Gloucestershire Regiment.

190 Ibid.

191 TNA: PRO WO95/2232 War Diary 25th Division CRE.

192 Ibid.

No. 1 Bridging Party arrived at the canal to find one out of the three single-plank bridges still standing.

The job of the 1/8th Worcestershire was to follow the leading battalions and, once the latter had secured the crossings over the Sambre, to leapfrog them, "capture Landrecies [and] occupy the Red Line".[193] The battalion's four companies were deployed as follows: on the left was C Company (Captain J.O. Walford); A Company (Captain L.R. Bomford) was in the centre, with B Company (Second-Lieutenant J.A. Bullock) slightly behind them in support, and D Company (Lieutenant E.Wedgbury) was on the right flank.

C Company's first task was to reach the canal bank south of Les Etoquies, but they were caught up in the fighting amongst the ruined houses of Faubourg Soyères and suffered a number of casualties, including two officers of the leading platoon wounded. Some of these casualties were caused by pushing on too quickly and getting too close to their own creeping barrage. "Sgt Faulkner took command of both platoons and led them resolutely forward".[194] Faulkner earned himself a DCM: when both platoons were held up by machine gun fire,[195] he led a Lewis Gun team round to a flank position and "opened a sharp burst of enfilade fire",[196] which dispersed the enemy machine gun team and allowed the rest of the company to move forward. Eventually, after clearing up more machine guns along the line of the railway, this time with the help of a tank, the canal was reached (about G 17 d 0.4). They came under fire from enemy field guns situated just across the water, but these were "silenced by LG fire".[197]

A Company, with B Company close behind, found themselves mixed up in the fighting for the enemy front line positions along with platoons of the Gloucesters. They were being held up by machine gun fire from a ruined Chateau on the outskirts of Faubourg Soyères, (G 16 a 1.1): "Captain Bomford went back quickly to find the supporting tanks. One tank was placed at his disposal, and he guided it personally to the Chateau. The rest of A Company followed close behind the tank as it rumbled forward up to the ruined building, terrorising the defenders; who surrendered in a few minutes – some 40 in all including a Battalion Commander".[198]

A Company was now somewhat behind schedule, and as they advanced from the railway station toward the main bridge at Landrecies, a German officer on a black horse was seen to gallop down to the canal edge, where he detonated a mine, blowing the bridge up.[199] The time was exactly 1030.

Lieutenant Wedgbury, commanding D Company on the right, led his men "rapidly down the slope through the mist, in the hope of securing the footbridges".[200] Four minutes into the

---

193 TNA: PRO WO95/2251 War Diary 1/8th Battalion Worcestershire Regiment.
194 H.F. Stacke, *The Worcestershire Regiment in the Great War* (Kidderminster: Cheshire & Sons, 1929) pp. 480-481.
195 Probably at either G 9 d 5.0 (TNA: PRO WO95/2251 War Diary 1/8th Battalion Worcestershire Regiment) or G 16 b 0.7.
196 Ibid.
197 Ibid.
198 Stacke, *The Worcestershire Regiment in the Great War*, p. 480.
199 Stacke, *The Worcestershire Regiment in the Great War*, p. 480; Kincaid-Smith, *25th Division*, p. 381; TNA: PRO WO95/2252 War Diary 25th Division CRE.
200 Stacke, *The Worcestershire Regiment in the Great War*, p. 480.

attack, at 0619, Wedgbury was wounded "by one of our MG bullets"[201] and Second-Lieutenant P.N. Coleman took command. They encountered enemy artillery and machine gun fire from the south bank of the canal as they crossed the railway line, but the fire was "largely unaimed, for the bank was smothered in dense clouds of smoke from shells and from bombs dropped by British aeroplanes".[202] A patrol was sent forward to the canal, and a footbridge at G 22 d 0.5 was found intact.[203]

As we pause, with soldiers poised at various points along the northern bank of the canal, the story of one particular tank is worth telling: Second-Lieutenant Donald Fraser Crosbie (Commander of Tank 6084) was in charge of three Supply Tanks of 2nd Tank Supply Company, which were carrying bridging material to the Lock at Landrecies.[204] As he approached the railway station, he realised that the infantry were held up by machine gun fire from a house nearby.

> As no good purpose could be served by remaining where he was, this officer pushed forward with his Tanks along the road west of the Station. The German machine gunners apparently thought that fighting tanks were upon them and surrendered.[205]

Crosbie then led his tanks on to the Lock, where he successfully unloaded his cargo. For this action, Crosbie was awarded the Military Cross.

The race to the canal had, it seems, many winners: the identity of those arriving first at its banks varies depending on the account read. On the left flank, to the north-east of Landrecies, No.3 Bridging Party RE was reported to have reached the canal bank at 1010, the party under Second-Lieutenant Petty. This officer had had a difference of opinion with an infantry company commander "as to the best line of approach",[206] had 'borrowed' a platoon of infantry, minus its officers, and headed for the canal: he left the infantry platoon at the railway embankment to cover his advance and took his bridging party to the water's edge. These, according to the 25th Division CRE War Diary were "the first troops to reach the canal bank".[207]

"The rafts were launched and the Sappers paddled across as per programme".[208] Two Sappers were hit by enemy machine gun fire from houses in Landrecies, but covering fire from 1/8th Worcestershire men "made the enemy shooting ineffective".[209]

---

201 TNA: PRO WO95/2251 War Diary 1/8th Battalion Worcestershire Regiment. 'Narrative of Operations'. Stacke's account (p. 480) has Wedgbury wounded later in the attack near the Ancient River.
202 Stacke, *The Worcestershire Regiment in the Great War*, p. 480.
203 TNA: PRO WO95/2251 War Diary 1/8th Battalion Worcestershire Regiment. This is the same bridge 'found' by the 1/5th Gloucestershire. The question of which unit found it first remains unsolved.
204 Supply Tanks were unarmed except for one machine gun.
205 TNA: PRO WO95/102 War Diary 2nd Tank Brigade.
206 TNA: PRO WO95/2232 War Dairy 25th Division CRE.
207 Ibid.
208 Ibid.
209 TNA: PRO WO95/2251 War Diary 1/8th Battalion Worcestershire Regiment. 'Narrative of Operations'.

If Stacke is to be believed, the first men across the canal at this point were from the 1/8th Worcestershire, who had passed through the Royal Warwickshires on their way to the canal, and "Corporal W. Roberts (C Company) actually won the race across", with Captain Walford close behind, the latter arranging the "ropes and tackle to pull the tin rafts to and fro".[210] In any case, within 10 minutes, "about a Company"[211] were ferried over, this being a mixture of a few Warwicks and a large number of Worcesters. The time was 1045. Second-Lieutenant Petty then collected the superstructures from the Supply Tanks and proceeded to build two floating footbridges. These were later used by more of the Worcesters.

As soon as the company of Worcesters was over the canal, they continued their advance "against desultory MG fire"[212] and captured the hospital at G 23 a 8.2, along with five officers, 40 men, three ambulances, two limbers and six horses, before pushing on to the Red Line objective. On the right, south-west of Landrecies, D Company 1/8th Worcestershire "rushed for the [intact] footbridge [over the canal], crossed it and seized the further bank"[213] at around 0950.[214] They were followed almost immediately by A Company of the Gloucesters, who formed up behind them.

D Company moved on again behind the artillery barrage at 1033, "meeting with little enemy resistance".[215] A strongpoint at G 22 d 7.5 was overrun, capturing over 50 prisoners "before they could man their weapons".[216] They had reached the Red Line by 1115. The rest of the Gloucesters then crossed the canal and formed a defensive flank on their right, facing south.

In the centre, in the town of Landrecies, units had been held up by the blowing of the main bridge. But not for long: the lock gates remained intact, however, and 130th Field Company RE (under Second-Lieutenant Wells) managed to get two footbridges in place across this narrow section. The artillery barrage now halted on a line 300 yards east of the canal. This curtain of shell fire and support from machine guns pushed forward, showering the southern bank with both direct and indirect fire, allowed men of 1/8th Warwickshire and 1/8th Worcestershire to cross at around 1245 and move into the town. The enemy garrison, realising that they were being outflanked on both sides by this time, "gradually slipped away"[217] and the town was mopped up with "many German stragglers [giving] themselves up".[218] The only real resistance was encountered at the crossroads south-east of the town centre: a sharp fight soon put an end to this, but both Captain Bomford and Captain Walford of 1/8th Worcestershire were wounded here.[219]

---

210 Stacke, *The Worcestershire Regiment in the Great War*, p. 481. It is possible, of course, that the operation was going as planned, and that more than one raft was being ferried back and forth.
211 TNA: PRO WO95/2232 War Diary 25th Division CRE.
212 TNA: PRO WO95/2251 War Diary 1/8th Battalion Worcestershire Regiment.
213 Stacke, *The Worcestershire Regiment in the Great War*, p. 480. The Bridging Party of Royal Engineers following up here, realising that rafting was not required, proceeded to install two floating footbridges.
214 TNA: PRO WO95/2251 War Diary 1/8th Battalion Worcestershire Regiment. 'Narrative of Operations'.
215 Ibid.
216 Ibid.
217 TNA: PRO WO95/2249 War Diary 75 Brigade HQ. 'Narrative'.
218 Stacke, *The Worcestershire Regiment in the Great War,* p. 481.
219 Bomford was awarded the DSO and Walford a Bar to his MC for their work that day.

Two German artillery batteries were situated on the high ground to the east of Landrecies and they continued to bombard the abandoned town. Second-Lieutenant A. Coe led B Company 1/8th Worcestershire forward to deal with them. He sent a Lewis Gun section out onto a flank to provide covering fire, whilst he and his men took the position in enfilade from the opposite flank, surprising the gunners and capturing both batteries intact, along with 40 prisoners. Coe was awarded the Military Cross for this action.

For such a bold enterprise, the casualty figures for 75 Brigade must be regarded as remarkably light: the 1/8th Warwickshire had lost one officer[220] and 21 other ranks killed. The Gloucesters had suffered two officers[221] and 19 other ranks killed. The Worcesters escaped with 11 other ranks killed. Total casualties for 75 Brigade for the day can be estimated at:

Second-Lieutenant Valentine Scroggie, 1/5th Battalion Gloucestershire Regiment. Landrecies British Cemetery. (Author)

	Officers			Other Ranks		
	K	W	M	K	W	M
1/8th Warwicks	1	2	–	21	108	–
1/8th Worcesters	–	4	–	11	48	7
1/5th Gloucesters	2	4	–	19	41	2
Total	3	10	–	51	197	9

They had taken 20 officers and 815 other ranks prisoner.

On the division's right, the 32nd Division had not made enough progress for the envisaged advance toward the Green Line objective on the 25th Division front to take place. The task of 74 Brigade therefore became much less demanding. A telephone message from 25th Division headquarters at 0925 resulted in 11th Sherwood Foresters [11/Sherwood Foresters] (Lieutenant-Colonel W.R. Corall) being ordered to follow 75 Brigade and "if not involved in

---

220 Captain Joseph Richards, age 26, is buried in Landrecies British Cemetery, grave A 31. Oddly, none of the contemporary or later accounts mention this officer's name, other than in a list of casualties compiled at the end of November by the 25th Division QMG. TNA: PRO WO95/2228 War Diary 25th Division QMG.
221 Second-Lieutenant Valentine Scroggie, age 26, and Captain Stanley Frederick Hill, age 30, are buried in Landrecies British Cemetery, graves A 59 and A 70 respectively.

fighting"[222] to cross the canal and take up positions in squares G 24 a & d. The 9th Yorkshire Regiment [9/Yorkshire] (Lieutenant-Colonel R.S. Hart) and 13th Durham Light Infantry [13/DLI] (Lieutenant-Colonel H.G. Faber) were ordered to move up to the railway in G 22 a and be ready to cross the canal when, or if, required to do so.

At 1240, the 11/Sherwood Foresters were able to report that they were over the canal and pushing forward to the Red Dotted Line. At 1530, 74 Brigade ordered its battalions forward to positions between Bouillette Farm and Catillon Farm. The 9/Yorkshire were to be on the left, 11/Sherwood Foresters on the right, straddling the Landrecies-Maroilles road. As the 11/Sherwood Foresters advanced, they did encounter some enemy opposition: they took harassing machine gun fire from their right flank and B Company captured one officer and 21 other ranks in the skirmish. At 1730, the three forward companies (A, B and D), on their way to their final deployments, concentrated on the road junction at G 30 a 9.8, just in time for a large delayed-action mine to blow up "just in front of 'A' Coy, making a huge crater in the centre of the road, but happily [this] did not cause any casualties".[223] The day's advance had cost them one other rank killed, however, with four wounded. It could have been much worse. Brigade casualties were negligible. The 13/DLI were not even required to cross the canal: they took up positions along the north-western bank of the canal in square G 22 b.

7 Brigade began the day in positions just south of Pommereuil (7,000 yards west of Landrecies). Two companies (A and C) of 21/Manchester, under Captain Miller MC, were placed temporarily under command of 74 Brigade, their task being to advance on the right flank of the attack and mop up the area around the hamlet of Happegarbes. This task was completed "without a hitch",[224] the companies reporting their objectives gained at 0745.[225] Thereafter, it joined its sister battalion, the 20/Manchester, on the railway line north-west of the canal. Signs of the recent fighting were evident: "There were many large buildings on fire in the area occupied by the Battn".[226]

The 9/Devonshire was the only battalion of 74 Brigade to cross the canal that day: they were ordered forward at 1635, crossed by a trestle footbridge near the Lock, and were in position by 2300. They had suffered 17 casualties, "all by one shell",[227] including two other ranks killed. One officer had been killed during the morning.[228]

A few days later, there was a ceremonial march through the town. The mayor of Landrecies issued a notice to its citizens, asking them to line the 'Grande Rue' at 1:30 p.m. for the march past. They were instructed to deck their houses with flags as best they could, and to give the soldiers the ovation they deserved, showering them with flowers as they passed. It was announced that day that one of the boulevards in the town would be renamed 'Boulevard Charles' in honour of the Division and its commander.[229]

222 TNA: PRO WO95/2245 War Diary 74 Brigade HQ.
223 TNA: PRO WO95/2247 War Diary 11th Battalion Sherwood Foresters (Nottinghamshire & Derbyshire Regiment).
224 TNA: PRO WO95/2242 War Diary 74 Brigade HQ. 'Narrative of Operations'.
225 TNA: PRO WO95/2244 War Diary 21st Battalion Manchester Regiment.
226 TNA: PRO WO95/2244 War Diary 20th Battalion Manchester Regiment.
227 TNA: PRO WO95/2244 War Diary 9th Battalion Devonshire Regiment.
228 Lieutenant Cecil Howard Brock, age 26, is buried in Pommereuil British Cemetery, grave A 3.
229 A monument to 25th Division and Major-General Charles still stands at the southern end of the main bridge over the canal in Landrecies, though its claim to be honouring the '600' who fell

25th Division Memorial, Landrecies. (Author)

Stacke concludes his account in typical dramatic style:

Everywhere the enemy's last line of resistance had been broken; everywhere the German armies were huddling back in confusion through the open country to the north-east. Behind them the whole British Army moved forward in pursuit.[230]

In essence, he was right.

drastically over-estimates the numbers. The author can find no evidence that the boulevard name-change ever took place. (Email communication with the office of the Mayor of Landrecies, June 2013)

230 Stacke, *The Worcestershire Regiment in the Great War*, p. 481.

Conclusion

XIII Corps' plan has been demonstrated to be audacious. The BEF showed itself capable of executing combined arms methodology with a high degree of competence, even if battle-field communications proved less than satisfactory in places. Isolated from higher command, battalion, company and platoon commanders were able to show initiative and improvise at the tactical level in order to ensure operational success.

7

IX Corps

Introduction

The basic nature of IX Corps' attacks was different to all of those executed further north: the entire frontage from 19th Division on the left flank of Third Army to 25th Division at Landrecies saw assaults on broad frontages, leaving no sections of the enemy's defences undisturbed. 32nd and 1st Divisions, directly facing the Sambre-Oise Canal, concentrated their forces and their efforts on a number of narrow sectors, leaving substantial stretches of the waterway unmolested.[1] Any German units along these sectors could be outflanked once crossings had been forced. Subsequent events demonstrate just how thin the line between success and failure can be. One canal crossing went exactly to plan; another was rescued by individual initiative and bravery, while a third failed, not for the lack of bravery, but owing to inferior bridging equipment and German obstinacy. The difficult situations along the Corps front were rectified by pragmatic decision-making in the face of setbacks and by a little luck. Decisions made by experienced and capable officers turned impending failure into ultimate victory.

*   *   *

The men of IX Corps (Lieutenant-General Sir Walter P. Braithwaite) were faced with one major task on the morning of 4 November 1918: forcing the crossing of the Sambre-Oise Canal. The German defences, consisting largely of machine gun teams, "concentrated in the forward area",[2] concealed amongst the hedges and orchards and lined up along some sectors of the eastern canal bank, were backed up by isolated batteries and sometimes single field guns. German units still held three positions west of the canal: the village of Catillon, the Happegarbes Spur and the site of the medieval castle motte known as Le Donjon.

The crossing of the canal was to be attempted at just five locations: on 32nd Division front, on the Corps left, 96 Brigade would bridge the waterway just south of the 90 degree bend in the canal two miles south-west of Landrecies and 14 Brigade would cross at the existing bridge in

---

1   See Maps 14 and 15.
2   TNA: PRO WO95/2372 War Diary 32nd Division HQ "Report on Operations".

Ors village. On 1st Division front, 3 Brigade would cross at Catillon after capturing the village, 1 Brigade would bridge the canal half way between Catillon and Lock No.1, the latter being where 2 Brigade would throw their bridges across the narrow lock walls.

IX Corps set the timing of the assault and the objective lines, but methods of attack, and more specifically the method of crossing the canal, were delegated to division and even brigade level. This necessity was dictated by the varied topography, the state of the enemy's defences and on a more mundane and practical basis, on the amount, quality and types of bridging materials available to the Royal Engineers in each sector. 1st Division had been lucky enough to capture a German engineering store intact at Bohain and its myriad contents were jealously guarded from other units, much to the detriment, so it turned out, of 32nd Division.

The planning of the artillery barrage was a divisional responsibility, though counter battery work and distribution of resources remained the domain of Corps. 32nd Division were allocated 35 batteries of field artillery,[3] and 1st Division 33.[4] Heavy artillery across the Corps frontage totalled 244 guns, well over half of these being 6" Howitzers.[5] The guns were to be brought forward gradually, under the cover of darkness if possible, camouflaged and "kept silent".[6] The amount of artillery action in the days leading up to the assault was to remain normal: any increase or diminution could alert the enemy to the imminent attack. Short periods of silence were also built in to the schedule to allow sound ranging units to locate hostile batteries.[7]

32nd Division[8]

On 2 November, 32nd Division (Major-General T.S. Lambert) issued, down to company and artillery battery level, a document entitled "Notes on Future Operations". These were to inform planning and tactics and included notes on enemy dispositions. Commanders down to platoon level were also issued with aerial reconnaissance photographs of ground to the east of the canal.[9] The notes concluded that there would be a "very large concentration of machine guns and infantry close to the canal and within about 2,000 yards of it", and the Germans had "orders to hold on to the Canal Bank at all costs", although we held "strong doubts as to the moral of his troops if surprised and attacked with determination".[10]

3   Three 13-pounder batteries, twenty 18-pounder batteries and seven 4.5" Howitzer batteries. TNA: PRO WO95/842 War Diary IX Corps HA.
4   Twenty-five 18-pounder batteries and eight 4.5" Howitzer batteries. Ibid.
5   60-pounders – 84; 6" Howitzers – 188; 8" Howitzers – 32; 9.2" Howitzers – 28; 6" Guns – 12.
6   TNA: PRO WO95/842 War Diary IX Corps HA.
7   The silent periods of half an hour were as follows:
      30/31 October: 2215–2245 & 0200–0230
      31 Oct-1 Nov: 2130–2200 & 0115–0145
      1 /2 November: 2300–2330 & 0230–0300
      2/3 November: 2230–2300 & 0130–0200
      3/4 November: 2100–2130 & 0030–0100.
8   See Map 14.
9   Imperial War Museum: Private Papers of Brigadier-General T.S. Lambert. Document 4723
10   TNA: PRO WO95/2372 War Diary 32nd Division HQ. "Notes on Future Operations".

Tellingly, it also said "we cannot expect every detail in the attack to take place as planned".[11] It goes on:

> The first phase[12] will require the highest determination of all ranks to force a landing with perhaps hand to hand fighting on the other bank". [...]
>
> The second and third phases[13] will largely depend on the initiative of individuals. [...] Farms, villages, hollow roads and crossroads are likely to be the chief centres of resistance. They should be dealt with by turning one or more flanks and concentrating Lewis and Machine Gun Fire on them, preferably at ranges of 300 yards or more if possible. Stokes Mortars and rifle grenades will be valuable if quickly available. [...]
>
> During the third phase, the enemy's resistance is likely to be almost entirely from machine guns. These are best attacked in flank or in rear.[14]

The advance to the Dotted Blue Line would be supported by a field artillery barrage. Its opening line, on which it would rest for five minutes, was the eastern bank of the canal. It would then lift 300 yards and stand for a further 30 minutes. Thereafter it would creep to the Yellow Line at a rate of 100 yards every six minutes. After a 15 minute pause 300 yards east of that line, it would recommence its movement, at the above rate, to the Dotted Blue Line, halting once more 300 yards to the east of it, for 45 minutes.

> East of this line Field Artillery action supporting the attack to the Blue Line will be arranged direct between Infantry Brigades concerned and their affiliated Artillery Group Commanders.[15]

In reality, for fear of bursting the canal banks and inundating the terrain into which the British were going to advance, the standing artillery barrage 'on the eastern bank' of the canal was in fact tens of yards beyond it. German machine gun positions on the bank, and also many of those within 300 yards of it, missed when the barrage lifted rather than crept to its next pause, were left untouched and were, in places, to provide severe opposition to the first waves of troops attempting to cross.

32nd Division lined up with 96 Brigade (Brigadier-General A.C. Girdwood) on the left and 14 Brigade (Brigadier-General L.P. Evans VC)[16] on the right. 97 Brigade (Brigadier-General G.A. Armytage) were held in reserve, except for two companies of 2nd King's Own Yorkshire Light Infantry [2/KOYLI], which were sent forward to reinforce the 15th Lancashire Fusiliers [15/Lancashire Fusiliers] on the extreme left of 96 Brigade's attack.[17]

---

11   Ibid.
12   Crossing the canal.
13   The advance to the Blue and then the Red Line.
14   Ibid.
15   TNA: PRO WO95/2376 War Diary 32nd Division CRA.
16   Evans won his VC at Zonnebeke on 4 October 1917.
17   96 Brigade had carried out operations on 2 & 3 November to try and take the Happegarbes Spur. Both times they had succeeded only to be driven out again by German counter-attacks. These had inflicted heavy casualties on the brigade. TNA: PRO WO95/2401 War Diary 97 Infantry Brigade HQ.

The 32nd Division's available fighting strength on 2 November 1918 was calculated as follows:

	Officers	Other Ranks
14 Brigade		
5/6th Royal Scots (Lothian Regt)	23	598
1st Dorsetshire Regt.	29	654
15th Highland Light Infantry	21	579
Total	73	1,831
96 Brigade		
15th Lancashire Fusiliers	29	621
16th Lancashire Fusiliers	25	621
2nd Manchester Regt.	28	701
Total	82	1,943
97 Brigade		
1/5th Border Regt.	33	721
2nd KOYLI	29	805
10th Argyll & Sutherland Highlanders	31	717
Total	93	2,243
16th Highland Light Infantry (Pioneers)	18	691
32nd Battalion Machine Gun Corps	33	726
Overall Total	299	7,434[18]

On the extreme left of 96 Brigade front, the 15/Lancashire Fusiliers (Lieutenant-Colonel G.E.R.G. Alban), with A and C Companies of 2/KOYLI (Lieutenant-Colonel L. Lamotte) were to advance onto the Happegarbes Spur and occupy the western bank of the canal. They were not to attempt to cross here,[19] but finally taking this ground would rob the Germans of high ground from which they were able to overlook the canal as far south as Catillon. The threat of enfilade fire from this location would be eliminated. The attack would be supported by two tanks from 10th Tank Battalion.[20]

The 15/Lancashire Fusiliers were being asked, fundamentally, to repeat their 'minor' operation of two days before: 2/KOYLI had received orders at 1135 on 3 November to "detach two companies to the aid of the 96th Brigade",[21] and accordingly C Company (Captain B.V. Pring)

---

18   TNA: PRO WO95/2374 War Diary 32nd Division QMG. The 15th Lancashire Fusiliers had suffered 52 fatalities on 2 and 3 November. The number of wounded is not recorded, but this probably exceeds 100.

19   Original orders (2 November) did include a crossing of the canal as a possibility, but left the final decision to the Brigadier-General. TNA: PRO WO95/2396 War Diary 96 Infantry Brigade HQ. Order No. 494.

20   The original plan was for three tanks. All three had gone in with the preliminary attack here on 2 November, but one had ditched in a pond in Happegarbes village. The successful German counter attack meant that this tank had to be abandoned. It was recovered, undamaged, two days later. TNA: PRO WO95/102 War Diary 2nd Tank Brigade.

21   TNA: PRO WO95/2402 War Diary 2nd King's Own Yorkshire Light Infantry.

slotted into the front line of the attack in the centre, with A Company (Captain H.J. Knight) in support. They were clearly destined for more than a supporting role.

The barrage opened at 0545 and the troops waiting in the jumping off positions caught "the fringe"[22] of it and suffered over 30 casualties before they could move off.

The war diary of 15/Lancashire Fusiliers describes the action in the briefest of terms, acknowledging the intensity and accuracy of the German defensive barrage and the heavy cost. The 96 Brigade diary states that "at 0700 the whole of the W. Bank of the CANAL […] was in our hands".[23]

The 2/KOYLI diarist allows himself considerably more latitude:

> In a dense natural fog the Companies moved forward through hedges and railway cuttings and across a marsh to the Canal Bank. The enemy's barrage came down with great intensity and caused many more casualties to the advancing Companies. In spite of the enemy's fire and difficulties of obstacles the Companies gallantly continued on their way and gained their objectives in quick time: the other Companies of the Lancashire Fusiliers were worn out somewhat with their previous heroic exertions and 'A' and 'C' companies were the only Companies who were able to cross the canal.[24] The two Companies most tenaciously stuck to their positions [and] the tenacity of Yorkshire troops secured the day.[25]

The two tanks, whilst receiving no mention in any of the infantry unit diaries, did good work, clearing up enemy strongpoints and machine gun posts in and around Happegarbes before "advanc[ing] parallel with the railway embankment, overcoming considerable opposition in that quarter, ultimately enabling the Infantry to cross the embankment. As had been proved by the heavy fighting in this area in the previous operations, the enemy laid great stress on retaining this portion of the high ground, and that [sic] fact that it was captured with such rapidity was largely due to the co-operation of tanks".[26] It was whilst returning to the rallying point after the action that 2nd Tank Brigade suffered its only officer fatality of the day, Major F.A. Robinson MC.[27]

The 15/Lancashire Fusiliers had lost a further five other ranks killed for the reclaiming of this high ground. The number of wounded other ranks is not recorded, but three officers were wounded.[28] The 2/KOYLI estimated their losses for the day at one officer killed,[29] with one wounded. Six other ranks were killed, with 80 wounded and 24 missing.[30]

22   Ibid.
23   TNA: PRO WO95/2396 War Diary 96 Infantry Brigade HQ.
24   This last statement is incorrect. No troops crossed the canal at *this* point. See below, however.
25   TNA: PRO WO95/2402 War Diary 2nd King's Own Yorkshire Light Infantry.
26   TNA: PRO WO95/102 War Diary 2nd Tank Brigade.
27   T/Captain A/Major Frederick Andrew Robinson MC and Bar is buried in Highland Cemetery, Le Cateau, grave VI E 2. Total Tank Brigade fatalities for 4 November 1918 amount to one officer and three other ranks, the other ranks coming from 9th Tank Battalion.
28   Between 1 & 4 November the 15th Lancashire Fusiliers suffered 15 officer casualties, killed, wounded or missing. This represents approximately half of their strength. TNA: PRO WO95/2374 War Diary 32nd Division QMG.
29   Second-Lieutenant Harry Leonard Colley MC, age 24, West Yorkshire Regiment (Prince of Wales' Own), attached 2nd KOYLI, is buried in Landrecies British Cemetery, grave A 20.
30   Commonwealth War Graves Commission records indicate 21 other ranks' fatalities for 4 November 1918.

By 0700 on 4 November, the canal bank from G27 c 1.1 to G28 a 1.6 was in the hands of the 32nd Division. Orders were later received for the 15/Lancashire Fusiliers to cross the canal at Landrecies and form a defensive flank on the right of 25th Division positions. By dusk they were on the line G29.a.0.0 to G34 a 4.9[31] and were able, after a quiet night, to advance to the Red Line (the Landrecies – Oisy road) at dawn on 5 November.

The main event for 96 Brigade was the crossing of the canal. Two battalions lined up between G26 c 4.7 and L36 c 7.2, 16th Lancashire Fusiliers [16/Lancashire Fusiliers] (Lieutenant-Colonel J.N. Marshall) on the left, and 2nd Manchester Regiment [2/Manchester] (Lieutenant-Colonel G.M. Robertson) on the right, their jumping off positions being about 400 yards from the canal bank. Their attempts to cross here were destined to fail.

Captain Frederick Andrew Robinson, MC & Bar, 2nd Tank Brigade. Highland Cemetery, Le Cateau. (Author)

The bridges over which the infantry were to cross had been constructed by 218th Field Company, Royal Engineers, and were of a pontoon style, resting on cork floats. The weight of the cork floats meant that the bridges could only be carried forward in sections and would have to be put together on the water. The engineers (42 of them) and A Company of 16th Highland Light Infantry (Pioneers) [16/HLI] would carry the two bridges forward and then push them out across the water under the covering fire of the infantry. They were to walk into a heavy enemy artillery barrage and intense machine gun fire from a range of about 30 yards coming from the opposite bank of the canal.

Some of the retaliatory barrage directed against both the Happegarbes Spur and the bank of the canal occupied by 96 Brigade came from a battery commanded by Leutnant Erich Alenfeld located some 600 yards from the canal opposite the Spur. His guns had helped to break up the earlier attempts to take the spur and his orders were to stay in position: his commanding officer, Major Wilhelmi, was confident that the British would not be able to force a crossing of the canal: "*Unsere M.G.'s und einige Karabiner würden jeden Engländer vertreiben*".[32] At six o'clock on the morning of 4 November Alenfeld was woken by the British artillery barrage and immediately replied, his men firing "*auf Teufel komm raus*" (like crazy). His battery was soon engulfed in the British smoke screen and news arrived that the enemy were on the canal bank.[33]

---

31   See Map 14.
32   "Our machine guns and a few riflemen would repulse all English attacks" Bundesarchiv-Militärarchiv, Freiburg, BA-MA: MSG 2/1291 p. 4. This document is a letter to his parents dated 6 November 1918 written by Battery Commander Leutnant Erich Alenfeld in which he details his experiences of the battle.
33   Ibid. p. 5

On the 16/Lancashire Fusiliers front, the engineers and pioneers somehow managed to get a bridge across the canal within around 30 minutes, but shell fire broke it before any of the infantry could cross. At this point, Lieutenant-Colonel Marshall came forward and began to organise parties of volunteers to repair the pontoons. His citation for the Victoria Cross continues the story:

> The first party were soon killed or wounded, but by personal example he inspired his command, and volunteers were instantly forthcoming. Under intense fire and with complete disregard for his own safety, he stood on the bank encouraging his men and assisting with the work, and when the bridge was repaired attempted to rush across at the head of his battalion, and was killed by so doing.[34]

Lieutenant-Colonel James Neville Marshall VC, MC & Bar, attached 16th Lancashire Fusiliers. Ors Communal Cemetery. (Author)

"The enemy's M.G.'s made it absolutely impossible to force a crossing"[35] and the 16/Lancashire Fusiliers remained pinned down behind the western bank of the canal.

The 2/Manchester on their right fared little better: they attacked with two companies in the front line, one in support and one in reserve. After the preliminary five minute bombardment of the far canal bank, they dashed forward into the same withering fire experienced by their colleagues on their left.

The men of 218th Field Company RE performed heroically to get a pontoon bridge across the canal. At this point, this bridge was also hit and destroyed by shell fire. Major A.H.S. Waters, commanding 218th Field Company RE, and one of his men, Sapper A. Archibald, rushed forward and worked desperately, under point blank machine gun fire, to repair it. "The fire was so intense that it seemed impossible that the two men could escape with their lives".[36] But escape they did, though Archibald collapsed from the effects of gas as soon as he had completed the work and made it back to the bank. Both men were awarded the Victoria Cross.[37]

34 Quoted in G.Gliddon, *VCs of the First World War The Final Days 1918* (Stroud: Sutton Publishing Ltd., 2000) p. 199. For the full citation, see Appendix IV. Lieutenant-Colonel James Neville Marshall VC MC & Bar, Irish Guards, attached 16th Lancashire Fusiliers, age 31, is buried in Ors Communal Cemetery, "in line with" A 22. The inscription on his headstone reads: "Splendid is death when thou fallest courageous leading the onslaught".
35 TNA: PRO WO95/2396 War Diary 96 Infantry Brigade HQ.
36 Gliddon, *VCs of the First World War: The Final Days 1918* p. 203.
37 See Appendix IV for their full citations.

They were helped by the efforts of Second-Lieutenant J. Kirk of the Manchesters. He paddled a raft across the canal, under intense fire, taking a Lewis Gun with him. He made it to the far bank and proceeded to fire at a German machine gun post at a range of 10 yards. Once all of his ammunition was expended, more was somehow got across to him on the raft and he continued to give covering fire to the engineers toiling in and on the water. The bridge was completed and two platoons of the Manchesters were able to rush across. In the meantime, however, Kirk had been wounded in the arm and face, yet had continued to fire until hit in the head and killed.[38]

It was decided, after suffering around 200 casualties, that further attempts to cross the canal here should be abandoned, and the remainder of the men retreated the few yards needed to take shelter behind the western canal bank. Under their covering fire, with the one repaired bridge still intact, the two platoons which had managed to get over the canal were withdrawn.[39]

Second-Lieutenant James Kirk VC, attached 2nd Battalion Manchester Regiment. Ors Communal Cemetery. (Author)

Four Victoria Crosses had been won, probably within sight of each other, during this abortive attempt to force the canal crossing. The action also cost the life of one other noteworthy officer. The poet Wilfred Owen, Lieutenant, 2/ Manchester, was shot and killed whilst on a raft with some of his men, ferrying planks out to assist with the repairs to the pontoon bridge.[40]

The battle was probably not yet much more than an hour old, and a decision had to be taken as to what to do next. Double runners were sent out in both directions along the canal to find out if it might be possible to cross elsewhere. There was no joy to be had to the north, of course, but it was soon learned that a successful crossing had been established south of Ors village. The 16/ Lancashire Fusiliers, now under the command of Captain J.B. Dunn, had also received orders to move south and cross by this bridge.

---

38   Second-Lieutenant James Kirk, 10th Battalion Manchester Regiment, attached 2nd Battalion, age 21, was awarded the Victoria Cross for this action. He is buried in Ors Communal Cemetery, grave A 22, just yards from Lieutenant-Colonel Marshall of 16th Lancashire Fusiliers. The full citation can be found in Appendix IV.

39   TNA: PRO WO95/2397 War Diary 2nd Manchester Regiment.

40   This is according to the account given by Dominic Hibberd in his biography of Owen. He adds that another version of events had Owen on the western bank when he was shot, but concludes that it "seems likely that he had in fact taken to a raft". D. Hibberd *Wilfred Owen: A New Biography* (London: Weidenfeld & Nicolson, 2002), p. 365. Lieutenant Wilfred Edward Salter Owen MC, age 25, is buried in Ors Communal Cemetery, grave A 3.

Both battalions crossed at Ors, 2/Manchester first. This battalion was instructed to turn sharp left and head north, before pushing on to the Yellow Line, which was reached by 1130.[41] There was opposition from the left flank in the vicinity of La Motte Farm, but orders came to push on to the Blue Line, leaving this pocket of resistance to the moppers up. By dusk they were 400 yards beyond the Blue Line.[42] The 'moppers up' turned out to be the 16/ Lancashire Fusiliers, who followed the Manchesters over the bridge at Ors and dealt with "stiff resistance from enemy MG nests and snipers",[43] finishing the day facing north-east, with its left on the canal and its right in touch with the Manchesters.[44]

Erich Alenfeld's artillery battery had not been directly assaulted and he was bothered more than anything else by the strafing he was taking from low-flying aircraft. The British barrage had long since moved on well behind his positions when he received the disconcerting news from a pale and breathless stretcher-bearer that Landrecies had been taken. Alenfeld gave the order to his nine surviving unwounded comrades to destroy the breechblocks on his two remaining serviceable guns and move out. He had no horses to haul his guns. He had reached Maroilles by 7 p.m. where he saw "countless columns of men marching" in the same direction – away from the front. He managed to acquire a lift in a lorry which took him as far as Marbaix, where he had chance to reflect on his day: he mourns the two dead, 17 wounded and five missing of his battery, bemoans the fact that his guns were placed too far forward, sure that from his previous position he could have helped to prevent the fall of Landrecies. "The end has come", he concludes, "our 'heroic' infantry can no longer hold on".[45]

The British advance had not reached the Red Line, but initial setbacks, which could have ended in complete disaster, were circumvented, literally, and the mission rescued. The attempt to cross the canal had been a valiant one, but commanders on the spot saw sense and allowed pragmatism to prevail.

The cost had been high, however: the 15/Lancashire Fusiliers on the extreme left had escaped relatively unscathed, suffering only five fatalities. The 16/Lancashire Fusiliers fared much worse: officer casualties were five killed,[46] five wounded and one missing. Other ranks fatalities totalled 47. The 2/Manchester estimated their casualties at three officers killed,[47] five wounded, with 22 other ranks killed,[48] 81 wounded and 18 missing.

96 Brigade casualties for 4 November were therefore as follows:

41   TNA: PRO WO95/2396 War Diary 96 Infantry Brigade HQ.
42   See Map 14.
43   TNA: PRO WO95/2397 War Diary 16th Lancashire Fusiliers.
44   See Map 14.
45   BA-MA: MSG 2/1291. Erich Alenfeld letter pp. 6-13.
46   Other than Marshall, these were: Captain Cecil Harry Joy Hulton MC, C Company, buried in Ors Communal Cemetery, grave B 15; Second-Lieutenant Alan Hugh Law, (Battalion Intelligence Officer), buried in Pommereuil British Cemetery, grave A 10; Second-Lieutenant Frederick Maurice Livingstone, age 20, buried in Busigny Communal Cemetery Extension, grave II C 19; Second-Lieutenant Joseph Morris, C Company, age 19, buried in Pommereuil British Cemetery, grave B 60.
47   The third officer was Captain Angus McKenzie MC & Bar, age 42, buried in Ors Communal Cemetery, grave A 5.
48   Commonwealth War Grave Commission records verify 23 other rank fatalities.

	Officers	Other Ranks
Killed	10	83
Wounded	24	373
Missing	6	157
Total	40	613[49]

14 Infantry Brigade, on the divisional right, had 1st Dorsetshire Regiment [1/Dorsetshire] (Lieutenant-Colonel H.D. Thwaytes) and 5/6th Royal Scots [5/6th R.Scots] (Lieutenant-Colonel J.A. Fraser) in the front line, left and right respectively, with 15th Highland Light Infantry [15/HLI] (Lieutenant-Colonel V.B. Ramsden) in support. The strengths of the units on 31 October 1918 were:

	Officers	Other Ranks
5/6th Royal Scots	30	755
1st Dorsets	42	794
15th HLI	35	737
Total	107	2,286[50]

The 1/Dorsetshire was to "force the passage of the canal and carry the first objective".[51] They would attack at the village of Ors and would also attempt a crossing of the canal by kerosene tin pontoon bridge some short distance to the south. The old bridge at the lock was not intact, but an attempt to seize it and span it with "an improvised bridge"[52] would be tried. One platoon of C Company was also to attempt to cross the canal to the north of the village using a collapsible boat.

Once over the water, the Dorsets would continue the advance to the Blue Dotted Line. The 5/6th R.Scots, on the right, were to launch what the Official Histories called "feints and small attacks".[53] Two platoons of A Company would attempt to seize Le Donjon, the ancient mound on the western bank of the canal by attacking at Zero plus 5 along the one causeway through the marshy land that surrounded it on three sides. They were to cross the canal "either here or behind the 1st Dorset Regt".[54] Should a crossing at Le Donjon prove impossible or impractical, the officer commanding A Company could decide to cross at Ors "without reference to Bn HQ except to notify the fact that he had done so".[55] Whichever way, Rue Vert hamlet (M12 a 3.6) was the battalion's first objective. They would then work south along the canal bank before turning east and advancing to the Red Line whilst acting as right flank guard. The 15/HLI

49   The officer fatalities include Lieutenant Ralph Miller Hardy, age 24, 16th HLI (Pioneers), buried in Ors British Cemetery, grave B 14. He was born in Sydney, Australia. The overall figure represents a casualty rate for the brigade of almost 32 per cent.
50   TNA: PRO WO95/2391 War Diary 14 Infantry Brigade HQ.
51   Ibid.
52   TNA: PRO WO95/2392 War Diary 1st Dorsetshire Regiment.
53   Military Operations France & Belgium 1918 Vol. V. p. 467.
54   TNA: PRO WO95/2391 War Diary 14 Infantry Brigade HQ.
55   TNA: PRO WO95/2392 War Diary 5/6th Royal Scots "Special Instructions".

would "cross the canal in rear of 96 or 14 Infantry Brigades, according to circumstances" and then "carry the Blue and Red Lines".[56]

The responsibility for forcing a crossing of the canal on 14 Brigade front fell squarely in the lap of 1/Dorsetshire. They were deployed as follows: B Company assembled "in an orchard in rear of 2/Manchester Regt".[57] One platoon of C Company was on the canal bank north of Ors, one platoon was behind a house close to the main bridge and two platoons were 60 yards from the canal, 200 yards south of the village. D Company had two platoons to the north of the church and two to the south, "ready to cross by whichever means was available".[58] A Company was in support to the west of the village.

In addition to the planned artillery barrage, one 18-pounder was brought up and placed near Ors church "from which it could fire point blank at the main [...] bridge if necessary".[59] Eight Vickers machine guns could also supply direct fire, four on the canal bank north of the village, four similarly placed to the south. Four Stokes Mortars near the church would deluge the eastern side of the village with rapid fire from Zero to Zero plus three minutes.[60]

At 0545, the morning mist was intensified by the opening of the artillery barrage and the Stokes Mortar shells. Three minutes later, the C Company platoon nearest the bridge rushed forward with the sappers, the latter carrying the improvised bridge with them. They were met not only by intense machine gun fire, but by rounds from a German field gun firing at them straight along the road from "point blank range".[61] Several attempts were made to get the bridge in place, but when one shell scored a direct hit on it, wounding the sapper officer, it was decided to abandon any further efforts. Seven other ranks had also been wounded in trying to force the crossing, and a message was sent back to Battalion Headquarters saying that it would be "impossible to get the bridge across".[62]

The mayhem at the main bridge kept the Germans' attention away from what was happening 200 yards to the south: the floating bridge was brought forward and launched "under the covering fire of the two platoons [of 'C' Company] detailed".[63]

> The enemy, while putting up an accurate fire on all known crossings, did not locate this work until too late, with the result that the whole of this battalion [1st Dorsets] were able to cross with but little opposition.[64]

The final C Company platoon, to the north of the village, succeeded in launching their collapsible boat in spite of heavy machine gun fire. The boat capsized at the cost of five casualties.

---

56   TNA: PRO WO95/2391 War Diary 14 Infantry Brigade HQ.
57   TNA: PRO WO95/2392 War Diary 1st Dorsetshire Regiment.
58   Ibid.
59   Ibid.
60   Can one presume that this was intended to deal with any isolated German positions still concealed on the western bank of the canal?
61   TNA: PRO WO95/2392 War Diary 1st Dorsetshire Regiment.
62   Ibid. Rather unkindly, 14 Brigade HQ Diary puts the failure of this action down to "the bridging material not being placed in position quick (sic) enough." TNA: PRO WO95/2391 War Diary 14 Infantry Brigade HQ.
63   Ibid.
64   TNA: PRO WO95/2372 War Diary 32nd Division HQ. 'Report on Operations'.

By 0610 C and D Companies had orders to cross immediately by the bridge south of the village and by 0700 were on the Yellow Line. B and A Companies were then ordered to wait until the 2/Manchester had crossed before joining their comrades on the eastern side, but the entire battalion was reported over the canal by 0800. Two platoons of D Company had meanwhile worked their way south as far as Rue Vert, "advanc[ing] through the main street of the village capturing 80 prisoners".[65]

An unplanned prolongation of the pause on the Yellow Line was ordered:

> … the Companies received order to reorganise and consolidate as a temporary measure until the position was less obscure on the 96th Bde front. The protective barrage 300ˣ in front of the Yellow Line was called for and continued until it was considered safe for it to die down.[66]

On the right brigade front, at Zero plus five minutes, two platoons of A Company, 5/6th R. Scots, attacked along the causeway towards Le Donjon. This was the only track across the marsh and attracted very concentrated defensive machine gun fire, this very quickly putting paid to the assault, despite one other platoon moving up in support.

Their orders stated that "if a crossing is impossible at this point, the canal will be crossed at Ors".[67] The remaining platoon of A Company and C Company did exactly that, but B Company were able to outflank Le Donjon on the right and cross by a bridge there. D Company had crossed "by a bridge NORTH OF CATILLON"[68] and by 1045 the troops in Le Donjon, realising that they were now surrounded, gave themselves up.

By 1330 the 15/HLI had crossed the pontoon bridge south of Ors: all three battalions of the brigade were now over the canal, and the advance to the Blue Line could begin. This move was timed at 1345 and "as there was very little enemy opposition no barrage was considered necessary".[69] This line was reached and the 15/HLI passed through the Dorsets "almost immediately".[70]

The 1/Dorsetshire set about consolidating their positions on the Blue Dotted Line and in effect settled down for the night.[71] The day's fighting had cost them seven other ranks killed, with around 50 wounded, including one officer.[72]

With 15/HLI on the left and 5/6th R.Scots on the right, the advanced continued toward the Blue Line. On arriving there, they were held up by machine gun fire from Wallaheim and Locquignol Farms, but these were successfully overcome by 15/HLI, their captures producing 30 prisoners. As night fell, it was decided that they and the Royal Scots should hold their positions on the Blue Line.[73]

---

65   TNA: PRO WO95/2392 War Diary 1st Dorsetshire Regiment.
66   Ibid.
67   TNA: PRO WO95/2392 War Diary 5/6th Royal Scots.
68   Ibid. All sources are vague on the nature and exact location of this bridge, and it is not mentioned at all in any of the Royal Engineer accounts.
69   TNA: PRO WO95/2392 War Diary 1st Dorsetshire Regiment.
70   Ibid.
71   Their final positions can be seen on Map 14.
72   Second-Lieutenant F.C. Casselman.
73   They were able to advance unopposed to the Red Line at 0530 on 5 November.

Casualties had been extremely light: the 5/6th R.Scots suffered only one fatality[74] and did not even bother to record the number of wounded. The "Germans were so utterly dispirited by their failure to prevent us from crossing the river [sic], that they put no sting into their resistance".[75] The 15/HLI suffered no fatalities and only 17 in total for the month of November 1918.[76]

The fate of 32nd Division fits neatly into the premise established by this book: initial resistance from German defenders was stiff along the front line, in defence, on this occasion, of the canal. The heavy casualties suffered by 96 Brigade, and by the two companies of 2/KOYLI (97 Brigade) were almost all inflicted on the canal bank where attempts to force the crossing failed. Initial resistance on 14 Brigade front, at Ors in particular and also at Le Donjon, were similarly fierce, but the successful bridging of the canal here and the subsequent outflanking of German front-line units resulted in the almost predictable dissipation of fighting spirit and the relative ease with which subsequent objectives were ceded. The successful forcing of the canal at this one point south of Ors saved the lives of many 14 Brigade men.

The overall divisional casualties for the day are impossible to calculate with any certainty due to the incomplete returns in the War Diaries, but they can be estimated at fewer than 50 officers and just over 700 other ranks. Fatalities can be confirmed at 125, if 16/HLI (Pioneers) and 32nd Battalion Machine Gun Company figures are included.

The last word on casualties can be left to 32nd Division diarist:

> Though the casualties in the left brigade had been severe, those of the right brigade had been insignificant and, taking into account the magnitude of the operation, the losses sustained by the Division in this day's fighting may be considered small in comparison with the great results obtained.[77]

And on the success:

> This success was undoubtedly due to the admirable co-ordination of all arms and to the readiness of all ranks to make bold decisions on the spot where occasion demanded without reference to higher authority.[78]

1st Division[79]

On 1 November Major-General E.P. Strickland, commanding 1st Division, held a conference at Divisional Headquarters at which "final arrangements"[80] for the forthcoming attack were

---

74 52758 Private John Doig Paterson, age 23, is buried in Cross Roads Cemetery, Fontaine au Bois, grave II I 23.
75 J. Ewing, *Royal Scots 1914-19* (Edinburgh: Oliver & Boyd, 1925), p. 734.
76 TNA: PRO WO95/2393 War Diary 15th Highland Light Infantry.
77 TNA: PRO WO95/2372 War Diary 32nd Division HQ. 'Report on Operations'.
78 Ibid.
79 See Map 15.
80 TNA: PRO WO95/1234 War Diary 1st Division HQ.

1st Division Memorial, Hautreve Crossroads. (Author)

made. Present were "all three Brigadiers, CRA, CRE, O.C. 1st Bn M.G.C., O.C. Signals and Army Wing Commander".[81]

On the following day, the 1st Battalion Cameron Highlanders [1/Cameron] (1 Brigade), in tandem with 23rd Field Company Royal Engineers, gave a demonstration of bridging arrangements to Strickland and his subordinates.

81   Ibid.

The three brigades of 1st Division, spread across a frontage of 7,000 yards, had essentially the same task before them on 4 November: to get across the canal. In detail, however, their under-takings were very different. On the left, 3 Brigade (Brigadier-General E.G. St Aubyn) was to capture the village of Catillon on the western bank of the canal, cross at the bridge by the lock that carried the *Route Nationale No. 39* and form a bridgehead to the east. To further complicate the issue, the village would be initially attacked from the south.

1 Brigade (Brigadier-General L.L. Wheatley) had a similar job to that of 96 Brigade, 32nd Division: cross the canal on pontoons in a relatively open, unpopulated area and then exploit the breakthrough.

2 Brigade (Lieutenant-Colonel D.G. Johnson, acting[82]) on the right, was tasked with similar exploitation on the eastern side of the canal, but was to cross at the relatively well-defended Lock No. 1.[83]

The artillery barrage was to be supplied by five brigades of Royal Field Artillery (298th, 39th, 25th, 30th & 23rd), supplemented by 5th Brigade Royal Horse Artillery, 3rd Australian & 46th Divisional Artillery. The initial barrage would stand for three minutes on the eastern bank of the canal, (within the distance limits discussed earlier), and then for seven minutes 300 yards further on, before advancing to the Blue Dotted Line. This barrage would be supplemented by over 100 Vickers Machine Guns. Specific arrangements between 298th Brigade RFA and 3 Infantry Brigade would produce an initial northward-creeping barrage through the village of Catillon. Once the Blue Dotted Line had been reached, there would be a pause of one and a half hours, during which 39th, 25th and 3rd Australian artillery brigades would move forward so as to be in position to supply the creeping barrage beyond it.

The Royal Engineers regarded it as their responsibility to get the infantry across the canal: a conference of Field Company commanders had been held on 21 October[84] to allow prelimi-nary discussions on how best to bridge it. Commanders were then to "go into the question thoroughly"[85] and submit their plans for consultation and approval. The previous day, cavalry patrols and aerial photography had confirmed an intelligence report that the bridges at Catillon (a swing bridge) and Ors had been blown by the Germans.[86]

These plans were crystallised into an initial plan on 27 October when the crossing sites for 2 & 1 Infantry Brigades were decided. Once the sites were identified, "it was possible to deter-mine the types of bridges to be used at each; some experimental material was prepared and a preliminary demonstration was given on 28th October".[87] Final instructions were issued the following day and bridge construction began in earnest. During this preparation time, "the

82 Brigadier-General G.C. Kelly had been wounded on 24 September 1918. Johnson remained in command of the brigade until 21 November. He also simultaneously retained command of his battalion, the 2nd Royal Sussex Regiment.
83 See Map 15.
84 This is the earliest conference specific to the 4 November attack that the author has found – and this nine days before formal orders for the attack were issued.
85 TNA: PRO WO95/1246 War Diary 1st Division CRE.
86 IWM: LBY 73281, 'Report on the Bridging Operations in connection with the forcing of the passage of the Sambre-Oise Canal 4th November 1918'. Lt-Col. C.E.P. Sankey CRE 1st Division.
87 Ibid.

battalions detailed for the assault carried out practices with some of the bridges, over a model of the canal constructed at one of the Field Company billets".[88]

It was decided that bridges for the 1 Brigade crossing north of the bend in the canal at M 31 central would be of a floating pontoon style, supported by German steel floats.[89] Four of these would be constructed:

> The several bays of each bridge were hinged together in such a way as to give the maximum vertical flexinility (sic), to avoid any difficulty in passing over the canal banks and the head of each bridge was fitted with a ladder, to enable the far bank to be scaled with ease".[90] It had been decided that these bridges would be "carried up bodily from the assembly positions to the site as <u>bridges</u> and that no constructional work should be necessary on arrival.[91]

For crossing the lock on 2 Brigade front, where the distance to be spanned was only 17 feet, single-span bridges were constructed "as light as possible consistent with their being able to support 4 to 6 men on them at one time. They were fitted with a lever and a pair of wheels so that they could be launched from the near abutment without requiring anyone on the far side to receive them".[92]

More substantial bridges would be brought up later which would fit into the lock walls, requiring coping stones to be prized out. A section of 1st Australian Tunnelling Company (Captain Woodward MC) would build a tank bridge over the lock later that day, "as soon as the tactical situation permitted".[93] A number of smaller bridges would be used to cross streams and ditches to both west and east of the canal.

The transportation of all this material to the assembly points on 3 November came to 44 wagon loads, all of which had then to be manhandled into positions to within 5–600 yards of the canal. Then, gaps had to be cut in the wire and the hedges. By the lock, all was ready by 0130, 4 November. To the north, it was 0330 by the time all was in place. All of the bridges were painted dark green to aid their concealment prior to the attack. At these two southern crossings, it would be the engineers that would spearhead the assault: they would be first to reach the canal bank.

On 3 Brigade front, at Catillon, the engineers of 26th Field Company RE (Lieutenant Fitzhenry) would move forward behind the infantry, ready to construct or repair bridges should they be needed. The attack by 1 & 2 Brigades would be led by 23rd Field Company RE (Major Smith) and 409th Field Company RE (Major Findlay MC) respectively. Their fortunes would prove to be very different.

3 Brigade consisted of 2nd Battalion Welch Regiment [2/Welch] (Lieutenant-Colonel J.F. Badham), 1st South Wales Borderers [1/SWB] (Lieutenant-Colonel C.L. Taylor) and 1st

88   Ibid.
89   Eighty of these floats were found at the captured German Engineer depot at Bohain.
90   TNA: PRO WO95/1246 War Diary 1st Division CRE 'Report on Operations'. See Diagrams 1 &
     2. Other bridges were built using various flotation devices: cork floats, barrels (these were collected
     locally from neighbouring villages), or 700 requisitioned petrol tins.
91   Ibid.
92   Ibid. See Diagram 3.
93   Ibid.

Gloucestershire Regiment [1/Gloucestershire] (Lieutenant-Colonel J.R. Guild).[94] 2/Welch, separated from the rest of the brigade, was placed in the line on the extreme right of the divisional front.[95] Their job was to protect the right flank of 2 Brigade's attack by firing at German units from their positions along the canal bank, and particularly to pin down the "German garrison at the house in S 9 c 0.5".[96] To help in this, two Stokes Mortars were attached to the battalion. In the event, this task was extended to forming a bridgehead over the canal on their extreme right, near Cambresis, crossing the waterway by the *route nationale* heading north towards Hautreve. This was accomplished by two platoons of C Company under Lieutenant J.A. Roberts at the cost of six other ranks wounded. The battalion remained there until relieved at 2130 that evening.

The operation by 3 Brigade to capture the village of Catillon is described in 1st Division HQ Diary as a "subsidiary" one,[97] but they would have one section of three tanks from 10th Tank Battalion to assist them. Once over the canal, troops would advance along the route nationale and "hold the houses in M 20a until touch is gained with 32nd Division on the left and 1st Inf. Bde. on the right".[98]

The main attack on the village was to be made by 1/Gloucestershire and two platoons of 1/SWB. The job of these two platoons was to clear the orchards to the west and south of the village. The rest of the Borderers were to "pin down any German garrison there may be in the Western outskirts of CATILLON until the mopping-up parties arrive".[99]

The Gloucesters were to "seize that part of Catillon which lies to the east of the road running North South through the church".[100] Their second task was to force a crossing of the canal at the bridge at M 19 b 6.8, form a bridgehead and simultaneously mop up the rest of the village. They were in their assembly positions, from the road junction at R 30 a 3.0 eastwards to the canal, by 30 minutes before Zero, with D and C Companies in the front line, left and right, B Company in support behind D Company and A Company in reserve. One section of D Company, 1st Battalion Machine Gun Corps, two Stokes Mortars and one section of 26th Field Company RE were attached to C Company and were to follow them into the village.

They moved off at 0545 behind a creeping barrage of shrapnel and indirect machine gun fire and made "excellent progress"[101] despite the heavy fog. D Company, with its left on the main north-south road, overran three machine gun posts in the orchards and then headed for the church. At this point they were overtaken by a tank.[102] The tank, with D Company now close on its heels, turned right at the church and worked around the south of the eastern sector

94   Battalion strengths were as follows:

	Officers	Other Ranks
1st South Wales Borderers	19	581
1st Gloucesters	20	651
2nd Welch	17	627
Total	56	1,859

95   See Map 15.
96   TNA: PRO WO95/1277 War Diary 3 Infantry Brigade HQ.
97   TNA: PRO WO95/1234 War Diary 1st Division HQ.
98   Ibid.
99   TNA: PRO WO95/1277 War Diary 3 Infantry Brigade HQ.
100 Ibid.
101 TNA: PRO WO95/1278 War Diary 1st Battalion Gloucestershire Regiment.
102 Only two of the three tanks went into action. One crewman was overcome by petrol fumes before reaching the village.

of the village until they reached the lock. C Company, meanwhile, advanced along the road running north-south around 100 yards west of the canal. "They encountered heavy machine gun fire from the hedgerows and orchards and eventually captured 9 or 10 machine guns with their teams".[103] They pushed on into the town and approached the bridge. There was a German machine gun post in a house nearby. This was communicated to 'their' tank, which engaged the strongpoint at close range, putting it out of action.

They had reached the crossing slightly ahead of time, as the creeping barrage was still falling on the canal. The company commanders decided not to wait for the barrage to lift, but agreed to "work round [it]"[104] and get across as quickly as possible. They succeeded in this venture, but were met on the bridge by "a formidable obstacle in the shape of a number of farm implements piled together and entwined with barbed wire".[105] As the barrage lifted, a number of Germans emerged from cellars in which they had been sheltering only to be immediately taken prisoner by the Gloucesters.

Now across the canal, D, C and B Companies pushed on along the *route nationale* "in the face of heavy machine gun fire"[106] and reached the road junction that was their final objective. Meanwhile, A Company had managed to mop up the rest of the village. This action had cost the Gloucesters two officers wounded, four other ranks killed and 36 wounded.[107]

1/SWB lined up to the west of Catillon with B and C Companies given the role of pinning down the Germans on the western edge of the village whilst two platoons of D Company tackled the orchards. This operation proved remarkably easy, despite the fog, against "very little opposition".[108] They did suffer casualties from shell fire, however. Later in the day, the companies closed in to form a cordon around the village and in doing so captured two officers and 121 men. The cost was seven other ranks killed, one officer and 15 other ranks wounded.

The 3 Brigade attack had gone very much to plan. All companies of both battalions had accomplished their allotted tasks and reached their objectives to time. The attempt by the German defenders to block the bridge by dumping farm machinery on it smacks of desperation from dispirited units effectively abandoned to their fate on the western bank of the canal, aware that the only certainty that day was their eventual envelopment. The machine gunners put up the expected resistance, but the haul of over 500 prisoners speaks volumes.

3 Brigade had suffered very minor losses:

	Officers			Other Ranks			Total
	K	W	M	K	W	M	
1st Gloucesters	–	2	–	5	36	–	
1st South Wales Borderers	–	1	–	7	15	–	
1st Welch	–	–	–	–	6	–	
Total	–	3	–	12	57	–	72

103 TNA: PRO WO95/1278 War Diary 1st Battalion Gloucestershire Regiment.
104 Ibid.
105 Ibid.
106 Ibid.
107 Commonwealth War Grave Commission records show five other ranks killed.
108 TNA: PRO WO95/1280 War Diary 1st Battalion South Wales Borderers.

On 1 Brigade front, the initial assault was entrusted to 1st Battalion Loyal North Lancashire Regiment [1/L. North Lancashire] (Lieutenant-Colonel R.E. Berkeley DSO) and 1st Queen's Own Cameron Highlanders [1/Cameron] (Lieutenant-Colonel H.C. Methuen), left and right respectively. The 1st Black Watch [1/Black Watch] (Lieutenant-Colonel F. Anderson) were in support and would subsequently move through the Loyal North Lancs on the Blue Dotted Line to resume the advance from there.

The canal crossing just north of the bend in the canal at M 31 b 0.0 was to be made across four pontoon bridges, two per battalion, put in position by 23rd Field Company RE.[109] They would be carried from jumping off positions just inside the orchards some 5 – 600 yards from the bank.[110] The bridges had been sent up over the previous three nights and "dumped under trees and hedges".[111] At 2130 on 3 November, the men of 23rd Field Company RE "began to put the bridges together and to carry them to their final assembly positions. This company also had to make the necessary holes in hedges, involving in some cases the cutting of trees up to 9 inches in diametre (sic), and to lay the subsidiary bridges over the small stream west of the canal".[112] All of the work was completed two and a quarter hours before Zero.

At 0540, the engineers "stood to at their bridges"[113] A platoon of D Company 1/L. North Lancashire accompanied the northern pair of bridges. The southern pair had a platoon of B Company 1/Cameron to assist. At 0545 the artillery barrage opened on the eastern canal bank and remained there for three minutes.[114] By 0550, the bridges were at the canal bank.

On the left, one other platoon of 1/L. North Lancashire "detailed as a covering party to hold the WEST (our bank) of the CANAL doubled forward and commenced to carry out their duties".[115] The two bridges were pushed across the canal into the mist that hung over the waterway and were in place within five minutes. A Lewis Gun section was sent across first to cover the crossing.[116] They came under retaliatory machine gun fire from short range, but were able to silence these guns and capture the teams. The rest of the battalion doubled forward and crossed the two bridges, A Company first, followed by B and C Companies. D Company remained on the western bank to help the engineers launch more bridges. The three companies were across the canal within 15 minutes of Zero.

On the right, one platoon of D Company 1/Cameron, under Second-Lieutenant G. Bryson, went to the canal bank ahead of the engineers to provide covering fire for the bridging operations. Unexpectedly, one German machine gun post, with its crew of five men, was found on the

---

109 These four bridges were built using the 80 German steel floats found at the store at Bohain. Eight bridges were launched later in the assault, four using wooden barrels as flotation devices, two with cork floats and two with petrol tins. The barrels came from local villages and were re-coopered and soaked in water to tauten them before use. IWM: LBY 73281 Sankey Report.

110 See Sketch Map 5.

111 TNA: PRO WO95/1246 War Diary 1st Division CRE.

112 Ibid.

113 Ibid. 'Narrative of Events'

114 The machine gun barrage had begun prematurely, pre-empting it by around half a minute. TNA: PRO WO95/1266 War Diary 1st Loyal North Lancashire Regiment & TNA: PRO WO95/1264 War Diary 1st The Queen's Own Cameron Highlanders.

115 TNA: PRO WO95/1266 War Diary 1st Loyal North Lancashire Regiment.

116 By this time, the artillery barrage had moved 100 yards to the east, remaining there for a further four minutes.

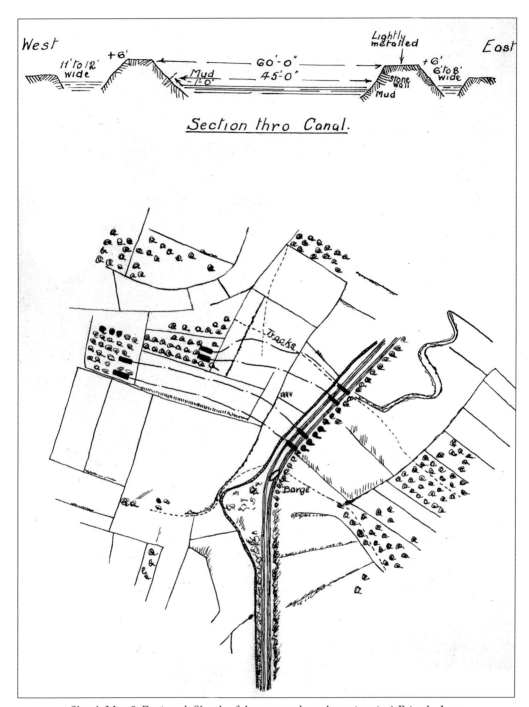

West

Lightly
metalled

East

+6'

11' to 12'
wide

60'-0"
45'-0"

+6'
6' to 8'
wide

Mud
1' 0"

stone
wall

Mud

Section thro Canal.

Tracks

Barge

Sketch Map 5 Engineer's Sketch of the proposed canal crossings in 1 Brigade Area.

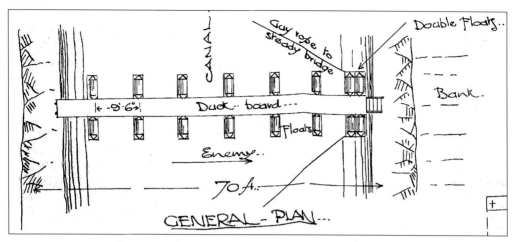

Diagram 1 Engineer's Sketch of 'Light Footbridge'. (IWM)

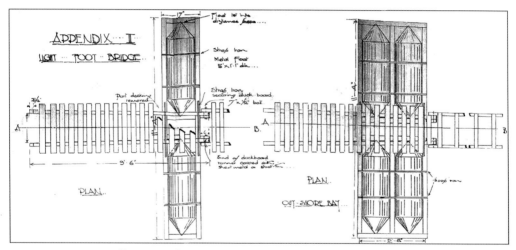

Diagram 2 Detailed drawing of 'Light Footbridge'. (IWM)

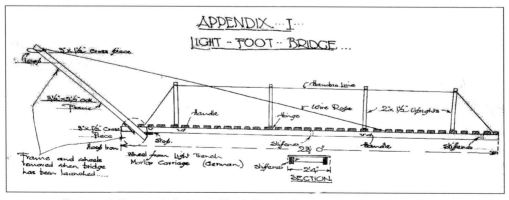

Diagram 3 Engineer's drawing of Light Footbridge for use at Lock No. 1. (IWM)

Pontoon Bridge in place across the Sambre-Oise Canal on 1 Brigade front. (IWM)

western bank here, exactly where the southernmost bridge was due to be launched. "Sgt Cook of 23 F Coy RE rushed them [single-handed], killing three and capturing the other two".[117] The bridging was completed in quick time and Second-Lieutenant Bryson, "the first man of any unit across the canal",[118] was on the far bank by Zero plus six minutes.[119] The 23rd Field Company RE had suffered one other rank killed,[120] one officer and eight other ranks wounded.

117 TNA: PRO WO95/1246 War Diary 1st Division CRE 'Narrative of Events at Crossing No. 2'. Sergeant J. Cook was awarded a Bar to his DCM for this action.
118 TNA: PRO WO95/1264 War Diary 1st The Queen's Own Cameron Highlanders.
119 Ibid. It was a matter of pride between the Loyal North Lancs and the Cameron Highlanders as to which got the first man across the canal. Whether it was the Loyal North Lancs' Lewis Gun team or the Highlanders' Second-Lieutenant Bryson is not clear, but Montgomery, *The Story of the Fourth Army in the Battles of the Hundred Days*, asserts on page 249, footnote 1, that the Camerons won the race by 30 seconds. The War Diary of 1st Division CRE times the first bridge across the canal at Zero plus nine minutes. The argument is irrelevant: the first men across were sappers: "All the first-wave bridges carried two Sappers at the head of the bridge, who threw up the storming ladder on arrival at the far bank, *went ashore,* and anchored the bridge. (My italics) These leading Sappers then captured 2 enemy posts behind the East bank of the Canal". TNA: PRO WO95/1246 War Diary 1st Division CRE 'Narrative of Operations'.
120 472031 Sapper Henry Almer Smith, age 29, is buried in La Vallée Mulatre Communal Cemetery Extension, grave A 42.

Three companies followed Bryson across the canal, C Company first, followed by A and B Companies: they were all on the eastern side by 0610 and quickly advanced on the hamlet of Bois de l'Abbaye, occupying it and capturing a number of prisoners.

It seems clear that the Germans did not have the manpower to defend every sector of the canal: the 1 Brigade troops had crossed almost unopposed, certainly helped by the mist, but mostly by the paucity of defenders. The enemy's retaliatory artillery barrage fell behind the attackers and "did no damage".[121]

Once across the canal, the units of 1/L. North Lancashire reorganised: A Company was to move north, parallel to the canal; B Company would be on their right, moving more or less north-east; C Company would advance due east and D Company would remain in reserve. Opposition to these moves once again proved less than robust. "The enemy, when seeing them-selves in danger of being outflanked, showed themselves disposed to surrender and only in a few cases put up a strong resistance".[122] The diarist describes the type of encounter experienced and praises the conduct of the new recruits:

> Owing to the thickness of the mist, the operations developed into a series of hand to hand combats between small parties. Although 50% of the men of the Bn had never been in action before, their superior morale & fine example set them by the experienced Officers, NCO's and men of the Bn, enabled them to deal, with slight loss, with these numerous parties. In several cases parties of 15 & 20 were surrounded in houses. The first few occu-pants who were encountered were disposed of with bomb & bayonet & the remainder surrendered.[123]

Companies reached their objectives on the Blue Dotted Line at around 0930 or slightly later, with A Company on the Catillon road and in touch with troops of 3 Brigade. The barrage now halted in front of this line for 90 minutes and thereafter 1/Black Watch leapfrogged the 1/L. North Lancashire and continued the advance to the Blue Line. The Loyal North Lancs were effectively "squeezed out"[124] and apart from C Company receiving orders to go forward in case they were required to assist the 1/Cameron,[125] "no further developments took place".[126] By 2300, all companies had been relieved and early on 5 November the battalion marched back to billets in Molain, some five miles west of the canal. The War diary claims seven other ranks killed, 41 wounded and four missing.[127] The battalion had fought its last action of the war.

The 1/Cameron reached their first objective, the Blue Dotted Line, by 0830, but "nothing could be seen on account of the mist which was still thick".[128] The mist began to clear rapidly at around 0900. During the 90 minute pause, they reorganised, putting B and A companies into the front line, left and right, ready to continue the assault. They moved off behind a barrage described

121 TNA: PRO WO95/1262 War Diary 1 Infantry Brigade HQ.
122 TNA: PRO WO95/1266 War Diary 1st Loyal North Lancashire Regiment.
123 Ibid.
124 Ibid.
125 They accordingly concentrated just west of the Hautreve crossroads.
126 Ibid.
127 Commonwealth War Graves Commission records show 13 fatalities.
128 TNA: PRO WO95/1264 War Diary 1st The Queen's Own Cameron Highlanders.

as "excellent to start with",[129] and were not held up until they reached the village of Robelmetre, where they came under heavy shelling. A Company stalled here, but B Company moved around the left flank of the shelled area, reached the road south of Grand Galop Farm and attempted to outflank a strongly held enemy position at La Cambotte. They came under heavy machine gun fire from three directions[130] and the decision was taken to withdraw a short distance and consolidate. A Company was eventually able to move up and continue the line to the south, but D Company had to throw back a defensive flank in order to conform with the left of 2nd Battalion Royal Sussex Regiment. The final line was therefore just to the east of Robelmetre.[131]

The battalion was relieved by 4th Battalion Leicestershire Regiment (46th Division) after dark and moved back to billets in Mazinghien. Their trophies amounted to 25 machine guns, four field guns, six trench mortars and around 500 prisoners. The War Diary does not mention casualty figures, but fatalities can be calculated at 15 other ranks.[132]

The 1/Black Watch had been in their assembly positions west of the canal in square R 35 since 2330 on 3 November. They crossed the canal the following morning at 0730 and moved up to their jumping off positions along the Catillon-Hautreve road. During the advance they were forced to capture two occupied houses that had been bypassed by the first wave: B Company mopped up 10 enemy soldiers in a house at M 26 d 4.4 and C Company were "compelled to organise an attack"[133] to take the house at M 27 a 4.0. The occupants did not resist for long, and three officers and 50 other ranks were captured, but at the cost of Lieutenant W. Wilson DCM, commanding C Company, being wounded by machine gun fire.

Companies lined up on the Blue Dotted Line as follows: B Company on the left, C in the centre and D on the right. The barrage that preceded them in their advance became ragged and slow, and as a result "many faint-hearted Germans, who would otherwise have been captured, were enabled to make good their escape".[134]

B Company, on the left, met little resistance until they reached the village of Mézières, but they caught the defenders by surprise and two German officers who tried to escape on horseback were killed. Fifty prisoners were taken, along with 12 horses, although two limber teams were shot at the road junction east of the village (M 22 b 9.9). Touch was made, eventually, at 1715, with 14 Brigade troops on the left, and a joint post established at the bridge just north of the settlement.

In the battalion centre, C Company advanced towards Boyau de Leu and then swung north, their left flank on the La Groise – Landrecies road. Their progression was untroubled until they came up against some stiff opposition from the houses in M 22 central. By 1215, all the houses as far as M 22 b 5.2 had been cleared, but the Germans were determined to hold the line of the stream where it crossed the main road. Their accurate machine gun fire effectively covered all northern exits from the village, and with no sign of 32nd Division advancing on the left, any attempts to

129 TNA: PRO WO95/1262 War Diary 1 Infantry Brigade HQ. The diarist continues: The barrage "later became ragged, some guns remaining on BOYAU DE LEU for an hour after the infantry had first entered the place".
130 TNA: PRO WO95/1264 War Diary 1st The Queen's Own Cameron Highlanders.
131 See Map 15.
132 According to Commonwealth War Graves Commission records and 'Soldiers Died in the Great War' CDRom.
133 TNA: PRO WO95/1263 War Diary 1st Battalion Black Watch (Royal Highlanders).
134 Ibid.

advance further along this road were abandoned. Instead, they attempted to capture some field guns a little further off to the east, around M 22 b 8.2: "indeed, the gunners held up a white flag, but as the party advanced the enemy opened rifle fire. 2/Lt W.H. GRANT was wounded in the arm and in the leg".[135] Two guns were captured. The fate of the crews was not recorded.

D Company, on the right, headed for Petit Galop and Grand Galop Farms, these situated neatly on the Blue Line, about 500 yards apart. On the way forward, one platoon had to be detached to deal with machine gun fire coming from orchards on their right flank. One platoon was detailed to capture Petit Galop Farm and it "secured its objective after a short struggle in which several of the enemy were killed. Four prisoners and three 77mm guns were taken".[136]

As the main body approached Grand Galop Farm, 30 or so of the enemy were seen "fleeing"[137] from the buildings. A number were brought down by Lewis Gun fire. The farm was in British hands by 1138, success flares fired, the rest of the garrison captured. This amounted to one officer and 10 other ranks, "each of whom wore the ribbon of the IRON CROSS".[138]

One enemy strongpoint near M 29 central seemed determined to hold out, retreating only marginally to a second prepared position after 50 rounds of trench mortar fire had dislodged them. From here they continued to fire with rifle and machine guns along the road running north-west to Grand Galop Farm, but once more it was deemed unnecessary for the Black Watch to push on further, and two Vickers machine guns and two platoons of A Company were brought up to face and contain this stubbornly held position, ready to attack should the need arise. It didn't, and the line solidified for the night. During the night, the battalion was relieved by 5th Battalion Lincolnshire Regiment (46th Division) and they withdrew to billets in Mazinghien. They had captured, in total, five officers and 128 men, 11 horses and five 77mm guns. Casualties amounted to three officers wounded, six other ranks killed, with 30 wounded.

1 Brigade had taken almost all its objectives, and the most dangerous part of the operation, the canal crossing, had passed with few alarms. The contrast with the experience of 96 Brigade to the north is startling. 1 Brigade had been very lucky: they had chosen a crossing point that was not well defended. The two crossing points share a similar topography, but on that day the fates of the attackers were wildly disparate. 96 Brigade had suffered 643 casualties (equivalent to a whole fighting battalion) on 4 November, 93 of them fatal. Figures for 1 Brigade are incomplete, but with a total of six officers and 146 other ranks,[139] they can be estimated at:

	Officers		Other Ranks		Total
	K	W	K	W	
1st Loyal North Lancs	–	?	13	41	
1st Cameron Highlanders	–	?	15	41?	
1st Black Watch	–	3	6	30	
Total	–	6	34	112	152

135 Ibid.
136 Ibid.
137 Ibid.
138 Ibid.
139 TNA: PRO WO95/1262 War Diary 1st Division HQ.

The 2 Brigade attack would be carried out by 2nd Royal Sussex [2/R.Sussex] (Lieutenant-Colonel D.G. Johnson) on the left, 2nd Kings Royal Rifle Corps [2/KRRC] (Lieutenant-Colonel H.F.E. Smith) on the right, with 1st Northamptonshire Regiment [1/Northamptonshire] (Lieutenant-Colonel G. St G. Robinson) in support. The actual bridging of the canal was the responsibility of 409th Field Company RE (Major G. de C. E. Findlay DSO, MC). 2/R.Sussex would cross at the lock, 3,000 yards south of Catillon (S 1 d 1.5). Sketch Map 6 shows the location in detail: there was one small derelict building on the western bank and three, including the lock keeper's house, on the eastern side. The lock itself was 17 feet wide and 170 feet long. To get there, the men would have to cross a stream some 15 feet wide and then climb a 16 foot high bank. Their final objective was 3,000 yards to the east.

The country on both sides of the canal was very enclosed with hedges and orchards making it impossible to distinguish any marked tactical features[140] or pick out any landmarks which would serve as distant direction guides during the advance. A liberal supply of excellent aeroplane photographs, however, were found to be of the greatest assistance and these were issued in time for officers and N.C.O.'s to make a thorough study of the ground they would be required to advance over.[141]

On the right, A Company of 2/KRRC would attempt a "subsidiary crossing",[142] using an existing wooden bridge 100 yards south of the lock. Should the bridge prove unusable, they should "endeavour to improvise a crossing with Berthen Boats".[143] They had been supplied with four of these by the Royal Engineers: they were collapsible rowing boats, in two sections, requiring assembly before use, each capable of carrying six men. They came with fore and aft tow ropes, but no oars. They would have to be propelled by shovels.[144]

The 1/Northamptonshire would cross the canal in the wake of its two sister battalions, 20 – 25 minutes after Zero and then be responsible for capturing the village of Fesmy on the right flank of the advance beyond the Blue Line and should "join hands with the French"[145] at La Justice (S 11 d 5.5).

The artillery barrage was as described earlier, supplemented by a machine gun barrage on the eastern bank of the canal for the first 30 seconds after Zero, and by eight 3 inch Stokes Mortars firing on the canal bank, extending 300 yards north and south of the lock from Zero to Zero plus three. Four 18-pounders had "been told off to deal by direct fire at ZERO Hour with the houses at the LOCK".[146] The engineers had called, in order to "greatly facilitate our task", for the lock buildings to be "razed to the ground. The debris would still afford a screen from machine gun bullets."[147] This piece of advice was not heeded.

140 See the photograph overleaf to view the approach to the lock. Major Findlay reconnoitred the area to the west of the canal on 29 October: with reference to the ground over which the troops would advance, he states: "Lock buildings dominate all ground […] which is all under direct view from windows." It was also reported that the Germans were felling trees on the canal banks in order to improve the fields of fire of their machine guns. TNA: PRO WO95/1246 War Diary 1st Division CRE & IWM: LBY 73281 Sankey Report.
141 TNA: PRO WO95/1269 War Diary 2nd Royal Sussex Regiment.
142 TNA: PRO WO95/1268 War Diary 2 Infantry Brigade HQ.
143 Ibid.
144 TNA: PRO WO95/1246 War Diary 1st Division CRE.
145 TNA: PRO WO95/1268 War Diary 2 Infantry Brigade HQ.
146 Ibid.
147 IWM: LBY 73281 Sankey Report.

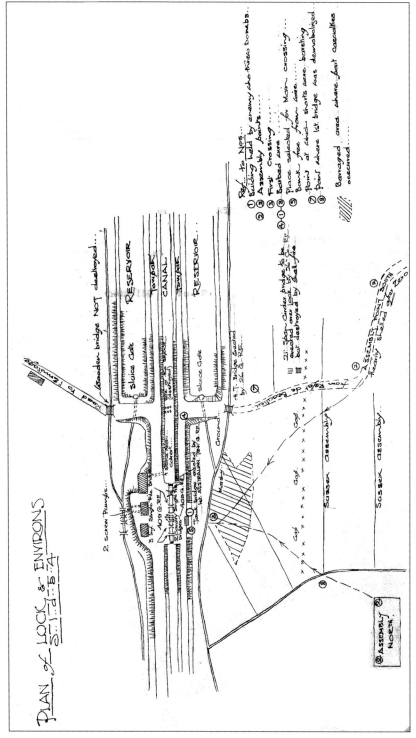

Sketch Map 6 Engineer's Sketch Map of Lock No. 1 & Environs.

Lock No. 1 approaches. (IWM)

The timings for the crossing at the lock were very tight: the whole of 2/R.Sussex and one section of 409th Field Company RE, along with one section of 1st Battalion Machine Gun Corps and two companies of 2/KRRC were to be across the water by Zero plus 15½ minutes. The bridges were to be clear, that is the whole brigade across, by Zero plus 33.

The assault bridges, the 'supplementary', shorter bridges for spanning the streams both west and east of the canal and the more substantial pack transport bridges were sent up in four wagon loads on the evening of 3 November and were taken to the forward dumps at X 5 a 7.2 and X 5 b 7.0, where they were unloaded at around 1800. Men of 409th Field Company RE then carried them forward to the final assembly positions where they were "all laid out in the proper order by 0130".[148]

The 2/R.Sussex had been practising "moving rapidly over dummy bridges"[149] and then deploying into their bridgehead positions for two days when they marched off in the late afternoon of 3 November, bivouacking for a few hours in the vicinity of La Vallée Mulatre. They approached the canal under cover of darkness along the road from the village of Rejet de Beaulieu[150] and were in their jumping off positions, 250 yards from the lock, at 0400. "Shelling was not heavy and no definite counter preparations fell upon the assembled troops. The assembly was so well and silently carried out that the enemy failed to notice anything unusual".[151]

148 TNA: PRO WO95/1246 War Diary 1st Division CRE.
149 TNA: PRO WO95/1268 War Diary 2 Infantry Brigade HQ.
150 See Sketch Map 6.
151 TNA: PRO WO95/1268 War Diary 2 Infantry Brigade HQ. This diary is rather dismissive of the artillery retaliation that fell amongst the advancing troops on the western bank on the morning of 4 November: in reality it was very disruptive – see TNA: PRO WO95/1246 War Diary 1st Division CRE and TNA: PRO WO95/1269 War Diary 2nd Royal Sussex and Montgomery, *The Story of the Fourth Army in the Battles of the Hundred Days*, p. 248. Perhaps the attack *was* expected.

They lined up with C Company on the left, B Company on the right, A in support and D in reserve. The barrage began on time, although the machine guns were a few seconds early again, and "length was excellent, with the exception of one gun on the right which was dropping about 150 yards short".[152] This meant that B Company had to edge slightly northwards as it began to advance in order to dodge the fall of these wayward shells, with C Company, "in two lines of platoons in single file".[153] The southern Royal Engineer bridging party, carrying the subsidiary bridges to put across the stream, under Sergeant McLaren, were reported to be "well away at zero"[154] and 50 to 100 yards ahead of the infantry. On the left, the northern bridging party under Lieutenants Elmslie and Kelly, came across a small stream.[155] They immediately used one of their smaller bridges to span this, to allow the assault bridges to be carried over. The first, Corporal Dow in charge, got across, but as the second one was about to be dragged over, an enemy shell landed amongst the party, wounding Lieutenant Elmslie and all but one of the men carrying it.

By around 0550 both leading engineer parties and infantry units were reaching the stream west of the lock: they found it clogged with fallen trees, tree roots and barbed wire. By this time, enemy shells were falling amongst the men and casualties were beginning to mount, as was the level of confusion thus caused, with the rear waves of infantry coming on and getting mixed up with those stalled at the stream. "So intense was the enemy's fire that even the stoutest troops hesitated, and it seemed impossible for any man to get to the lock and yet live".[156]

It was discovered that the section of the stream to the north of the ruined house on the western bank was largely clear of debris, and a crossing was attempted there. The stream was wider than anticipated, however, and two of the smaller bridges had to be placed together in a 'V' shape in order to span it. One of the assault bridges meant for the lock was also placed over the stream.[157] While this was happening, some infantry had waded the stream, scrambled up the bank and "silenced the enemy post in the ruined house [...] which up to this time had caused much trouble and some casualties by bombs".[158]

Back at the stream, under the shelling, the situation remained very confused. It fell to Lieutenant-Colonel Johnson and Major Findlay to restore order, by organising "scratch parties"[159] to manhandle the bridges and by getting some infantry across to cover the next stage of the advance. "Men soon crossed [the stream] and lined the bank of the canal,[160] engaging the enemy on the opposite bank with fire – some of the Lewis Gunners standing on top of the bank

152 TNA: PRO WO95/1246 1st Division CRE. See Sketch Map 6, reference point 7.
153 TNA: PRO WO95/1269 War Diary 2nd Royal Sussex Regiment.
154 TNA: PRO WO95/1246 1st Division CRE.
155 See Sketch Map 6, reference point 8. The CRE account uses the word "encountered", which may suggest that the stream was not expected. It is, however, mentioned in Major Findlay's report following his reconnaissance of the area on 29 October, and is marked on the accompanying sketch map. Original maps had, however, incorrectly marked the stream as a hedge. (IWM: LBY 73281 Sankey Report)
156 Montgomery, *The Story of the Fourth Army in the Battles of the Hundred Days*, p. 248.
157 Sketch Map 6, reference point 5.
158 TNA: PRO WO95/1246 1st Division CRE.
159 TNA: PRO WO95/1269 War Diary 2nd Royal Sussex Regiment.
160 The War Diary of 2nd Royal Sussex reports one man scrambling over the lock gates at this point, but he is not mentioned again, nor indeed elsewhere.

The stream to the west of Lock No. 1. (IWM)

firing their Lewis Guns from the hip, traversing as they did so".[161] The diarist of 409th Field Company RE substantiates this almost hero comic-book scenario, praising the Lewis Gunners, who "stuck their ground throughout, even when others fell back and it is largely due to them that the bridging was able to proceed".[162]

Under this covering fire, Major Findlay organised a mixed party of sappers and infantry to drag Corporal Dow's assault bridge across the other one already laid across the stream and up the canal bank. It was almost 0610. They quickly attached the wheels[163] and the launching lever, but one of the steel guys had been shot away, requiring it to be lowered rather more gently than originally envisaged across the lock. It was successfully placed, however, and Major Findlay and two of his NCOs rushed across, closely followed by men of 2/R.Sussex, including Lieutenant-Colonel Johnson, and set about neutralising the Germans in the lock buildings. It was a "brisk fight [that] ensued at the Lock houses with the enemy garrison, but these quickly surrendered themselves".[164] Even whilst this was going on, Corporals Wardrop and White of 409th Field Company RE crossed the lock and managed to place two subsidiary bridges over the stream *east* of the canal behind the lock buildings. By 0613, three more bridges had been placed over

161 Ibid.
162 TNA: PRO WO95/1254 War Diary 409th Field Company Royal Engineers.
163 The wheels came from German Light Trench Mortar carriages.
164 TNA: PRO WO95/1268 War Diary 2 Infantry Brigade HQ.

Lock No. 1. (IWM)

Present-day Lock No. 1. (Author)

the lock, and with a further three there by 0625, and the enemy position overrun, the rest of the infantry were able to cross.[165]

On the right, A Company of 2/KRRC had advanced to the canal at Zero plus six, but reconnaissance the previous afternoon had shown that the wooden bridge by which they were hoping to be able to cross the canal had been badly damaged. Any crossing here would have to be by boat. They had dragged the Berthen boats across a six foot dyke and up a six foot bank only to discover on arrival at the bank that their assembly was far from straightforward. "A quarter of an hour was spent toiling at these unwieldy engines, and then, as they were still unassembled, the Company Commander decided to waste no further time, dumped the boats and led his men to the Lock".[166] Here, they were able to cross with the rest of their battalion.

The infantry crossings were completed by around 0635,[167] and the engineers set about tidying the lock crossings, spacing the bridges out and checking the area for hidden mines. It was whilst completing these tasks that Lieutenant Kelly was killed by an enemy shell.[168] At 0720, a Pack Transport Bridge was across the canal and at 0800 the 1st Australian Tunnelling Company started work on the Tank Bridge, which was completed, under intermittent shell fire, by 10 o'clock.[169]

The Engineers had suffered the following casualties during the day:

	Officers		Other Ranks		Total
	K	W	K	W	
23rd Field Company Royal Engineers	–	1	1	10	
26th Field Company Royal Engineers	–	–	1	8	
409th Field Company Royal Engineers	1	3	12	18	
1st Australian Tunnelling Company	–	–	3	8	
Total	1	4	17	44	66

The 409th Field Company RE casualties represented 45 percent of Other Ranks engaged.[170]

---

165 Major George de Cardonnel Elmsall Findlay, commanding 409th Field Company Royal Engineers, and Lieutenant-Colonel Dudley Graham Johnson, commanding 2nd Battalion Royal Sussex Regiment, were awarded the Victoria Cross for their exploits at Lock No. 1. See Appendix IV for the full citations.
166 TNA: PRO WO95/1268 War Diary 2 Infantry Brigade HQ.
167 This was only 18 minutes behind schedule.
168 Lieutenant John Lawson Kelly MC, age 24, is buried in Le Rejet de Beaulieu Communal Cemetery, grave B 11.
169 One supply tank came forward along the road from Le Rejet de Beaulieu to use this bridge, having a load of supplies to dump near Bois de l'Abbaye, but no-one had seen the necessity of constructing a bridge over the stream west of the canal strong enough to take a tank. The tank commander proceeded to try to cross by the Horse Transport Bridge and both bridge and tank ended up in the stream, the latter completely 'ditched'.
170 TNA: PRO WO95/1246 1st Division CRE. Gallantry awards to the men of the RE Field Companies were numerous: one Victoria Cross, one Bar to a DSO, one DSO, eight MCs, eight Bars to DCMs, four Bars to MMs and 42 MMs.

2 Brigade had a little catching up to do: although the crossing of the lock had resulted in "a certain amount of confusion of Units", because "all the men had been thoroughly instructed in what direction (right or left) to go, by the time the battalions reached the line of the road in S 2 a & c, they were fairly reorganised and were covering their full frontages according to plan".[171] Enemy resistance "was small and beyond rounding up a few machine guns which gave battle here and there, there was no infantry fight worthy of mention as the enemy infantry seemed only too ready to 'Kamerad'".[172] When the fog lifted at 0900 the men were on the Blue Dotted Line, along the road running through Sans Fond, having caught up with the barrage. "It was clear that there was no enemy immediately in front".[173]

The men of 1/Northamptonshire had crossed the canal at about 0615[174] and took up positions in support to the west of the Blue Dotted Line, though they were asked to send two companies forward to bolster the depleted 2/R.Sussex. After the 90 minute pause on this line, the artillery barrage resumed its forward movement, the infantry following, 2/R.Sussex on the left, 2/KRRC in the centre and 1/Northamptonshire on the right. The "enemy surrendered freely and put up a poor fight".[175] The 2/R.Sussex and 2/KRRC took up final positions a little short of the original objectives[176] and it was noted that "there were no counter-attacks" and enemy shelling was "negligible".[177]

At 1400 the 1/Northamptonshire went forward to capture the village of Fesmy. B and D Companies were able to clear all but the eastern outskirts where resistance from German machine guns proved "determined",[178] but by 1630, after trench mortar fire had been directed onto these strongpoints, the entire village was in British hands. It was beginning to get dark, and there was still one pocket of Germans out on the right and this made liaison with the French 66th Division problematic. A patrol was sent out to the pre-arranged 'international post' at La Justice, but there was no French presence. It was decided that the Northants should consolidate their current positions, with B, C and D Companies in the front line and A Company remaining behind in support. A link with the French was established at La Justice at 0500 on 5 November.

1/Northamptonshire had lost one officer killed,[179] and three wounded, with 11 other ranks killed and 22 wounded. 2/KRRC had lost two officers killed,[180] 2/R.Sussex one.[181]

Total casualties for 2 Brigade can be calculated at:

---

171 TNA: PRO WO95/1268 War Diary 2 Infantry Brigade HQ.

172 TNA: PRO WO95/1269 War Diary 2nd Royal Sussex Regiment.

173 Ibid.

174 According to the battalion diary (TNA: PRO WO95/1271 War Diary 1st Northamptonshire Regiment). This is quite optimistic. It was probably nearer 0630.

175 TNA: PRO WO95/1273 War Diary 2nd King's Royal Rifle Corps.

176 See Map 15.

177 TNA: PRO WO95/1273 War Diary 2nd King's Royal Rifle Corps.

178 TNA: PRO WO95/1271 War Diary 1st Northamptonshire Regiment.

179 Second-Lieutenant Lewis James Morten, age 26, is buried in Le Rejet de Beaulieu Communal Cemetery, grave D 15. His wife, Charlotte, lived in Slough, in a house called "Catillon".

180 Lieutenant Herman Grant Oxley, age 25, and Second-Lieutenant S. Burroughes are buried side by side in Highland Cemetery, Le Cateau, graves VI E 6 and VI E 5 respectively.

181 Second-Lieutenant Ernest Stanley Loader is buried in Le Rejet de Beaulieu Communal Cemetery, grave D13.

	Officers		Other Ranks		Total
	K	W	K	W	
2nd Royal Sussex	1	7	12	86	
1st Northamptonshire Regt	1	3	11	22	
2nd KRRC	2	1	12	60	
Total	4	11	35	168	218

1st Division, despite the perceived difficulty of the tasks given them, rank only eighth in the list of divisional fatal casualties for 4 November.

	Officers		Other Ranks		Total
	K	W	K	W	
1 Brigade	–	6	34	112	
2 Brigade	4	11	35	168	
3 Brigade	–	3	12	57	
Total	4	20	81	337	442

The division had advanced its line over 4,000 yards on a 5,000 yard frontage, forced the passage of the Sambre canal and liberated nine villages and hamlets. They had taken 49 officers and 1,649 other ranks prisoner, and captured over 20 field guns.[182] Major-General Strickland, in his 'Special Order of the Day', dated 5 November, is quite sure of the reasons for success:

> The task that the Division was called upon to perform yesterday was one entailing the utmost forethought for every detail, the most careful and precise Staff work in all branches, a thorough and precise organisation in BNs of the most minute detail, and gallantry, tact and endurance on the part of all troops engaged.
> The complete success of the operations is very greatly due to the skill, ability, rapidity and completeness with which the Bridging arrangements were completed and perfected.[183]

IX Corps, in the end, got away with it. The crossing at Lock No. 1 succeeded, but it took the resolve of the commanding officers to redeem a plan that was in danger of becoming, if not a failure, a more costly enterprise. The forcing of the canal at Ors by 14 Brigade was only courtesy of a secondary bridge veiled in the morning mist and thus not spotted by the defenders, a crossing in the end used by many more units than had originally been envisaged. The attempt by 96 Brigade to cross the canal further north was a disaster rescued only by the pragmatism of officers willing to call off the frontal attacks and, in effect, outflank the problem. Lieutenant-Colonel Sankey, in his report on the crossings, explains, though not implicitly, the main reason

182 TNA: PRO WO95/1262 War Diary 1st Division HQ.
183 Ibid.

for 32nd Division's difficulties: he condemns the use of the cork float bridges, asserting that "no constructional work should be necessary on arrival [at the canal bank]".[184] When the half hour needed to get one bridge across the canal in the 96 Brigade sector is compared to the five minutes taken to have four in place on 1 Brigade frontage, the lesson, hard learnt, is obvious. The taking of the Happegarbes Spur was a third, and still relatively costly attempt at this operation. Only at Catillon did everything go more or less to plan, and here the objectives were much more closely defined, the bridgehead being the limit of the day's work.

As in many other places along the front, the German forward positions provided the only real solid opposition to the attackers: once this crust was broken through, it became apparent that there was little behind it. Is this assessment too harsh? Battle plans rarely survive first contact with the enemy, and the resourcefulness through which the eventual success was achieved should also be trumpeted alongside the misgivings. The British Army of 1918 has received praise[185] for the pragmatism of its leaders, for the attributes of its 'middle leaders', those in command at division, brigade and even battalion level, for the ability of the 'man on the spot' to assess, plan, and then adapt an operation in order to ensure its ultimate success. IX Corps men certainly exhibited these traits on 4 November and should be recognised for this.

Conclusion

This all serves to confirm the assertion that the combined arms methodology was not only well understood by the officers and men tasked to implement it, but also that those men were skilled enough in the arts of war not to be tied irrevocably to plans that, during the middle years of the war, often proved to be an immovable millstone around the neck of flexibility.

184 IWM: LBY 73281 Sankey Report.
185 See the works of John Bourne, Gary Sheffield, Peter Simkins, Jonathan Boff, Andy Simpson, Simon Robbins, Paddy Griffith.

Conclusion

In battle, you do not have to be perfect, just better than your enemy.[1]

The plan for the Battle of the Sambre was still evolving as officers' whistles blew to send their men forward, reflecting the dynamic nature of the fighting of the last weeks of the Great War. It continued to do so as the battle progressed: in every chapter of this work there are examples of alterations and adjustments to the original plans, of decisions taken 'on the spot' to extend, curtail or re-direct a unit's efforts, to react to the efficacy of enemy resistance, and a seemingly instinctive knowledge – either conscious or unconscious – amongst commanders that it was fine to call a halt, where necessary, before final objectives had been reached, knowing that the job had been done.

This account has shown that the Battle of the Sambre did not go entirely to plan, but also that it was not essential that it do so in order to be counted as a success. Of the 13 divisions in the front line on 4 November, only five reached or exceeded their final objectives.[2] The relative 'failures' of the other seven were, in the end, irrelevant: it was vital that the forward German defences be overrun, but the lack of available German reserves rendered the risk of counter-attack negligible. 'Bite and hold' became a series of 'bites' with the 'hold' phase largely untested. Where the British settled for positions short of their objectives on the evening of the battle, the Germans, knowing they were beaten, mostly melted away during the hours of darkness, allowing units to move forward largely unopposed onto and beyond their original targets in the early hours of the next morning.

Ultimate operational success was therefore achieved, but performance at tactical level was uneven. The BEF was probably at its operational and tactical zenith during August and September 1918:[3] by November, logistical, meteorological and topographical issues restricted the range of new technologies available to planners, thus limiting the tactical scope for forth-coming attacks.

---

1   Dr Peter Lieb, Senior Lecturer at the Royal Military Academy, Sandhurst, during a lecture at the Western Front Association's President's Conference held in Birmingham on 5 July 2014. Dr. Lieb was lecturing on the Eastern Front 1914, but his remark is universally applicable. To strive toward perfection is laudable, but to believe that it is attainable in war is delusional.

2   These were the 19th, 24th, New Zealand, 37th and 38th Divisions. 18th and 50th Divisions came close.

3   Boff, *Winning and Losing*, p. 245

Aerial support was restricted by diminishing hours of daylight and deteriorating weather conditions and much of the RAF's work was done prior to the day of the attack: it provided hundreds of aerial photographs which gave invaluable information to the attacking units on the ground. By the time the aircraft were able to become airborne on the day of the attack, once daylight had arrived and fog had dispersed, much of the infantry's work had been completed. The planes were able to fly contact patrols to check on the rate of the infantry advance, to spot German troop concentrations and therefore warn of impending counter attack and to help direct artillery fire. Offensive actions appear to have been limited largely to bombing and strafing columns of retreating German infantry and vehicles.

The use of armour was curtailed by the limited availability of serviceable machines and by the topography of the battlefield. That tanks were not a decisive element in this battle is down to the small number of serviceable machines available, the difficulties in delivering these machines over long distances to the battlefield, and by the terrain they would face. It proved impractical to supply tanks any further north than 37th Division. They were then restricted by orders not to enter the forest[4] and by the impossibility of crossing the canal. They proved useful against hedgerows, machine gun posts and fortified positions in villages, but were still plagued by mechanical unreliability, navigational difficulties and vulnerability to basic anti-tank measures. Infantry commanders welcomed the assistance, but their plans were careful not to rely on the tanks' presence. They undoubtedly saved lives of attacking infantry at places like Landrecies, Preux-au-Bois, Catillon, Jolimetz and Hecq, and in places were able to speed up or reinvigorate a stalled advance, but it is difficult to argue that they were vital to the ultimate success of the battle. Attacks, it seems, were no less successful where no tanks were available. The infantry's opinion of them is perhaps best summed up by the 17th Division orders which reminded troops that the role of the tank was "entirely separate yet supplementary to that of the infantry." The men were not to "wait for the tanks".[5]

The major players on 4 November 1918 were therefore the infantry, the artillery and the engineers. The question of where the BEF lay on the 'learning curve' in the final days of the war does not rely for its answer solely on the range of the latest weaponry available and the inventiveness or efficacy of its deployment, but on the fact that the abilities of the BEF's commanders, who were experienced enough and skilled enough to go with what they had, allowed them – sometimes in the face of impending failure – to win the day.

Small unit infantry tactics were well understood, and it is tempting to adopt the view that British infantry of late 1918 was a cohesive, well-trained and innovative fighting force. This was true to a certain extent: the army had come a long way since the summer of 1916 and had learnt many lessons. Increased firepower and better tactics had changed the nature of the attack beyond recognition and German machine gun posts were no longer insuperable obstacles to a successful advance: suppressing fire, infiltration and the flanking manoeuvre were by then not only instinctive, but very effective. The brevity with which successful assaults on machine gun posts, farm buildings and various other strongpoints are described in numerous battalion war diaries demonstrates just how 'unremarkable' such small-scale tactical victories were regarded by this stage of the war. However, Jonathan Boff asserts[6] that training and the subsequent

4   One that did almost immediately 'bellied' itself on a tree stump.
5   TNA: PRO WO95/1985 War Diary 17th Division HQ
6   Boff, *Winning and Losing*, pp. 39-73. (In particular pp. 63-67).

adoption and successful implementation of such tactics was patchy. A brief re-evaluation of the work of two divisions (both V Corps) on 4 November will serve as examples.

17th and 38th Divisions attacked side by side through the Forêt de Mormal. Their fates were quite different.[7] On 17th Division front, an initial re-alignment manoeuvre had cost a large number of casualties as units fell victim to an effective enemy counter barrage. Orders had directed troops to bypass areas of strong resistance, but 50 Brigade, hampered by less than effective artillery support, was held up in the forest when confronted by German machine gun fire and when units were reluctant to manoeuvre, preferring the comfort of secure flanks. 38th Division, to their south, employed the very tactics recommended: 114 Brigade, in particular, used the tracks and rides to great effect and reached their objectives with limited casualties.[8]

17th Division should be viewed as something of an anomaly, however: most attacks demonstrated that the BEF had learnt its lessons, was able to adapt and improve its tactics and use its increased firepower effectively – there are many examples in the text of the very effective use of rifle grenades, mortars and Lewis Guns as German positions were repeatedly overrun.

The engineers are deserving of praise: they worked wonders to clear paths through hedgerows, to bridge rivers and streams behind the lines to facilitate the movement of troops, and to come up with the ideas and the hardware required to force the passage of the canal. If they can be criticised, it would be for not sharing ideas, knowledge and, crucially, materiel, across divisions. The fact that 32nd Division was not able to approach the waterway with pre-constructed pontoons – they were left with the heavy and unwieldy cork floats that other divisions[9] did not want and which required bridges to be constructed from their constituent parts once the canal was reached, and therefore under enemy fire – cost them dear. As illustrated by the successful crossings of the canal at other points, the speed with which the bridging operations were completed was the vital element crucial to the success of the undertaking.

Artillery provision for the 4 November attack was more than ample. Thirty-one Royal Field Artillery brigades, 19 heavy and 13 siege batteries added up to over 1,000 guns. Arrangements for artillery support for the later phases of the assault, once infantry had passed beyond the range of the initial creeping barrage, were down to liaison between gunners and brigade or battalion commanders. Some plans were very effective, some less so, but in places enemy opposition was so slight that infantry were able to move forward with minimal or no support from the guns. There was no artillery bombardment prior to Zero Hour, thus helping to ensure surprise. Silent registration on targets was accepted practice. The creeping barrage had become a sophisticated entity by this time in the war, and gunners were able to provide barrages at right angles to the general axis of advance, such as at Preux-au-Bois and Catillon. Towns and villages were only subject to shrapnel fire, in order to prevent civilian casualties and Le Quesnoy was not bombarded at all.[10] Counter battery work had been hampered by poor visibility prior to the assault – the RAF were unable to fly on 2 and 3 November – and infantry were greeted by stiff enemy barrages in a number of sectors. When combined with Trench Mortars and long-range indirect fire from Machine Gun Companies, the overall effect of British creeping barrages was demoralising for the defenders.

7   See Chapter 5 for a detailed account.
8   A glance at the bar chart in Appendix C will reveal the relative costs of these two approaches.
9   1st and 25th Divisions.
10   See Map 7a.

Was it necessary for the BEF to fight the Battle of the Sambre? It is possible, with hindsight, to suggest that the Germans were already beaten and that the Allies were by this time pushing against an already open door, that an armistice was imminent anyway. Neither politicians nor military leaders of the time were blessed with infallible clairvoyance, however: Field-Marshal Haig wrote on 2 November that "the determined fight put up by the Enemy today shows that the German Army is not yet demoralised!"[11] On 3 November, General Rawlinson wrote in his diary that "He [the Germans] evidently means to put up a fight tomorrow" and on the day of the battle "I don't think the Boche can stick out very much longer".[12] They could not have known that this major offensive was to be the last on that scale, even if that was what they were hoping. Politicians were still contemplating the possibility of the war lasting into the spring and summer of 1919 and orders for vast numbers of tanks for the next spring offensive were being considered. The German Army was not about to withdraw voluntarily from its defensive positions west of the Forêt de Mormal and along the Sambre-Oise Canal: the BEF was obliged to force the issue and found their opponent to be no push-over: the determined and tenacious defence of the canal opposite 32nd Division serves as an example of how difficult a task the British faced on that misty morning. The victory, it must be remembered, had cost the British over 1,200 infantry fatalities and around 5,000 wounded.[13]

The BEF's victory on the Sambre was decisive. On a tactical level, the growing reliance on the part of the Germans on machine guns and artillery, combined with the limited number of troops available to man support and reserve positions – behind the canal these consisted mainly of fortified farmhouses and hamlets – meant that the overwhelming strength of British artillery, the tried and tested infantry tactics for dealing with such strongpoints, and numerical superiority coupled with better morale, were always going to prove successful. Even where tactics were less than cutting-edge, the final result was the same. With objectives mostly, or almost, reached on the day, or at least by the following morning, the battle must also be declared an operational success. The Germans were pushed off what was to be their final 'prepared' defensive line: subsequent actions had all the attributes of a pursuit. At the strategic level, the British success removed any chance of the Germans holding out for a negotiated peace in the spring of 1919 and OHL leaders knew that it was vital to secure an armistice as quickly as possible and at any price.

This book illustrates the dynamic and complicated nature of war. It is important to show that by 4 November 1918 the BEF was no longer at the high-point of its 'learning curve': the logistics system was strained; manpower was limited; tactical competence could be variable and all-arms tactics were curtailed by the unavailability or paucity of aircraft and tanks, unsuitable ground and the autumn weather. The stubborn resistance of a depleted enemy determined to hold the line of the forest and the canal required confidence in the planning, along with superiority of method, morale and materiel, but these prerequisites had to be combined with improvisation, ingenuity and pragmatism in order for the BEF to prevail. The facts are that the attack on 4 November finally broke the will of the German Army, effectively destroyed its means of resisting any longer and brought the Great War to a precipitous end.

11   Sheffield & Bourne (eds), *Douglas Haig*, p. 484.
12   Churchill College Archives, Cambridge. Rawlinson Papers.
13   The latter figure is an estimate, as some units did not report full casualty figures for the day. The overall figure is approximately one tenth of that for the Somme on 1 July 1916.

Appendix I

Order of Battle

The formations and units are listed, down to divisional level, in the order in which they occupied the front line on 4 November 1918, moving north to south.

Third Army	GOC	General Hon. Sir J.H.G. Byng
	MGGS	Major-General L.R. Vaughan
	MGRA	Major-General A.E. Wardrop
	DA & QMG	Major-General A.F. Sillem
	CRE	Major-General W.A. Liddell
XVII Corps	GOC	Lieutenant-General Sir C. Fergusson
	BGGS	Brigadier-General W.D. Wright VC
	BGRA	Brigadier-General E.H. Willis
	CHA	Brigadier-General N.G. Barron
	DA & QMG	Brigadier-General R.F.A. Hobbs
19th Division	GOC	Major-General G.D. Jeffreys
	GSO1	Lieutenant-Colonel H.F. Montgomery
	BGRA	Brigadier-General E.J.R. Pell
	AA & QMG	Lieutenant-Colonel G.E. Hawes

56 Brigade	Brigadier-General R.M. Heath
1/4th Shropshire L.I.	Lieutenant-Colonel W.A. Bowen[1]
8th North Staffordshire Regt	Lieutenant-Colonel H.W. Dakeyne
9th Cheshire Regt	Lieutenant-Colonel R.R. Raymer[2]

1   Bowen was in command up to 2 November 1918. The author has been unable to trace the name of his replacement.
2   Raymer was in command up to 14 October 1918. The author has been unable to trace the name of his replacement.

57 Brigade — Brigadier-General A.J.F. Eden
10th Royal Warwickshire Regt — Lieutenant-Colonel F.B Follett
8th Gloucestershire Regt — Lieutenant-Colonel W. Parkes
3rd Worcestershire Regt — Lieutenant-Colonel P.R. Whalley

58 Brigade — Brigadier-General A.E. Glasgow
9th Royal Welsh Fusiliers — Lieutenant-Colonel Lt-Col L.F. Smeathman
9th Welsh Regt — Major L. Hammill
2nd Wiltshire Regt — Lieutenant-Colonel P.S.L. Beaver

24th Division	GOC	Major-General A.C. Daly
	GSO1	Lieutenant-Colonel C.M. Longmore
	BGRA	Brigadier-General H.G. Lloyd
	AA & QMG	Lieutenant-Colonel Hon. R.H. Collins

17 Brigade — Brigadier-General G. Thorpe
1st Royal Fusiliers — Lieutenant-Colonel W.W. Chard
8th Queen's — Lieutenant-Colonel H.J.C. Peirs
3rd Rifle Brigade — Lieutenant-Colonel E.R. Kewley

72 Brigade — Brigadier-General R.W. Morgan
9th East Surrey Regt — Lieutenant-Colonel E.W. Cameron
8th Royal West Kent Regt — Lieutenant-Colonel H.J. Wenyon
1st North Staffordshire Regt — Lieutenant-Colonel W.D. Stamer

73 Brigade — Brigadier-General R.J. Collins
9th Royal Sussex Regt — Lieutenant-Colonel M.V.B.Hill
7th Northamptonshire Regt — Lieutenant-Colonel E.S.C. Grune
13th Middlesex Regt — Major R.S. Dove

VI Corps	GOC	Lieutenant-General Sir J.A.L. Haldane
	BGGS	Brigadier-General R.H. Kearsley
	BGRA	Brigadier-General J.G. Rotton
	CHA	Brigadier-General A. Ellershaw
	DA & QMG	Brigadier-General J.B.G. Tulloch

Guards Division	GOC	Major-General T.G. Matheson
	GSO1	Lieutenant-Colonel E.W.M. Grigg
	BGRA	Brigadier-General F.A. Wilson
	AA & QMG	Lieutenant-Colonel F.G. Alston

1 Guards Brigade — Brigadier-General C.R. Champion de Crespigny
2nd Grenadier Guards — Lieutenant-Colonel C.F.A. Walker
2nd Coldstream Guards — Lieutenant-Colonel E.P. Brassey
1st Irish Guards — Lieutenant-Colonel R.R.C.Baggallay

2 Guards Brigade		Brigadier-General B.N. Sergisson-Brooke
3rd Grenadier Guards		Lieutenant-Colonel Viscount Lascelles
1st Coldstream Guards		Lieutenant-Colonel Hon. E.K. Digby
1st Scots Guards		Lieutenant-Colonel V.A.F. Mackenzie

3 Guards Brigade		Brigadier-General C.P.Heywood
1st Grenadier Guards		Lieutenant-Colonel Hon. W.R. Bailey
2nd Scots Guards		Lieutenant-Colonel J.A. Stirling
1st Welsh Guards		Lieutenant-Colonel R.E.C. Luxmoore-Ball

62nd Division	GOC	Major-General Sir R.D. Whigham
	GSO1	Lieutenant-Colonel F.W. Gossett
	BGRA	Brigadier-General A.T. Anderson
	AA & QMG	Lieutenant-Colonel H.F. Lea

185 Brigade		Brigadier-General Viscount Hampden
1/5th Devonshire Regt		Lieutenant-Colonel H.V. Bastow
1/8th West Yorkshire Regt		Lieutenant-Colonel N.A. England
2/20th London Regiment		Lieutenant-Colonel W.M. Craddock

186 Brigade		Brigadier-General J.L.G. Burnett
5th Duke of Wellington's		Lieutenant-Colonel J. Walker
2/4th Duke of Wellington's		Lieutenant-Colonel P.P. Wilson
2/4th Hampshire Regt		Lieutenant-Colonel F. Brook

187 Brigade		Brigadier-General A.J. Reddie
2/4th K.O.Y.L.I.		Lieutenant-Colonel C.A. Chaytor
2/5th K.O.Y.L.I.		Lieutenant-Colonel F.H. Peter
2/4th York & Lancaster Regt		Major J.E.D. Stickney

IV Corps	GOC	Lieutenant-General Sir G.M. Harper
	BGGS	Brigadier-General R.G. Parker
	BGRA	Brigadier-General J.G. Geddes
	CHA	Brigadier-General T.E. Marshall
	DA & QMG	Brigadier-General W.H.V. Darell

N. Zealand Division	GOC	Major-General Sir A.H. Russell
	GSO1	Lieutenant-Colonel H.M. Wilson
	BGRA	Brigadier-General G.N. Johnston
	AA & QMG	Lieutenant-Colonel H.E. Avery

1 New Zealand Brigade		Brigadier-General C.W. Melvill
1st Wellington Battalion		Lieutenant-Colonel F.K. Turnbull
2nd Wellington Battalion		Major H.E. McKinnon
1st Auckland Battalion		Lieutenant-Colonel W.H. Alderman

2nd Auckland Battalion		Major W.C. Sind
3rd New Zealand (Rifles) Brigade		Brigadier-General H.E. Hart
1st New Zealand Rifle Brigade		Captain E.A. Harding
2nd New Zealand Rifle Brigade		Lieutenant-Colonel L.H. Jardine
3rd New Zealand Rifle Brigade		Major G.W. Cockroft
4th New Zealand Rifle Brigade		Lieutenant-Colonel H.E. Barrowclough
37th Division	GOC	Major-General H. Bruce Williams
	GSO1	Lieutenant-Colonel W. Platt
	BGRA	Brigadier-General F. Potts
	AA & QMG	Lieutenant-Colonel H.G. Reid
63 Brigade		Brigadier-General A.B. Hubbock
8th Lincolnshire Regt		Lieutenant-Colonel A.T. Hitch
8th Somerset Light Infantry		Lieutenant-Colonel C.J. de B. Sheringham
4th Middlesex Regt		Lieutenant-Colonel W.G. Chapman
111 Brigade		Brigadier-General S.G. Francis
10th Royal Fusiliers		Lieutenant-Colonel J.D. Waters
13th King's Royal Rifle Corps		Lieutenant-Colonel W.G. Johns
13th Rifle Brigade		Lieutenant-Colonel R.A. Mostyn-Owen
112 Brigade		Brigadier-General W.N. Herbert
13th Royal Fusiliers		Lieutenant-Colonel R.A. Smith
1st Essex Regt		Lieutenant-Colonel T.J.E. Blake
1/1st Hertfordshire Regt		Lieutenant-Colonel J.L. Heselton
V Corps	GOC	Lieutenant-General C.D. Shute
	BGGS	Brigadier-General R.H. Mangles
	BGRA	Brigadier-General R.P. Benson
	CHA	Brigadier-General A.M. Tyler
	DA & QMG	Brigadier-General H.M. de F. Montgomery
17th Division	GOC	Major-General P.R. Robertson
	GSO1	Lieutenant-Colonel E.M. Birch
	BGRA	Brigadier-General P. Wheatley
	AA & QMG	Lieutenant-Colonel A.E.J. Wilson
50 Brigade		Brigadier-General J.F.R. Hope
6th Dorsetshire Regt		Lieutenant-Colonel E.S. Weldon
7th East Yorkshire Regt		Lieutenant-Colonel G.E. King
10th West Yorkshire Regt		Lieutenant-Colonel W.Gibson

51 Brigade		Brigadier-General R.M. Dudgeon
7th Lincolnshire Regt		Lieutenant-Colonel H.Sargent
7th Border Regt		Lieutenant-Colonel P. Kirkup
10th Notts & Derby Regt		Lieutenant-Colonel T.W. Daniel

52 Brigade		Brigadier-General W. Allason
10th Lancashire Fusiliers		Lieutenant-Colonel G.L. Torrens
12th Manchester Regt		Lieutenant-Colonel S. Danby
9th Duke of Wellington's		Lieutenant-Colonel A. Driver

38th Division	GOC	Major-General T.A. Cubitt
	GSO1	Lieutenant-Colonel J.E. Munby
	BGRA	Brigadier-General T.E. Topping
	AA & QMG	Lieutenant-Colonel H.R. Lee

113 Brigade		Brigadier-General H.E. ap Rhys-Price
13th Royal Welsh Fusiliers		Lieutenant-Colonel J.F. Leman
14th Royal Welsh Fusiliers		Major W.P. Wheldon
16th Royal Welsh Fusiliers		Lieutenant-Colonel C.E. Davies

114 Brigade		Brigadier-General T.R.C. Price
13th Welsh Regt		Lieutenant-Colonel H.F. Hobbs
14th Welsh Regt		Lieutenant-Colonel G.F. Brooke
15th Welsh Regt		Lieutenant-Colonel E. Helme

115 Brigade		Brigadier-General H.D. dc Pree
10th South Wales Borderers		Lieutenant-Colonel A.L. Bowen
2nd Royal Welsh Fusiliers		Lieutenant-Colonel G.E.R. de Miremont
17th Royal Welsh Fusiliers		Lieutenant-Colonel R.L. Beasley

Fourth Army	GOC	General Sir H.S. Rawlinson
	MGGS	Major-General A.A. Montgomery
	MGRA	Major-General C.E.D. Budworth
	DA & QMG	Major-General H.C. Holman
	CRE	Major-General R.U.H. Buckland

XIII Corps	GOC	Lieutenant-General Sir T.L.N. Morland
	BGGS	Brigadier-General I. Stewart
	CHA	Brigadier-General J.D. Sherer
	DA & QMG	Brigadier-General S.W. Robinson

18th Division	GOC	Major-General R.P. Lee
	GSO1	Lieutenant-Colonel G. Blewitt
	BGRA	Brigadier-General T.O. Seagram

| | AA & QMG | Lieutenant-Colonel R.H.L. Cutbill |

53 Brigade — Brigadier-General M.G.H. Barker
7th Royal West Kent Regt — Lieutenant-Colonel L.H. Hickson
10th Essex Regt — Lieutenant-Colonel R. Forbes
8th Royal Berkshire Regt — Lieutenant-Colonel N.B. Hudson

54 Brigade — Lieutenant-Colonel K.C. Weldon
2nd Bedfordshire Regt — Lieutenant-Colonel A.E. Percival
6th Northamptonshire Regt — Lieutenant-Colonel R. Turner
11th Royal Fusiliers — Lieutenant-Colonel K.D.H. Gwynn

55 Brigade — Lieutenant-Colonel A.P.B. Irwin
7th Queen's — Major H.J. Tortise
7th East Kent Regt — Major W.H. Stronge
8th East Surrey Regt — Lieutenant-Colonel W.H. Baddeley

50th Division
GOC — Major-General H.C. Jackson
GSO1 — Lieutenant-Colonel A.K. Grant
BGRA — Brigadier-General W. Stirling
AA & QMG — Lieutenant-Colonel A.C.H. Duke

149 Brigade — Brigadier-General P.M. Robinson
3rd Royal Fusiliers — Lieutenant-Colonel M.O. Clarke
13th Black Watch — Lieutenant-Colonel P.J. Blair
2nd Royal Dublin Fusiliers — Major J. Luke

150 Brigade — Brigadier-General G. Rollo
7th Wiltshire Regt — Lieutenant-Colonel H.J. Hodgson
2nd Northumberland Fusiliers — Lieutenant-Colonel A.C.L.H. Jones
2nd Royal Munster Fusiliers — Lieutenant-Colonel C.R. Williams

151 Brigade — Brigadier-General R.E. Sugden
6th Royal Inniskilling Fusiliers — Lieutenant-Colonel G.G.F.F. Greville
1st K.O.Y.L.I. — Lieutenant-Colonel H. Mallinson
4th King's Royal Rifle Corps — Major G.A. Tryon

25th Division
GOC — Major-General J.R.E. Charles
GSO1 — Lieutenant-Colonel D.F. Anderson
BGRA — Brigadier-General K.J. Kincaid-Smith
AA &QMG — Lieutenant-Colonel Hon. E.P.J. Stourton

7 Brigade — Brigadier-General C.J. Hickie
9th Devonshire Regt — Lieutenant-Colonel H.I. Storey
20th Manchester Regt — Lieutenant-Colonel C.R. Pilkington

21st Manchester Regt		Lieutenant-Colonel C.E.N. Lomax
74 Brigade		Brigadier-General H.M. Craigie-Halkett
11th Notts & Derby Regt		Lieutenant-Colonel W.R. Corall
9th Yorkshire Regt		Lieutenant-Colonel R.S. Hart
13th Durham Light Infantry		Lieutenant-Colonel H.G. Faber
75 Brigade		Brigadier-General C.W. Frizell
1/8th Worcestershire Regt		Lieutenant-Colonel H.T. Clarke
1/5th Gloucestershire Regt		Lieutenant-Colonel D.Lewis
1/8th Royal Warwickshire Regt		Lieutenant-Colonel P.H. Whitehouse
IX Corps	GOC	Lieutenant-General Sir W.P. Braithwaite
	BGGS	Brigadier-General A.R. Cameron
	BGRA	Brigadier-General G. Humphreys
	CHA	Brigadier-General G.B. Mackenzie
	DA & QMG	Brigadier-General J.C. Harding-Newman
32nd Division	GOC	Major-General T.S. Lambert
	GSO1	Lieutenant-Colonel E. FitzG. Dillon
	BGRA	Brigadier-General J.A. Tyler
	AA &QMG	Lieutenant-Colonel J.P.B. Robinson
14 Brigade		Brigadier-General L.P. Evans VC
5/6th Royal Scots		Lieutenant-Colonel J.A. Fraser
1st Dorsetshire Regt		Lieutenant-Colonel H.D. Thwaytes
15th Highland Light Infantry		Lieutenant-Colonel V.B. Ramsden
96 Brigade		Brigadier-General A.C. Girdwood
2nd Manchester Regt		Lieutenant-Colonel G.M. Robertson
15th Lancashire Fusiliers		Lieutenant-Colonel C.E.R.G. Alban
16th Lancashire Fusiliers		Lieutenant-Colonel J.N. Marshall
97 Brigade		Brigadier-General G.A. Armytage
2nd K.O.Y.L.I.		Lieutenant-Colonel L.Lamotte
1/5th Border Regt		Lieutenant-Colonel H.N. Vinen
10thArgyll & Sutherland H'landers		Lieutenant-Colonel H.G. Sotheby
1st Division	GOC	Major-General E.P. Strickland
	GSO1	Lieutenant-Colonel E.N. Tandy
	BGRA	Brigadier-General H.F.E. Lewin
	AA & QMG	Lieutenant-Colonel H.H. Spender-Clay
1 Brigade		Brigadier-General L.L. Wheatley
1st Cameron Highlanders		Lieutenant-Colonel H.C. Methuen

1st Loyal North Lancashire Regt	Lieutenant-Colonel R.E. Berkeley
1st Black Watch	Lieutenant-Colonel F. Anderson

2 Brigade	Lieutenant-Colonel D.G. Johnson
2nd Royal Sussex Regt	Lieutenant-Colonel D.G. Johnson
2nd King's Royal Rifle Corps	Lieutenant-Colonel H.F.E. Smith
1st Northamptonshire Regt	Lieutenant-Colonel G. St G. Robinson

3 Brigade	Brigadier-General E.G. St Aubyn
1st Gloucestershire Regt	Lieutenant-Colonel J.R. Guild
1st South Wales Borderers	Lieutenant-Colonel C.L.Taylor
2nd Welch Regt	Lieutenant-Colonel J.F. Badham

Royal Engineers

XVII Corps	Brigadier-General W.D. Waghorn
19th Division (81/82/94 Field Companies)	Lieutenant-Colonel P.E. Hodgson
24th Division (103/104/129 Field Companies)	Lieutenant-Colonel J.H. Prior

VI Corps	Brigadier-General R.N. Harvey
Guards Division (55 / 75 / 76 Field Companies)	Lieutenant-Colonel E.F.W. Lees
62nd Division (457 / 460 / 461 Field Companies)	Lieutenant-Colonel L. Chenevix-Trench

IV Corps	Brigadier-General C.M. Carpenter
NZ Division (1 / 3 Field Companies, NZ RE)	Lieutenant-Colonel H.L. Bingay
37th Division (152 / 153 / 154 Field Companies)	Lieutenant-Colonel R.D. Jackson

V Corps	Brigadier-General A.G. Stevenson
17th Division (77 / 78 / 93 Field Companies)	Lieutenant-Colonel F.A. Ferguson
38th Division (123 / 124 / 151 Field Companies)	Lieutenant-Colonel T.E. Kelsall

XIII Corps	Brigadier-General C.A. Elliott
18th Division (80 / 81 / 82 Field Companies)	Lieutenant-Colonel C.B.O. Symons
50th Division (7 / 446 / 447 Field Companies)	Lieutenant-Colonel P. de H. Hall
25th Division (105 / 106 / 130 Field Companies)	Lieutenant-Colonel R.J. Done

IX Corps	Brigadier-General R.A. Gillam
32nd Division (218 / 206 Field Companies)	Lieutenant-Colonel G.C. Pollard
& (465 / 466 / 468 Field Companies)	Lieutenant-Colonel W. Garforth
1st Division (23 / 26 / 409 Field Companies)	Lieutenant-Colonel C.E.P. Sankey

Appendix II

Commanders' Length of Service

Commanding Officers down to Brigade level are listed with date of appointment to that post and number of days in post. Where the exact day is not known*, the 15th of the month is assumed to be date of appointment, thus giving an accuracy of plus or minus 15 days.

			(Days)
Third Army	General Hon. Sir J.H.G. Byng	9.6.17	514
XVII Corps	Lieutenant-General Sir C. Fergusson	25.5.16	894
19th Division	Major-General G.D. Jeffreys	22.9.17	410
56 Brigade	Brigadier-General R.M. Heath	7.4.18	212
57 Brigade	Brigadier-General A.J.F. Eden	30.8.18	67
58 Brigade	Brigadier-General A.E. Glasgow	10.1.17	664
24th Division	Major-General A.C. Daly	15.9.17	416
17 Brigade	Brigadier-General G. Thorpe	7.6.18	151
72 Brigade	Brigadier-General R.W. Morgan	13.12.17	327
73 Brigade	Brigadier-General R.J. Collins	15.7.18	113
VI Corps	Lieutenant-General Sir J.A.L. Haldane	8.8.16	819
Guards Division	Major-General T.G. Matheson	11.9.18	55
1 Guards Brigade	Brigadier-General C.R. Ch. de Crespigny	22.9.17	409
2 Guards Brigade	Brigadier-General B.N. Sergisson-Brooke	25.4.18	194
3 Guards Brigade	Brigadier-General C.P.Heywood	26.10.18	10
62nd Division	Major-General Sir R.D. Whigham	28.8.18	69
185 Brigade	Brigadier-General Viscount Hampden	21.8.17	441
186 Brigade	Brigadier-General J.L.G. Burnett	3.12.17	337
187 Brigade	Brigadier-General A.J. Reddie	3.4.18	216
IV Corps	Lieutenant-General Sir G.M. Harper	11.3.18	239
New Zealand Division	Major-General Sir A.H. Russell	?.11.15	1,086*
1 NZ Brigade	Brigadier-General C.W. Melvill	8.6.17	515
3 NZ Rifle Brigade	Brigadier-General H.E. Hart	?.2.17	628*

37th Division	Major-General H. Bruce Williams	9.11.16	726
63 Brigade	Brigadier-General A.B. Hubbock	21.10.18	15
111 Brigade	Brigadier-General S.G. Francis	19.10.17	382
112 Brigade	Brigadier-General W.N. Herbert	27.9.18	39
V Corps	Lieutenant-General C.D. Shute	28.4.18	191
17th Division	Major-General P.R. Robertson	13.7.16	845
50 Brigade	Brigadier-General J.F.R. Hope	23.9.18	43
51 Brigade	Brigadier-General R.M. Dudgeon	30.5.18	159
52 Brigade	Brigadier-General W. Allason	14.4.18	205
38th Division	Major-General T.A. Cubitt	23.5.18	166
113 Brigade	Brigadier-General H.E. ap Rhys-Price	17.10.17	384
114 Brigade	Brigadier-General T.R.C. Price	6.8.18	91
115 Brigade	Brigadier-General H.D. de Pree	5.9.18	61
Fourth Army	General Sir H.S. Rawlinson	5.2.16	1,004
XIII Corps	Lieutenant-General Sir T.L.N. Morland	12.4.18	207
18th Division	Major-General R.P. Lee	15.1.17	659
53 Brigade	Brigadier-General M.G.H. Barker	24.4.18	560
54 Brigade	Lt-Col K.C. Weldon	25.10.18	11
55 Brigade	Lt-Col A.P.B. Irwin	24.10.18	12
50th Division	Major-General H.C. Jackson	23.3.18	227
149 Brigade	Brigadier-General P.M. Robinson	7.6.18	151
150 Brigade	Brigadier-General G. Rollo	29.9.18	37
151 Brigade	Brigadier-General R.E. Sugden	7.6.18	151
25th Division	Major-General J.R.E. Charles	4.8.18	93
7 Brigade	Brigadier-General C.J. Hickie	31.5.18	158
74 Brigade	Brigadier-General H.M. Craigie-Halkett	31.3.18	219
75 Brigade	Brigadier-General C.W. Frizell	1.10.18	35
IX Corps	Lieutenant-General Sir W.P. Braithwaite	13.9.18	53
32nd Division	Major-General T.S. Lambert	31.5.18	158
14 Brigade	Brigadier-General L.P. Evans VC	10.6.18	148
96 Brigade	Brigadier-General A.C. Girdwood	20.8.17	442
97 Brigade	Brigadier-General G.A. Armytage	6.10.18	30
1st Division	Major-General E.P. Strickland	12.6.16	876
1 Brigade	Brigadier-General L.L. Wheatley	22.9.18	44
2 Brigade	Lt-Col D.G. Johnson	26.9.18	40
3 Brigade	Brigadier-General E.G. St Aubyn	6.10.18	30

Corps Commanders' average time in post:	400 days	(c. 13½ months)
Divisional Commanders' average time in post:	445 days	(c. 14½ months)
Brigade Commanders' average time in post:	203 days	(c. 6½ months)

Numbers who took up post in:

	1915	1916	1917	1918
Divisional Commanders	1	3	3	6
Brigade Commanders	0	0	10	28

Appendix III

Divisional Fatalities, November 1918

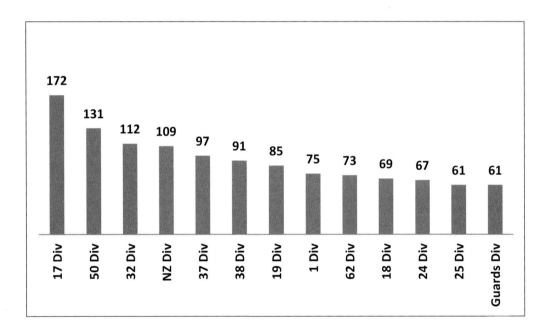

Total fatalities: 1203.

Appendix IV

Victoria Cross Winners, 4 November 1918

Seven Victoria Crosses were won on 4 November 1918. They are listed here north to south by location of action and citations are quoted in full.

Lance-Corporal W. Amey.
1/8th Battalion, Royal Warwickshire Regiment.

For most conspicuous bravery on 4 November 1918 during the attack on Landrecies, when owing to fog many hostile machine-gun nests were missed by the leading troops. On his own initiative he led his section against a machine-gun nest, under heavy fire, drove the garrison into a neighbouring farm, and finally captured about 50 prisoners and several machine-guns. Later, single-handed, and under heavy fire, he attacked a machine-gun post in a farm house, killed two of the garrison and drove the remainder into a cellar until assistance arrived. Subsequently, single-handed, he rushed a strongly held post, capturing 20 prisoners. He displayed throughout the day the highest degree of valour and determination.

William Amey was born on 5 March 1881 in Duddeston, Birmingham. He joined the Royal Warwickshires in 1914 and had earned a Military Medal before winning his VC. He was demobilised in 1919 with the rank of Corporal and lived for the rest of his life in Leamington Spa. He died on 28 May 1940 and was buried with full military honours in All Saints Cemetery, Leamington Spa.

Lieutenant-Colonel J.N. Marshall
Attached 16th Battalion, Lancashire Fusiliers

For most conspicuous bravery, determination and leadership in the attack on the Sambre-Oise Canal, near Catillon, on the 4th November 1918, when a partly constructed bridge came under concentrated fire and was broken before the advanced troops of his battalion could cross. Lieut-Colonel Marshall at once went forward and organized parties to repair the bridge. The first party were soon killed or

wounded, but by personal example he inspired his command, and volunteers were instantly forthcoming. Under intense fire and with complete disregard of his own safety, he stood on the bank encouraging his men and assisting in the work, and when the bridge was repaired attempted to rush across at the head of his battalion, and was killed by so doing. The passage of the canal was of vital importance, and the gallantry displayed by all ranks was largely due to the inspiring example set by Lieut-Colonel Marshall.

John Neville Marshall was born on 12 June 1887 in Stretford, Manchester. The family moved to Birmingham in 1891 and Neville attended King Edward VI Grammar School, Camp Hill before working in the Medical Faculty of the University of Birmingham. Though unqualified, he later worked as a vet in Harlow, Essex. He married Edith Maud Taylor on 20 September 1911.

In September 1914 he was serving in the 1st Division of the Belgian Army, was wounded several times and discharged as medically unfit. In 1915 he volunteered for service in the British Army and was commissioned into the Irish Guards. He served with a number of different regiments before being finally attached to the 16th Lancashire Fusiliers on 11 October 1918.

Marshall's VC was presented to his widow at Buckingham Palace on 12 April 1919.

Major A.H.S. Waters
218th Field Company, Royal Engineers

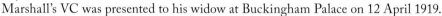

For most conspicuous bravery and devotion to duty on the 4th November 1918, near Ors, when bridging with his Field Company the Oise-Sambre canal. From the outset the task was under artillery and machine-gun fire at close range, the bridge being damaged and the building party suffering severe casualties. Major Waters, hearing that all his officers had been killed or wounded, at once went forward and personally supervised the completion of the bridge, working on cork-floats while under fire at point-blank range. So intense was the fire that it seemed impossible that he could escape being killed. The success of the operation was due entirely to his valour and example.

Arnold Horatio Santo Waters was born on 23 September 1886 in Plymouth. He attended the Hoe Grammar School in Plymouth before training as an engineer at University Tutorial College, London. He joined the army on 30 January 1915 as a Second-Lieutenant in the Royal Engineers. He won an MC in July 1917 and a DSO in 1918.

After the war, he set up his own engineering business and was active in the British Legion. He married Gladys Barribau in 1924 and had three sons. He became Deputy Lieutenant for the County of Warwick after the Second World War and was a JP in Sutton Coldfield. He was made a CBE in 1948 and was knighted in 1954.

He died at his home in Four Oaks, Sutton Coldfield on 22 January 1981.

Sapper A. Archibald
218th Field Company, Royal Engineers.

For most conspicuous bravery and self-sacrifice on 4th November 1918, near Ors, when with a party building a floating bridge across the canal. He was foremost in the work under a very heavy artillery barrage and machine-gun fire. The later was directed at him from a few yards' distance while he was working on the cork floats; nevertheless, he persevered in his task, and his example and efforts were such that the bridge, which was essential to the success of the operations, was very quickly completed. The supreme devotion to duty of this gallant sapper, who collapsed from gas-poisoning on completion of his work, was beyond all praise.

Adam Archibald was born on 14 January 1879 in Leith, Scotland. He married Margaret Lander Sinclair in Edinburgh on 6 June 1902: they had four children, three girls and a boy. He joined the Army under the Derby scheme on 4 November 1915 and after initial service with the Durham Light Infantry joined the Royal Engineers. He went to France in September 1917.

His recovery from gas-poisoning delayed his return home until April 1919, but he still managed to serve in the allied expedition to Archangel before demobilisation later the same year.

He returned to his pre-war employers, Stuart's Granolithic Works in Edinburgh, becoming manager of the Duff Street Works. He retired in the early 1940s and died at his Edinburgh home on 10 March 1957.

Second-Lieutenant J. Kirk
Attached 2nd Battalion, Manchester Regiment.

For most conspicuous bravery and devotion to duty north of Ors on 4 November 1918, whilst attempting to bridge the Oise Canal. To cover the bridging of the canal he took a Lewis Gun, and under intense machine-gun fire paddled across the canal in a raft, and at a range of 10 yards expended all his ammunition. Further ammunition was paddled across to him, and he continuously maintained covering fire for the bridging party from a most exposed position till killed at his gun. The supreme contempt for danger and magnificent self-sacrifice displayed by this gallant officer prevented many casualties and enabled two platoons to cross the bridge before it was destroyed.

James Kirk was born on 27 January 1897 in Cheadle Hulme, Cheshire. He enlisted with the 2/6th Battalion, Manchester Regiment on 10 October 1914 and set off for Gallipoli in July 1915. He was in action at the storming of Achi Baba in September, but was evacuated two months later with frostbite. After six weeks' convalescence in Cairo he joined the 1st Camel Corps, remaining with them for just over a year and being promoted to Quartermaster-Sergeant. He rejoined the Manchester Regiment in February 1917 and in December was recommended for a commission. He returned to France in October 1918 as a second-lieutenant.

His parents learned of his death on Armistice Day and were presented with his medal at Buckingham Palace on 1 March 1919.

Major G. De C.E. Findlay
409th Lowland Field Company, Royal Engineers.

For most conspicuous bravery and devotion to duty during the forcing of the Sambre-Oise Canal at the lock, two miles south of Catillon, on 4 November 1918, when in charge of the bridging operations at this crossing. Major Findlay was with the leading bridging and assaulting parties which came under heavy fire while trying to cross the dyke between the forming-up line and the lock. The casualties were severe, and the advance was stopped. Nevertheless, under heavy and incessant fire he collected what men he could and repaired the bridges, in spite of heavy casualties in officers and other ranks. Although wounded, Major Findlay continued his task and after unsuccessful efforts, owing to his men being swept down, he eventually placed the bridge in position across the lock, and was the first man across, subsequently remaining at this post of danger till further work was completed. His cool and gallant behaviour inspired volunteers from different units at a critical time when men became casualties almost as soon as they joined him in the fire-swept zone, and it was due to Major Findlay's gallantry and devotion to duty that this most important crossing was effected.

George de Cardonnel Elmsall Findlay was born on 20 August 1889 in Cardross, Scotland. He was educated at Harrow School, where he won the Spencer Cup at Bisley in 1907. He entered the Royal Military Academy, Woolwich in 1910 and served with 5th Field Troop until a riding accident resulted in 10 months' sick leave. He trained recruits in musketry until February 1915 and then worked on lines of communication. He was appointed Staff Officer to the CRE, V Corps, in May 1916 and later became O.C. of 409th Lowland Field Company, receiving an MC for his work during Third Ypres. At the Hindenburg Line in October 1918 he was awarded a Bar to his MC.

He married Dorothy Gordon in 1921, but the marriage was annulled. He was appointed Captain & Adjutant of the 52nd Divisional Engineers and served in India, reaching the rank of Lieutenant-Colonel before retiring in 1939. He was called back to duty twice as temporary colonel before finally retiring in 1945. He became Deputy Lieutenant of Dunbartonshire in 1957 and was a prominent member of the local British Legion. He married Nellie Constance Barclay Clark in Glasgow at the age of 70, and died on 26 June 1967.

Lieutenant-Colonel D.G. Johnson
Attached 2nd Battalion, Royal Sussex Regiment.

For most conspicuous bravery and leadership during the forcing of the Sambre Canal on the 4th November 1918. The 2nd Infantry Brigade, of which the 2nd Battn. Royal Sussex Regt formed part, was ordered to cross by the lock south of Catillon. The position was strong, and before the bridge could be thrown a steep bank leading up to the lock and the waterway about 100 yards short of the canal had to be crossed. The assaulting platoons and bridging parties, Royal Engineers, on their arrival at the waterway were thrown into confusion by a heavy barrage and machine-gun fire, and heavy casualties were caused. At this moment Lieut-Colonel Johnson arrived, and, realizing the situation, at once collected men to man the bridges and assist the Royal Engineers, and personally led the assault. In spite of his efforts heavy enemy fire again broke up the assaulting and bridging parties. Without any hesitation, he again reorganized the platoons and bridging parties, and led them at the lock, this time succeeding in effecting a crossing, after which all went well. During all this time, Lieut-Colonel Johnson was under a very heavy fire, which, though it nearly decimated the assaulting columns, left him untouched. His conduct was a fine example of great valour, coolness and intrepidity, which, added to his splendid leadership and the offensive spirit that he had inspired in his battalion, were entirely responsible for the successful crossing.

Dudley Graham Johnson was born on 13 February 1884 in Bourton-on-the-Water, Gloucestershire. He joined the army as an officer in the South Wales Borderers in July 1903. He was promoted Captain in March 1914 and Major in December 1917, before assuming command of 2nd Royal Sussex in April 1918.

He won his first DSO in China in 1914, his MC in 1917, and a Bar to his DSO at Pontruet, France, in September 1918. He had been wounded on the Gallipoli Peninsula in 1915.

He married Marjorie Grisewood on 12 June 1912 and his son was born the day before the outbreak of the First World War. Two daughters followed.

After the war he commanded 2nd Royal Sussex as part of the Army of Occupation in Germany. Further commands included the 2nd North Staffs and the 12th (Secunderbad) Infantry Brigade. He was ADC to King George VI from September 1936 to January 1939.

He was GOC of 4th Division at the outbreak of the Second World War and served in France and Belgium, being evacuated from Dunkirk.

He was GOC Aldershot Command from 1940 and Colonel of the South Wales Borderers from 1944 until 1949. After retirement, he became a borough councillor in Fleet, Hampshire.

Johnson died on 21 December 1975 at the age of 91 and is buried in Church Crookham Churchyard in the same grave as his wife, who had died in 1950.

Appendix V

Trench Map References and How to Interpret Them

The method of using map references is explained below, allowing the reader to find locations on the maps referred to in the text by First World War-style coordinates.

The areas shown on the maps are divided into large rectangles, each identified by a capital letter of the alphabet. These are, in turn, divided into smaller squares (1000 yards by 1000 yards on the ground) identified by a number.

Each numbered square is divided into four quarters, referred to as a, b, c & d, though only rarely marked as such on the maps. Each side of these 500 yard x 500 yard 'sub-squares' are considered to be divided into ten.

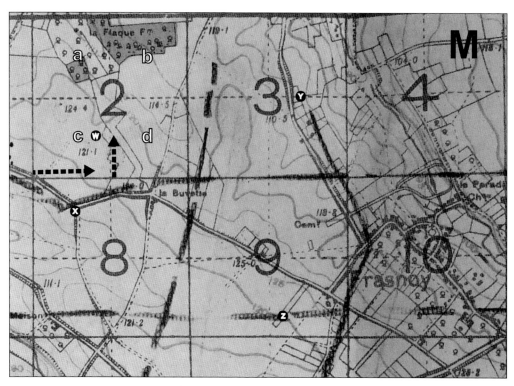

Examples will now serve best:

The dot marked 'W' is in square M.2. It is in sub-square c, therefore M.2 c.

Count from left to right along the southern horizontal boundary of that sub-square – the dot is above the eighth division. Count upwards along the eastern vertical boundary and it is adjacent to the fifth division.

Therefore, this point can be described as being at **M.2 c 8.5**. Similarly, the dot marked 'X' is at **M.8 a 5.6**. The dot marked 'Y' is at **M.3 b 4.0** and the dot marked 'Z' is at **M.9 d 2.3**.

Any point on the map can therefore thus be identified to within 50 yards on the ground. On larger scale maps, each side of a sub-square is divided not into ten, but one hundred, therefore M.2 c 82.51 locates the centre of 'W' to an accuracy of five yards. (This notation is not generally used in the text of this work.)

Bibliography

This bibliography is organised as follows:

1. ARCHIVAL SOURCES

1.1 National Archives of the United Kingdom: Public Record Office, Kew

1.1.1 War Diaries

WO158/228	Third Army Headquarters
WO95/231	Third Army Headquarters
WO95/375	Third Army Headquarters
WO95/719	IV Corps HQ, Staff
WO95/730	IV Corps CRA
WO95/733	IV Corps Heavy Artillery
WO95/2515	37th Division HQ, General Staff
WO95/2517	37th Division CRA
WO95/2519	37th Division CRE
WO95/2524	37th Bn Machine Gun Corps

WO95/2522	CLII & CLIII Bdes Royal Field Artillery
WO95/2523	CLIV Bde Royal Field Artillery
WO95/2531	111 Brigade
WO95/2532	10th Royal Fusiliers (City of London Regiment)
WO95/2533	13th King's Royal Rifle Corps
WO95/2534	13th Rifle Brigade (The Prince Consort's Own)
WO95/2536	112 Brigade
WO95/2538	13th Royal Fusiliers (City of London Regiment)
WO95/2537	1st Essex Regiment
WO95/2537	1/1st Hertfordshire Regiment
WO95/2528	63 Brigade
WO95/2529	8th Lincolnshire Regiment
WO95/2529	8th Prince Albert's (Somerset Light Infantry)
WO95/2528	4th The Duke of Cambridge's Own (Middlesex Regiment)
WO95/3661	New Zealand Division HQ
WO95/3665	New Zealand Division CRA
WO95/3668	New Zealand Division CRE
WO95/3679	New Zealand Bn Machine Gun Corps
WO95/3675	1st New Zealand Field Company Royal Engineers
WO95/3677	3rd New Zealand Field Company Royal Engineers
WO95/3670	1st New Zealand Field Artillery Brigade
WO95/3673	3rd New Zealand Field Artillery Brigade
WO95/3707	3 New Zealand Rifle Brigade
WO95/3708	1st Bn Rifle Brigade
WO95/3709	2nd Bn Rifle Brigade
WO95/3710	3rd Bn Rifle Brigade
WO95/3711	4th Bn Rifle Brigade
WO95/3687	1 New Zealand Infantry Brigade HQ
WO95/3688	1st Aukland Bn
WO95/3688	2nd Aukland Bn
WO95/3689	1st Wellington Bn
WO95/3690	2nd Wellington Bn
WO95/752	V Corps HQ, General Staff
WO95/2540	38th Division HQ, General Staff
WO95/2542	38th Division CRA
WO95/2544	38th Division CRE
WO95/2548	38th Bn Machine Gun Corps
WO95/2546	CXXI Bde Royal Field Artillery
WO95/2545	CXXII Bde Royal Field Artillery
WO95/2554	113 Brigade
WO95/2555	13th Royal Welsh Fusiliers
WO95/2555	14th Royal Welsh Fusiliers
WO95/2556	16th Royal Welsh Fusiliers
WO95/2558	114 Brigade
WO95/2559	13th Welsh Regiment
WO95/2559	14th Welsh Regiment
WO95/2559	15th Welsh Regiment
WO95/2560	115 Brigade
WO95/2562	10th South Wales Borderers

WO95/2561	17th Royal Welsh Fusiliers
WO95/2561	2nd Royal Welsh Fusiliers
WO95/1985	17th Division HQ, General Staff
WO95/1988	17th Division CRA
WO95/1990	17th Division CRE
WO95/1986	17th Division QMG
WO95/1995	17th Bn Machine Gun Corps
WO95/2547	123rd, 124th & 151st Field Companies, Royal Engineers
WO95/1991	LXXVIII Bde Royal Field Artillery
WO95/1991	LXXIX Bde Royal Field Artillery
WO95/1999	50 Brigade
WO95/2001	6th Dorsetshire Regiment
WO95/2005	7th East Yorkshire Regiment
WO95/2004	10th The Prince of Wales's Own (West Yorkshire Regiment)
WO95/2006	51 Brigade
WO95/2007	7th Lincolnshire Regiment
WO95/2008	7th Border Regiment
WO95/2008	10th Sherwood Foresters (Nottinghamshire & Derbyshire Regiment)
WO95/2011	52 Brigade
WO95/2012	10th Lancashire Fusiliers
WO95/2012	12th Manchester Regiment
WO95/2014	9th Duke of Wellington's (West Riding Regiment)
WO95/775	VI Corps HQ, General Staff
WO95/783	VI Corps CRA
WO95/789	VI Corps Heavy Artillery
WO95/3071	62nd Division General Staff
WO95/3073	62nd Division CRA
WO95/3074	62nd Division CRE
WO95/3072	62nd Division QMG
WO95/3077	62nd Bn Machine Gun Corps
WO95/3076	457th, 460th & 461st Field Companies, Royal Engineers
WO95/3075	CCCX Bde Royal Field Artillery
WO95/3075	CCCXII Bde Royal Field Artillery
WO95/3080	185 Brigade
WO95/3083	1/5th Devonshire Regiment
WO95/3083	1/8th The Prince of Wales's Own (West Yorkshire Regiment)
WO95/3083	2/20th London Regiment
WO95/3085	186 Brigade
WO95/3086	5th Duke of Wellington's (West Riding Regiment)
WO95/3086	2/4th Duke of Wellington's (West Riding Regiment)
WO95/3087	2/4th Hampshire Regiment
WO95/3089	187 Brigade
WO95/3091	2/4th King's Own (Yorkshire Light Infantry)
WO95/3091	2/5th King's Own (Yorkshire Light Infantry)
WO95/3090	2/4th The York & Lancaster Regiment
WO95/1195	Guards Division HQ, General Staff
WO95/1196	Guards Division CRA
WO95/1202	Guards Division CRE
WO95/1197	Guards Division QMG

WO95/1200	Guards Division Heavy Artillery
WO95/1206	4th Bn Guard's Machine Gun Regiment
WO95/1205	55th, 75th & 76th Field Companies, Royal Engineers
WO95/1203	LXXIV Bde Royal Field Artillery
WO95/1203	LXXV Bde Royal Field Artillery
WO95/1214	1 Guards Brigade
WO95/1215	2nd Grenadier Guards
WO95/1215	2nd Coldstream Guards
WO95/1216	1st Irish Guards
WO95/1218	2 Guards Brigade
WO95/1219	3rd Grenadier Guards
WO95/1219	1st Coldstream Guards
WO95/1219	1st Scots Guards
WO95/1222	3 Guards Brigade
WO95/1223	1st Grenadier Guards
WO95/1223	2nd Scots Guards
WO95/1224	1st Welsh Guards
WO95/936	XVII Corps HQ, General Staff
WO95/943	XVII Corps CRA
WO95/944	XVII Corps Heavy Artillery
WO95/2057	19th Division HQ, General Staff
WO95/2062	19th Division CRA
WO95/2066	19th Division CRE
WO95/2058	19th Division QMG
WO95/2071	19th Bn Machine Gun Corps
WO95/2069	81st & 82nd Field Companies Royal Engineers
WO95/2070	94th Field Company Royal Engineers
WO95/2067	LXXXVII Bde Royal Field Artillery
WO95/2067	LXXXVIII Bde Royal Field Artillery
WO95/2077	56 Brigade
WO95/2078	1/4th King's (Shropshire Light Infantry)
WO95/2082	8th The Prince of Wales's (North Staffordshire Regiment)
WO95/2079	9th Cheshire Regiment
WO95/2084	57 Brigade
WO95/2085	10th Royal Warwickshire Regiment
WO95/2085	8th Gloucestershire Regiment
WO95/2086	3rd Worcestershire Regiment
WO95/2089	58 Brigade
WO95/2092	9th Royal Welsh Fusiliers
WO95/2092	9th Welsh Regiment
WO95/2093	2nd Wiltshire Regiment
WO95/2192	24th Division HQ, General Staff
WO95/2195	24th Division CRA
WO95/2196	24th Division CRE
WO95/2194	24th Division QMG
WO95/2201	24th Bn Machine Gun Corps
WO95/2199	103rd, 104th & 129th Field Companies Royal Engineers
WO95/2197	CVI Bde Royal Field Artillery
WO95/2197	CVII Bde Royal Field Artillery

WO95/2205	17 Brigade
WO95/2207	1st Royal Fusiliers (City of London Regiment)
WO95/2208	8th Queens (Royal West Surrey Regiment)
WO95/2206	3rd Rifle Brigade (The Prince Consort's Own)
WO95/2212	72 Brigade
WO95/2215	9th East Surrey Regiment
WO95/2213	8th The Queen's Own (Royal West Kent Regiment)
WO95/2213	1st The Prince of Wales's (North Staffordshire Regiment)
WO95/2217	73 Brigade
WO95/2219	9th Royal Sussex Regiment
WO95/2218	7th Northamptonshire Regiment
WO95/2219	13th The Duke of Cambridge's Own (Middlesex Regiment)
WO95/439	Fourth Army Headquarters
WO95/440	Fourth Army Headquarters
WO158/242	Fourth Army Headquarters
WO53/572	Fourth Army Headquarters
WO95/579	Fourth Army Headquarters
WO95/837	IX Corps HQ, General Staff
WO95/841	IX Corps CRA
WO95/842	IX Corps Heavy Artillery
WO95/1234	1st Division HQ, General Staff
WO95/1241	1st Division CRA
WO95/1246	1st Division CRE
WO95/1238	1st Division QMG
WO95/1256	1st Bn Machine Gun Corps
WO95/1252	23rd Field Company Royal Engineers
WO95/1253	26th Field Company Royal Engineers
WO95/1254	409th Field Company Royal Engineers
WO95/1248	XXV Bde Royal Field Artillery
WO95/1249	XXXIX Bde Royal Field Artillery
WO95/1139	2nd Dragoons, Scots Greys
WO95/1262	1 Brigade
WO95/1264	1st The Queen's Own Cameron Highlanders
WO95/1266	1st Loyal North Lancashire Regiment
WO95/1263	1st Black Watch (Royal Highlanders)
WO95/1268	2 Brigade
WO95/1269	2nd Royal Sussex Regiment
WO95/1273	2nd King's Royal Rifle Corps
WO95/1271	1st Northamptonshire Regiment
WO95/1277	3 Brigade
WO95/1278	1st Gloucestershire Regiment
WO95/1280	1st South Wales Borderers
WO95/1281	2nd Welsh Regiment
WO95/2372	32nd Division HQ, General Staff
WO95/2376	32nd Division CRA
WO95/2379	32nd Division CRE
WO95/2374	32nd Division QMG
WO95/2385	32nd Bn Machine Gun Corps
WO95/2383	218th Field Company Royal Engineers

WO95/2383	206th Field Company Royal Engineers
WO95/2676	465th Field Company Royal Engineers
WO95/2677	466th Field Company Royal Engineers
WO95/2678	468th Field Company Royal Engineers
WO95/2380	CLXI Bde Royal Field Artillery
WO95/2381	CLXVIII Bde Royal Field Artillery
WO95/2391	14 Brigade
WO95/2392	5/6th Royal Scots (Lothian Regiment)
WO95/2392	1st Dorsetshire Regiment
WO95/2393	15th Highland Light Infantry
WO95/2396	96 Brigade
WO95/2397	2nd Manchester Regiment
WO95/2397	15th Lancashire Fusiliers
WO95/2397	16th Lancashire Fusiliers
WO95/2401	97 Brigade
WO95/2402	2nd King's Own (Yorkshire Light Infantry)
WO95/2402	1/5th Border Regiment
WO95/2402	10th (Princess Louise's) Argyll & Sutherland Highlanders
WO95/897	XIII Corps HQ, General Staff
WO95/900	XIII Corps HQ, A & Q
WO95/902	XIII Corps CRA
WO95/2227	25th Division HQ, General Staff
WO95/2230	25th Division CRA
WO95/2232	25th Division CRE
WO95/2228	25th Division QMG
WO95/2235	25th Bn Machine Gun Corps
WO95/2235	105th & 106th Field Companies Royal Engineers
WO95/2237	130th Field Company Royal Engineers
WO95/2233	CX Bde Royal Field Artillery
WO95/2234	CXII Bde Royal Field Artillery
WO95/2245	74 Brigade
WO95/2247	11th Sherwood Foresters (Nottinghamshire & Derbyshire Regiment)
WO95/2247	9th Green Howards. Alexandra, Princess of Wales's Own (Yorkshire Regiment)
WO95/2247	13th Durham Light Infantry
WO95/2249	75 Brigade
WO95/2251	1/8th Worcestershire Regiment
WO95/2251	1/5th Gloucestershire Regiment
WO95/2251	1/8th Royal Warwickshire Regiment
WO95/2242	7 Brigade
WO95/2244	9th Devonshire Regiment
WO95/2244	20th Manchester Regiment
WO95/2244	21st Manchester Regiment
WO95/2812	50th Division HQ, General Staff
WO95/2814	50th Division HQ CRA
WO95/2816	50th Division CRE
WO95/2813	50th Division QMG
WO95/2823	50th Bn Machine Gun Corps
WO95/2821	7th, 446th & 447th Field Companies Royal Engineers
WO95/2817	CCL Bde Royal Field Artillery

WO95/2819	CCLI Bde Royal Field Artillery
WO95/2827	149 Brigade
WO95/2831	3rd Royal Fusiliers (City of London Regiment)
WO95/2831	13th Black Watch (Royal Highlanders)
WO95/2831	2nd Royal Dublin Fusiliers
WO95/2833	150 Brigade
WO95/2836	7th The Duke of Edinburgh's (Wiltshire Regiment)
WO95/2836	2nd Northumberland Fusiliers
WO95/2837	2nd Royal Munster Fusiliers
WO95/2839	151 Brigade
WO95/2843	6th Royal Inniskilling Fusiliers
WO95/2843	1st King's Own (Yorkshire Light Infantry)
WO95/2843	4th King's Royal Rifle Corps
WO95/2840	6th Durham Light Infantry
WO95/2017	18th Division HQ, General Staff
WO95/2021	18th Division HQ CRA
WO95/2023	18th Division CRE
WO95/2018	18th Division QMG
WO95/2028	18th Bn Machine Gun Corps
WO95/2027	80th Field Company Royal Engineers
WO95/2069	81st & 82nd Field Companies Royal Engineers
WO95/2024	LXXXII Bde Royal Field Artillery
WO95/2025	LXXXIII Bde Royal Field Artillery
WO95/2036	53 Brigade
WO95/2040	7th The Queen's Own (Royal West Kent Regiment)
WO95/2038	10th Essex Regiment
WO95/2037	8th Princess Charlotte of Wales's (Royal Berkshire Regiment)
WO95/2042	54 Brigade
WO95/2042	2nd Bedfordshire Regiment
WO95/2044	6th Northamptonshire Regiment
WO95/2045	11th Royal Fusiliers
WO95/2048	55 Brigade
WO95/2049	7th Queens (Royal West Surrey Regiment)
WO95/2049	7th Buffs (East Kent Regiment)
WO95/2050	8th East Surrey Regiment
WO158/332	Machine Gun HQ
WO95/95	Tank Corps Headquarters
WO95/102	2nd Tank Brigade
WO95/107	9th Tank Battalion
WO95/103	10th Tank Battalion
WO95/103	14th Tank Battalion
WO95/103	1st Company 14th Tank Battalion
WO95/106	17th (Armoured Car) Tank Battalion

1.1.2 Maps

WO153/333	Sambre: Situation Map
WO153/332	1st & 3rd Armies' Objectives
WO153/330	XIII Corps Artillery Barrage
WO153/331	XXII Corps Dispositions

1.2 Bundesarchiv-Militärarchiv, Freiburg, Germany
BA-MA MSG 2/1291: Letter written by Battery Commander Leutnant Erich Alenfeld, Feldartillerie-Regiment 280, on 6.11.1918.

1.3 Churchill College, University of Cambridge
Private Papers of Field Marshal Sir Henry Rawlinson.

1.4 Imperial War Museum
Private Papers of Brigadier-General T.S. Lambert. Doc. 4723.
Lt-Col C.E.P. Sankey, CRE 1st Division, 'Report on the Bridging Operations in connection with the forcing of the passage of the Sambre-Oise Canal 4th November 1918'. Ref: LBY 73281.

2. PUBLISHED SOURCES

2.1 Journals
Boff, J., 'Combined Arms during the Hundred Days Campaign, August–November 1918', *War in History*, 17, (4) (2010) pp. 459-478.
Harris, P. & Marble, S., 'The Step-by-Step Approach: British Military Thought And Operational Method on the Western Front, 1915-1917', *War in History*, 15 (1) (2008) pp.17-42.
Travers, T., 'The Evolution of British Strategy and Tactics on the Western Front in 1918: GHQ, Manpower and Technology', *Journal of Military History*, 54 (April 1990) pp. 173-200.

2.2 Contemporary Diaries & Letters
Ludendorff, E., *My War Memories, 1914-1918, Vol. 2* (London: Hutchinson & Co, 1919).
Sheffield, G. & Bourne, J. (eds), *Douglas Haig: War Diaries & Letters 1914-1918* (London: Weidenfeld & Nicolson, 2005).

2.3 General Works & Special Studies
Beckett, I.F.W., *The Great War 1914-1918* (London: Longman, 2001).
Beckett, I.F.W. & Corvi, S.J. (eds), *Haig's Generals* (Barnsley: Pen & Sword, 2006).
Bidwell, S. & Graham, D., *Firepower: British Army Weapons and Theories of War 1904-1945* (George Allen & Unwin Publishers, 1982).
Boff, J., *Winning & Losing on the Western Front* (Cambridge: Cambridge University Press, 2012).
Bourne, J.M., *Britain and the Great War 1914-1918* (London: Arnold, 1989).
Brown, I.M., *British Logistics on the Western Front 1914-1919* (Praeger, Westport, Connecticut, USA, 1998).
Brown, M., *The Imperial War Museum Book of 1918 – The Year of Victory* (London: Sidgwick & Jackson, 1998).
Dennis, P. & Grey, J. (eds), *1918 Defining Victory* (Canberra: Army History Unit, 1999).
Farndale, M., *History of the Royal Regiment of Artillery: Western Front 1914-1918* (Dorchester: Henry Ling Ltd, 1986).
Fuller, J.F.C., *Tanks in the Great War 1914-1918* (Nashville: The Battery Press 2003).
Gliddon, G., *VCs of the First World War: The Final Days 1918* (Stroud: Sutton Publishing, 2000).
Griffith, P., *Battle Tactics of the Western Front: The British Army's Art of Attack 1916-1918* (London: Yale University Press, 1994).
Griffith, P., (ed) *British Fighting Methods in the Great War* (London: Frank Cass, 1996).
Harris, J.P. with Barr, N., *Amiens to the Armistice* (London: Brassey's, 1998).

Hart, P., *1918. A Very British Victory* (London: Weidenfeld & Nicholson, 2008).

Johnson, J.H., *1918: The Unexpected Victory* (London: Arms & Armour Press, 1997).

Lloyd, N., *Hundred Days: The End of the Great War* (London: Viking, 2013).

Neillands, R., *The Great War Generals on the Western Front 1914-18* (London: Robinson, 1998).

Passingham, I., *All the Kaiser's Men: The Life & Death of the German Army on the Western Front 1914-1918* (Stroud: Sutton Publishing, 2003).

Philpott, W., *Attrition: Fighting the First World War* (London: Little, Brown& Co., 2014).

Prior, R. & Wilson, T., *Command on the Western Front* (Oxford: Blackwell, 1992).

Robbins, S., *British Generalship on the Western Front 1914-18: Defeat into Victory* (London: Frank Cass, 2005).

Sheffield, G., *Forgotten Victory* (London: Headline, 2001).

Sheffield, G. & Todman, D. (eds), *Command and Control on the Western Front* (Staplehurst: Spellmount, 2004).

Sheffield, G. & Gray, P. (eds), *Changing War* (London: Bloomsbury Academic, 2013).

Simpson, A., *The Evolution of Victory: British Battles on the Western Front 1914-18* (London: Tom Donovan, 1995).

Stevenson, D., *1914-18* (London: Penguin, 2004).

Terraine, J., *Douglas Haig: The Educated Soldier* (London: Leo Cooper, 1963).

—— *To Win a War: 1918, The Year of Victory* (London: Papermac, 1978).

Travers, T., *The Killing Ground: The British Army, the Western Front & the Emergence of Modern Warfare 1900-1918* (London: Routledge, 1987).

—— *How the War was Won* (London: Routledge 1992).

Williams, J., *Byng of Vimy: General and Governor General* (London: Leo Cooper, 1983).

2.4 Official Histories

Bundesarchiv, *Der Weltkrieg 1914-1918 Vol. XIV, Die Kriegführung an der Westfront im Jahre 1918* (Berlin: Mittler & Sohn, 1944).

Edmonds, J.E. & Maxwell-Hyslop, R., *Military Operations France & Belgium 1918 Vol. V* (London: HMSO, 1947).

Pritchard, H.L. (ed), *The History of the Corps of Royal Engineers Vol. V* (Chatham: The Institution of Royal Engineers, 1952).

Stewart, H., *The New Zealand Division 1916-1919* (Uckfield: Naval & Military reprint of 1921 edition).

2.5 Formation Histories

Atteridge, A.H., *History of the 17th (Northern) Division* (Glasgow: Maclehose, 1929).

De Pree, H.D., *The 38th (Welsh) Division in the last five weeks of the Great War* (Reprinted from Royal Artillery Journal,, 1933).

Headlam, C., *History of the Guards Division in the Great War* (London: John Murray, 1924).

Kincaid-Smith, M., *The 25th Division in France and Flanders* (London: Harrison, 1920).

Montgomery, Sir A., *The Story of the Fourth Army in the Battles of the Hundred Days, August 8th to November 11th 1918* (London: Hodder & Stoughton, 1919).

Munby, J.E., *A History of the 38th Division* (London: Rees, 1920).

Nichols, G.H.F., *The 18th Division in the Great War* (London: Blackwood, 1922).

Wyrall, E., *History of the 19th Division 1914-1918* (London: Arnold, 1932).

—— *The History of the Fiftieth Division 1914-1919* (London: Percy Lund Humphries, 1939).

—— *The History of the 62nd (West Riding) Division, 1914-1919*, 2 Vols (London: Lane, 1924-5).

2.6 Unit Histories

Atkinson, C.T., *The Devonshire Regiment 1914-1918* (Exeter: Eland Brothers, 1926).

Bales, P.G., *The History of the 1/4th Battalion Duke of Wellington's (West Riding) Regiment 1914-1919)* (Halifax: Mortimer, 1920).

Bond, R.C., *The King's Own Yorkshire Light Infantry in the Great War* (London: Percy Lund Humphries, 1929).

Buchan, J., *The Royal Scots Fusiliers 1678-1918* (Edinburgh, Nelson, 1928).

Clarke, H.T. & Peake, W.K., *1/8th Battalion The Worcester Regiment, 1914-1918* (London: War Narrative Publishing Company, 1919).

Dudley Ward, C.H., *History of the Welsh Guards* (London: The London Stamp Exchange, 1920).

Ewing, J., *Royal Scots 1914-1918* (Edinburgh: Oliver & Boyd, 1925).

Johnson, M.K., *Saturday Soldiers. The Territorial Battalions of the King's Own Yorkshire Light Infantry (1908-1919)* (Doncaster: Doncaster Museum Services, 2004).

Magnus, L., *The West Riding Territorials in the Great War* (London: Kegan Paul, Trench, Trubner & Co, 1920).

Ponsonby Sir F., *The Grenadier Guards in the Great War, 1914-1918* (3v. London: Macmillan, 1920).

Ross-of-Bladenburg, Sir J., *The Coldstream Guards 1914-1918 Vol II.* (London: Humphrey Milford, 1928).

Stacke, H. FitzM., *The Worcestershire Regiment in the Great War* (Kidderminster: Cheshire & Sons, 1929).

Stedman, M., *Manchester Pals. 16th, 17th, 18th, 19th, 20th, 21st, 22nd & 23rd Battalions of the Manchester Regiment: A History of the Two Manchester Brigades.* (London: Leo Cooper, 2004).

Wylly, H.C., *History of the Manchester Regiment. Volume 2: 1883-1922* (London: Forster & Groom, 1925).

Wyrall, E., *The Gloucestershire Regiment in the War, 1914-1918: The Records of the 1st, (28th), 2nd, (61st), 3rd (Special Reserve), and the 4th, 5th and 6th (First Line T.A.) Bns*
(London: Methuen, 1931).

—— *The East Yorkshire Regiment in the Great War* (London: Harrison, 1918).

—— *The West Yorkshire Regiment in the War 1914-1918* (2v) (London: Lane, 1924).

2.7 Reference Works

Becke, A.F., *Order of Battle of Divisions* (1937-45).

Naval & Military Press, *Soldiers Died in the Great War CD Rom. Version 2.0* (2004).

War Office, *Statistics of the Military Effort of the British Empire during the Great War 1914-1920* (London: War Office, 1920).

3. THESES

Cook, M.N., 'Evaluating the Learning Curve: the 38th (Welsh) Division on the Western Front 1916-1918' (Unpublished MPhil Thesis, University of Birmingham, 2005).

4. OTHER SOURCES

SS143 *Instructions for the Training of Platoons for Offensive Action* 1917 (February 1917)
SS135 *Instructions for the Training of Divisions for Offensive Action* (November 1918)

Index

INDEX OF PEOPLE

INDEX OF PLACES

INDEX OF MILITARY FORMATIONS & UNITS